To Audra and Mare

ROMUALD J. MISIUNAS
REIN TAAGEPERA

The Baltic States
Years of Dependence
1940–1990

EXPANDED AND UPDATED EDITION

UNIVERSITY OF CALIFORNIA PRESS
BERKELEY AND LOS ANGELES

University of California Press
Berkeley and Los Angeles, California

Library of Congress Cataloging-in-Publication Data

Misiunas, Romuald J.
  The Baltic states, years of dependence, 1940–1990/Romuald J.
Misiunas and Rein Taagepera.
    p.   cm.
  Rev. ed. of: The Baltic states, years of dependence,
1940–1980. 1983.
  Includes bibliographical references and index.
  ISBN 0–520–08227–3. — ISBN 0–520–08228–1 (pbk.)
  1. Baltic States—History—1940–1990.   I. Taagepera, Rein.
II. Misiunas, Romuald J. Baltic states, years of dependence,
1940–1990.   III. Title.
DK502.7.M57 1992
947′.4—dc20

                                           92–39806

CONTENTS

PLATES

Between pages 132 and 133

Between pages 274 and 275

PREFACE TO THE SECOND EDITION

A decade ago, we completed our survey of post-war Baltic history, *The Baltic States: Years of Dependence, 1940–1980*. The dramatic developments during the subsequent decade warrant an updated edition. Throughout most of the 1980s, Baltic history did not differ radically from the preceding period of all-Union stagnation. However, by 1987 the rumblings of change had become noticeable. Three years later, all three states declared their independence. Its practical implementation, including successful resistance to several dramatic attempts at reconstituting the earlier Soviet structure, had to await the collapse of the USSR in the aftermath of the failed coup of August 1991. The reconstruction of modern Baltic nation-states is currently progressing.

The new situation in the Baltic region has evoked attention to the Kaliningrad province of Russia which, from the end of the Second World War, was one of the most obscure corners of the USSR. We have accordingly added a postscript surveying the region's postwar history. Kaliningrad is, in all likelihood, slated to become increasingly integrated into the region as a distinct entity. Considerably more material has become available on the territory since that chapter was written, and continues to do so. The curse of writing contemporary history is rapid obsolescence; however, because of the overall paucity of attention to the subject, we have elected to include the chapter as it stands.

The new edition has allowed for the correction of many errors and infelicities which were noted in the earlier survey after its publication. While we have updated the appendixes listing office-holders, we have decided not to update most of the statistical data. The new circumstances have not allowed publication of statistical information to be as systematic as it was earlier. Moreover, it now appears that much of the earlier data in itself may be suspect. Accordingly, a proper updated statistical survey is not feasible under current conditions and will have to await separate revision in the future.

The original work was undertaken at the request of the British publisher, Christopher Hurst, as a sequel to Georg von Rauch's *The*

Baltic States: The Years of Independence, 1917–1940 (1974). It sought to fill a gap in scholarly literature. Apart from a seventy-page appendix by Evald Uustalu, "Events After 1940," to the second edition of August Rei, *The Drama of the Baltic Peoples* (1970), there was no overview of the area in Soviet times. Most of the histories of the individual countries in English do not cover the period after the Second World War. Significant overviews of the Soviet period — Tönu Parming and Elmar Järvesoo (eds), *A Case Study of a Soviet Republic: The Estonian SSR* (1978), and V. Stanley Vardys (ed.), *Lithuania under the Soviets, 1940–1965* (1965) — are multi-author efforts which cover these particular republics by specific topics rather than by chronological survey. In recent times, some overviews have appeared, but most are extremely general.

Like von Rauch, we approached the Baltic countries as an entity. Treating each republic separately would have simplified our task considerably, but would have yielded a less useful survey and doubtless a somewhat repetitious one. Even more than in the interwar period, the Baltic peoples have come to identify themselves as a unit, and others came to view them as a particularly distinct entity within the USSR. Such perceptions argue for a unitary approach.

A common approach stresses the similarities in the histories of the three countries, and to a large extent there were indeed such similarities in their recent experience: occupation by the Soviets, collectivization, deportations, Sovietization of culture, and a search for Western ties. On the other hand, the three countries were also significantly different in their postwar development. The Estonian purge of 1950 and that in Latvia in 1959 proved unique for both republics. And in many ways Lithuania tended to exhibit a markedly different pattern of postwar Sovietization: a later industrialization, a native Communist Party leadership and membership, and the existence of the Catholic Church as a strong focal point for national resistance. Although our approach is one of synthesis, which by its very nature tends to downplay distinctions, we hope that such major differences have received sufficient attention.

Postwar periodization emerged as a major problem. Both Soviet and émigré treatments tended to avoid subdivisions of these years, considering them as one happy or unhappy period, as the case might be. But it is evident that forty-five years cannot be so uneventful as to become practically indivisible in historiography. Some Soviet works, operating on the Marxist principle that historical periods should be based on the economic organization of the society they treat, use 1950 as one such divide. Collectivization was then nearly complete and guerrilla resistance was waning. Consistency in application of this principle of historical division would have implied a need for subsequent divisions in 1958 and 1965, when the *sovnarkhozy* (regional economic councils) were established and abolished. But such division never materialized, since it could have detracted from the aura of infallibility of the party which was so assiduously nurtured by the regime.

Western periodization of Soviet history has also not been readily adaptable to the Baltic scene. It tends to be based on changes in all-Union leadership: the Stalin, Khrushchev and Brezhnev years, which are not always consonant with developments on the republic scene.

We chose our own subdivisions. The postwar Stalinist years are continued to the end of 1953 and, in some aspects, even to 1955. Even though an appreciable change in mood can be said to have appeared in 1953, it took some time for concrete changes to filter down significantly to the republic level. The replacement of Krushchev by Brezhnev in 1964 did not seem to have any immediately noticeable impact on the Baltic republics. Therefore, we somewhat arbitrarily chose 1968 as a dividing line. Admittedly, the invasion of Czechoslovakia also did not have any immediate tangible repercussions on the Baltic scene. However, we chose to view it as a sort of psychological watershed in moods and expectations of improvement, particularly on the cultural scene — a focal point in the national lives of the three republics. Such change in mood or perception is admittedly hard to measure, define or delineate — by its nature it remains subjective — but we are nevertheless of the opinion that change can definitely be said to have occurred in the aftermath of the events in Czechoslovakia, altering the guarded optimism which appeared pervasive up to that time. Its concrete manifestations took some time to surface, yet surface they did. The resignation and the dissent of the 1970s were both markedly different in quality from the hidden hopes of the 1960s.

The first of the new chapters is a continuation of the general processes noted during the 1970s. A definite break seems to have occurred in 1987–8 with the ecology movements and the formation of the national fronts. The declarations of independence in 1990 ushered in a new era.

We realize that our subdivisions are arbitrary and debatable. Moreover, they might not always best suit developments in each of the three countries. However, they should be viewed as an attempt to integrate developments in each republic into a Baltic unit as well as into the history of the whole USSR of which such developments perforce formed a part.

One obvious difficulty has been our inability to use Latvian-language literature in any detailed way. We found secondary literature in other languages sufficient to allow us to proceed with the overview; however, our inability to operate with original Latvian material, and our being less familiar with the distinctness of the Latvian scene, may have introduced some imbalance in examples and illustrations. We hope this will not detract too much from the validity of the survey in general.

The paucity of primary sources hindered the writing of Baltic history in the West. Within the three Baltic republics themselves, primary sources are more readily available, but synthesis was frequently restricted by a whole host of impediments typical of Soviet academic life: restricted access to archives, self-censorship and formal censorship. Yet many valuable Soviet secondary sources were produced. Taken in conjunction with corroborating evidence available outside the USSR, we were able to construct a fairly accurate overall picture which did not have to be changed in view of revelations during the most recent period.

The present volume cannot pretend to be a definitive picture of the Baltic states since 1940. The time-perspective for the 1970s and 1980s is too short to make valid generalizations. Except for the most recent period, key primary sources were frequently unavailable, and often, even when they were available, they were buried among considerable chaff in secondary Soviet works. It has not always proved feasible to sift through this bulk, particularly for the Stalin years. But even when perspective is sufficient and documentation adequate, there remains a marked absence of detailed analytical study on many very important questions which would bring together all extant primary and secondary sources, and the findings of which could be generalized in a survey such as this.

This work can be said to be, in many sections, a condensation of as-yet nonexistent specific studies. We earnestly hope that in-depth research might be catalyzed by the numerous tenuously documented statements, necessitated by the overview nature of the work, which are included in preference to total silence on the topics in question. We originally noted that perhaps a second edition, a decade later, would be able to utilize such studies to rectify some of these instances of incompleteness, imbalance, and possible error in the present text. This has indeed become possible in many cases, but not in all. Obvious errors have been corrected. But many doubtless remain to be unearthed.

All data tables are located in Appendix B. Footnote citations at the end of the paragraph usually apply to the entire paragraph, or to that part which follows the previous note.

We are grateful to all who read and commented on the original and revised manuscripts. Many extremely useful suggestions have come from these people and have shaped the final appearance of the work. We are particularly indebted to Karl Aun, Nicholas Balabkins, Juris Dreifelds, Andreivs Ezergailis, Uldis Germanis, Walter Hanchett, Gundar King, Benedict Mačiuika, Hain Rebas, Aleksandras Shtromas, Evald Uustalu and Tomas Venclova. Valuable comments have also been received from Yaroslav Bilinsky, David Crowe, Neil Dale, Elmar Jarvesoo, Ivar Ivask, Austra Jurašas, Atis Lejiņš, Imre Lipping, Dietrich Loeber, Vita Matiss, Jānis Penikis, Jaan Pennar, Arnold Purre, Thomas Remeikis, Veljo Salo, Rimvydas Šilbajoris, Adolfs Sprudzs, Dagmar Vallens, V. Stanley Vardys, George Viksnins and Pranas Zunde. Important source materials were given or loaned to us by Edgar Anderson, Jaan Puhvel, Toivo Raun, and Andris Trapans. Jānis Borgs, Ilze Brands, Stephanie Komkow, Hedwig Kraus, Hilja Kukk, Edžus Liniņš, Stephen Rodgers, and Robert Scott helped with the indexing. We should further like to thank Uldis Briedis, Klaudijus Driskius, Rolfs Ekmanis, Jurgis Anysas, Tõnu Krünvald, Bronius Kviklys, Zenonas Nekrošius, Valdis Semjonovs, Reino Sepp, Antanas Sutkus, Kalju Suur, Vitolis Vengris, the Lithuanian Information Center, the Estonian Archives in the United States, the Relief Centre for Estonian Prisoners of Conscience in the USSR and Vitauts Simanis, who lent us some of their photographs for the illustrations. We also thank Lorraine Thompson and various individuals at the UCI Social Services Word Processing Center — Kathy Alberti, Donna Dill, Cheryl Larsson, Jayne Putman, Marjorie Robinson, Dave Westhoff, Lillian White, and Helen Wildman — who struggled so valiantly with the Baltic spellings. Needless to say, any shortcomings remain our responsiblity.

October 1992   ROMUALD J. MISIUNAS
                                                          REIN TAAGEPERA

FINLAND

GULF OF FINLAND

Paldiski · Tallinn

HIIUMAA

Kohtla-Järve

Narva

ESTONIA

·Kautla

BALTIC

Lake
Peipsi

SAAREMAA

Pärnu · Viljandi

Tartu

RUSSIA

Kilingi-Nõmme

Emajõgi

SEA

GULF
OF
RIGA

LIVONIA

Petseri · Pskov

Haanja
Kuusmäe

Valmiera

Ventspils

Cēsis

ABRENE

**KURZEME
(COURLAND)**

LATVIA

Augspils

Rīga

Madona

Jūrmala · Ogre

·Liepāja

Dobele.

LATGALE

Jelgava

Plaviņas

Daugava

Rēzekne

Mažeikiai

Žagarė

Venta

Akmenė

Klaipėda

Minija

Šiauliai

Daugavpils

Panevėžys

LITHUANIA

Zarasai · Lake
Drukštai

Jurbarkas · Kėdainiai

Nevėžis

Sovetsk
(Tilsit)

Nemunas

Jonava

**KALININGRAD
OBLAST (RSFSR)**

Šešupė

Kaunas

Žiežmariai

BELORUSSIA

Elektrėnai · Vilnius

Trakai

**EAST
PRUSSIA**

Skardupiai

Pirčiupis

Suwałki

Varėna

Minsk

POLAND

0   100 KM

---- 1938 borders
········ June 1940 border of
          Lithuania
— — Post-1945 borders

⧄ Lithuania's gains in
   1939 and 1940
☰ Estonia's and Latvia's
   losses in 1945

1

INTRODUCTION
HISTORICAL BACKGROUND

Before the Modern Age

The three Baltic republics formed a distinct and unique cultural unit — a Western enclave within the multi-national Soviet state. They were the only areas of the USSR to have experienced an independent modern national life and modernization not patterned on the Soviet model. Although bound by geographic proximity and a modern history of inclusion in the same empire, the Estonians, Latvians and Lithuanians are ethnically and culturally diverse peoples. The Estonians speak a Finno-Ugrian language, related to Finnish, which is radically different from those of their two neighbors to the south. Latvian and Lithuanian are the only living varieties of the Indo-European Baltic family of languages. Estonia and Latvia developed within the North European Protestant world, while Lithuanian culture was shaped by the Central and Eastern European Catholic milieu. The histories of the three peoples during the twentieth century, their emergence as independent nation-states after the First World War, their mutual experiences during the interwar period, and their fate during the Second World War and its aftermath have served, however, to affirm a common identity which in some ways has superseded the cultural differentiation of the past.

The homeland of the Baltic peoples, the eastern littoral of the Baltic Sea, was medieval Europe's last pagan backwater. Although it straddled the commercially important waterway between the Varangians and the Greeks, its distance from the two European centers of civilization of the time, the Latin West and the Orthodox East, limited cultural contact between its indigenous inhabitants and the world of Christendom.

The first serious outside incursions into the area date from the beginning of the present millennium. While the occasional campaigns for booty and tribute by several princes of the East Slav Kiev realm failed to introduce lasting political dominance, the expansion of the Latin West was accompanied by settlement and the imposition of suzerainty. The thrust began toward the end of the twelfth century and first touched the westernmost Baltic people, the Prussians. Within a few decades their lands were subjugated by the military monastic Order of the Teutonic Knights, which had transferred their crusades to this region after suffering reverses in the Near East. A few centuries later the Prussians became extinct, leaving only their name (until 1945) to the lands they had once inhabited. At around the same time the maritime Danish monarchy entrenched itself in northern Estonia, and German merchants colonized the region of the Daugava (Dvina) River. In 1201, a bishopric was established at the core of their operations, Riga. Another German military order, the Brothers of the Sword, pursued the conquest of the hinterland. As had happened with the Prussians, native resistance based on a rudimentary political organization proved sporadic and disunited. Within a century, the conquest of what would subsequently become Latvia and Estonia was completed. Their peoples were absorbed into the social and cultural structures of the world of Western Christendom of the High Middle Ages before they could develop a native political system. The invaders colonized, baptized and gradually enserfed the indigenous population, reducing their identity to an ethnic character, politically dormant until the age of modern nationalism. After the Danes sold their holdings in Estonia to the Teutonic Order in 1346, the area became a loose confederation of the domains of the Order, ecclesiastical estates ruled by princes of the Holy Roman Empire, and a few independent Hansa towns.

During their initial drive of the thirteenth century, the Latin Christians were unable to overwhelm the less accessible Lithuanians. A native chief, Mindaugas (Mindovg), successfully forged the Baltic tribes in the area of present-day Lithuania and parts of Belorussia into a lasting political entity. He inflicted a crushing defeat on the Brothers of the Sword, which led, in 1237, to their amalgamation into the Teutonic Order. Seeking peace with the Germanic invaders, he attempted to integrate his newly established realm into the West European political system. He converted to Latin Christianity and was crowned King on the authority of Pope Innocent IV. But internal strife thwarted his efforts. The Lithuanian state survived his violent end in 1263 at the hands of political opponents. Its society, however, returned to the pagan customs of its ancestors.

During the fourteenth century, a series of particularly able Lithuanian rulers — Gediminas (Gedimyn), Algirdas (Olgerd) and Kęstutis (Kenstut) — managed not only to contain the assaults of the Teutonic Order but also to expand eastward in the wake of the recession of Tatar power. Considerable East Slav territory was absorbed into Lithuania, making it a major power in Eastern Europe. The extensive state, whose rulers and ethnic core maintained their pagan religion, became a cultural battleground between Latin influences and the Orthodox traditions of the incorporated East Slav population. A resolution of this conflict came in 1386. Great Prince Jogaila (Jagiełło), pressed by continuing incursions of the Order, sought Polish support. As a condition of his marriage to the heiress of Poland, Jadwyga, and his accession to the Polish throne, he agreed to the baptism of his pagan Lithuanian subjects into the Latin rite. The rule of Jogaila's cousin Vytautas (Vitovt), as Viceroy according to theoretical West European designation but as an independent Great Prince in practice, saw the apogee of Lithuanian power. The realm stretched from the Baltic to the Black Sea, from the outskirts of Moscow to Poland. In 1410 the combined armies of Poland and Lithuania inflicted a crushing blow on the Teutonic Order at Grünwald (Tannenberg). It was never able to recover, and thereafter ceased to be the threat to Lithuania that it had been for two centuries.

The nearly 200 years of personal union with Poland, never clearly defined in the political sense, lasted until 1569 and had two long-term cultural effects on the ethnic core of the Lithuanian state: the Christianization of the Lithuanians according to the Latin Rite and the Polonization of the Lithuanian nobility. The older and culturally richer Polish society proved irresistible to the Lithuanian nobles. While a sense of distinct political identity was preserved for a long time, the Lithuanian nobility became culturally indistinguishable from their Polish counterpart. The effect on the peasantry was similar to that in Estonia and Latvia — enforced Christianization and enserfment to a nobility which could not speak their language.

As a result of the Reformation, the Teutonic Order and the ecclesiastical domains in the Estonian and Latvian lands became politically anachronistic. Their secularization coincided in time with the colonization of the New World, which attracted adventurous Europeans, and led to a manpower problem in the successors to the Order. Unable to defend themselves adequately, they began to seek foreign protection. The major political realignments were triggered by a Russian push toward the Baltic launched by Ivan IV. In reaction, the rulers of northern Estonia preferred to submit to Sweden in 1561. The nobility of Livonia (southern Estonia and eastern Latvia) sought Lithuanian protection in 1560. Their lands were incorporated into the Lithuanian state; the western part of Latvia became the Duchy of Courland, a personal fief of the Lithuanian and Polish sovereign. Not long thereafter, also in a reaction to the Muscovite push, Lithuania regularized its personal political union with Poland into a formal constitutional arrangement. While duality of sovereignty was retained, a new Commonwealth structure with a joint sovereign and legislature was established at the Union of Lublin (1569).

The Commonwealth successfully resisted the Russian drive. However, it was not able to contain the Swedes. In 1629, Livonia was divided. Its northwestern half, including the city of Riga, came under Swedish overlordship; its eastern portion, Latgale, remained under Lithuanian rule. The status of the Duchy of Courland did not change. Except for Latgale, whose association with Lithuania for two centuries made it distinct from the rest of Latvia, the cultural boundary between Lithuania and the north acquired a long-standing character as one between Catholic and Lutheran worlds, and between Polish and German social and administrative practices.

Although Sweden itself had never experienced enserfment, the system of peasant bondage continued in its Baltic provinces. As a result, the sympathies of the government were not always automatically on the side of the Baltic barons. However, Sweden depended on the barons for military service and on uninterrupted grain imports from the region, and could not afford wholly to alienate the local seigneurs. On the whole, conditions among the peasants worsened during the course of the seventeenth century. However, in view of even worse times later, Estonians and Latvians have come to regard the Swedish period in their history rather warmly.

The next major change in the political configuration of the region came with the renewed and successful Russian push to the Baltic Sea during the Great Northern War. The Treaty of Nystad (1721) confirmed Russian possession of Livonia and Estland (northern Estonia). The imposition of Russian rule allowed the local nobility to reassert some of their former prerogatives which had been whittled down during Swedish times. Among its provisions, the peace settlement guaranteed all former noble rights, among them self-government and unlimited rule over the peasants, which had fallen into disuse. It is doubtful whether any other area in Europe at the time produced quite the extent of legal argumentation designed to redefine and, in so doing, expand nobles' rights over their peasants. As a practical consequence, a closed corporation of 324 families established a monopoly of landholding in the area. The Baltic German barons proved loyal subjects of the Russian Empire. New opportunities for advancement in the administrative, diplomatic and military service developed, allowing them to expand their influence in St. Petersburg far beyond what their relatively small numbers warranted. For the Latvian and Estonian peasants, however, the late eighteenth century marked the nadir of their rights and living conditions.

In addition to the annexation of Livonia and Estland, the Russian Empire established *de facto* control over the Duchy of Courland, which had become virtually an independent state during the preceding century. Likewise, Russia managed to exercise preponderant influence over the decadent Polish-Lithuanian Commonwealth. Internal attempts at reform in this state triggered foreign intervention and its extinction as a political unit. During the course of the three partitions of the Commonwealth (1772, 1793 and 1795), the Lithuanian state fell almost entirely under Russian rule.

The Road to the Modern Nation-States

In all three Baltic countries the appearance and growth of national consciousness during the nineteenth century accompanied the social struggle of the peasantry against a culturally alien entrenched nobility. Matters were complicated by the desire of the Russian government to turn the region into a culturally integral part of the Russian state. The policy of Russification pursued by the Tsarist government, particularly during the latter part of the century, was aimed primarily at the old local élites and thus unwittingly facilitated the emergence of the indigenous peasant nations.

The Baltic provinces of Estland, Livonia and Courland were the first regions of the Russian Empire in which serfdom was abolished. The first attempt to limit this institution was made by Alexander I in 1804, but the Baltic barons managed to minimize any practical results from his measure. By 1819, however, personal emancipation had been effected. The trend of the previous five centuries was reversed. Although the peasants were legally free, they had not been endowed with land. Changes in the agrarian economy coupled with a series of measures from the 1840s to the 1860s enabled many peasants to acquire as personal holdings much of the land which they had formerly been forced to lease from the barons. At the same time, the abolition of compulsory guild membership among urban crafts-men allowed Estonian and Latvian peasants to settle in the hitherto mainly German cities.

Proselytizing for the Russian Orthodox Church, which proved quite successful in some districts among the peasantry, established a counterweight to the German-dominated Lutheran Church. The competition between the two churches led to an expansion of publications in Latvian and Estonian.

The railway age saw a considerable expansion of the cities. Riga, Liepāja (Libau) and Tallinn (Reval) grew significantly with an increase in their importance as ports and industrial centers. In both Latvia and Estonia a middle class as well as a proletariat made their appearance. Tallinn, already more than half Estonian in 1871, was about two-thirds Estonian by 1897. The Latvian share in the population of Riga nearly doubled during the same period, from 23 to 42 per cent. This expansion of urbanization was accompanied by the introduction of education in the native languages. By the end of the century, the Baltic provinces were unique within the Russian Empire in having almost eliminated illiteracy.

The growth of national consciousness fostered by such socio-economic tendencies was furthered by the Russification policy pursued by the Imperial government during the reign of Alexander III. Its targets were the provincial administration, the courts and the educational system, which were the bastions of the privileged German elements. This pressure helped the fledgling political activity of the rising Estonian and Latvian elements, although forced imposition of Russian as the language of instruction in Latvian and Estonian schools resulted in an educational setback for the native languages. By the turn of the century, there were successes at the municipal level. In 1904, Estonians gained a majority in the municipal council of Tallinn. Between 1897 and 1906, Latvian majorities were elected to the municipal councils of four large towns.

A somewhat different socio-economic development occurred in Lithuania. In one portion of the country — the area southwest of the Nemunas River, which had belonged to Napoleon's Grand Duchy of Warsaw — the peasants were freed during the first decade of the nineteenth century. Emancipation, with the right to limited land-holding, came to the rest of the country in 1861, along with the general abolition of serfdom throughout the Russian Empire. A social struggle with the Polonized nobility ensued.

The policy of Russification began earlier in Lithuania than in the other two Baltic countries. It became a marked feature of cultural life after the 1831 uprising which accompanied a revolt in Poland. Initially it was aimed at the Polonized nobility; after the 1863 revolt, however, its measures also hindered the Lithuanian national renaissance. The Lithuanian peasantry had shown themselves to be more revolutionary than their counterpart in Poland. In 1865, the publication of Latin alphabet books in the Lithuanian language was prohibited, a measure not repealed until 1904. Policies of settling Russians in rural areas and of proselytizing for the Russian Orthodox Church were undertaken. The rights of the Roman Catholic Church were curtailed; in 1894, Roman Catholics were excluded from administrative positions in local government organs. A struggle for religious equality turned into one facet of the Lithuanian nationalist movement, in contrast to its Latvian and Estonian counterparts. The close identification of Catholicism with nationalism has persisted in Lithuania to the present day.

Cultural persecution by the Russian authorities led to the use of the compact ethnic Lithuanian population living across the border within the more liberal structure of Prussia as a *point d'appui*. The first journal in the Lithuanian language was published here, and books printed in Tilsit and elsewhere in that region were smuggled across the Russian frontier. These helped to nourish a system of *ad hoc*, almost secret "schools of the hearth" through which the level of rural literacy was raised and national values were fostered during a half-century of intense Russification.

Unlike Estonia and Latvia, Lithuania remained an almost entirely agrarian country. Its few urban centers were not populated by the ethnic Lithuanian majority. As a result, by the turn of the century there was virtually no Lithuanian middle class or proletariat. Rural overpopulation at a time of rising anti-Russian sentiment fostered emigration — mostly to the United States and Canada. It is estimated that on the eve of the First World War, one out of every three Lithuanians lived in North America.

The disorders which swept the Russian Empire in 1905 affected the entire Baltic area, though to different degrees. In Latvia and Estonia, the protests were heavily socio-political. Urban unrest was particularly severe in Riga and Tallinn. Freedom of the press and of assembly as well as a universal franchise were the principal goals of the strikers and demonstrators. Nationwide assemblies (1,000 Latvian delegates in Riga, 800 Estonian delegates in Tartu) convened in November and called for national autonomy. The situation in the countryside was even more turbulent. German nobles and clergymen were particular targets for the jacqueries; nearly 200 manor houses were burned and about 100 noblemen killed. The brutal suppression of the uprising included the execution of several thousand people and the imprisonment and exile to Siberia of thousands more.

The revolution in Lithuania was considerably less dramatic and remained largely confined to rural areas. It appeared to be aimed more at perceived cultural enemies. Its targets were mostly Russian schoolteachers and members of the Orthodox clergy; excesses were relatively few. The events in Lithuania were highlighted by the massive National Congress of 2,000 delegates which met in Vilnius (Vilna) in December 1905. The resolutions of the Congress sought autonomy, a centralized administration for the ethnic Lithuanian region of the Russian Empire, and the use of the Lithuanian language in administration. The reaction in Lithuania was likewise relatively mild. The Stolypin reform, which sought to create a rural class of prosperous farmers throughout the Empire as a social bulwark of the system, even benefited many Lithuanian peasants.

In spite of setbacks, the general political and cultural relaxation which set in after 1906 allowed for a steady intensification of the national consciousness of the Baltic peoples. Although the events of 1905 had forced many leaders into exile and emigration, Estonians and Latvians acquired representation through delegates to the Imperial Duma. The Lithuanians also acquired a group of experienced national politicians through this new Russian legislature. The elimination of restrictions on the press in the national languages affected all three republics, but was an especially pronounced cultural development in Lithuania.

The Years of Independence, 1918–1940

Modern Baltic history has been shaped by the conflict among great powers in the region. The simultaneous collapse of the Russian and German empires during the First World War allowed the three Baltic peoples to seize a rare opportunity of creating their own nation-states. Before the end of the war, on 16 and 24 February 1918 respectively, Lithuania and Estonia declared their independence. An analogous Latvian declaration appeared on 18 November, shortly after the end of hostilities in the West. The circumstances under which each of the three countries established its independence differed considerably.

The Estonian movement for separate statehood emerged from the dissolution of the Russian Empire. Estonia was the only national region to which the Provisional Government of 1917, after a massive demonstration of Estonians in Petrograd, granted autonomy. The organ of autonomous self-government unilaterally declared complete independence one day before advancing German troops occupied Tallinn. The collapse of Germany in November 1918 allowed for a reassertion of this proclamation. An invasion by the Red Army in December seriously threatened Estonia's independence, although a Soviet naval attack on Tallinn was foiled by a British naval squadron. While an appreciable minority of the population favored the Bolsheviks, the wide majority rallied to the cause of national statehood. By March 1919, Estonian territory had been cleared of foreign forces, although hostilities continued at the frontiers.

Circumstances in Latvia were far more complex. As the most industrialized part of the Russian Empire, Latvia had developed a strong working-class movement which had been affected by the revolution. Moreover, the Tsarist government had formed Latvian rifle regiments in the summer of 1915 after the German armies reached the Daugava (Dvina) River. These soldiers, along with the rest of the old Russian army, were affected by the revolutionary mood of 1917 and split their loyalties between a crystallizing national movement and the Bolsheviks. Such a division of sympathies immensely complicated the incursion of the Red Army into Latvia after the German collapse. Matters were further complicated by German attempts in 1919 to preserve a foothold in the Baltic lands. Utilizing the desperate Latvian nationalist need to stem the Red tide, a commander of the German *Freikorps*, General Rüdiger von der Goltz, tried to set up a puppet Latvian regime. The defeat of his army by Estonian-Latvian forces, British diplomatic and naval pressures, and the subsequent defeat of another German attempt to utilize a White Russian adventurer, Colonel Pavel Bermondt-Avalov, as a cover for their operations allowed the Latvians to concentrate on clearing their country of the Red Army. By 1920 this had been achieved.

The Lithuanian declaration of independence came while the entire country was still under German occupation. The Lithuanian National Council (*Taryba*), a group of nationalist leaders whom the Germans had originally sought to use as a cover for their expansionist aims, issued the resolution unilaterally. However, it could not be implemented because of German refusal to recognize any arrangement which would not permanently tie Lithuania to Germany. The German collapse in 1918 made possible the organization of an administration and an army. In early 1919, an invading Red force was repulsed. Later that year, the German forces of Bermondt-Avalov were also pushed back into Latvia.

The establishment of Lithuanian independence was also complicated by pressures from the newly arisen Polish state for a restoration of the political union of historic times. Although they were resisted, these demands delayed Lithuania's recognition by the Western powers. Matters were exacerbated by the conflicting territorial claims of the two states. The capital of the historic Lithuanian state, Vilnius, was occupied by the Poles after conclusion of an armistice leaving the city in Lithuanian hands. As a result, Polish-Lithuanian relations remained strained throughout the interwar period, and diplomatic relations between the two countries were not established until 1938.

In 1920, the three Baltic countries concluded peace treaties with the Soviet state: Estonia on 2 February, Lithuania on 12 July and Latvia on 1 August. Russian claims to sovereignty over their territories were renounced in perpetuity. Nation-building could now proceed unhindered, although in Lithuania continuing problems with unsettled frontiers delayed this process.

The achievement of independence brought similar problems to all three countries. They needed to reform their social, economic and political structures to conform with their new status as nation-states. In societies which were still predominantly agrarian, the question of land ownership was a pivotal one, from the social as well as the economic point of view. Economies which had suffered during the years of war needed adaptation to new international circumstances. And new constitutional structures had to be devised for an independent state life.

Land reform proved most drastic in Estonia and Latvia. There the holdings of the large landed estates were redistributed to peasants, particularly to volunteers in the war for independence, thus ending the economic and political power of the Baltic barons. Their legal corporations, which had dominated social life in the area, had already been dispersed in 1917. Land reform in Lithuania, where the local nobility had been considerably more repressed in Tsarist times, was less sweeping. Although the large estates disappeared, their former owners were left with somewhat larger portions of the land they had once owned.

Loss of their Russian markets led to some hardship for the

Estonian and Latvian industries. Realignment came slowly, but it was successfully achieved. Estonia developed a new oil-shale industry. Timber and related enterprises were built up as export industries. In 1930, manufacturing engaged 17.4 per cent of Estonia's labor force and 13.5 per cent of Latvia's, but only 6 per cent of Lithuania's, which remained largely unindustrialized.

The principal economic effort in all three countries was to create an export economy based on agricultural produce and specializing in meat, poultry and dairy products. Government-sponsored cooperatives appeared in all three countries to handle the collection, processing and marketing of farm produce. Britain and Germany became the two principal export markets. These moves were intended to benefit the new independent farming class which had been created through land redistribution and which emerged as the principal component in the socio-economic structures of the three states.

In accordance with prevailing Western political currents of the time, all three countries adopted liberal democratic constitutions. Their legislatures clearly predominated over their executives. Single-chamber parliaments emerged in all three. In Estonia the Prime Minister was simultaneously head of state, and thus a vote of no-confidence in Parliament would leave the country without even a titular head. Such assembly structures are perhaps the most difficult of all to operate, and none of the three societies possessed a proper social, economic or political culture or tradition necessary to support their functioning. The radical parliamentary constitutions and electoral rules hampered the creation of stable governments. The pressures of radical interests and ideologies soon led, as they did throughout the rest of Eastern Europe, to the emergence of some sort of authoritarian system.

The earliest change came in Lithuania. A precarious political stability had been possible as long as the Christian Democrats and their allies managed to win majorities among the predominantly Catholic electorate. In 1926, however, a series of scandals led to their defeat. Later that year, the small Nationalist Union, supported by the passivity of the opposition Christian Democrats, was installed by the army, overthrowing a coalition government of Populists, Socialists and minorities which had been in power barely half a year. An authoritarian presidential regime, similar to that of Piłsudski in Poland, emerged under the leadership of Antanas Smetona.

The process of democratic disintegration was somewhat more long-drawn-out in Estonia and Latvia. Fragmentation into numerous small political parties made the formation of stable coalitions a difficult task. In Estonia, governments between 1919 and 1933 lasted eight months on average. Political instability was aggravated by the social effects of the Great Depression. Pressures for political reform mounted, particularly from the right-wing League of Freedom Fighters, an association of veterans of the war for independence. In October 1933, their proposal for constitutional reform won by 72.7 per cent of the votes in a referendum. The following March, the Acting President, Konstantin Päts, made use of the new authoritarian Constitution to declare a state of emergency, deactivate Parliament and disband the League of Freedom Fighters. He ruled by presidential decree until 1938.

A similar change occurred in Latvia a few months later. In a situation of extreme polarization between right- and left-wing forces, Prime Minister Kārlis Ulmanis declared a state of emergency, formed a government of national unity, dissolved all political parties and governed without the legislature.

There were noticeable differences in the styles of the new regimes in the three countries. Authoritarianism proved somewhat milder in Estonia and Lithuania than in Latvia. The moderate Estonian leader considered his system as a transition to a more stable democratic system. A referendum on a new Constituent Assembly implicitly legalized his caretaker regime in 1936, and another new Constitution provided for a Parliament, which convened in 1938. Electoral rules were designed to favor Päts and his Patriotic League. However, elections to the lower house were basically fair. Despite their fragmentation, opposition groups won 17 of the 80 seats. In Lithuania, the more dictatorially inclined rightist Prime Minister Augustinas Voldemaras, who had been installed along with Antanas Smetona during the coup of 1926, was dismissed in 1929. Thereafter Smetona, casting himself as the "nation's leader," tried to fashion his regime on the fascist Italian model. Although his Nationalist Union, the only political group allowed to function openly, was expanded into a mass organization, many politicians from the previously important political parties continued their activity unofficially. The worsening international climate during the late 1930s led Smetona to allow the *de facto* emergence of "coalition" governments of national unity, even though the parties represented in them could not legally function as such. Authoritarianism in Latvia proved more straightforward. Ulmanis did not bother to legalize his regime by a referendum or to organize his supporters into an official party. Adopting a policy of "a strong and

Latvian Latvia," he combined the offices of President and Prime Minister. In his search for a base of support, he pursued a policy of enlarging the state sector of the economy, primarily at the expense of the German minority.

No significant opposition to the suppression of the parliamentary governments arose. Many former politicians proved quite willing to cooperate with the new regimes, whose introduction was rationalized by a need to prevent foreign influence or takeovers by extreme local rightist or leftist elements. The continued support of the professional officer corps assured their stability. While the liberal-minded intelligentsia could not be won over, and chafed under the relatively mild restraints on political expression, the rural population and the business establishment welcomed the prosperity accompanying stability — which was largely due, however, to the passing of the world Depression. From the mid-1930s, foreign trade showed a steady increase in all three countries. While political dissatisfaction was not absent, potentially serious internal dissension did not arise. In Estonia, the general amnesty of 1938 left only a few dozen "political" prisoners, nearly all of them espionage cases. Even the Lithuanian regime proved able to weather two grave blows to its prestige in foreign relations. In 1938, following a frontier incident, Poland presented an ultimatum demanding recognition of the Polish possession of Vilnius, and in March 1939 Hitler reannexed Klaipėda (Memel), which had been part of the pre-1918 German state.

The political authoritarianism was too mild to affect culture significantly. Indeed, the regimes supported the development of the national cultural life which had begun with the achivement of independence. The twenty-two-year period of independence was one of significant cultural advance for the Baltic peoples. Literary, artistic and musical life flourished. The increase in numbers of schools was phenomenal. Each of the three countries maintained a national university, where higher education in the native language became available for the first time. In Estonia the German-Russian University of Iurev (Dorpat) became the University of Tartu. In Latvia the Polytechnic Institute of Riga was expanded to become a full university. In Lithuania, since Vilnius was controlled by Poland, a new university was established at Kaunas in 1922.

The three Baltic countries attempted to pursue a path of neutrality in foreign policy as the war clouds gathered during the late 1930s. Even regional cooperation among the smaller states between Germany and the USSR proved minimal. Irreconcilable differences between

Lithuania and Poland hampered cooperation in that quarter, and Finland was not interested in any southern alliance. An Estonian-Latvian defensive alliance of 1923 was supplemented in 1934 by a Baltic Entente including Lithuania. However, the level of practical cooperation remained minimal. This may have been due partly to differences in opinion as to where the principal danger lay. Lithuania and Latvia inclined toward a predominant fear of Germany, while Estonia, which was further away from Germany and which had experienced an abortive Communist coup in 1924, was more concerned with the threat from the USSR.

All three countries eventually signed non-aggression or neutrality agreements with the Soviet Union (Lithuania in 1926, Latvia and Estonia in 1932), and with Germany (Latvia and Estonia in June 1939, and Lithuania in the context of the Act of March 1939 ceding Klaipėda). Neutrality laws patterned on the Swedish law of 1938 were adopted by Latvia and Estonia in December 1938, and by Lithuania a month later.

If the foreign policies of the Baltic states can be said to have been inclined toward any of the great powers, it was toward Britain which, while far away, could supposedly exercise its naval power in the area, as it had done in 1919. However, by 1939 Britain appeared increasingly weak. It also seemed to be moving in the direction of willingness to accept some sort of Soviet predominance in the Baltic states as a safeguard against German influence. The extent to which Britain was ready to tolerate Soviet control is unclear; one of the reasons for the failure of the Anglo-French military mission to the USSR in the summer of 1939 was its inability to grant the Soviets a free hand in the area.

The Baltic leaders strove to minimize and to balance both German and Soviet influences. Their attempts to maintain neutrality came to be criticized as pro-German by both Britain and the Soviet Union, which wanted the Baltic states to participate in collective defense against Germany. The sole area of direct German interest, Klaipėda, was wrested from Lithuania by force in March 1939, and German economic pressure on Lithuania increased; but German attempts to promote a military alliance with Lithuania directed against Poland, with Vilnius as a prize, were resisted by the Kaunas government. Baltic independence, however, was less dependent on efforts of the local governments than on arrangements among the great powers.

2

THE WAR YEARS, 1940–1945

The Coming of the Soviets

The End of Baltic Independence. The fate of Baltic independence was sealed with the conclusion of the Molotov-Ribbentrop Pact on 23 August 1939 between Nazi Germany and the Soviet Union. Its secret "additional protocol" assigned Estonia and Latvia to the Soviet sphere of influence, while Lithuania was left to Germany. A subsequent modification concluded after the collapse of Poland placed most of Lithuania in the Soviet sphere as well. By late September, with the Baltic states completely cut off from Britain and France, Stalin could begin the process of annexation. He started with Estonia, which (in contrast to Latvia and Lithuania) had not mobilized even partly during the Polish campaign. About 160,000 Soviet troops were brought to the Estonian border.[1]

The first step on the road to loss of independence was the least painful. With Soviet warplanes flying low over Tallinn, and Germany taking a stance of pro-Soviet neutrality,[2] Estonia was forced to accept, on 28 September, a Pact of Defense and Mutual Assistance with the USSR. Latvia's turn came on 5 October, and Lithuania's on 10 October. The pacts provided for sizeable Soviet garrisons as well as naval bases on Baltic territory. The 30,000 Soviet troops in Latvia and 25,000 in Estonia surpassed in size the national armies (20,000

1. For texts of Nazi-Soviet agreements, see Raymond Sontag and James Beddie (eds), *Nazi-Soviet Relations, 1939–1941* (Washington, DC, 1948; henceforth cited as *Nazi-Soviet Relations*), pp. 76–8; or *Documents on German Foreign Policy, 1918–1945*, ser. D, vol. VIII (US Department of State, 1954), p. 166; also Bronis Kaslas (ed.), *The USSR-German Aggression against Lithuania* (New York, 1973), pp. 109–12 and 129–30. For Baltic mobilizations and Soviet troops, see Seppo Myllyniemi, *Die baltische Krise, 1938–1941* (Stuttgart, 1979), pp. 54–5 and 59.

2. German representatives not only refused any support, but also said they would not allow sea transport of arms to Estonia from the West. See *Eesti NSV ajalugu*, III (Tallinn, 1971), p. 365.

and 16,000, respectively); Lithuania haggled its share down to 20,000 Soviet troops. The Baltic governments could not verify the actual numbers brought to the Soviet bases. The treaties guaranteed Baltic independence and reiterated Soviet non-interference in Baltic internal affairs. Lithuania, which during September had resisted German promptings to become a satellite and to retake its claimed capital city Vilnius from Polish control, now received that city together with some surrounding territory as a "gift" from the USSR, which had occupied the area on 17 September.[3]

During the first few months following the pacts, the Soviet military and naval presence was kept at an unobtrusively low level. Stalin, having to face unexpectedly stiff resistance to his attempt to impose a similar arrangement on Finland, was also no doubt waiting to see which way the Germans' war with the West would go.

It is not clear how much the Baltic governments knew about the secret protocols in the Molotov-Ribbentrop Pact. Rumors were circulating already in August. The published documents seem to indicate that in Latvia and Lithuania the governments had been at least partially apprised of the clauses by the Soviets in early October.[4] The lack of German protest over the military arrangements in the Pacts of Mutual Assistance provided sufficient indication of German cognizance of and acquiescence in the matter. Repatriation of about 65,000 Germans from Latvia and Estonia in late 1939 was also ominous. What most likely remained unclear was the degree to which the USSR would effectively seek to impose its dominance. If the Baltic governments were aware of the gravity of the situation, their attempts to reassure their populations provided little indication of it. For instance, on 20 October the Lithuanian paper *Lietuvos aidas*, considered a mouthpiece for government opinion, reasoned:

The present war shakes the foundations of our old order. Certainly the new peace radically changes its exterior physionomy. Many new principles will be found and applied, not only in international relations, but also in the internal organization of many free and independent peoples. The new principles will equally affect our country.[5]

---

3. Kaslas 1973, pp. 148–58; see also Myllyniemi 1979, pp. 59–69. For Latvian and Estonian figures, see Arnolds Spekke, *History of Latvia* (Stockholm, 1957), p. 380, and Evald Uustalu, "Events after 1940," in the Appendix to August Rei, *The Drama of the Baltic Peoples*, 2nd ed. (Stockholm, 1970), p. 239.

4. *Nazi-Soviet Relations*, pp. 114–17.

5. Cited in Henry de Chambon, *La tragédie des nations baltiques* (Paris, 1946), p. 34.

The policy of all three governments was to maintain good relations with the USSR and to avoid incidents with the garrisons until the international political climate improved. Since Baltic independence had originally been made possible in part by a German-Russian conflict, not much could be done as long as Germany supported the Soviet presence in the three states. The Finnish Winter War confirmed that the Western powers could not be counted upon. Perhaps the leading circles in Riga and Kaunas shared Estonian President Päts' conviction of the inevitability of a German-Soviet clash by late 1940.[6] Such reasoning affirmed the prudence of docility *vis-à-vis* the USSR. It also dictated efforts at a slow strengthening of the German stake in the area as a counterbalance. Increased trade arrangements with the Reich reflected such a policy. The war had interrupted Baltic trade with the West, and new outlets were badly needed. Between December 1939 and April 1940, all three states had concluded trade treaties according to which Germany was supposed to buy about 70 per cent of all Baltic exports.[7] The Soviets voiced no objections; their own trade with Germany was brisk.

The winter of 1939–40 also saw the first meaningful and intensive, albeit belated, collaboration among the three states, even though the formal framework for such communality, the Baltic Entente, dated from 1934. However, in view of the general attempt on the part of all three governments to placate the Soviets, no concrete preparations were undertaken. In May 1940 some instructions on contingency situations were issued to the diplomatic services of Latvia and Lithuania. On 17 May 1940, plenipotentiary power was issued to the Latvian Minister in Britain, Kārlis Zariņš. He was authorized, should contact with the home-country be broken, to exercise full authority over Latvia's resources and representatives abroad and to liquidate all diplomatic missions save that in the United States if he saw fit.[8] The Lithuanian Envoy in Rome, the former Foreign Minister Stasys Lozoraitis, was designated on 30 May head of the service in the event that the home government should cease to exist or be unable to carry

---

6. Heinrich Laretei, *Saatuse mängukanniks* (Lund, 1970), p. 241; Myllyniemi 1979, p. 102.

7. Actual figures were lower: e.g. Germany accounted for 53 per cent of Estonia's exports in May 1940, and 42 per cent from January to May. The USSR actually urged Latvia to export more to Germany. See Myllyniemi 1979, pp. 108–10.

8. *Third Interim Report of the Select Committee on Communist Aggression*, 83rd Congress, 2nd Session (Washington, DC, 1954; henceforth cited as *Third Interim Report*), p. 433.

out its duties. A portion of the Latvian and Estonian gold reserve was sent to the United States and Britain, and some Estonian archives were shipped to the Legation in Stockholm.[9]

The Soviets obviously realized that in the case of any military conflict they could not depend on the Baltic states as allies — any hope for a genuine alliance had been wrecked by the methods whereby Soviet bases had been forced upon them. A decision to occupy them fully may have been made in early February 1940, at a Moscow meeting attended by Soviet envoys in the Baltics, since Baltic Communist underground activity increased sharply in March.[10]

The Battle of France gave Stalin a unique opportunity for total occupation of the Baltic states; both German and Western forces were tied up far from Eastern Europe. Lithuania was singled out for the first blow. On 25 May, a Soviet note to the Kaunas government accused Lithuanian authorities of kidnapping two Soviet garrison soldiers. The Lithuanians proposed an extraordinary investigatory commission including a representative of the Red Army garrisons, as well as an order for an energetic search for the two, but there was no Soviet reaction. On 30 May, Moscow published a communiqué on allegedly provocative activities by the Lithuanian authorities. The Lithuanian Minister of Foreign Affairs, Juozas Urbšys, went to Moscow in an attempt to settle the incident through direct negotiations. Molotov agreed to discuss the matter, but only with the Prime Minister, Antanas Merkys, who also flew to Moscow on 7 June. In two meetings with Merkys, Molotov castigated the Lithuanian Minister of the Interior as well as the Director of its Security Department for their allegedly hostile anti-Soviet attitudes. The Prime Minister himself was reproached for transforming the Baltic Entente into a military alliance directed against the USSR. Subsequent efforts by the Lithuanian government included a personal message from the President of the Republic to the Chairman of the Presidium of the Supreme Soviet giving explicit assurances of having at all times honored the Pact of Mutual Defense with the USSR.

After Merkys' empty-handed return to Kaunas, Molotov, at midnight on 14 June, handed the Foreign Minister (who had stayed in Moscow) the Soviet proposal for settling the issue. It came in the form of an ultimatum: (1) the arrest and trial of the two officials against

9. Hain Rebas, "Tallinn-Stockholm-Tallinn, 1940: Estonian Diplomatic Records on a Mysterious Round Trip," JBS, VIII/3 (Fall 1977), pp. 205–13.

10. Myllyniemi 1979, pp. 114–17.

whom Molotov had levelled charges; (2) the formation of a government "capable of assuring proper fulfillment" of the pact with the USSR; and (3) the entry into Lithuania of additional units of the Red Army, to be stationed at important centers "in numbers sufficient to ensure proper enforcement" of the pacts. The numbers were not specified, but since the country was to be occupied, this was irrelevant.

The emergency Lithuanian cabinet session that followed decided to comply with the Soviet demands. President Smetona found himself in a minority in urging at least symbolic military resistance, to be followed by a collective withdrawal of the government from the country.[11] In accordance with Soviet wishes, Prime Minister Merkys resigned and Smetona asked the erstwhile Commander-in-Chief of the army, General Stasys Raštikis, who had left that post not long before over political differences with Smetona, to form a new government. A few hours later, the Foreign Minister, still in Moscow, informed the government that Raštikis was also unacceptable to the Kremlin and that the Soviet Deputy Commissar for Foreign Affairs, Vladimir Dekanozov, would be sent to Lithuania as special emissary. He would supervise the formation of a new cabinet. Smetona, accompanied by a few high officials, left his country. The Red Army streamed into Lithuania. On the same day (15 June 1940), the Germans entered Paris.

On the following day, Molotov sent similar notes to Latvia and Estonia accusing their governments of breaking their pacts with the USSR and of plotting to turn the Baltic Entente into an anti-Soviet alliance. His proof consisted in pointing to the December 1939 and March 1940 meetings of the Foreign Ministers of the three countries, which had hardly been secret, and publication of the *Baltic Review*, a journal which had appeared since February 1939 with articles in English, French and German. Molotov's notes demanded the formation of governments capable of carrying out the pacts with the USSR and the introduction of unlimited additional Soviet military and naval units. Each ultimatum carried a six- to eight-hour time limit.

Latvia and Estonia also yielded to the Soviet demands, and on 17 June Soviet forces marched into both countries. The futility of any resistance had been increased by the Lithuanian surrender. Latvian combat preparations were called off when the Soviets threatened to bomb the cities, and when it became clear that Germany would not agree to sell any arms; President Päts of Estonia also seems to have

11. Stasys Raštikis, *Kovose dėl Lietuvos* (Los Angeles, 1957), II, pp. 23–5.

tried through his unofficial contacts with the German Legation in Tallinn to persuade Germany to intercede.[12] Two special emissaries, Andrei Vyshinskii for Latvia and Andrei Zhdanov for Estonia, accompanied the Red Army to supervise the formation of new pro-Soviet governments. By 18 June the occupation of the Baltic states was complete.

At no time in May–June did the USSR accuse the Baltic governments of collusion with Germany. Indeed, a 28 May 1940 article in *Pravda* on "political feelings in Estonia" had chided the Estonians for their liking England and disliking Germany. Germany did not protest at the Soviet occupation of the Baltic states. On 18 June, the German Ambassador in Moscow reported Molotov's comment on the necessity to put "an end to all intrigues by which England and France had tried to sow discord and mistrust between Germany and the Soviet Union in the Baltic states."[13]

The Formation of People's Governments. The first step tóward a "constitutional" metamorphosis of the Baltic states into constituent republics of the USSR was the formation of transitional "People's Governments." Cabinet lists were presented by the Soviet emissaries, who refused to sanction even minor changes.[14] The Communist Parties in all three states were minuscule (see details in next section). During the first days of Soviet occupation, they were still officially illegal. Their leaders were not widely known. So, for the sake of appearance, the new governments were coalitions of broadly left-wing "popular" forces including several prominent opponents of the previous regimes. Only a few Communists received ministerial portfolios, albeit ones of key significance. In theory, the cabinets were installed according to constitutions still in force.

From the legal point of view, this task of forming a cabinet "normally" was most problematic in Lithuania. The President had left. Antanas Merkys was Acting President by virtue of a position, that of Prime Minister, which he had already resigned. His ability to fulfill presidential functions, including the appointment of a new cabi-

---

12. Jānis Jūrmalnieks, "Die Einverleibung Lettlands in die Sowjetunion," AB, XVII (1977), p. 152; Georg von Rauch, *The Baltic States: The Years of Independence, 1917–1940* (London, Berkeley and Los Angeles, 1974), p. 221.

13. *Nazi-Soviet Relations*, p. 154.

14. Boris Meissner, *Die Sowjetunion, die Baltischen Staaten und das Völkerrecht* (Cologne, 1956), pp. 71–81. The only exception seems to be the inclusion of Kruus in Estonia, on the insistence of Vares; cf. Myllyniemi 1979, p. 131.

net, could be questioned. Dekanozov overcame this obstacle with a blatantly untrue announcement that the Lithuanian government considered Smetona's departure as his resignation.[15] The new Lithuanian cabinet was headed by Justas Paleckis, a journalist whose political sympathies could be best described as moderate left-wing populist. He also replaced Merkys as Acting President, an act of dubious constitutional validity. The Prime Minister's functions were taken over by his deputy who was simultaneously Minister of Foreign Affairs, the writer and literary scholar Vincas Krėvė-Mickevičius, the most eminent and widely known personage in the new administration and the only one with genuine popularity throughout the land. His participation gave credence to the official line that the new government was only a replacement for the overthrown "fascist" regime. The retention of the Minister of Finance of the previous cabinet, Ernestas Galvanauskas, also served this purpose. Although the new Minister of Internal Affairs, Mečys Gedvilas, was a Communist, he was publicly known only as a left-wing activist. Somewhat later, three other Communists — Mykolas Junčas-Kučinskas, Karolis Didžiulis and Stasys Pupeikis — were added to the cabinet, though not in prominent positions.

From the constitutional point of view, the tasks in Riga and Tallinn were somewhat simpler. Vyshinskii and Zhdanov presented Presidents Ulmanis and Päts, respectively, with Soviet-proposed cabinet lists. The initial refusal of both incumbents to sanction such governments led to the organization of "popular" demonstrations by the "masses" — a *mélange* of Communist sympathizers, some of the recently released prisoners, civilian Soviet workers at Soviet bases, and Soviet military and naval personnel specially lent out and accompanied by armored cars for the occasion. In Riga, where on 18 June the cruiser *Marat* had brought a shipload of Soviet demonstrators, 25,000 people in all may have been involved in demonstrations. Their activity led to some bloody street disturbances. In Tallinn, there was a brief skirmish, with some shots fired between Estonian soldiers and civilians invading their barracks with armed Soviet support. Demonstrators and bystanders amounted to anything between 2,000 and 7,000 people.[16] The futility of noncompliance

15. Juozas Brazaitis, "Pirmoji sovietinė okupacija (1940–1941)," *Lietuvių enciklopedija* (Boston, Mass., 1968), XV, p. 360.

16. Alfred Bilmanis, *A History of Latvia* (Princeton, 1951), p. 394; August Rei, "Traagiliste sündmuste tunnistajana," in *Eesti riik ja rahvas teises maailmasõjas* (Stockholm, 1954–62; henceforth cited as *Eesti riik*), 10 vols, III, pp. 17–25; A. Kurgvel,

became evident to both Presidents. In Latvia, an "announcement of the Secretariat of the President of the Republic" to the effect that a new cabinet had been formed was published in the official government gazette on 20 June, but without the signature of Ulmanis or of any other official.[17] Initially, the new government, led by the Liberal Augusts Kirhenšteins, a professor of bacteriology, also included, in addition to two Communists (Vilis Lācis and Vikentijs Latkovskis), Social Democrats, Populists and various left-wing cultural figures.

Only in Estonia were the constitutional formalities observed, as Päts, under coercion, approved the Soviet-proposed cabinet. Johannes Vares, a physician and poet, was the new Prime Minister; Professor Hans Kruus, a well-known historian from the University of Tartu, was appointed Deputy Prime Minister. The cabinet represented a coalition of three former social revolutionary intellectuals (Vares, Kruus and Johannes Semper), four leftist members of the Estonian Parliament, and several non-party specialists. The Soviet-imposed cabinet of Estonia initially included no known Communists.

Presidents Ulmanis and Päts formally headed their respective countries until both were forced to resign in mid-July. But in a political sense, neither was of any significance once the new cabinets had been installed. After their resignations, both were deported to the USSR, Kārlis Ulmanis to Voroshilovsk on 22 July, and Konstantin Päts to Ufa on 30 July; the locations became known only years later. Antanas Merkys, the former Lithuanian Acting President, was deported on 16 July.[18] Several other high officials of the previous Baltic governments were also taken to the USSR around this time. Lithuanian Foreign Minister Juozas Urbšys, who was in Moscow on 15 June, was simply not allowed to return home.

The formal incorporation of the Baltic states into the USSR had not yet taken place, and from the official Soviet point of view they were still independent states. The arrest and deportation of leading statesmen of one state by another state was perhaps an unprecedented event in the history of modern international relations.

"Sõjavägede staabis 21 juunil," *ibid.*, pp. 32–7, Myllyniemi 1979, pp. 128–31. A demonstration attendance of 30,000 to 40,000 people in Tallinn is claimed in *Eesti NSV ajalugu*, III, p. 489, but a picture on p. 487 shows a half-empty square with only a few thousand people.

17. *Latvju enciklopēdija* (Stockholm, 1950–1), I, pp. 804–5; *Valdības vēstnesis*, 20 June 1940.

18. Rauch, p. 226.

People's Assemblies and Formal Incorporations.   The earliest statements of the new cabinets denied any intention of setting up Soviet regimes, not to mention incorporation into the USSR.[19] The declared purpose of the invasion and of political changes was merely to remove the "fascist" politicians from office. Vyshinskii, in an address from the balcony of the Soviet Legation in Riga, rebuked overzealous pro-Soviet demonstrators demanding the incorporation of Latvia into the USSR. He even finished his speech in Latvian: "Long live free Latvia! Long live the unbreakable friendship between Latvia and the Soviet Union!" Lithuanian Minister of the Interior Gedvilas, one of the Communists in the new cabinet, declared on 21 June:

The essential fundamentals of our country have not been changed. No one threatens rightful private property or wealth. The Red Army came to our country not to change our way of life, but only to protect us from the dangers of war and to help us maintain our independence.[20]

On the other hand, it should also be stressed that Communist Party appeals did not eschew allusions to the incorporation which was to come. Slogans like "Long live Soviet Lithuania — the Thirteenth Soviet Socialist Republic" began to appear in party leaflets.[21]

Nevertheless, the initial uncertainty among the populations of the Baltic states over Soviet intentions following the events of mid-June soon gave way to realization that establishment of the "coalition cabinets" was not the end of the process. Real power lay not with these governments but rather with the three Soviet emissaries operating from the Soviet Legations.

Significant alterations in the political and social structures of the three countries were begun soon after the occupations. In late June and early July, the Communist parties, which had been visibly active (though still illegal) since the first days of the arrival of the Red Army, emerged as the countries' only legal political parties. Their position was somewhat anomalous. As all three countries were predominantly agrarian, none had developed a Communist movement of any significance. Moreover, most of the more prominent Baltic Communists who had remained in the USSR during the interwar period had

19. See *Third Interim Report*, pp. 220, 301 and 338, as well as the speech of J. Paleckis, 18 June 1940, in V. Kancevičius (ed.), *Lithuania in 1939–1940: The Historic Turn to Socialism* (Vilnius, 1976), pp. 160–2.

20. *Third Interim Report*, pp. 338–9; cited from *Lietuvos žinios*, 22 June 1940.

21. *Istoriia Litovskoi SSR* (Vilnius, 1978), p. 422. Mentions of the currency of such slogans in June 1940 seem to have been avoided in earlier Soviet sources.

perished during the purges of 1936–8. The Lithuanian party of some 1,500 members was numerically the largest of the three. A significant portion of its membership consisted of individuals from minority groups. The Latvian party had about 1,000 members at the time of its legalization. The supreme irony was that its traditions were still those of 1905 and 1917–18. Soviet "liberation" galvanized the remnants of such traditional political action: the distribution of leaflets, hoisting of red flags and the agitation of crowds. The Muscovite functionaries who were running the show, however, had emerged from the USSR of the 1930s and tended to view such "old-fashioned" spontaneous ebullience disapprovingly. According to the official party history, the Estonian party numbered only 133 members.[22]

All non-Communist-controlled public activity was proscribed; political, social, ideological and religious groups which could not be subsumed into the circle of Communist fronts were disbanded. In late June, the process touched groups which were evidently political. By the end of the following month, even the Boy Scouts had ceased to exist. Changes in the administrative apparatus of all three countries began immediately after the occupation. There were massive layoffs

22. It is difficult to find exact figures for party memberships in June 1940. More recent Lithuanian sources place the number at around 2,000; viz. K. Surblys, *Lietuvos KP veikla ugdant socialistinę darbininkų klasę, 1940–1975* (Vilnius, 1976), p. 12. Another source, *Lietuvos Komunistų Partija skaičiais, 1918–1975: statistikos duomenų rinkinys* (Vilnius, 1976), p. 10, claims 2,000 upon legalization on 25 June 1940; on p. 42, however, the figure of 1,690 is given for 15 June 1940. It also provides the puzzling explanation that, in late 1940, party cards could not be issued to 1,011 individuals for a variety of reasons. Of these, more than 500 had belonged to the underground before the occupation; therefore actual membership must have reached some 2,200. The prominent party historian R. Sharmaitis (Šarmaitis), in "Kommunisticheskoi Partii Litvy — 50 let," *Kommunist* (Litvy), 1968, p. 69, also claims 2,000 upon legalization. However, at the bottom of the same page, he gives the figure of 1,470 for party membership from 1934 up to 1940, which would indicate that the underground party increased by a third during the first half of 1940, which is rather hard to believe. An earlier source, A. Butkutė-Ramelienė, *Lietuvos KP kova už tarybų valdžios įtvirtinimą respublikoje* (Vilnius, 1958), p. 166, estimates 1,500 for mid-June 1940 and adds that 673 were admitted soon after legalization. The Latvian figure is taken from *Ocherki istorii Kommunisticheskoi Partii Latvii*, II (Riga, 1966), p. 444. Myllyniemi 1979, p. 84, tabulates 1,150 LaCP members in 1934, only 400 in 1939 and 1,000 in June 1940, with the latter figure possibly applying to late June when the Soviet army was already in. The Estonian figure of 133 is from Aleksander Panksejev, in *Töid EKP ajaloo alalt*, II (Tallinn, 1966), p. 156. On 1 September 1940 only 124 pre-July ECP members received the new membership cards, according to Johannes Jakobson et al., *Ülevaade Eestimaa Kommunistliku Partei ajaloost*, III (Tallinn, 1972; henceforth cited as Ülevaade EKP), p. 13.

of leading officers, district chairmen, police commanders and school principals. In Lithuania, 11 of the 12 mayors of principal cities, 19 of the 23 mayors of towns, and 175 out of 261 county heads were replaced by 18 July.[23] At the end of the month, the police force was replaced by a militia specially recruited from among workers in factories with workforces of more than fifty. The newly renamed "People's Armies," though still technically distinct from the Red Army, were rapidly Sovietized in preparation for their absorption into the Red Army. Already in late June, massive layoffs of senior officers began. Early the following month, Institutes for Political Instruction were established in the three armies. Their soldiers were "allowed to participate" in politics during their off-duty time. In effect, they were marshalled as participants in the ever-increasing "spontaneous" demonstrations. By mid-July, the auxiliary Home Guard militias which had been conceived as a volunteer ready reserve were disbanded.

The course of Sovietization gave overwhelming and unmistakable evidence of a rapidly approaching loss even of formal independence. It most alarmed those Baltic leaders who had felt that collaboration with the USSR was the only sensible way of riding out the crisis. Lithuanian Foreign Minister Vincas Krėvė-Mickevičius acted on such considerations in seeking an interview with the Kremlin leadership. Molotov saw no need for talks and refused his initial request. But Mickevičius' persistence changed Molotov's mind, and an interview was granted on 30 June. At first, according to his memoirs, the Lithuanian official presented a picture of the actual state of affairs in Lithuania and the impotence of the People's Government in running the country in the face of activity by Soviet officials. He requested a new convention to regulate Soviet-Lithuanian affairs more precisely. Molotov was quite blunt about the Soviet intention to occupy the whole region permanently, and defended the move as a historical necessity for the development of the Russian state which had been understood by the Tsars. But historical imperative was not the sole criterion conditioning the Kremlin's actions. Molotov continued:

You must take a good look at reality and understand that in the future small nations will have to disappear. Your Lithuania along with the other Baltic nations, including Finland, will have to join the glorious family of the Soviet Union. Therefore you should begin now to initiate your people into the

---

23. A. Rakūnas, *Klasių kova Lietuvoje, 1940–1951 m.* (Vilnius, 1976), p. 22.

Soviet system, which in the future shall reign everywhere, throughout all Europe; put into practice earlier in some places, as in the Baltic nations, later in others.[24]

Mickevičius tried to raise objections on practical grounds. He argued that Sovietization would merely introduce chaos into the Lithuanian economy, a situation obviously detrimental to Soviet interests. But such observations were useless. Not wanting to officiate over the burial of his country, a thoroughly disillusioned Krėvė-Mickevičius submitted his resignation on his return·to Lithuania. It was rejected, though he was given leave of absence ostensibly for health reasons. The Minister of Finance, Ernestas Galvanauskas, also resigned and fled abroad.

In order to prevent *de facto* Sovietization from outpacing the formal constitutional structures by too wide margins, elections for "People's Assemblies" to be held on 14 July (and continuing to 15 July in Latvia and Estonia) were announced early that month. Changes in the electoral laws by decrees which accompanied the announcements contravened the constitutions then still formally in force. In Latvia the period for presentation of candidates was drastically shortened from 40 to 4–6 days after promulgation of the decree; in Estonia the period was reduced from 35 to 3 days. Candidates were to be "nominated" by cultural, educational, labor and other legally functioning organizations — and, for practical purposes, by that time only organizations dominated by the Communist parties were legal. The obvious intention was the staging of a Soviet-style election with the unanimous victory of a single slate of candidates. The approved slates of the "Working People's Leagues" were heavily non-Communist in composition. As parliaments under the Soviet system were a formality anyway, such a ratio made no difference. In Lithuania, at least two candidates appeared on the slate without the knowledge of the individuals involved;[25] it is unlikely that they were an exception. At that stage, any talk of incorporation into the USSR was vehemently denied by the new rulers.

Efforts to organize alternate electoral slates in all three countries were the last attempts to maintain some autonomy within the new

---

24. *Third Interim Report*, p. 458.
25. Liudas Dovydėnas, "Mano kelias į Liaudies Seimą," *Lietuvių archyvas: Bolševizmo metai* (Kaunas, 1942), III, p. 51; Dovydėnas, *Mes valdysim pasaulį* (Woodhaven, N.Y., 1970), I, pp. 193ff.; A. Garmus, "Lietuvos įjungimas į SSSR — Maskvos diktatas," *Lietuvių archyvas*, ed. J. Prunskis (Brooklyn, NY, 1952), p. 8.

system. In Estonia, where only three-and-a-half days had been allotted for nominations, opposition groups nonetheless managed to present 78 candidates in 66 of the 80 electoral districts. The cabinet, acting on instructions from Zhdanov and without any legal basis, required all candidates to submit a platform within a few hours. Most of the alternate candidates managed to comply, but they were removed by a combination of threats and violence as well as invalidations by district electoral commissions. As orders were received at the last minute, some alternate candidates did manage to obtain certification in several districts; this had to be summarily nullified. In Latvia, an abortive attempt was made to include on the ballot a Democratic bloc representing a coalition of all significant, but by then banned, Latvian political parties with the exception of the Social Democrats. The organizers were arrested soon after. It has been claimed that the formally dissolved Populist Party proposed a distinct slate in Lithuania; we are unable to verify this assertion.[26]

The goal of the occupation authorities was that the greatest number of individuals should vote and thus legitimize the new system. Along with Latvian and Lithuanian newspapers, Estonia's main daily *Rahva Hääl* openly threatened non-voters on 14 July: "It would be extremely unwise to shirk elections. . . . Only people's enemies stay at home on election day." As results had, according to Soviet practice, most likely been decided in advance, scrupulous care in the electoral procedure itself was not warranted. In Lithuania, no lists of eligible voters were drawn up; in effect, anyone could vote, and several times if he so desired. In all three countries, a stamp in the internal passports identified, for future purposes, those who had voted. However, even with this practical threat, the turnout was so low as to induce the Lithuanian cabinet to extend balloting by one day, 15 July.

The ballot carried only the Soviet-assigned candidate's name. The only way to register opposition was to strike it out. Use of an isolated booth was discouraged or prevented; in many places, open ballots had to be handed to an official who dropped them in the box. The vote-count was often cynical. In one Estonian case, doubtless typical throughout the three countries, election officials computed the number of votes needed to show 99.6 per cent participation, counted out

26. At the Estonian government meeting of 9 July, Prime Minister Vares apparently showed a note from Zhdanov ordering elimination of alternate candidates; see Myllyniemi 1979, p. 133. On Latvian arrests, see Spekke, p. 386. Lithuanian Populist list: Leonas Sabaliūnas, *Lithuania in Crisis, 1939–1940* (Bloomington, Ind., 1972), p. 285, note 44.

the necessary number of used and unused ballots for that result, and submitted the appropriate return to the district committee. In Narva, Red Army troops guarded the ballot boxes overnight; in Tartu, they were even present in the polling room.[27] Thus the elections in one sovereign state were physically conducted by the armed forces of another.

Officially, the results were to the Kremlin's satisfaction: in Lithuania 95.5 per cent of the electorate allegedly voted and gave 99.2 per cent of its vote to the League; in Latvia the figures were 94.7 and 97.6 per cent; in Estonia 81.6 and 92.2 per cent. Privately, several leading members of the Lithuanian administration were quoted as having claimed a real total turnout no higher than 32 per cent.[28] Archives left behind by the Soviets during their retreat in 1941 indicate that Estonia's Central Electoral Committee forged 35,119 votes.[29] This was apparently in addition to the widespread tampering at lower levels.

Once the elections had been staged, open reference to Sovietization and to incorporation into the USSR, which until then had not been justifiable according to the circumstances, became commonplace. Indeed, exhortations along such lines now provided the topics for "discussion" of the principal tasks facing the elected assemblies. Before the elections, there had been virtual silence on the questions which those bodies would have to tackle. "Popular voices," consisting of organized street demonstrations, began increasingly to express the "demand of the people" for the introduction of the Stalin Constitution in all three countries as well as their incorporation into the USSR.

All three People's Assemblies convened on 21 July 1940. In Estonia Soviet troops were present in the assembly hall at least part of the time.[30] Within the first hour, the Estonian Assembly had passed by acclamation the establishment of a Soviet socialist form of govern-

27. For Tartu: eyewitness report by Ants Oras, *Baltic Eclipse* (London, 1948), p. 73. For Narva: eyewitness report by A. Soom, "Seadusevastased valimised," *Eesti riik*, III, p. 42. For ballot-box stuffing: eyewitness report by E. Kuik, "Valimis-võltsimine Viljandimaal," *ibid*, p. 48.

28. Sabaliūnas, pp. 206–7. Acting President Paleckis of Lithuania is supposed to have expressed privately his opinion that the actual voter turnout in Lithuania stood at 15–16 per cent: Brazaitis, "Pirmoji sovietinė," p. 362.

29. Evald Uustalu, *The History of the Estonian People* (London, 1952), p. 242.

30. *Eesti riik*, III, p. 59, has an unambiguous photo; pp. 21, 41 and 65 have photos of Soviet troops and armored cars participating in the 21 June demonstrations in Tallinn.

ment. The following day, it formulated an application for membership of the USSR. In Latvia and Lithuania, both acts took place on
the first day. The rest of the initial sessions were devoted to remaining
essentials, such as the nationalization of most urban and rural property, together with all industrial concerns and banks. Because there
was no real debate and everything was passed unanimously, the
assemblies completed their assigned tasks within a few days. Before
adjourning, they "elected" delegates to go to Moscow to present their
countries' applications for membership in the fraternal Soviet
brotherhood of nations.

The Supreme Soviet met on 1 August. After a lengthy exposition
of Soviet foreign policy by Molotov, the recent tangible benefits of
that policy were presented to the Soviet legislators. The Baltic delegations applied, on behalf of their governments and peoples, for membership of the USSR. The Supreme Soviet apparently "deliberated"
the merits of their cases. It decided to grant the Lithuanian request
on 3 August, the Latvian request two days later, and held out on the
Estonian request till 6 August.

Thus in the space of less than two months, the Kremlin completed
its formal takeover of the Baltic states. The Soviet military establishment in the region, which had been considerably augmented since
June 1940, kept increasing now that the area had become a forward
position. Russia's loss of a broad littoral along the Baltic in the First
World War had been reversed.

Lithuania, which had been "awarded" Vilnius in November 1939,
now gained additional districts in the east. However, the sum total
of Lithuanian territorial acquisitions, consisting of previously Polish-
controlled territory, represented only about one-third of the total area
which the Soviet state had recognized as Lithuanian in 1920, but
which had not been part of the interwar republic. The incorporation
of Lithuania also included the southwest region of that state which,
according to the September 1939 secret "supplementary protocol" to
the German-Soviet Boundary and Friendship Treaty, had remained in
the German sphere of influence. Not willing for the moment to raise
the issue, Berlin agreed to a Soviet payment of 7,500,000 gold dollars
for these "rights."[31]

Most of the Baltic diplomats stationed abroad ignored the instructions and threats of the new regimes to return home. Of the foreign
powers, only Germany and Sweden recognized the annexation. While

31. *Nazi-Soviet Relations*, pp. 176, 186–8, 237, 267–8.

some governments subsequently extended *de facto* recognition, others (e.g. the United States) did not and continued to accept the official continued functioning of the Baltic legations in their capitals.

The First Year of Soviet Occupation

In comparison to what had gone before, the formal aspects of Sovietization after Moscow's acceptance of the Baltic "petitions" were an anticlimax. The People's Assemblies unanimously adopted new Soviet constitutions giving themselves, as well as other offices and organs of state power, proper Soviet nomenclature. No new elections to these bodies were held until 1947. In January 1941, however, all three republics elected their representatives to the USSR Supreme Soviet. The results more closely resembled the Soviet averages of popular approval in the upper-90s percentages than had the July 1940 elections.

According to Soviet practice, the First Secretaries of the republics' Communist parties became the ranking focuses of power in theory as well as in practice: Karl Säre in Estonia, Jānis Kalnbērziņš in Latvia, and Antanas Sniečkus in Lithuania, all local Communists. While the state structure of the USSR was formally federal, the party organization in whose hands the monopoly of political power rested was centralized. The republic Council of Ministers (until 1946, Council of People's Commissars) did not govern, but was rather a channel for the implementation of decisions by a strictly disciplined body controlled by Moscow. Likewise, the Supreme Soviets of the republics served merely to legitimize legislation frequently devised outside the republic. The transitional Prime Ministers were kicked upstairs to become Chairmen of the Presidium of the Supreme Soviet, i.e. the formal heads of state. (For a systematic list of Baltic leaders and administrators, see Appendix A.) In November, the legal codes of the republics were changed; or rather, the code of the Russian Soviet Federated Socialist Republic (RSFSR) was adopted by each of them.

The Communist parties which had emerged during the first weeks of occupation as the sole political organizations continued to grow rapidly (see Table 6 in Appendix B). The Estonian party mushroomed from 133 members in mid-June to 1,344 in early September; by 1 June 1941 it had grown to 3,732. By 1 January 1941 the Lithuanian party counted 2,504 members and 634 candidate members; six months later, the number of Communists in the republic stood at 4,625. The rapid increase was due largely to the influx of officials from the other parts of the USSR whose party memberships were automatically transferred to the new Baltic republics once their parties had been integrated into the all-Union party in October 1940. In Estonia, 37 per cent of the membership (1,009 people) were imports. However, the great need for party members in the situation of reorganization and expansion began to attract careerists of all types. Not everyone was accepted. Of the 133 pre-July Estonian CP members, only 124 had received CP membership cards by September 1.[32]

Changes in the civil service varied. Those institutions least concerned with the exercise of political power and most likely to be staffed by hard-to-replace experts tended to keep their former personnel. In Lithuania, for instance, as late as April 1941, 81.7 per cent of the staff of the Ministry of Finance and 60 per cent of the Ministry of Agriculture's personnel had been appointed before the occupation.[33]

The Sovietization of Economic Life.   Although formal rearrangements in the economic structures of the Baltic states had to wait until the convocation of the People's Assemblies, dislocations affecting everyday life began with the arrival of the additional large numbers of Soviet military and political personnel. In Lithuania, the 15 June ultimatum led to lines at food stores, which were virtually empty by the following day. Chronic shortages can thus be said to have come with the Red Army. Later, hoarding and speculation began to have their effect as well. Demand was intensified by large-scale purchases by newly-arrived Soviet personnel. A drop in production followed even the initial steps of Sovietization. The disruption of distribution also affected availability of goods, as did large-scale requisitions for other parts of the USSR. Shipment to the Baltic states of quantities of some foods, such as watermelons, in boxcars allegedly decorated with slogans such as "for the starving *Pribaltika*," had no marked effect on the shortage which developed.

Expropriation of industry began in early July, even several weeks before the promulgation of the appropriate decrees by the People's Assemblies. The first step consisted of the appointment of commissars, usually individuals without any experience in industrial management but with the "proper" social backgrounds, to positions of complete supervisory control. In early 1941, only 4 per cent of enterprise managers in Latvian light industry had a college education, and 64

32. *Ülevaade EKP*, pp. 13–19; Rakūnas, p. 47.
33. Rakūnas, p. 41.

per cent had only attended primary schools.[34] The effect on practical operations is not hard to imagine.

Formal expropriation came in late July; this affected all factories employing more than 20 workers, and mechanized enterprises with 10 or more workers. In Latvia and Lithuania, but not in Estonia, all concerns exceeding a specified annual turnover (150,000 *litas* and 100,000 *lats*) were also expropriated. Although in theory small firms were excluded, they were expropriated for all practical purposes if they possessed machinery needed by some trust or organization. Repair shops for agricultural machinery provided the most frequent examples of this — they tended to be converted into machine-tractor stations (MTS). By early 1941, the state takeover of industry had been all but completed. In May of that year, over 1,000 enterprises in Lithuania had been nationalized.

Expropriation of commercial enterprises began in the fall of 1940. At first, only larger units exceeding a specified annual turnover were affected. In Lithuania, 1,597 stores, restaurants and warehouses along with 43 hotels and 2,555 buildings were taken over. By June 1941, only 10 per cent of private shops in the country remained in private hands.[35]

From the first days of Sovietization, the Russian *ruble* appeared as legal tender, circulating alongside the local currencies. However, the rates of exchange were extremely unfavorable. The Estonian *kroon* (then valued at approximately 18 to one British pound) was pegged at 1.25 rubles; its earlier value had been between 10 and 15 rubles. The Latvian *lat*, which had officially been worth 10 rubles, was made equal in value. The Lithuanian *litas* was set at 0.9 rubles, whereas its earlier value had been 3 to 5 rubles. Such rates of exchange provided windfall profits for Soviet military and political *apparatchiks* (party officials) with high ruble incomes and little to spend them on in the rest of the USSR. The Baltic currencies were eventually abolished in late 1940.

The situation in banking paralleled that in industry and in commerce. Bank panics broke out with the Soviet ultimatums. In Lithuania, withdrawals soon had to be limited to 250 litas per week unless the account-holder could show a concrete business need for a larger withdrawal. The number of litas notes in circulation increased

---

34. Gundar J. King, *Economic Policies in Occupied Latvia* (Tacoma, Wash., 1965), p. 60.

35. Details on Lithuanian expropriations are provided in Rakūnas, pp. 54ff.

by 9 per cent in June and by 13 per cent at the end of the first month of Soviet occupation.[36] In spite of the phenomenal growth in business sales, deposits into bank accounts virtually ceased. With the state takeover of banks in late July, all accounts were effectively frozen for several months. When they reopened, only 1,000 rubles could be withdrawn from any account. The rest had been confiscated.

In July and August, salary increases were announced for individuals at the low end of the economic scale. These were, however, usually accompanied by "Stakhanovite" campaigns requiring considerable unpaid overtime. Prices also rose, resulting in an overall decrease in the purchasing power of money at a time when the availability of goods had become patchy. The semi-official explanations of the disappearance of goods as having been caused by a growth in the purchasing power of the population tended to be met with scorn. By November, further increases had tripled the money wages of Latvian industrial workers (compared to 1939) and nearly doubled most other wages. However, by May 1941 food prices had tripled and textile and shoe prices had increased sixfold. In Estonia, the relative purchasing power of median wages fell by 15 per cent for food and by 65 per cent for textiles between early 1940 and early 1941.[37]

Expropriation also affected housing. The aim was not merely the sequestration of property, but also the ruin of its owners. Real estate was classified as business. Houses exceeding 220 square meters in the cities and 170 sq. m. in the rural areas were affected. In Kaunas, housing had been in chronically short supply during the period of independence. In 1937 rents had been stabilized, though at a high level. On 5 July 1940 they were lowered by 15–25 per cent in Kaunas and 10 per cent in other cities. However, the demand had skyrocketed with the advent of Soviet bureaucrats and officials. The housing shortage was aggravated by the construction slowdown which accompanied the overall drop in production. The 1941 plan called for only 1,148 new apartments in Kaunas, while 3,376 had been completed in 1939.[38] In order to make room for the new ruling class, the so-called parasite elements and their families — former real estate

36. Albert Tarulis, "Lietuvos ūkio katastrofos pradžia, 1940. VI.15–1940. VIII. 25," *Lietuvių archyvas*, II, p. 133.

37. For Latvia: King, p. 58; for Estonia: calculations based on price lists given by H. Nurk, "Eesti majandus punasel aastal," *Eesti riik*, III, pp. 124–5.

38. Brazaitis, "Pirmoji Sovietinė," p. 364.

owners, merchants, clergymen, pensioners and unemployed — were forced to relocate in the far suburbs. This situation was paralleled in Riga and Tallinn, which had been less squeezed for housing during the independence period. The introduction of Soviet cadres resulted in the eviction of many urban residents, creating a housing shortage almost overnight.

All those who either left after the arrival of the Soviets or who had been abroad at the time and refused to return had their property confiscated. Individual craftsmen were pushed into cooperative artels through threats and high taxes. All existing consumer and producer cooperatives as well as credit unions were made state property. Only nonvoluntary cooperatives seemed to be acceptable.

The working class lost not only purchasing power but also its autonomous institutions. Trade unions which had organized many successful strikes during independence now became management tools to strengthen labor discipline. Unexcused absence, or even being 20 minutes late for work, could mean six months' work at wages reduced by one-quarter. The Stalinist labor laws made the workers pay for damage or loss caused by carelessness (as determined by the management), sometimes at a punitive rate of five times the actual cost. Leaving employment without the manager's permission was punishable by two to four months in prison. The same applied to those refusing transfer to another plant. In December 1940, the workers at "Red Krull" in Tallinn went on a three-day strike against high prices, shortages, overtime and abolition of workers' councils. They were broken through attrition tactics, and only won a two-day Christmas holiday which was abolished elsewhere.[39]

The Sovietization of Agriculture.   All three Baltic states were predominantly agricultural countries. The expropriation of industrial, commercial and banking institutions affected only a small portion of the population directly. As the likelihood of a backlash over these acts was minimal, the regime could proceed with impunity. This was not so with agricultural holdings, which did involve the majority of the population. Land reforms had been enacted in all three states during the first years of independence, and there were really no latifundia to provide convenient objects for negative Soviet propaganda. The regime certainly possessed sufficient power to enforce collectiviza-

---

39. Uustalu 1952, p. 246; Aleksander Kaelas, *The Worker in the Soviet Paradise* (London, 1947), pp. 42–3.

tion, which was its ultimate goal in agricultural planning. It realized, perhaps as a practical result of experience gained during collectivization of the USSR in the early 1930s, the dislocations and interruption in production which would result. The People's Assembly of Lithuania specifically expressed its condemnation of any collectivization attempts:

Any attempts to infringe upon the personal property of peasants or to impose on them collective farms against their will shall be severely punished as harmful to the interests of the people and the state.[40]

Apparently collectivization rumors were widespread.

Although collectivization was not on the immediate program for the Soviet Baltic countryside in 1940, it is hard not to discern from concrete measures enacted that it was a long-term goal. According to the land legislation of the new Soviet Baltic governments, those portions exceeding 30 hectares (75 acres) were taken away from their former owners. In Lithuania, this affected only some 28,000 owners (10 per cent of the total), who as a group lost 604,000 ha. out of their total holdings of 1,440,000 ha. In Latvia about 15 per cent and in Estonia about 20 per cent of farms were affected by the measure. About 3,700 Estonian farms were seized in their entirety. The untouched land remained in "perpetual tenure"; it could not be bought, sold or given away. Significant portions of the sequestered land were slated for parcelling out to small landholders or to landless peasants. In Lithuania, 607,600 ha. were made available, and by November some 75,000 landless peasants or small landholders had received 394,000 ha. In Latvia, 52,000 landless peasants received land, and 23,000 small farms were increased in size. The plots granted by the Soviet regime were small; the maximums of 10 ha. in Latvia and Lithuania and 12 ha. in Estonia were too small to support a family. The grants were evidently meant to be temporary and were intended more to splinter the farmers as a class than to provide social justice in the countryside. Such a rationale was virtually admitted by Antanas Snieckus, First Secretary of the Lithuanian Communist Party.[41]

---

40. Kancevičius, p. 218.

41. *Tarybų Lietuvos valstietija: istorijos apybraiža* (Vilnius, 1979), pp. 39–40; M. Gregorauskas, *Tarybų Lietuvos žemės ūkis, 1940–1960* (Vilnius, 1960), p. 82; taken from A. Snieckus, *Ataskaitinis pranešimas V-me LKP(b) suvažiavime apie LKP(b) darbą* (Kaunas, 1941), pp. 24–7.

Other practical measures in agriculture undertaken during the first year of the Soviet regime also seem to confirm collectivization as an eventual goal. Production levels had dropped in the summer of 1940 as a result of the loss of work incentive coupled with rumors of all kinds. Public appeals by the new governments did not succeed in solving the problem. In early 1941, requisition norms appeared. In Lithuania, a 30-ha. farm with 20 ha. of plowed land worked by hired farmhands was assessed: 15 tonnes of grain, 11 tonnes of potatoes, 4,680 liters of milk, 390 kilos of meat, and 13 kilos of wool. Depending on farm size, 30–50 per cent of total production went to the state; local authorities had the right to increase these figures by up to 30 per cent if they saw fit. The farms were to receive 2,500 rubles for their produce, the market value of which was about 15,500 rubles. A further indication of planned collectivization was the appearance by early 1941 of about 50 machine-tractor stations in Latvia, 42 in Lithuania, and 25 in Estonia. At the same time, the press began to devote attention to the subject.

A few kolkhozes (collective farms) were actually founded during this period, starting as early as 25 September 1940 in Estonia's eastern borderland. Lithuania's first, named after Lenin, appeared in January 1941 in the Akmenė district. It was a small enterprise worked by 16 families consisting of 250 ha. (625 acres) of land, 20 horses and 60 head of cattle. One week before the German attack, a kolkhoz named after Stalin cropped up near Augspils in northeast Latvia. Altogether, 9 kolkhozes were created in eastern Estonia and 12 in Lithuania.[42]

The Sovietization of Society and Culture.   Changes in economic life were paralleled by those in education and culture. All private schools were taken over; the organizational systems of education and scholarship were somewhat altered. Latvia's 12-year and Lithuania's 13-year primary and secondary school systems were reduced to an 11-year system, similar to the Soviet Union's. Estonia already had an 11-year system.

The curricula saw more drastic revisions. Many writers in the native

---

42. Gregorauskas, p. 101; *Ülevaade EKP*, p. 77; *Lietuvos TSR istorija*, IV (Vilnius, 1975), pp. 44–5; Alfreds Ceichners, *Was Europa drohte: die Bolschewisierung Lettlands, 1940–1941* (Riga, 1943), pp. 400–2. Lithuania received 4 kolkhozes with territory transferred from Belorussia in 1940; the total number has been stated as 20 in a recent source, *Tarybų Lietuvos valstietija*, p. 49. The existence of Latvian and Estonian kolkhozes has been downplayed in Soviet historiography, possibly because most of them were located in territory transferred to the Russian republic in 1945.

literary traditions had to be deleted from syllabuses. Others, though not nearly as many, had to be introduced. Most had to undergo selective presentation. In Lithuania, for instance, the liberal turn-of-the-century poet Vincas Kudirka, author of the national anthem, could not be totally excluded, though some of his work was demonstrably excised from plans of study. As it would have been a major and practically insurmountable effort to prepare new textbooks for the fall 1940 school year, the Lithuanian People's Commissar for Education issued a circular on 30 September instructing teachers to tear out unsuitable pages from old textbooks. In Estonia, bookstores were instructed to do this.

Press control appeared early. On 7 August (two days after formal annexation) all publishing houses and printing shops in Latvia were taken over by the Soviet state. They were consolidated into a single State Publishing House run by three expatriate Communists returning from Russia. As in the rest of the USSR, the function of newspapers became primarily the dissemination of official views rather than the reporting and discussion of events from a variety of viewpoints. Their total circulation of pre-Soviet times was not matched; the diversity reflected in the larger circulations was not needed. Only the major newspapers were allowed to continue, although their names and the tone of their coverage were altered. Pre-war Lithuania had had 7 daily newspapers, 27 weeklies, 15 biweekly reviews and 27 monthly magazines, with a combined total circulation of around a million copies. During the Soviet regime, the total number of all titles in these categories shrank to 33.

An official *List of Banned Books and Brochures* was issued in Latvia in November 1940. Additional lists in February and March 1941 brought the total number of proscribed titles to 4,000: books on history, politics, philosophy and sociology, and any fiction by "nationalist authors." The pattern was similar in Estonia and Lithuania. All such books were to be removed from all bookstores and libraries. In many places throughout the three countries, the proscribed books were burned. Most writers, including many a leftist, were classified as "reactionary," and their work was banned. Among major writers, Latvia's Vilis Veldre, who had sung about chains, equality and fraternity, committed suicide; Aleksandrs Grīns was shot; Atis Ķeniņš and Līgotnu Jēkabs were deported, and Jēkabs soon perished.[43]

43. Rolfs Ekmanis, *Latvian Literature Under the Soviets, 1940–1975* (Belmont, Mass., 1978), pp. 45–9. Banned book lists: *Aizliegto grāmatu un brošūru saraksts*, nos 1, 2 and 3 (Riga, 1940, 1941).

At least in the short run, the organization of culture along Soviet patterns was a more difficult task than the reshaping of education. Creative artists lend themselves least to bureaucratic regimentation. Nevertheless, the foundations were laid in this domain as well, with the establishment of Baltic branches of the all-Union societies of writers, composers, etc. This transformation presented some difficulties to the cultural bureaucrats. In Latvia, which had some 200 active members of the writing profession, only 9 joined the Writers' Union at the time of its foundation. Most of the previously existing cultural organizations were disbanded, and Stalinist oddities began to be featured frequently and prominently at the operas and theatres.

For a variety of reasons, including personal ones, some prominent cultural figures did initially welcome the new order, forswearing some of their own previous writings and serving as the regime's minstrels within their forms of artistic endeavor. Three Latvians — the poet Jānis Sudrabkalns and novelists Andrejs Upīts and Vilis Lācis, a member of the People's Government — fall into this group, as does the Estonian writer Johannes Semper. The Lithuanian poet Salomēja Neris provides another example, especially with her now-downplayed ode to Stalin. But these readily appeared as exceptions. The majority chose silence or wrote, though not for publication. A number sought refuge in translating Russian and world classics. In spite of the frequently reiterated wishes of the party, nothing original, apart from two poems, appeared in Lithuania to glorify the events of the summer of 1940. The Estonian cultural monthly *Looming* presented a curious mix of fully non-Marxist works and strident Sovietese. In Latvia, a group of poets published in March, following official suggestion, a "Writers' Promise"

to create, within a month, a poem about the liberated Latvian people and their Great Friend, the Leader of the whole world.[44]

Results of such planned poetry rarely surpassed the level of sycophantic praise of the dictator:

> Like beautiful red yarn into our hearts we wove,
> Stalin, our brother and father, your name.[45]

Officially the churches were untouched insofar as clerical organization was concerned. In Lithuania, all government support for religious

44. *Padomju Latvija*, 18 March 1941.
45. V. Lukss, *Dzejas* (Riga, 1951), pp. 29–32; translation from Ekmanis 1978, p. 58.

bodies and payment of the clergy's salaries ceased; civil registration of births, deaths and marriages was introduced. Church holidays were abolished in all three republics. Clergy were excluded from the army, the educational system and other government institutions. Social and informal educational church functions were curtailed by the new laws on organizations and the reorganization of the press. In addition, church services and the faithful began to be harassed by "atheist brigades," no doubt overfulfilling their plans. Most theological institutes were closed. In Tartu, 70,000 volumes of theological literature were destroyed. The clergy lost their pensions. They and their congregations had to pay extra taxes, rents and utility fees.

Repression and Deportations. The significant decline in the standard of living, and the general confusion affecting the quality of life of most citizens which accompanied the imposition of Sovietization, were perhaps not the worst aspects of the process. Those most heavily affected on that score certainly belonged to the more enterprising elements of the Baltic populations. Left to their own devices, they would no doubt have managed to reconstruct their lives, albeit at a much lower level of material wellbeing than they had become used to during the relatively prosperous years of independence. Yet the Soviet system — particularly its Stalinist variant, then at a peak — was by its very nature specifically ordered so as to prevent any such development. The insecurity of the individual, irrespective of his social standing, became a cardinal element in the maintenance of social order. It affected loyal bureaucrats and party activists equally with common workers and peasants. The inculcation of fear had to be pervasive in order to fulfill effectively its task as a method of social control.

By the time Soviet forces arrived in the Baltic, the Great Purge in the USSR had subsided. The dramatic events in the USSR, including the massive arrests and several spectacular show trials, were not reenacted in the newly annexed Baltic republics. Indeed, on the whole the Soviet regime seemed at first to avoid such blatantly indiscriminate repression. That began only with the massive deportations initiated in June 1941, and was interrupted only by the German invasion of the USSR. However, these deportations had been planned for much longer and had been adumbrated by various other events during the first year of Soviet occupation.

The Soviet security organ (NKVD) arrived in the Baltic states together with the garrison troops in the fall of 1939, but its overt operations did not begin until after reinforcement by additional Soviet military in June 1940. At first, arrests were limited to some of the more prominent figures in the old regimes plus some in special categories of Kremlin concern, like Trotskyites, of whom there were only a handful in the Baltic countries.

The first wider arrests came on the eve of the first elections. In Lithuania, some 2,000 individuals were arrested on the night of 11–12 July 1940. Most received summary eight-year terms, though not through any personal trials, and were deported. The pace of arrests — nocturnal knocks on the door for people never to be heard from again — reached an average of 200–300 a month by the end of the year. Several newly-made high Soviet officials were affected. Maksim Unt, Minister of the Interior in the People's Government of Estonia, who had been Acting President while his colleagues were in Moscow petitioning the Supreme Soviet to admit Estonia to the USSR, disappeared in early 1941 and was executed later for acts committed in 1920. Other arrested members of the People's Governments included Julijs Lācis (who died in 1941) and Pēteris Blaus in Latvia, and Juhan Narma-Nihtig in Estonia. No ethnic group was spared. Among others, the future Prime Minister of Israel, Menachem Begin, was arrested in Vilnius, six weeks after the Soviet annexation, and was sent to the Soviet Arctic.[46]

The possibility of wider deportations appeared sporadically as a topic of private discussion from the midsummer of 1940 onwards. The rumor might have been used as added insurance for smooth performance of the necessary electoral and legislative shows of July and August. The Lithuanian Acting President Justas Paleckis supposedly told an acquaintance at the time that the deportation of 50,000 was under consideration and could be triggered by a bad move.[47] Such arguments might have had some effect on those among the Lithuanian public who considered Paleckis, not yet formally a Communist, as an alternative preferable to some satrap imported from Russia.

Deportation rumors and actual arrests enhanced interest in evacuation among those who could claim any faint German ties. The Soviets and the Nazis agreed on such a "repatriation" in January 1941. Most Latvian and Estonian Germans had left in late 1939, but 16,000 people

---

46. Myllyniemi 1979, pp. 135 and 145; Herbert-Armin Lebbin, *Sotsiaaldemokratismi pankrot Eestis* (Tallinn, 1970), pp. 319–20; Lithuanian Security Office Order of 7 July 1940 regarding arrests is translated in *Third Interim Report*, pp. 468–70; Menachem Begin, *White Nights: The Story of a Prisoner in Russia* (New York, 1979).

47. A. Merkelis, "Masinis lietuvių išvežimas į SSSR," *Lietuvių archyvas*, II, p. 16.

made use of the new opportunity, bringing the total to 80,000, compared to a total pre-war declaredly German population of 78,000. Lithuania, which had 35,000 declared Germans left after Hitler's seizure of Klaipėda, saw 50,167 people leave for Germany in January 1941.[48]

Soviet documents which became known as a result of dislocations caused by the sudden German attack seem to indicate interest on the Kremlin's part in massive population shifts, especially from Lithuania, situated on the German border. One such document, numbered 0054 and signed by the People's Commissar for the Interior of the Lithuanian SSR, Aleksandras Guzevičius, on 28 November 1940, lists 14 categories of individuals slated for deportation:

(1) members of leftist anti-Soviet parties
(2) members of nationalist anti-Soviet parties
(3) gendarmes and jail guards
(4) Tsarist and White Army officers
(5) officers of the Lithuanian and Polish armies
(6) White Russian volunteers
(7) those who had been expelled from the party or the Komsomol
(8) all political émigrés and unstable elements
(9) all foreign citizens and individuals with foreign connections
(10) all those with personal foreign ties, viz. philatelists, Esperantists etc.
(11) high civil servants
(12) Red Cross officials and refugees from Poland
(13) clergymen
(14) former noblemen, estate-owners, industrialists and merchants[49]

The chief handicap of the NKVD in carrying out instructions like these to draw up lists of candidates was a poor and possibly inaccurate system of intelligence necessarily based on native informers. The archives, including those of the Foreign Affairs ministries which had been specifically carted to Moscow during the summer of 1940, were mostly in the local languages. The circle of natives suitable for this kind of NKVD work was extremely small. It is doubtful whether considerable, systematic and accurate classification could have made significant progress by the summer of 1941, and it is more likely that

48. Seppo Myllyniemi, *Die Neuordnung der baltischen Länder, 1941–1944* (Helsinki, 1973), pp. 44–5, 161 and 293.
49. *Third Interim Report*, p. 471.

NKVD officials were fulfilling their tasks haphazardly. While the appropriate numbers of individuals did appear on their lists, the rationale for their inclusion could have been arbitrary.

Massive deportations according to prepared lists began on the night of 13–14 June 1941, but a series of practical difficulties in execution prevented their completion as planned. It is very likely that not all the listed individuals could be readily located; some, realizing their situation, began to filter to the woods or to move around frequently — maneuvers with which the still largely alien NKVD personnel could not cope adequately.

It is difficult to determine the actual number of persons deported. Figures vary according to methods of calculation and estimation. One Latvian study concludes that specifically 662 boxcars containing 15,081 individuals (of whom 3,332 were children under 16) were dispatched from Latvia before the outbreak of the war; for Estonia, the figures were 490 boxcars and 10,205 individuals (including 3,018 under 16), of whom 28 per cent were workers and 26 per cent salaried personnel or their family members. A Lithuanian calculation posits a total figure of 34,260 deported from Lithuania between 14 and 18 June 1941.[50]

The full number of persons involved, however, must in all likelihood have been greater. Many had been arrested and deported earlier. Others were still detained at the outbreak of German-Soviet hostilities. Some massacres of prisoners by NKVD personnel are known to have taken place shortly after 22 June. The general estimates of population losses from all causes — deportations, mobilizations, massacres and unexplained disappearances during the first year of Soviet rule — hover around 60,000 for Estonia, where Soviet forces stayed longest and where some conscription into the Red Army could be effected; 35,000 for Latvia; and 34,000 for Lithuania.[51] If these figures are accurate, Estonia can be said to have lost about 4 per cent of its prewar population and the other two Baltic states 1.5 to 2 per cent each. It should be remembered that, had the outbreak of the war

50. *Latvju enciklopēdija*, I, pp. 476–7; Arveds Švābe, *Lettlands historia* (Stockholm, 1961), p. 171; Uustalu 1970, p. 320; M. Kuldkepp, "Inimkaotused punasel aastal," *Eesti riik*, III, pp. 230–4; Brazaitis, "Primoji sovietinė," p. 369. According to these figures, deportations affected 0.9 per cent of the population in Estonia, 0.8 per cent in Latvia and 1.1 per cent in Lithuania. About 46,000 deportees from Lithuania are estimated, with 19,000 names actually listed, by Leonardas Kerelis (ed.), *Išvežtųjų lietuvių sąrašas: Stalino teroras, 1940–1941* (Chicago, 1981).

51. Uustalu 1970, p. 323; Spekke, p. 396; Brazaitis, "Pirmoji sovietinė," p. 369.

not intervened, the deportation figures would in all likelihood have been much higher. Jurgis Glušauskas, People's Commissar for Communications of the Lithuanian SSR, who did not leave for Russia during the Soviet retreat, claims to have seen a document envisaging the deportation of 700,000 from Lithuania.[52] There is no documentary evidence to substantiate such a claim. However, in view of the massive relocations which accompanied collectivization during the 1930s and the national deportations actually effected elsewhere in the USSR in 1944–5, such a figure, roughly one-quarter of the pre-war population, does not appear exaggerated.

The deportations served as a massive shock to the citizens of the Baltic republics, which no doubt had been the intention. Now it was no longer select individuals whose disappearance without a trace could be explained by some system of logic, but large groups representing various sections of the population. Many of the deportees died on their way to exile during the trips to northern Russia or Siberia which lasted several weeks. The crowding in the boxcars, and the minimal sanitary and eating arrangements, naturally had this result with the frail members of the groups. Families were separated, men being sent to one location and women and children to another. While the men were considered under arrest, and as such destined for labor camps where many died, women and children were as a rule merely exiled. Eventually, relatives did get some news from those exiled, but only after the war.

The deportations, coming as they did on the eve of the outbreak of the German-Soviet war, no doubt had an effect opposite from that intended by those who conceived them. While they undoubtedly instilled fear in the population, they also deepened hatred for the regime, especially among those who might otherwise have remained neutral. Despite the efforts of the regime's propaganda in heralding popular Soviet resistance to the German onslaught, there are hardly any known instances of spontaneous native Baltic opposition to the German advance. This developed only after some time, as the negative side of the German occupation came to be felt.

Resistance to Sovietization. The period of independence, 1918 to 1940, had successfully entrenched among the Baltic peoples a strong sense of national identity, as well as the corollary that this could only be properly expressed and preserved through maintenance of an

---

52. Brazaitis, "Pirmoji sovietinė," p. 369.

independent state entity. The Soviet preservation of a formal national political existence, albeit at a "higher" level of sovereignty, failed to satisfy national aspirations. Coupled with a rapid and marked decline in living standards, plus the high-handedness of Soviet officials and the system of terror they represented, this served to foster opposition to Soviet rule. Such anti-Soviet feelings were bolstered by expectations of an imminent Soviet-German conflict as well as by the refusal of the Western powers to recognize the incorporations.

The most widespread resistance was passive, mainly through boycotts of the formal political activity of the new regimes, such as the elections, and through verbal ridicule of the system and of the Russians. The old holidays, even though formally abolished, continued to be observed by the populace. In Lithuania, the graves of soldiers who had fallen during the independence struggle in 1918–20 were as usual fully decorated on All Souls' Day (2 November). Christmas 1940 was still a *de facto* holiday.

Some acts of spontaneous symbolic opposition went beyond mere passivity. In Lithuania, the Teachers' Congress of 14–15 August was held soon after incorporation and planned as a demonstration of loyalty to the new system. At one point during the proceedings, someone intoned the old national anthem and the teachers joined in. Even some of the ranking members of the new government on the podium are said to have instinctively risen, only sheepishly to sit down again.[53]

Soon after the coming of the Soviets, a variety of organized resistance groups were formed. As early as July 1940, leaflets phrased in extremely emotional language appeared in Lithuania, urging a boycott of the elections. Several distinct opposition groups engaged in memorable activity during the second half of 1940. The most widespread was the Lithuanian Activist Front (LAF), some of whose cells were formed as early as October 1940. Later, beginning in December, these managed to establish contact with the foreign cell established by the erstwhile Lithuanian Minister in Berlin, Colonel Kazys Škirpa, with German approval. Geographical difficulties prevented contacts with the West. The group in Germany included intellectuals, officers and politicians who had managed to escape from Lithuania at various stages of Sovietization or who had been abroad in mid-June 1940 and

53. Zenonas Ivinskis, "Lithuania during the War," in V. Stanley Vardys (ed.), *Lithuania under the Soviets, 1940–1965* (New York, 1965), p. 63; Iu. Paletskis (Paleckis), *V dvukh mirakh* (Moscow, 1974), pp. 353–4.

never returned. It did not include President Antanas Smetona, who had by then left Germany for the United States.

The LAF worked out systematic rules for a widespread underground organization as well as a political program for the reestablishment of a Lithuanian state. It was considering plans for an armed uprising at a favorable moment — the outbreak of a Soviet-German war — and the establishment of a provisional government. The German agencies which approved of the existence of the LAF in Berlin did not sanction its plans for a provisional government. A network of LAF cells combed Lithuania, and membership is estimated to have reached 36,000 by 1941. Although somewhat impaired by the June 1941 deportations, the LAF managed to rise in force on the outbreak of the war.[54]

The resistance in Latvia and Estonia was more limited. Unarmed underground groups formed in several Estonian towns, and by March 1941 some of them had begun to interact. Armed guerrilla resistance in the forests was triggered by the mid-June 1941 deportations.

War and Revolt

The German attack on the USSR came during the early morning hours of 22 June 1941. Lithuania, situated astride East Prussia, was immediately affected, and within a week the Red Army had been pushed out. The German columns reached Daugavpils in Latvia on 26 June, and Riga fell to them on 1 July. By the ninth, the German armed forces were already in Pskov, and by 21 July a thrust east of Lake Peipsi nearly cut Estonia off from Russia. The rapid advance, which had taken place with a minimum of fighting, was halted for two weeks along a line running through mid-Estonia. Soviet reinforcements sent to that area during this lull stiffened opposition to the renewed German advance in late July. As a result, much fighting took place in northern Estonia. Tallinn fell on 28 August, but some Soviet detachments held out in the islands of Saaremaa and Hiiumaa until October.

If the goal of Soviet diplomatic pressure on the Baltic states since 1937 and military action in 1939–40 was to ensure the immunity of its northern flank to German attack, the results were counterproductive. The speed of the initial German thrust through the Baltic states (the 480 kilometers from East Prussia to Pskov were covered in

54. Ivinskis, pp. 64–5.

17 days) surpassed that of most German offensives during the Second World War. This advance could not possibly have been much faster in face of the weak Baltic armies defending their homelands against the traditional German enemy, and it could have been slower. In any event, the Soviet forces now destroyed in the Baltic states would have been spared for the defense of Leningrad. The unusual speed of the German thrust is at least partly explained by the Stalinist feat of making the Baltic populations friendly toward the Germans.

The German attack came during the first period of massive arrests and deportations undertaken by the Soviet regime. That, taken together with the other experiences of Sovietization, tended to identify Germany with the West in the minds of ordinary Baltic people. The feeling seems to have been pervasive that the overthrow of the Soviet yoke by the Germans would enable the Baltic peoples to reassert their national independence. The majority of the native populations welcomed the arrival of the Germans at least passively. In some instances, the *Wehrmacht* was greeted with flowers, but, from the beginning, the German actions did nothing to preserve such feelings.

A revolt against the Soviet system broke out in Lithuania on the first day of the war. A detachment of insurgents took over the Kaunas radio station and broadcast a proclamation of the reestablishment of independence and formation of a provisional government, as had been envisaged in LAF plans. The provisional government, an *ad hoc* coalition of individuals from every major political trend in the independent state, claimed, as such, to represent the will of the nation. Units of the former Lithuanian army were also reported to have mutinied against their Soviet commanders and to have gone over to the Germans *en masse*. Local uprisings in various parts of Lithuania harassed retreating Red Army columns. It has been estimated that some 100,000 insurgents were active. Casualties reached some 2,000, with 200 in Kaunas alone.[55] While much of this activity had been planned by the LAF, much more, especially in the countryside, proved spontaneous.

The Provisional Government officially reinstated the administrative structure which had existed on 15 June 1940 and began to appoint personnel to fill the posts. The German occupation authorities did not welcome the appearance of such a body, which had not been planned in their designs. The designated head of the Provisional Government,

55. *Ibid.*, pp. 67–8.

the former Envoy to Berlin, Colonel Škirpa, was not allowed to return to his country. In his absence, Juozas Ambrazevičius, a literary scholar, became Acting Prime Minister and chaired the daily cabinet sessions.

The *Wehrmacht* entered Kaunas almost in parade formation on 25 June and found the Provisional Government in control. Hoping to secure recognition from Germany as the government of an independent state, albeit one allied to Germany, the Provisional Government cooperated fully with the transient German military administration. The German commandant of Kaunas, however, was not authorized to deal with any government. Still, General Robert von Pohl was an Austrian and perhaps appreciative of the Lithuanian striving for a national state identity. He took no action against the reconstituted Lithuanian authorities as long as they were not in his way.

Coexistence became more problematic as the Germans sought to reestablish civilian control. The Provisional Government continued to cooperate; indeed, this was its only choice for survival. German plans, though never clearly formulated, did not however envisage any independent or semi-independent status for the Baltic countries. It would have proved needlessly unpopular in Lithuania, and possibly detrimental abroad, to disband the Provisional Government by force. Rather, the decision was to effect a quiet removal by forcing the authorities either to disband of their own accord or to reconstitute themselves into the *Zivilverwaltung* which the Reich leadership had envisaged for the area. The Provisional Government was denied access to the press, the radio and other means of communication, but ties to the provinces were dependent on the couriers which had been used by the underground during the Soviet period, and thus Provisional Government decrees were on occasion published in some provincial papers not subject to German military censorship.

German designs to change the Provisional Government, by force or by deceit, into its planned civil administration proved unsuccessful. A Gestapo attempt to foment a split within the LAF ranks through the use of some extreme nationalists also proved abortive. Goodwill efforts such as the release of Lithuanian army personnel in Soviet uniform who had gone over to the Germans were equally of no avail. The Provisional Government refused to compromise on its goal of an independent state, which the Reich was not willing to recognize.

While it was not ready to metamorphose into an open instrument of German domination, the Provisional Government had neither the will nor the means to confront the Germans. And it was internally split over the extent to which collaboration was advisable. In early August, after a public declaration of inability to pursue its functions, the Provisional Government was disbanded. On the whole, it had not been able to influence German occupation policies, and its annulment of the confiscatory Soviet nationalization laws was stillborn. Its only concrete achievements came in areas of least immediate interest to the German authorities, such as reorganization of the educational system. However, its six-week existence was testimony to the striving by the Lithuanian population for national independence, and it inspired continued passive resistance.[56]

In Latvia and Estonia, insurgency against the Soviet administration and Red Army presence also broke out before the Germans arrived. On 28 June there was an insurrection in Riga, and its radio station announced the formation of a Latvian government. The Soviets regained control the next day. Some Latvian military units managed to reorganize themselves after the outbreak of war, but they were dissolved soon after the arrival of the Germans, who reached Riga on 1 July. Two separate quasi-governmental bodies had meanwhile been formed: the Central Organizing Committee for Liberated Latvia, and the Provisional State Council (led by the former Transport Minister, Bernhards Einbergs). The Germans avoided direct contacts with them, but used them to get the economy going again. The former Finance Minister (1938–9), Alfreds Valdmanis, emerged as the strongest Latvian figure. Much to the dismay of the German administration's advance party, he succeeded in presenting them with a reopened Riga University and Opera — national institutions which the Germans preferred to see closed.[57]

Guerrilla units of varying size and organization were especially active in Estonia. Some numbered several hundred men and were organized by former army officers into fairly disciplined units. In large parts of southern Estonia, Soviet local administration was replaced by an Estonian one, days and even weeks before the arrival of German main forces. Tartu was under full or partial Estonian control from 10 to 28 July. The last Premier before the occupation, Jüri Uluots, convened a council which met repeatedly but never proclaimed itself a government. They had learned from Lithuanian and Ukrainian precedents that such an act would lead to direct confron-

56. *Ibid.*, pp. 68–72.
57. Bilmanis 1951, pp. 403–4; Myllyniemi 1973, pp. 78 and 84.

tation with the Germans, and possibly to arrests (as in the Ukraine, on 30 June). In northern Estonia, the guerrillas amounted to 5,000 active fighters, with 1,500 in a single armed forest base in Kautla (near the present Ardu, 50 km. northeast of Tallinn). Countrywide losses by the guerrillas amounted to 541 dead and missing, with comparable losses inflicted on Soviet forces during the two months of fighting.[58] The Germans disbanded all Estonian units as soon as they had established firm central control. Attempts by Uluots to present a memorandum arguing for the reestablishment of the sovereignty which the Soviets had removed were brushed aside by the new masters.

The German Occupation

It is quite clear from the documents in German archives that the long-range goal of the Nazi leadership was to annex the Baltic region to the Reich, to expel two-thirds of the population, and to fuse the remainder gradually with German immigrants. The competing plans by various staffs all agreed on this broad outline, and alteration of details by the top leaders always tended to make the plans even harsher. *Ostminister* Alfred Rosenberg's favored ploy in 1941 was to double the size of the Baltic republics at the expense of Russia and Belorussia, and then deport most of the Balts into the newly-annexed areas. The *Generalplan Ost* (1942) of the SS Chief Heinrich Himmler envisaged the deportation of almost 50 per cent of Estonians, all Latgalians, over 50 per cent of other Latvians and 85 per cent of Lithuanians. The remaining fraction was evaluated racially as Nordic (and thus worth Germanization) by a 1942 Anthropological Commission field study. Due to the limited number of Germans available, immigration was expected to be rather slow: 520,000 within 20–25 years after the end of the war.[59]

The immediate goal of Nazi Germany, however, was to win the war. Major deportation, immigration and denationalization were to start only after military victory. Meanwhile, such plans were ordered to be kept strictly secret so as not to upset the Baltic populations, whose maximum support for the "anti-Bolshevik struggle" was

58. K. Talpak, "Eesti metsavendlus 1941 aastal," *Eesti riik*, IV, pp. 25–7.

59. See Alexander Dallin, *German Rule in Russia, 1941–1945: A Study in Occupation Policies* (London, 1957), pp. 182–98, for the broad outline of German Eastern policies. For details regarding the Baltic states, see Myllyniemi 1973, especially pp. 57–9, 69–70, 89 and 146–60. See also Ekmanis 1978, pp. 82–3; Spekke, pp. 398–400; Uustalu 1970, p. 328; and Ivinskis, pp. 74–5.

desirable.[60] On the other hand, absolutely no independence or meaningful autonomy was to be given or promised to the Baltic nations, so that Germany would not have to break its Germanic word of honor in the postwar reckoning. The Baltic states were to be treated as just another piece of the USSR, with no regard to their independence only one year earlier. The more immediate German goal was to exploit the area economically as part of the war effort.

German Administration. On 17 July 1941, Alfred Rosenberg, a Baltic German, was appointed Reich Minister for the Occupied Eastern Territories. One of his deputies, the Gauleiter of Schleswig-Holstein Hinrich Lohse, became Reich Commissioner for the *Ostland* with his seat in Riga. His fief, which came into administrative existence on 28 July 1941, included the three Baltic countries and Belorussia, each of which constituted a General District headed by a General Commissioner resident in the respective capitals (see list in Appendix A). Various lower-level officials — Area Commissioner, County Head and a host of special-interest officers (*Sonderführer*) — filled out the formal German administrative structure. Paralleling the Soviet pattern, two other elements, the party and the police, were also actively present, and reported to Himmler. As under the Soviets, both were capable, under various circumstances, of wielding greater power than the administrative apparatus. Furthermore, the economy was handled by Hermann Göring's *Wirtschaftsstab Ost*. Although the manpower level was frequently below that required for optimal performance, the presence of several agencies transferred aspects of the widespread intra-agency rivalry, apparently tacitly favored by the Führer in Berlin as a practical means for rule, into the realm of the *Ostland* operations as well. Rosenberg gradually lost most of his power to Himmler.

In addition to the administrative apparatus introduced from above by the Reich, German plans also included indigenous "Directorates"

---

60. Settlement of 16,300 German colonists in southwest Lithuania has been reported by J. Dobrovolskis, "Lietuviškųjų buržuazinių nacionalistų antiliaudinis veikimas okupaciniame hitlerininkų valdžios aparate, 1941–1944 m.," *LTSR Mokslo Akademijos Darbai*, ser A-2(13), 1962, p. 162. Actually this was part of the return of 30,000 Lithuanian residents from among those who had left during the January 1941 evacuation of Germans to the Reich. They received large farms and were meant to be the first link in a "land bridge" connecting East Prussia to Courland. Also, 400 Dutch farmers were settled in the Vilnius area. The Jelgava District Commander in Latvia reported confidentially, in March 1942, that he had already reserved 1,100 farmsteads for German front soldiers. See Myllyniemi 1973, pp. 161–75 and 97.

or "Self-Administrations" (*Selbstverwaltungen*). They consisted of 5
to 12 "Country Directors" (*Landesdirektoren*) in Estonia, "General
Directors" (*Generaldirektoren*) in Latvia, and "General Counselors"
(*Generalräte*) in Lithuania. These entities had only a narrowly administrative and advisory function. They were headed by a First Director
(*Erster Direktor*) or First General Counselor (*Erster Generalrat*) respectively, and consisted of a group of experts each of whom was responsible for administrative functions corresponding to the ministries of
independent states.

Efforts were made to find prominent individuals to undertake
these roles. After Theodor Adrian von Renteln, the newly-appointed
General Commissioner for Lithuania, failed to convince the Lithuanian Provisional Government that it should turn itself into such a body
of counselors, he was forced to appoint one himself. General Petras
Kubiliūnas, a man of extreme nationalist views who had led an unsuccessful coup in 1934, became First General Counselor. Three of the
other 11 Lithuanian Counselors had been members of the Provisional
Government.

The selection of retired General Oskars Dankers as Latvian First
Director was also not a smooth operation. Dankers had left for Germany in January 1941, and become a German citizen. The Germans
wanted yes-men, but also realized that such people would be useless
unless they enjoyed some popular prestige. In November, Alfreds
Valdmanis was accepted as Director of Law Administration, despite
misgivings among several German factions, some of whom even
opposed the whole notion of a native body dealing with all of Latvia:
they recommended separate "self-administrations" for Courland,
Livonia and Latgale, and felt that none of the Latvian Directors
was "German-minded." The city of Riga, however, was put under
direct German control, with a Baltic German mayor, and completely
excluded from the reach of the Latvian Directorate. This dismember-
ment of the national territory remained a sore point about which
the Latvian Directors never stopped protesting — on the cautious
grounds of administrative efficiency.[61]

Estonia's Directors were mostly picked from among those who
had gone to Germany during the repatriation of January 1941. First
Director Hjalmar Mäe, belonging to this group, had spent time in
prison before the war for pro-fascist subversion. No nationally known
pre-war politicians agreed to serve. The Germans felt that the rapid

61. Myllyniemi 1973, pp. 107–15 and 137.

self-restoration of Baltic institutions had made them accept too many untrustworthy elements into the Latvian and Lithuanian self-administrations; in Estonia they took their time, and felt much more satisfied with Mäe and his team than with Dankers or Kubiliūnas. The city of Narva remained under military administration, largely outside Directorate influence.[62]

As advisory and administrative bodies, the Directorates had little if any say in formulation of the important decisions governing the daily lives of the people whom they were called upon to administer. In this sense their position was similar to the governments of the Soviet Baltic republics in 1940–1. On occasion they did manage, through bureaucratic interpretation as well as by taking advantage of opportunities presented by rivalry among German officials, to blunt some of the more detrimental features of German occupation exactions. The existence of the Directorates, however, allowed the Germans to channel their demands through native bodies, thus somewhat masking the fact of occupation. The price which the Directors had to pay for their limited ability to soften the German occupation regime was public identification with, and thus in a sense a share in, the onus of all German occupation measures, even those in which they had no say or whose severity they were unable to soften. They often had an unenviable role, alternating between being tools of German rule fleecing their own countries and patriots trying to keep the worst from happening. It is not surprising that under such circumstances appearances could and did prove deceptive. For instance, Pranas Germantas, the Lithuanian Counselor for Education, seemed to be close to the Nazis. However, this image facilitated his reintroduction of the old educational system which indirectly fostered the growth of resistance. In mid-1943, as the institutes of higher education were being closed by the German occupation authorities, Germantas was en route to the Stutthof concentration camp.

Formally, the Directorates headed reestablished pre-war administrative and judicial systems, including some police power. These could operate fairly normally as long as the questions involved were of little concern to the German authorities. The pre-war legal codes regained validity, although Germans on the one hand and Jews on the other were specifically excluded from their scope. In practice, there was generally a preference in the administration of justice for using the

62. *Ibid.*, pp. 109–10.

police, at times even military units, as well as administrative measures, rather than the courts.

Economic and Cultural Life.   In the short run, the Germans considered Baltic territory as an occupied region open to maximum exploitation of its resources for the general pursuit of the war effort, and the Baltic peoples were viewed primarily as providers of agricultural products and labor. This attitude was clearly reflected in the socio-economic policies of the occupation administration.

The first key economic measure radically affecting the everyday life of the people was introduced during the short initial period of German military administration. On 26 June, the German mark was officially valued at 10 rubles. The Baltic peoples, already stung by the earlier Soviet fiscal reevaluation, were totally fleeced by this second round. For instance, the pre-war Lithuanian litas had officially been worth 40 pfennigs. After the two confiscatory currency exchanges coming during the space of a year, the holder of a litas was left with roughly 9 pfennigs in a special *Ostmark* currency.

Private property was not restored. All enterprises expropriated by the Soviets were taken over by German firms specially created for the purpose. Some were extensive companies like the *Zentralhandelsgesellschaft Ost*, which ran all slaughterhouses, sugar and flour mills, and breweries, or the *Landbewirtschaftungsgesellschaft Ost*, which took over all the land which the Soviets had expropriated. Other industrial enterprises such as textile and paper mills and cigarette factories functioned as shareholding companies run by a German trustee whose position was usually one of patronage due to NSDAP (Nazi Party) membership.

Some reprivatization was effected on the basis of an 18 February 1943 order, as part of propaganda and morale-boosting campaigns when the tide of war had shifted against the Reich. In Lithuania on 11 May 1943, for instance, 50 farmers received land which had been expropriated by the Soviets. Such measures were frequently coupled with increased requisitions and harsher penalties for failure to carry them out. On the whole, they remained entirely token moves. Most owners of expropriated industrial and commercial property did not even undertake the petty and humiliating application procedure to have it restored (which included a written promise to support Germany). Of those who did, only a quarter in Latvia and Estonia and

4 per cent in Lithuania saw their property returned. The outcome for farms was similar.[63]

Rationing of food and goods was introduced in the cities in July 1941. In practice, the black markets which had appeared under the Soviets continued under the Germans. City wages and prices for obligatory farm-produce deliveries were set at 60 per cent of those in East Prussia, the closest German area.

On the whole, cultural life was the area of national existence least affected by the German occupation. Although cultural and religious affairs were strictly supervised, the Nazis, unlike the Soviets, did not act on a perceived need to infuse them immediately with a particular ideology. The requirements of waging war obviously took precedence over those of eventual Germanization, and so these concerns were left largely in the hands of the local authorities.

This does not mean that the conditions of occupation and the economic exactions which went with them did not affect cultural life. Riga University, reopened by the Latvians in the summer of 1941, was ordered to be closed on 15 September, and was reluctantly reopened only in early 1942, along with Tartu University. Kaunas and Vilnius Universities, opened in the fall of 1941, were closed early in 1943. School history and biology textbooks were subject to direct German control, and Nazi tenets were introduced. Censorship combined with paper shortages to decimate the press. Even *Faust* in Latvian translation was forbidden; it was not for peasants who could not read German. Few newspapers and periodicals and few worthwhile books were published. The absence of individual security in the face of the repeated manpower mobilizations directly affected educational and cultural institutions. Especially in Lithuania, these bore the brunt of German reprisals for mobilization failures. The performing arts were somewhat less affected. The theatre and opera functioned more or less as could be expected during wartime conditions. New youth organizations were created in Latvia and Estonia under district-level German control, with Directorates strictly kept out.

In the absence of any widespread armed anti-German resistance which could have been based on the religious establishments, the German authorities mostly did not interfere with organized religion. The significant exceptions concerned individual clergy, some of high rank, who had become involved in anti-German activities and were there-

63. Juozas Brazaitis, "Vokiečių okupacija (1941–1944)," *Lietuvių encikeopedija* (Boston, Mass., 1968), XV, p. 375; Myllyniemi 1973, pp. 223–6.

fore subject to repression. Theological institutes were allowed to function in Tartu and Kaunas, but not in Latvia.

German Mobilization of Manpower. The first German attempt to
utilize Baltic labor resources came in mid-July 1941 in Lithuania.
Invitations were issued for voluntary work in East Prussia. This
opportunity was largely utilized by individuals who had in some
way been compromised during the Soviet occupation and who wished
to be away from their home areas.

Compulsory drafts for labor service took on a more extensive as
well as a more coercive scope when, on 19 December 1941, Rosenberg decreed a general work obligation for those aged from 18 to
45. Failure to register would be punished by three months' imprisonment and a 1,000-mark fine. Later, in 1942, university freshmen
were required first to serve a year in the German youth labor force
(*Reichsarbeitsdienst*), which in 1942–3 recruited 950 Estonians, 4,576
Latvians, and 1,645 Lithuanians. About 30 per cent of the applicants
were refused for racial reasons.[64]

Decreed exactions on the labor force continued in various forms
throughout the German occupation. By early 1944, it was announced
in Lithuania that 15 ha. of farmland could be farmed by no more than
one individual. Surplus farm labor was to be sent to the Reich. The
quotas were lower in Latvia and Estonia, which were short of labor,
but still 30,000 had been conscripted by February 1943.

Efforts to sabotage these drafts greatly diluted their value to the
German economy. In Lithuania, only 5 per cent of a first quota of
100,000 in early 1942 was actually filled. Various means of evasion
were soon discovered. At the lower levels, the administrators as well
as the police were staffed by natives who were not eager to carry out
their tasks conscientiously. At higher levels, officials, even Germans,
could be bribed. Furthermore, the Directorates found ways of con-
vincing orderly German bureaucrats to limit the coercive aspects of
the mobilizations somewhat by arguing that such activities would
introduce disorder into the smooth functioning of the local economies,
which was also deemed of interest to the Reich. A demand for 3,000
Estonian and 10,000 Latvian women in April 1943 was very strongly
opposed by the Latvian Directorate, and abandoned. The failure
to meet set quotas usually led to an imposition of new and higher
figures. And the cycle began anew as the Directorates managed to

64. Myllyniemi 1973, pp. 191–2 and 294.

renegotiate these downward to figures which still could never be met. Early in 1944, for instance, the Lithuanian quota of 100,000 (about 5,000 weekly) was reduced to 80,000. About 8,000 were actually provided.[65]

Conscription methods grew harsher as resistance increased. In the fall of 1942, 8,000 Latgalians were forcibly dispatched to Germany. The Gestapo encircled selected villages, and all able-bodied adults were taken by truck to the nearest railway station. According to the post-war report by First Director Dankers, families were often separated, and only under-age children were left behind. Beginning in the fall of 1943, the German authorities in Lithuania also began to bypass the Directorates in their quest for laborers. The church at Žiežmariai was surrounded on Sunday morning, 10 September, to gather able-bodied men, and such "church actions" became almost weekly occurrences thereafter. In all, it is estimated that some 75,000 Lithuanian were netted for forced labor in this way.[66]

According to a Rosenberg memo to Himmler on 20 July 1944, a total of 126,000 Baltic workers had been sent to Germany. The national breakdown may have been 75,000 Lithuanians, 35,000 Latvians (especially from Latgale) and 15,000 Estonians. Conscription caused flight to the woods and decreased local production, especially in Lithuania. The above figures do not include those sent to the concentration camps. The total killed or deported by the Nazis from Latvia alone has been estimated at 120,000, half of them Jews (see next section) and half mainly ethnic Latvians.[67]

The German mobilization of Baltic manpower was also designed to provide recruits for military and paramilitary units. Although such activity clearly conflicted with international law, the measures were so couched as to make the draftees "voluntary associates." The first such units consisted of the so-called Defense Battalions ("Security Units" in Estonia), later renamed Police Battalions, which were largely staffed by volunteers. The motives of those who signed on were various. A few were genuinely pro-Nazi, while others sought revenge against Bolshevism for the deportations or murders of dear ones and the indignities inflicted on their homelands. Some tried to cover up their earlier collaboration with the Soviets or to escape false accusations to that effect.

65. Brazaitis, "Vokiečių," p. 375; *ibid:*, pp. 239–42.
66. *Ibid.*
67. *Ibid.*; Ekmanis 1978, p. 83.

In Lithuania, where almost the entire pre-war army which had been turned into a Soviet unit surrendered *en masse* during the first days of the war, recruitment for the Defense Battalions was frequently presented to its members in the form of a choice between joining or being sent to a POW camp; thus it is not surprising that many joined. It has been estimated that during the period of their operation some 20,000 Lithuanians served in these battalions; their manpower averaged around 8,000 at any one time. In August 1941 there were 20 Lithuanian battalions with 8,388 officers and men; in March 1944 the figure stood at 8,000.[68]

The Sovietized old Latvian and Estonian armies also surrendered *en masse* to the Germans. The Latvian Defense Battalions included about 15,000 men. At first, 27 undersized battalions were formed in Estonia, later to be consolidated into 13, with a total of approximately 10,000 men.[69]

According to official pledges issued in all three countries, these battalions should have been used only within their homelands, principally for duty against Soviet stragglers, parachutists, and escaped POWs. This promise was soon broken, and almost all the battalions were sent east for support duty behind the German lines, and later at the front. Some even saw service eventually in Poland, Yugoslavia and Italy. As tactical rather than combat units, they were frequently given unpleasant tasks of civilian population control or anti-guerrilla operations. Some among them were reported to have done ghetto guard duty in Poland. Overall, their rate of attrition was high. Estonian Police Battalion 36 was sent to Stalingrad with 450 men, and returned with 72.[70]

A second attempt at raising military personnel was the creation of the *Waffen*-SS National Legions from the fall of 1942 to the spring of 1943. In Latvia and Estonia, recruitment for such units was again connected with compulsory labor drafts; in theory, individuals had a choice, but the widely-known poor conditions in the Labor Battalions, combined with various pressures exerted by local recruitment

68. Brazaitis, "Vokiečių," p. 376; *Masinės žudynės Lietuvoje: dokumentų rinkinys* (Vilnius, 1965), I, p. 323; A Rakūnas, "Lietuvos liaudies kova prieš mobilizaciją į hitlerinę kariuomenę ir jos sužlugdymas, 1941–1944 m.," *Istorija*, VII (Vilnius, 1965), p. 41.

69. Latvia: Myllyniemi 1973, p. 228; Estonia: Arnold Purre, "Eesti sõda Nõuk. Liiduga," *Eesti riik*, VII, pp. 25–6.

70. Brazaitis, "Vokiečių," p. 376; *Masinės žudynės*, I, p. 323; Purre, "Eesti sõda," p. 26.

officers, induced over half the "volunteers" to choose Legion service. The Estonian Legion at its peak size was one division numbering some 11,000 men, while the Latvians eventually manned two divisions. By August 1943 the German Security Service reported strongly anti-German attitudes in the Latvian Legion, especially among officers.[71]

Attempts to form a Lithuanian Legion floundered, along with most of the other German manpower-mobilization efforts in that country. On 17 March 1943, SS recruitment efforts in Lithuania were stopped, and Lithuanians were declared unworthy of wearing the SS uniform. The brunt of German reprisals which followed fell on the intelligentsia, and three incumbent General Counselors — Pranas Germantas, Mečislovas Mackevičius and Stasys Puodžius — were among the 46 prominent individuals sent to the Stutthof concentration camp. All institutes of higher learning were closed, with the exception of several branches which the Directorate managed to save through an argument based on the letter of the German instructions rather than on its spirit.

In Latvia and Estonia, the Germans called for a new mobilization in October–November 1943. Latvia's Directorate was not even consulted. A mobilization appeal was published under the name of Latvian General Rudolfs Bangerskis, without his knowledge. He protested in writing, and refused to supervise the draft. Estonia's Directorate refused to discuss a mobilization under conditions of non-sovereignty, but Mäe published the order under his name alone, and the other Directors yielded.

New attempts to form Lithuanian military units followed the abortive Legion. An "All Lithuanian Conference" sponsored by the German occupation authorities was convened in the summer of 1943. A *Taryba* (council), linguistically evocative of the body which had declared Lithuania's independence in 1918, was formed and attached to First General Counselor Kubiliūnas. It was hoped that such mollification might smooth the new mobilization efforts which soon followed.

An agreement was reached between high officials of the SS in Lithuania and General Povilas Plechavičius of the former Lithuanian

71. In Latvia, 14,800 chose the Legion and 5,600 went to Labor Battalions; in Estonia, the numbers were 5,300 and 6,800. For 1942–3 mobilizations, the most detailed source is Myllyniemi 1973, esp. pp. 433–8 and 252. See also Ivinskis, pp. 79–80; and Purre, "Eesti sõda," pp. 19–40.

army, on the formation of "Local Detachments"; this was announced on 16 February 1944, the anniversary of Lithuanian independence. These were to be Lithuanian military units, manned and officered by natives. Their use was to be restricted to the Baltic area, from Narva to Vilnius, and their operations would be directed against Soviet partisan and bandit activities. This effort, unlike previous mobilization efforts, enjoyed the blessing of many native notables who saw in it the nucleus for a reestablished Lithuanian army at a time when the Soviets were approaching; and the considerable personal magnetism of General Plechavičius added another dimension of attraction. The actual level of volunteers exceeded expectations; some 30,000 came forward, and the originally planned number of battalions was somewhat increased.

Experience showed that the organizing officers were naive to trust German assurances. Manpower demands on the Eastern front overruled any promises, which may not have been made in good faith anyway. In May, the transfer of the new units into the Auxiliary Police Services of the SS was initiated. However, it triggered an immediate self-demobilization of the remaining units, most of whose personnel managed to slip away into the woods. General Plechavičius and his staff were arrested on 15 May, and some 100 of his men were indiscriminately shot. Those who did not succeed in escaping (about 3,500) were transferred for *Luftwaffe* ground duty in Germany and Norway. All later German recruitment efforts in Lithuania failed.[72]

In Latvia, military mobilization efforts continued to center around the Legion. The Soviet advance toward the Latvian border made the native administration reconsider its stand of no mobilization without autonomy. A conference of Latvian administrators (including those at the district level), called on 15 November 1943, reluctantly decided to support mobilization anyway, and the total strength of Latvian units jumped to 40,000. The peak strength, around mid-1944, has been estimated at 60,000, but may have been higher. Throughout the German occupation, up to 150,000 were inducted or recruited. At least 50,000 were killed, wounded or missing in action. About 80,000 men were captured by the Soviets, mainly after the collapse of the Courland front in May 1945. About 20,000 reached the West at the end of the war.[73]

72. Ivinskis, p. 84.
73. King, pp. 87–9, based on *Latvju enciklopēdija*, II, pp. 1317–18; Ekmanis 1978, pp. 84–5; Myllyniemi 1973, pp. 254–5 and 276.

In Estonia, the pre-war Prime Minister Uluots (whom the Germans alternatively ignored and tried to coopt) switched his stand on mobilization in February 1944 when the Soviet army reached the Estonian border. At that time the Estonian units under German control had about 14,000 men. Counting on a German debacle, Uluots considered it imperative to have large numbers of Estonians armed, through any means, and grouped in Estonia to guard against Soviet invasion, and to wrench independence from the retreating Germans. It was a desperate ploy of a weasel facing two wolves — the only alternative to passive surrender. Uluots even managed to tell it to the nation through the German-controlled radio: Estonian troops on Estonian soil have "a significance much wider than what I could and would be able to disclose here." The nation understood and responded. The Germans had set an upper limit of 15,000, but 38,000 registered and 28,000 actually received poor arms and hasty training. Six border-defense regiments were formed, headed by Estonian officers, and the SS Division received reinforcements, bringing the total of Estonian units up to 50,000 or 60,000 men. During the whole period of the German occupation, at least 70,000 Estonians joined the German army, and more than 10,000 may have died in action. The Estonian Division was reorganized in Germany after the Soviet conquest of Estonia. About 10,000 men reached the West after the war ended.[74]

Unlike their confreres to the south, Estonians facing the German draft had the alternative possibility of flight to Finland. The Gulf of Finland could be crossed overnight in a boat. A sentence of hard labor waited for those caught trying to flee; nevertheless, mostly between April and December 1943, about 5,000 men, some of them with their families, succeeded in making the crossing. About 3,000 of these were persuaded to volunteer for the Finnish armed forces, and a special Estonian regiment saw service on the Karelian front. In August 1944, in the face of a new Soviet invasion of Estonia, 1,800 agreed to a German amnesty arranged through Finnish mediation, and returned to their homeland to join local units.[75]

74. Text of Uluots radio speech in *Eesti riik*, VII, pp. 45–6; military detail from Richard Maasing, "Katseid Eesti sõjaväe uuestiloomiseks," *ibid.*, VII, pp. 17–51; Myllyniemi 1973, p. 276. The total number in the German army and casualties are our estimates.

75. Evald Uustalu, *For Freedom Only: The Story of Estonian Volunteers in the Finnish Wars of 1940–1944* (Toronto, 1977).

The Fate of the Jewish Population.   The Reich's policy toward the Jewish population of areas which fell under its control is well known, and the Baltic region was no exception. While the Jewish community of Estonia was minuscule (5,000), in 1939 Lithuania, including Vilnius, had over 200,000 and Latvia 93,000 Jews.

Some outbreaks of indiscriminate killing of Jews occurred in Lithuania soon after the German attack, and several bands of *ad hoc* executioners are known to have perpetrated such massacres. The connection between their activity and the LAF's organized uprising is hard to establish, with no indication of any definite relationship except in time and circumstance. However, the Soviet destruction of national élites had eliminated one element of social control over the most primitive segments of the population.

A German task force of 1,000 men (*Einsatzgruppe A*) was charged with liquidating Jews and Communists in the Baltic lands.[76] Its first groups went into action in Kaunas on 28 June — four days after the entry of German armed forces. The Germans made conscious efforts in Kaunas and Riga to take photos and films that would suggest popular initiative in the pogroms, and they urged the new local auxiliary units to participate, with some success. Nonetheless, the German *Sicherheitspolizei* reported that incitement was surprisingly difficult in Lithuania, and even more so in Riga. Altogether, German confidential reports in July estimated 7,000 Jews murdered in Kaunas, and 400 in Riga, by German *Einsatzgruppen* and local henchmen. By 15 October, one of the *Einsatzgruppen* reported having killed 71,105 Jews in Lithuania and 30,025 in Latvia, in addition to 3,387 non-Jews. Protests by people like the Latvian Lutheran Archbishop Teodors Grünbergs were of no avail.[77]

The introduction of formal anti-Jewish measures followed the German advance. As long as the front-line military administration functioned, these were quite circumscribed. The establishment of civil government was accompanied by specifics regulating the lives of the Jewish communities. At first these were relatively minor, such as prohibitions on the use of parks or sidewalks by Jews, or the regulation that they wear the indentifying yellow Star of David. Within a

76. *Einsatzgruppe A* also operated in northern Russia (Pskov, Novgorod), while eastern Lithuania (including Vilnius) was part of the territory assigned to *Einsatzgruppe B*.

77. Myllyniemi 1973, pp. 76–8, based mainly on *Trials of the Major War Criminals before the International Military Tribunal* (Nuremberg, 1947–9; 42 vols), 180-L, XXXVII, pp. 670–83; Spekke, p. 402.

month, however, ghettos, paralleling those in other German-occupied
East European areas, had been established in Lithuania. As elsewhere,
these proved to be but a temporary stage in the so-called final solution.
With time, ghettos were liquidated and their residents either executed
or transferred to the death camps for eventual extermination. In comparison with the better-known SS death factories erected on occupied
Polish territory, the camps established in the Baltic region were of
modest proportions. The largest of them was at Salaspils, near Riga;
another was at Klooga, near Tallinn. The Ninth Fort outside Kaunas,
one in a ring of fortifications dating from Tsarist times, and Aukštieji
Panèriai, outside Vilnius, were also turned into notorious locales for
mass executions.

In their capacity as fronts for the German occupation, the Directorates have later acquired a "guilt by association" with all German
policies carried out on their territory, whether they had any say in
them or not. Soviet propaganda was quite active in equating any anti-
Soviet activity pursued by Baltic political bodies with concurrence in
the Reich's genocide policy. Such charges imply participation and
approval. While participation of the Directorates in the administration
of German measures against the Jews cannot be questioned, it is
somewhat more difficult to establish wholehearted concurrence.
Doubtless some of their members agreed with the moves, but it is hard
to say that all, or for that matter even a majority, in the three Directorates were so disposed.

As in most East European areas under German control, a handful of local rabble actively joined in carrying out the Nazi genocide
policy. A complex series of circumstances can be said to have motivated such activity, and among them two were paramount. The first
was anti-Semitism inherited from the Tsarist period, although its
manifestations in Latvia and Lithuania were far milder than in other
areas of the former Pale of Jewish settlement. Some of their policies,
aimed at development of an ethnically Baltic professional and middle
class, tended by their very nature to discriminate against the Jewish
urban population which was disproportionately represented in these
groups, but neither the Ulmanis nor the Smetona regime can be
accused of anti-Semitism. Conditions for the Jewish minorities in pre-
war Latvia and Lithuania had been among the best in Eastern Europe
of that time, and the same was true of the tiny Jewish population in
Estonia.

The second and by far the greater impetus for violent anti-Semitism
was provided by the socially disruptive first year of Soviet domina-

tion, which introduced a syndrome of murder and revenge accompanied by destruction of the normal structure of social control. The pent-up native hostilities naturally directed against Communists and their sympathizers were in many cases deflected on to the Jews. The Lithuanian and Latvian Communist parties, although with extremely small memberships, were disproportionately composed of individuals of Jewish background. While Lithuania's population was about 7 per cent Jewish in early 1941, about 15 per cent of the local Communist Party were Jews.[78] This small number could not in any logical way reflect the Jewish community as a whole, but the visibility of such Communists as well as of the numerous newly-installed non-party officials who were Jewish led some who had been personally affected by the trauma of the deportations to identify "Soviet" with "Jewish".[79] The more actively inclined among these individuals joined the terrorist bands formed, in the first days of the war, to execute any real or imagined collaborators. Many in these small circles automatically placed all Jews in such a category. It is difficult to estimate the numbers of participants or of victims. These bands should not be summarily identified with the wider national resistance forces, which had no means to discipline terrorists supported by the Germans.

While the social circumstances which surround such activity can be explained, that does not condone indiscriminate murder. It is perhaps somewhat easier to understand the predicament of those who had joined the various German-sponsored military units with the intention

78. The number of Jews in the Lithuanian CP on 1 January 1941 is given as 412 in *Lietuvos Komunistų Partija skaičiais*, p. 55, and as 479 (including candidate members) in *Mažoji lietuviškoji tarybinė enciklopedija*, II (Vilnius, 1968), p. 386. Either figure is about 15 per cent of the total.

79. Most people in the Baltic countries did not realize that the Jews, overwhelmingly city-dwellers and often relatively well-off, were also more heavily affected by Soviet deportations than the majority nationalities. The number of Lithuanian Jews deported could have been 5,000, as given in *Kniga o russkom evreistve, 1917–1967* (New York, 1968), p. 97, or even 7,000, as claimed by Dov Levin, "Participation of the Lithuanian Jews in the Second World War," JBS, VI/4 (Winter 1975), p. 310. Even if the number were 3,000, this would still mean close to 1.5 per cent of the total Jewish population of somewhat over 200,000, while the deportation losses of the country as a whole were about 1.1 per cent (34,000 out of 3,100,000). A figure of approximately 5,000 Latvian Jews deported (i.e. 5 per cent of all Jews) has been given by Max Kaufmann, "The War Years," in Mendel Bobe *et al.* (eds), *The Jews in Latvia* (Tel Aviv, 1971), p. 351. This seems high, compared to even the highest estimates for Lithuania. However, even 1,000 Latvian Jews deported would lead to a higher percentage (1 per cent) than for the country as a whole (0.8 per cent).

of fighting the Soviets and who found themselves transferred away from their home countries to carry out aspects of the German genocide operations, under circumstances where disobedience to orders would entail courtmartial.

The Jewish communities of the Baltic states suffered tremendous losses. It is estimated that at least 170,000 from among the Lithuanian Jewish population perished. The exact pre-war figure is difficult to ascertain: the 1923 census indicates 153,743, but this of course includes neither the natural increase up to 1940 nor the sizeable Jewish population of Vilnius, which came under Lithuanian control in 1939. It is not unlikely that at the time of the Soviet takeover there were over 200,000 Jews in Lithuania.

In 1939, the Latvian Jewish population stood at approximately 93,000. Up to 5,000 were affected by the Soviet deportations of June 1941. About 18,000 Latvian Jews were either drafted into the Red Army or evacuated by the Soviets. The arrival of the Germans occasioned mass-murders of allegedly pro-Soviet elements. About 3,500 ethnic Latvians perished, along with several thousand Jews. The *Einsatzgruppen* liquidated 30,000 more before the German occupation regime concentrated the remaining Jewish population in ghettos, in October. By the end of 1941, about 30,000 of these were slaughtered. In late 1943, the Latvian ghettos were liquidated and their surviving residents sent first to Salaspils and later, as the German occupation drew to a close, to the Stutthof concentration camp. Of approximately 70,000 Jews who remained in Latvia after the Soviet retreat, only about 4,000 survived.[80]

Estonia had fewer than 5,000 Jews in 1939. Of these, only about 1,000 remained after the Soviet retreat. Most of them perished. In total about 250,000 Baltic Jews, of whom only about 10,000 survived, were deported or killed during the German occupation. Among the ethnic Lithuanians, Latvians and Estonians, an estimated 25,000 were killed in local camps, and 10,000 were transferred to concentration camps in Germany.[81]

Resistance to the Germans.   During the occupation, the rump press of the three countries was filled with exhortations for greater grati-

80. Our calculations, based on indirect figures given by Kaufmann, pp. 353–67, and King, p. 83.

81. See Tönu Parming, "The Jewish Community and Inter-Ethnic Relations in Estonia, 1918–1940," JBS, X/3 (Fall 1979), pp. 257–9; and Spekke, p. 402.

tude toward Germany as the liberator from Bolshevism. On the whole, such a mood prevailed among the majority of the native populations during the first months of the war. German occupation policies soon dissipated this reservoir of goodwill, making the mood either resignedly indifferent or actively hostile. Hopes among many leading elements for attaining formal sovereignty if not real independence once more quickly proved to be illusory. The majority might have settled for some sort of quasi-independence along the lines of Slovakia. As it was, the clear German refusal to satisfy the strong yearning for statehood, even as a formality, tended to fix the relationship between the new occupiers and the occupied. A Dutch Nazi visitor (to whom the "self-administration" officials may have talked more frankly than to Germans) reported in June 1942 that "chauvinist national consciousness" dominated in all layers of the population in Latvia and Estonia, and that he encountered no genuinely Germanophile circles or individuals. The apparent differences in attitudes merely reflected varying degrees of ability to hide one's thoughts.[82]

An underground press began to sprout, answering the Germans' demand for gratitude for liberation with observations on the initial complicity of the Reich in the Soviet invasion. The incessant severity of economic exploitation, and in particular the attempts at mobilization of manpower, eventually gave rise to an active opposition in all population groups. When the Germans invited the Latvian Directorate to ask for "permission" to form a Latvian SS Legion, Valdmanis responded with a memo on "The Latvian Problem" to Latvia's German SS Commander, saying that the situation of Latvians was unbearable:

Every Latvian, including those who have never given any thought to politics, is clearly faced with the question of what is actually happening. Have the Germans effectively come as liberators or as conquerors?[83]

By the middle of 1943, the influential Lithuanian underground newspaper *Nepriklausoma Lietuva* was wondering whether the Nazis or the Bolsheviks "were the more inveterate murderers of innocent people."[84] The organized anti-German oppositions did not encourage armed resistance, which could only help the Soviets. Rather, the

82. Myllyniemi 1973, p. 156, based on Rost van Tonningen's report in Bundesarchiv R6/441.

83. Alfreds Valdmanis, "Das Lettische Problem" (November 1942), in Bundesarchiv R6/5, as reported in Myllyniemi 1973, p. 210.

84. *Nepriklausoma Lietuva*, nos. 11–12 (1943), as cited by Ivinskis, p. 76

aim was to sabotage German occupation measures and to keep alive an organized national political body capable of representing each nation's interest during the postwar settlement. Hope was placed in the Western powers. As one of the underground Lithuanian papers expressed it on 16 February 1944, the anniversary of Lithuanian independence:

We are convinced that the Western nations who have formed the Atlantic Charter . . . will help us, at the right time, to secure and to defend from National Socialism as well as from Communism that for which we are prepared to sacrifice all.[85]

In Lithuania, a formal resistance began to crystallize by the fall of 1941. The LAF had organized the Provisional Government, disbanded in early August. Later that summer it presented Hitler, through the German military command, with a memorandum on Lithuania's independence. In September, the LAF Chief, Leonas Prapuolenis, was deported to Dachau and the organization was suppressed. One of its factions, the extreme right-wing Lithuanian Nationalist Party which had crystallized in late June, attempted to achieve some independence through collaboration and participation in the Directorate, but by late October it too had been proscribed for criticism of certain faults in the *Zivilverwaltung* system. From then on, organized political life continued only in the underground.

The Lithuanian resistance movement formed principally along two axes, a Catholic-oriented *Lietuvių Frontas* (Lithuanian Front) and a more secular *Laisvės Kovotojų Sąjunga* (Union of Freedom Fighters). Both published their own underground newspapers and maintained a liaison with the outside world. In early 1944, the latter even operated a clandestine radio station. By late 1943, these groups united in a Supreme Committee for the Liberation of Lithuania organized along the lines of the pre-war political parties. The Supreme Committee functioned as a center of the Lithuanian resistance until the summer of 1944, when one of its couriers, enroute to Stockholm, fell into a Gestapo net aimed at the Estonian underground. His arrest led to others throughout Lithuania, affecting the Supreme Committee's leadership. Although alternates took the places of those arrested, the activities of the body were severely restricted and it faded soon after the return of the Soviets. Although the Supreme Committee was obviously intended eventually to become a provisional government,

85. Brazaitis, "Vokiečių," p. 379; taken from *Laisvės kovotojas*, 16 February 1944.

the experience of the summer of 1941 must have dissuaded the Lithuanians from any renewed attempts at establishing such a body under the conditions of German occupation.[86]

Latvian attempts to form a provisional government arose from two quarters. The first emanated from within the Latvian Directorate. In his memo on "The Latvian Question," Valdmanis proposed the formation of a Latvian army to fight the USSR in exchange for the establishment of a formally independent state entity, albeit one with somewhat circumscribed sovereignty. The Latvian Directorate declared its support for the memo. Otto Drechsler, the German General Commissioner for Latvia, admonished Valdmanis, but confidentially suggested autonomy along Slovakian or at least Bohemian–Moravian lines to his superior, Lohse, on 7 December 1942. Contrary advice came from *Ostland* Political Section Leader Friedrich Trampedach:

The politically leading circles of the Baltic people . . . would use an increased independence not for rapproachment with the Reich but with the Anglo-Saxon powers.[87]

Nonetheless, the German armed-manpower problem was becoming so severe that by 26 January 1943 Rosenberg himself drafted proposals to Hitler, covering all three Baltic states: (1) total and rapid restoration of private property; (2) creation of autonomous governments; and (3) national troops based on general mobilization. These proposals, which reflected the minimal demands of Valdmanis, met Hitler's uncompromising veto on 8 February (except for reprivatization), and again on 5 May: "Subjected peoples cannot be used as allies." Meanwhile, Lohse accused the Latvian Directors of anti-Germanism, and reminded them that 80 prominent Dutchmen had been shot for such behavior. In mid-1943, Valdmanis resigned from the Directorate. Failure also met various later attempts in Germany by members of the former Directorate who in late 1944 and early 1945 envisaged the establishment of a provisional Latvian government in Courland, which remained under German control until the end of the war.[88]

The second Latvian approach avoided collaboration. It centered around the seven-man Latvian Central Council (founded on 13 August

86. Ivinskis, pp. 76–83; Myllyniemi 1973, pp. 81–3 and 265.

87. Drechsler to Lohse, 7 December 1942; Trampedach memo, 19 November 1942. Cf. Myllyniemi 1971.

88. Rosenberg, "Entwurf einer Führervorschlag," 26 January 1943, in Bundesarchiv R6/35. Full documentation in Myllyniemi 1973, pp. 207–18 and 243.

1943), an underground body representing the four largest political parties of the pre-war Parliament as well as some individuals from its presiding board. The presupposition for its existence was that the end of the war would leave both Germany and the USSR weakened, allowing Latvia to regain its independence with the aid of the Western powers. The Council had contacts in the West, and it published an underground newspaper, *Independent Latvia*. A Lithuanian-Latvian resistance conference took place in January 1944, and there were two all-Baltic ones in April, all in Riga. The Germans discovered the Latvian Council's existence in the fall of 1944, and arrested and deported most of the leaders. The Council's leader, the Liberal Konstantins Čakste, died while he was being deported in 1945. A Latvian unit of the German army had 8 officers shot and 545 men sent to the Stutthof concentration camp. On 7 May 1945, as the German power in Courland was collapsing, the National Council, consisting of 73 elected members, endorsed a provisional government led by Colonel Roberts Osis. During the following days, the Soviet forces occupied all of Courland.[89]

In Estonia, the Directorate was rather submissive. Still, the Director for Internal Affairs, Oskar Angelus, recommended in March 1943 a declaration of independence to facilitate mobilization:

The average Estonian is saying: If I am treated badly in my own homeland now, during an exhausting war, then what will they start doing with me when peace comes?[90]

Karl Litzmann, the German General Commissioner for Estonia, also supported Slovakian-type autonomy, an idea vetoed by Hitler. By February 1944 even Mäe started to ask for sovereignty, and came to be considered by some Germans as a secret Anglophile.[91]

Estonian resistance was favored by the geographical proximity of Finland and Sweden. Traces of organized political resistance formed around underground circles in Tartu and Tallinn, which were able to maintain contact with the still-resident Estonian Envoy to Finland and through him with Stockholm and London. These circles were instrumental in the creation in early 1944 of a blanket underground

89. Ekmanis 1978, p. 85; Myllyniemi 1973, p. 267; Bilmanis 1951, pp. 405–6; Uustalu 1970, p. 338.

90. Angelus memo, 15 March 1943, in Bundesarchiv R6/76.

91. Litzmann to Himmler, 31 March 1943; Mäe to Himmler, 9 February 1944. Full documentation in Myllyniemi 1973, pp. 213–14 and 269.

organization — the Republic National Committee — a coalition of all pre-war political tendencies which in many ways resembled the Latvian Central Council. Cooptation attempts by the Germans had begun in 1943, and were countered by demands for military autonomy which the Germans refused. The increased Estonian underground activity resulted in 200 arrests by the Gestapo in April. This impaired operations until mid-June 1944, by which time foreign connections were beginning to play a significant role in the activity of the Committee. Traffic by fast motorboat was organized more or less twice a month between Tallinn and Stockholm, where August Rei, a leading Social Democrat, was active. The ability to maintain a foreign connection gave the Estonian Committee some visibility abroad. On 23 June 1944 it released, in Stockholm, a manifesto which caught the attention of foreign correspondents and the ire of German occupation authorities.

The aim of the Committee was the installation of a provisional government during the interval between the German retreat and the Soviet arrival. It managed to accomplish this on 18 September, despite German opposition. It was not possible to organize any potentially successful resistance. Some Estonian units clashed with retreating Germans and set up defense positions east of Tallinn. On 22 September 1944, Soviet troops broke through these defenses and occupied Tallinn. The government decided to withdraw to Sweden — only Acting President Uluots succeeded.[92]

In all three countries, then, the bulk of anti-German resistance was channeled along the lines of political organization and the sabotage of occupation exactions. Armed resistance was minimal, as it had been against the Soviets in 1940–1. Some Soviet partisan activity, although greatly inflated by Soviet historiography, did exist, but its ties with the indigenous populations were extremely limited. The greatest concentration seems to have been in the eastern Lithuanian woods, where contact with the genuinely widespread Belorussian partisan activity was easiest. The earliest groups consisted of stranded Red Army personnel as well as some Communists who had not succeeded in withdrawing to the interior of the USSR. Later, these were joined by some Jews who had managed to escape from the ghettos or from train convoys enroute to concentration camps. Eventually some Soviet parachutists also joined.

---

92. Johannes Klesment, "Kolm aastat iseseisvuse võitlust võõra okupatsiooni all," *Eesti riik*, VIII, pp. 7–33; Evald Uustalu, "The National Committee of the Estonian Republic," JBS, VII/3 (Fall 1976), pp. 209–19.

The activities of the Soviet partisans provided one of the reasons for German reprisals, at times indiscriminate, against the country-side. In Latvia's Rēzekne district, all 235 inhabitants of Audrini village were executed, some of them publicly in the Rēzekne marketplace. Perhaps there was a rationale on the part of the Soviet planners that provocation of German reprisals could engender a genuine armed anti-German resistance in the countryside. The tragedy of the village of Pirčiupis, the Lithuanian Lidice, where 119 peasants were burnt to death by the Germans, was triggered by a Soviet partisan attack on 3 June 1944.[93]

In Russia, the Soviet Baltic institutions headed by their evacuated local leaderships continued to have a shadow existence. Most of the Baltic Red Army conscripts were considered unreliable and were sent to die in labor camps. Later (in early 1942), specifically Baltic com-bat units were established. Toward the end of the war, native Balts tended to be a minority in those units which saw some symbolic activity during the Soviet reoccupation of the Baltic states. The peak number of native Balts in the Red Army combat units may have been 18,000 Estonians (800 of whom surrendered to the Germans at Velikie Luki in December 1942), 10,000 Latvians and 5,000 Lithuanians.[94]

Unlike most occupied nations of the Second World War, the Baltics were in the unenviable situation of facing not one but two occupying powers. Of these, the one coming second had an unfair advantage: it did not have to destroy the national élite, because that had already been done. Therefore it generated relatively little resentment. The Baltic people could suspect Hitler of wanting to deport them east, but Stalin had actually started doing so. They saw no advantage in weakening Hitler against Stalin.

The Return of the Soviets

The return of the Soviets in 1944, unlike their orderly arrival in 1940, was a nightmare for the Baltic populations. Occasionally it was preceded by severe military action, as the Germans made several

---

93. Myllyniemi 1973, p. 141; Brazaitis, "Vokiečių," p. 377.

94. For Estonia: estimates based on Lembit Pärn, *Sõjakeerises* (Tallinn, 1968), pp. 88–118; Arnold Purre, "Eesti rahvastik okupeeritud Eestis," in Richard Maasing *et al.* (eds), *Eesti saatusaastad, 1945–1960* (Stockholm, 1963–7; henceforth cited as *Eesti saatusaastad*), V, pp. 12–15. For Lithuania: Levin, "Participation," p. 310, note 14. For Latvia, very approximately: King, p. 83.

attempts at stabilizing the front lines on Baltic territory.

The reappearance of the Red Army can be said to date from 20 January 1944 at Narva. The front there, however, remained immobile until the summer. The collapse of the German Army Group Center in Belorussia in June led to Soviet reoccupation of most Baltic territory by the fall. The eastern border of Lithuania was crossed in early July. Vilnius fell on 13 July, and by 1 August the *Wehrmacht* had abandoned Kaunas. A German counterattack temporarily halted the Soviet advance and secured German control over the Klaipėda area until January 1945. Further north, the Red Army had reached the Gulf of Riga in late July 1944, temporarily severing German land connections with Estonia. These were restored, allowing a relatively orderly withdrawal, in September. Riga fell on 13 October. By late October, only Courland was still occupied by German forces, which remained bottled up there until the end of the war.

The passing of the front was immediately followed, as later in Germany, by a wave of robbery, looting and rape. Summary executions of 400 to 700 people were reported in Kaunas, Zarasai and Šiauliai in Lithuania.[95] However, such occurrences appear to have been exceptional in the immediate aftermath of the Soviet reconquest.

Effective Soviet control was initially patchy and superficial. The forests were full of dispersed Germans, Baltic units of the German army and Lithuanian nationalist guerrillas, as well as Estonian Finnish army veterans opposing both Germans and Russians. There were also people simply hiding from the war, uncertain about Soviet intentions. Roads were crowded with refugees returning home. Soviet patrols stopped younger men, but in general did not try to find out who had been evacuated by the Germans and who had tried to flee Soviet rule on their own initiative.

Even in the partly destroyed cities, the establishment of effective control was hampered by an extreme shortage of trustworthy personnel. The pro-Soviet activists and careerists of 1941 were either dead, evacuated to Russia or mobilized into the Red Army. A large portion of the active population had fled to the West, been evacuated by the Germans or gone into hiding. Those who remained tended to be passively hostile or apprehensive and could not be trusted.

The Soviet response was a gradual tightening of control. Red Army rule was replaced by civilian administration as the front moved west.

95. Evald Uustalu, "Events after 1940," appendix to 2nd edn of August Rei, *The Drama of the Baltic Peoples* (Stockholm, 1970), p. 350.

People willing to cooperate were initially accepted with few questions, in order to reactivate the basic food distribution, transport and production systems. Food ration cards were issued in the cities through places of work and the Bureau of Employment. German money was collected from among the population against receipts rather than being exchanged for rubles. For a short moneyless period, barter trade prevailed, especially for food, along with earning vouchers issued by enterprises. Consumer goods were in shorter supply than ever before. Although much housing had been destroyed, city living was not overcrowded, since many people had left and few had arrived. But the fuel shortage became extreme during the winter of 1944–5. In buildings with central heating systems, people slept in their winter clothes. Courland, conquered only in May 1945, seemed to be especially hardhit by hunger and the general destruction.

The general mood can perhaps be best described as one of wait-and-see. In fall 1944, a dozen Moscow-based foreign correspondents were allowed a unique trip to Tallinn, and could walk around unattended. A British newsman later wrote:

The Estonians, it soon became evident, despised and feared the Russians. . . . I don't think a single one of us spoke to a single person during the whole trip who had a good word to say for the Russian re-occupation — except, of course, the spokesmen produced by the Russians. . . . [96]

There was some relief that the worst expectations, based on Soviet behavior in 1941 and on German propaganda, did not fully materialize immediately. Some joyfully discovered that relatives evacuated to the USSR in 1941 or mobilized were, after all, still alive. The Soviets promised to maintain private farming and promoted the use of some secondary national symbols. Physical hardship could not become any worse, as bombing and military activity had ceased. The rumor mill even promised an eventual Soviet withdrawal under pressure from the Western Allies.

However, the reestablishment of Soviet control was accompanied by activity from the political police (NKVD, renamed MVD in 1946). The agency rapidly established branches down to the township level. These were frequently headed by experienced Russian personnel, symbolically supervised by native Balts at the ministerial level. Three-to-four-member screening commissions investigated the past and the political views of every inhabitant above the age of 12 in order to

96. Paul Winterton, *Report on Russia* (London, 1945), pp. 85–6.

decide whom to deport and whom to arrest. Formal charges fell into two categories: "war criminal" and "enemy of the people." Presumably the first category involved Nazi collaborators, and the second anti-Nazi Baltic patriots.

The first major wave of deportations involved mainly Baltic members of the German army sent to "labor service" outside the labor-starved Baltic republics. A figure of 30,000 was mentioned on the Soviet Estonian radio in late 1944, and 38,000 in Soviet Latvian sources of early 1945, before the capture of Courland.[97] These figures were increased by the capture in 1945 of numerous Baltic soldiers in the German army. Few outright executions can be documented; death from starvation, cold and disease seem to have been the prevalent methods.

Some retribution against people serving with the competing occupation forces could be expected. But the war against the Baltic population continued and escalated, due partly to guerrilla resistance, partly to deliberate passive resistance, and mostly to the sheer inability of a Western-oriented population to adjust within only a few years to the Stalinist Soviet system.

In August and September 1945 an estimated 60,000 men, women and children were deported from Lithuania, followed by 40,000 in February 1946, and the worst was still to come. About 60,000 people may have been deported from Latvia in 1945-6.[98]

If the goal of the deportations was to break national resistance, the results were mixed. Expectations of being next in line for deportation made many desperate people join the guerrillas in order to die fighting on native ground rather than of starvation in Siberia. Instead of slowly subsiding after the war, the guerrillas continued to gather strength in 1945 and 1946.

The reestablishment of Soviet rule was also accompanied by Red Army mobilizations. Estonia, which had been cleared of Germans earliest, was most affected. In August 1944, men aged 18 to 33 were called up. Success was apparently only partial, in that the call was repeated in March 1945. This time the age-span was extended, from 18 to 37. Many of the draftees had previously served in the German army, but backgrounds tended not to be fully checked. Those who

97. Tönu Parming, "Population Changes in Estonia, 1935–1970," *Population Studies*, XXVI/1 (March 1972), p. 56; Bilmanis 1951, p. 406.

98. Thomas Remeikis, "The Armed Struggle against the Sovietization of Lithuania after 1944," *Lituanus*, VIII/1–2 (1962), p. 38; George Carson (ed.), *Latvia: An Area Study* (New Haven, Conn., 1956), p. 82.

admitted to front-line German service were sent to hard-labor battalions in Russia. Those with auxiliary non-armed service with the Germans were deemed redeemable and faced labor duty in Estonia. Those claiming no German ties were sent to the Courland front and suffered heavy casualties. It is not surprising that as time passed some reportedly preferred to claim non-armed German service. The extent of the mobilization in Estonia is unclear; most likely fewer than 10,000 were thus affected. Soviet sources provide figures in excess of 100,000 for Lithuania.

Estonia and Latvia suffered some formal territorial losses. In January 1945, the right bank of the Narva River and most of the Petseri district in southeastern Estonia were ceded to the Russian Soviet republic. The area involved 5 per cent of Estonia's pre-war territory and 6 per cent of its population. The Latvian loss was smaller, involving the detachment of part of the Abrene district in the northeast, about 2 per cent of the pre-war territory and population. The Klaipėda (Memel) region, which had been forcibly taken by Germany in March 1939, now reverted to Lithuania.

All three states emerged from the war with considerable population and property losses inflicted by Soviet as well as German policies and activities, by internal reactions and by the course of the war. Material losses were difficult to overcome. In Estonia, industrial capacity was down to 55 per cent, means of transport to 7 per cent, city housing down to 45 per cent, and area under cultivation down to 60 per cent of the pre-war figures. *Per capita* losses were estimated at around 6,000 rubles in Lithuania, 10,000 rubles in Latvia and 15,000 rubles in Estonia. There is little reason to doubt Soviet estimates that in Lithuania 21 villages had been burned by the Germans, 86,300 buildings destroyed, and 56 electricity stations and 1,148 bridges blown up by 1944.[99]

Psychologically, the population losses due to the war were perhaps not as devastatingly unexpected as the deportations during the first Soviet occupation. In real terms, however, they proved far greater. The blame is often hard to place on any particular quarter. Estimates are inevitably based on weak foundations, since those best placed to know certain figures are also those most interested in hiding them. Soviet sources have never given any estimates of the number of

99. Leonid Lentsman (chief ed.), *Eesti rahvas Suures Isamaasõjas* (Tallinn, 1977), II, p. 439; K. Meškauskas, V. Januškevičius, V. Puronas, *Lietuvos debartis ir ateitis* (Vilnius, 1973), p. 12.

deportees to the USSR, even though the deportations have been acknowledged. Their overviews of population losses tend blithely to ignore this category or possibly to reassign it to Germany deportation. Some Baltic refugee sources tend to underestimate the voluntary evacuation to the USSR and the extent of German-sponsored executions and deportations. The latter cannot be evaluated separately from the anarchistic executions by Baltic gangs who operated outside any German (or Baltic) organized control in the summer of 1941.

The very approximate estimates in Table 2 suggest that the Baltic states lost about 20 per cent of their population during the Second World War, due partly to people fleeing to the West and partly to losses of territory in 1945. About 9 per cent of the population, as shown in Table 3, suffered premature deaths caused by war and occupation. Again these estimates are very approximate.

How do the Baltic war and occupation deathrates compare with those of other European countries? A French overview presents the following list of undefined "human losses" as a percentage of each country's total population:[100]

Poland	20
Yugoslavia	12
USSR	9
Greece	7
Austria	6
Germany	5
Hungary	4
Romania	4
Netherlands	2.1
Czechoslovakia	2.1
France	1.5
Belgium	1.2
United Kingdom	0.8
Italy	0.5
Bulgaria	0.2

Even assuming that all these losses represent deaths, Baltic losses figure among the largest in Europe.

100. Larousse, *La Seconde Guerre mondiale* (Paris, 1951), p. 232. Civilian losses surpass the military ones for most countries in this list, as is the case for the Baltic states. The Soviet losses clearly include deaths in Stalin's labor camps and prisons, and many countries may have listed nonreturned refugees and prisoners of war, as of 1951, among the losses.

3

POSTWAR STALINISM, 1945–1953

Administration

The Reestablishment of Soviet Control. The Soviet Baltic leaders returned from Russia as soon as it became possible to reestablish even symbolic control. The first sessions of the Supreme Soviets of all three republics were held between August and October 1944 in the portions of each recaptured by the Red Army. Symbolic legitimation of the regimes through the standard one-candidate elections with upper-90s percentages of "yes" votes had, however, to be delayed. USSR Supreme Soviet elections were held in February 1946, the Baltic republics' Supreme Soviet elections in February 1947, and local Soviet elections only in January 1948. Official explanations of the delays mention remnants of the exploiting classes; one can only wonder where these had been in 1940. We may assume that only by 1946–8 did the regime feel it safe enough to proclaim inflated results without the threat of open challenge. Resistance estimates claim turnouts of less than 50 per cent in Lithuania.[1]

Overall control from Moscow was exerted mainly through the Lithuanian, Latvian and Estonian bureaux, which were formed on 11 November 1944 at the Central Committee of the Communist Party of the Soviet Union (CPSU CC). This seemed to be the main policy-making level for Sovietization of the Baltic countries (see Appendix A for names of various powerholders). The ranking native executors of these policies were the First Secretaries of each republic's Communist Party (CP) organization. Jānis Kalnbērziņš in Latvia and Antanas Sniečkus in Lithuania had occupied these posts since 1940. In Estonia, Nikolai Karotamm replaced Karl Säre, who had been captured by the Germans and declared a traitor by the Soviets for divulging information to the Germans; Karotamm had emigrated to the

---

1. K.V. Tauras, *Guerrilla Warfare on the Amber Coast* (New York, 1962), p. 58.

USSR in 1930 and returned in 1940 as Second Secretary of the Estonian CP. Despite their spotless party records ever since underground days, the native First Secretaries were now assigned Russian Second Secretaries to act as Moscow's watchdogs.

Next in rank were the Chairmen of the Councils of People's Commissars (renamed Council of Ministers in 1946). These were native Communists: Vilis Lācis in Latvia and Mečys Gedvilas in Lithuania, who continued from 1940; and Arnold Veimer in Estonia, replacing Johannes Lauristin, who died at sea during the 1941 evacuation. The ceremonial figurehead position of Chairman of each republic's Supreme Soviet Presidium continued to be held by the 1940 incumbents. Johannes Vares either committed suicide or was murdered by the MVD on 19 November 1946, and was replaced as Chairman in Estonia by a former linguist, Eduard Päll, who had grown up in Russia.

The top leadership of the Lithuanian party had changed slightly. A Russian, Aleksandr Isachenko, occupied the position of Second Secretary; the office had previously been held by a Lithuanian, Icikas Meskupas-Adomas. In practice, the Lithuanian leadership became an adjunct to the CPSU CC Special Bureau for Lithuania, which was headed by Mikhail Suslov until the spring of 1946.[2] Suslov — who was to become CPSU CC Secretary in 1947 and Politburo member in 1955 — may also have supervised the heads of the other two special Baltic bureaux.

The pattern was the same in Latvia. During the immediate postwar period, two representatives of the CPSU CC, Vasilii Riazanov and Sergei Grigorevich Zelenev, were dispatched there to keep a close watch on developments, and throughout 1946, the Latvian press documented their presence at all significant public and party functions. Riazanov's listing seems to imply a position superior to that of the Second Secretary, Ivan Lebedev, and following those of Kalnbērziņš, the First Secretary, Lācis, Chairman of the Council of Ministers, and Kirhenšteins, Chairman of the Presidium of the Supreme Soviet. Both Riazonov and Zelenev disappeared from press accounts in early 1947.[3]

2. *Lietuvos TSR istorija*, IV, pp. 145–6; Z. Zalepuga, "Lietuvos KP veikla atkuriant tarybinius organus respublikoje," *LKP istorijos klausimai*, XII (Vilnius, 1973), pp. 50–2.

3. Michael Widmer, "Nationalism and Communism in Latvia: The Latvian Communist Party under Soviet Rule" (Ph.D. diss., Harvard, 1969), pp. 177–8.

Control remained arbitrary, even by Soviet standards, and as Sniečkus admitted in 1961, it had to be exercised by force and terror.[4] On the local level, officials were appointed by the Presidium of the Supreme Soviet. There was a shortage of qualified and politically reliable personnel. Complaints of inefficiency, especially in rural administrative control, appeared endemic during the immediate postwar years.[5] "Enemies of the people" were continuously discovered and weeded out from the ranks. The peak of such activity came with the Estonian purge discussed in the next section.

The Soviet rulers clearly distrusted anyone who had not undergone the 20 years of Sovietization in the USSR. This distrust also extended to the local Communists, whose small number had been further decimated during the war. On the other hand, the need to know the local language restricted the utility of imported Russians. A large pool of suitable personnel was available in the form of Latvians and Estonians whose families had emigrated to Russia during the half-century preceding the Baltic independence period. Some of them had been dispatched to their ancestral lands already in 1940–1. After the war, tens of thousands returned at the command of Soviet agencies, or because of superior living conditions and major advancement opportunities. These "Russian Latvians" and "Russian Estonians" were often considered uncouth and arrogant by the local population. In Estonia they were at times called *jeestlased* (which might be translated as "Yestonians"), because that was how their Russian accent made them pronounce the word *eestlased* (Estonians).

Few Lithuanians resided in Russia before the war, and thus thousands of completely non-native cadres were imported at all levels. They included one-third of the ministers (32 per cent in 1947, plus 13 per cent who were Russian Lithuanians), most of the deputy ministers and various supervisory assistants to Lithuanian functionaries. Russian officials were used heavily even in Latvia and Estonia; in Estonia, 376 "leading cadres" were imported as early as 1945: the Vice-Chairmen of the Council of People's Commissars and of the republic's Planning Committee, the Second Secretaries of the Estonian Communist Party (ECP) and of the Komsomol (Communist Youth), and the three ECP Acting Secretaries were all Russians.[6]

4. *Tiesa*, 24 October 1961.

5. *Sovetskaia Latviia*, 30 May and 29 June 1946; *Sovetskaia Estoniia*, 28 September 1946.

6. Thomas Remeikis, "Berücksichtigung der nationalen und verwaltungsmässigen Interessen . . .," AB, X (1970), p. 142; Lentsman, p. 447.

The pre-war territorial administrative units (which had not been changed in 1940–1) continued to be maintained long into the post-war period. As a result, the Baltic subdivisions for both government and party institutions differed from the rest of the USSR (see Table 9). From March 1945 on, Soviet-type "village council areas" were gradually superimposed on the existing units. Traditional counties were at times subdivided, and cities were separated from them. The townships and counties (some of them with folklore-hallowed names going back to the pre-Christian era) were abolished in 1950. The new *raions* (the Soviet term for district) were much smaller than the previous counties, and their large number (39 to 87 per republic) presented a rationale for dividing the republics into a few provinces or *oblasts* (four in Lithuania in 1950, and three each in Latvia and Estonia in the spring of 1952). These larger units seemed seriously to undermine the administrative significance of the national republics. In April 1953, however, the *oblasts* were liquidated. The constant revamping of administrative units increased confusion, but made for great office politics.

The Communist Parties and the Estonian Purge.   Party membership continued to be heavily non-indigenous long into the postwar period, and the proportion of party members among the populations of the three republics stayed well below the USSR average. Membership grew slowly (see Table 6). Recruits who had lived under German occupation were distrusted, and the majority of the population considered the Communist Party as alien. During the last quarter of 1944, only 56 new party members were enrolled in Estonia, and local recruitment during 1945 probably totalled a few hundred. In early 1944, the ECP and the Communists in the Red Army Estonian Corps (who were not administratively part of the ECP) numbered around 7,400. By January 1946, after demobilization and disbanding of the Corps, the ECP counted 7,139 members, 52 per cent of them Russian, about 21 per cent Estonians from Russia and only about 27 per cent (1,900 members) home-grown Estonians.[7] The ECP was not only taking its orders from the outside; it also consisted largely of outsiders.

The Lithuanian CP (LiCP) emerged from the war with 8,060 members in January 1946 (as opposed to 1,500 in June 1940). By

---

7. Lentsman, p. 447; Jaan Pennar, "Soviet Nationality Policy and the Estonian Communist Elite," in Tönu Parming and Elmar Järvesoo (eds), *A Case Study of a Soviet Republic: The Estonian SSR* (Boulder, Colo., 1978), p. 118.

January 1949 the figure had risen to 24,000, the majority of its membership being non-Lithuanian. Indeed, even 46 per cent of the staff of its Central Committee (CC) were non-indigenous. Such a low numerical strength of locals was grossly inadequate for effective exercise of control over the country. The dominance of the Special Bureau of the CPSU CC was paralleled at the lower levels by political control exercised by thousands of non-native cadres and government officials specially imported for the purpose. In 1945, Lithuanians made up less than 31 per cent of the LiCP, a figure which had risen to 38 per cent by 1953.

On 1 January 1946, the Latvian CP (LaCP) had 10,987 members, about half of Latvian origin. The pre-war underground members still alive probably numbered a few hundred. Of those who joined in 1940–1, up to 2,000 may have survived the war. A third group consisted of those who had joined during the war from among the evacuees and army units. They probably numbered less than 1,000. The rest of the Latvian half of the LaCP was accounted for by the "Russian Latvians." From early 1945 to early 1951, at least 9,000 Communists were transferred to Latvia from elsewhere. In early 1950, the membership figure stood at 34,224 (about 1.5 per cent of the population). In 1949, Latvians maintained a narrow majority of 53 per cent in their party membership. As descendants of emigrants to Russia are included in these figures, home-grown Communists formed only about a quarter to one-third of the total membership. During the period between 1945 and 1950, only 9,561 individuals from within the republic were accepted for party membership. In late 1945, the great majority of those who served in district party organizations had come from the outside. Most could not have been proficient in Latvian. In March 1949, of the 30 non-staff lecturers in the Agitprop Department of the City of Riga Lenin District Committee, only eight knew Latvian — and these were people whose task it was to spread Soviet ideology among the population.[8]

The preponderance of non-native elements was similar in the Estonian party, which in 1946 was 48 per cent Estonian (including "Yestonian" immigrants from outside the republic), and which in January 1949 numbered about 17,000. These low figures suggest a reluctance of the population, as in the other two Baltic republics, to join in the occupation regime politically at this early date of Soviet control.

8. *Sovetskaia Latviia*, 26 January 1949; Widmer, pp. 123 and 552; King, p. 183; Carson, p. 354. See also sources in Table 6.

They also probably indicate a preference by the regime for importing a new ruling élite rather than recruiting it from among an untrustworthy population.

Around 1949, home-grown Communists in all three countries represented only about one-third of the total membership. Despite the career opportunities involved, only 0.3 per cent of the Lithuanians and 0.7 per cent of the Latvians and Estonians had joined the CP after five years of continuous Soviet occupation. This rate was 5 to 10 times less than the USSR average at that time.

In 1950–1, nearly all home-grown Estonian CP leaders lost their positions, and some vanished without a trace. They were replaced by Yestonians. Unlike other upheavals such as the collectivization of agriculture (to be described later), which simultaneously affected all newly-acquired Soviet western territories, the leadership purge did not spread to Latvia or Lithuania, and it is still unclear what triggered it in Estonia.[9]

It may be that of the three Baltic Communist leaders, Karotamm pleaded most actively for a slower pace of collectivization, for moderation in the deportation of farmers and for keeping the deportees within Estonia, where the oil-shale mines needed labor. Once Stalin's suspicion had been aroused, Karotamm's obedient execution of collectivization through deportation might actually have worked against him. Estonia's record-breaking pace in this activity may have suggested to Stalin that Karotamm had been timorous and could have achieved a breakthrough even earlier. Once Karotamm was demoted, every underling whom he had at times praised became suspect in turn. The sequence of events was as follows.

In February 1950, an Estonian Minister of Security, despite his keenness in doing his job, was replaced by a Ukrainian from Siberia. In March, the Soviet Politburo passed a resolution on "The Shortcomings and Errors in the Work of the Estonian Communist (Bolshevik) Party CC." This resolution, which was presented at an Estonian party plenum, "helped to unmask a bourgeois nationalist anti-popular group who had forced their way into the party and caused great harm,

9. A possible connection with the purge of supporters of Zhdanov in nearby Leningrad has been suggested by Benedict Mačiuika, "The Baltic States under Soviet Russia: A Case Study in Sovietization" (Ph.D. diss., University of Chicago, 1963), pp. 266–9. However, there is no evidence that Zhdanov maintained any special influence in Estonia after July 1940, and a power struggle among basically Russian factions in the CPSU leadership would not explain the heavy purge of non-party intellectuals in Estonia.

especially on the ideological front."[10] A CC member, Lembit Lüüs, was declared "dangerous to the Estonian people," expelled from the party, and sentenced to 25 years of forced labor; so too was Trade Minister August Hansen (who died in 1952). Hans Kruus, Foreign Minister and President of the Academy of Sciences, was expelled but not deported (although some of his fingerbones were broken during torture in Leningrad).

The charge against Karotamm was that he

did not ensure implementation of the correct political line regarding the most important issues of ideological work and socialist reconstruction, committed rightist opportunist errors, and guided the party organization toward peaceful coexistence with class-hostile elements.[11]

Karotamm was dismissed and finished his days as an economics researcher in Moscow. He was replaced by Ivan Käbin, whose family had emigrated to St Petersburg in 1910. The thoroughly Russianized Käbin, who had become a professional party organizer, was sent to Estonia in 1941 and by 1948 had become one of the ECP Secretaries. He was fully prepared to implement the denationalization of culture, appointment of Russians to key positions, extended use of the Russian language, and subservience to everything Russian; or, in the words of *The History of Soviet Estonia*, to

fight against the bourgeois nationalist ideology, for the implementation of the Leninist policy of cadres, and for the education of all workers in the spirit of Soviet patriotism and proletarian internationalism.[12]

Among those active in condemning Karotamm was the Vice-Chairman of the Council of Ministers, Hendrik Allik, who had been sentenced to 25 years in prison in 1924 for subversive Communist activities against the Republic of Estonia. In July 1950 he was awarded the Order of Lenin, but in December received his second 25-year sentence, this time for alleged bourgeois nationalism. The Chairman of the Council of Ministers, Arnold Veimer, with a similar background, was dismissed in April 1951 but maintained some public functions. Major officials who vanished or were deported in 1951 included the Party Secretaries Villem Kuusik and Aleksander Kelberg. Hundreds

10. *Rahva Hääl*, 4 April 1951. The major source on Estonian purges is Arnold Purre, "Teine punane okupatsioon Eestis: Aastad 1944–1950," in *Eesti saatusaastad*, II, pp. 7–65.

11. *Rahva Hääl*, 23 March 1953.

12. *Eesti NSV ajalugu*, III, p. 684.

of other functionaries and intellectuals were deported. The purge extended from Tallinn to Tartu University and to minor cities. The Estonian share of ECP membership fell to 41 per cent (including Yestonians). By late 1952, not a single home-grown ethnic Estonian was left among the four ECP secretaries and the 26 ministers.

Nevertheless, Baltic CP membership continued to grow. By the early 1950s it was becoming evident that Soviet power was likely to stay and that career opportunities required party membership. Guerrilla activities (to be discussed in the next section), which had at times made such membership dangerous, were subsiding. Moral condemnation of collaboration with the enemy also became muted, as deportations made people shut up. At Stalin's death in March 1953, the total CP membership was 36,000 in Lithuania, 42,000 in Latvia and 22,000 in Estonia. In their own republic, Lithuanians formed 38 per cent of the members, and the percentage was probably slowly increasing. The Latvian figure was around 50 per cent, and probably decreasing. The Estonian share stood at around 42 per cent, slowly recovering from the purge.

Guerrilla Warfare and Collectivization

Guerilla Resistance. "Forest Brothers" was the name by which the population called the guerrillas in all three countries and languages. At peak size they involved 0.5 to 1 per cent of the total population. This is comparable to the peak Viet Cong strength in South Vietnam (discounting the North Vietnamese supplements) of about 170,000 fighters and supply-runners out of a population of 20 million. Lithuania emerged from the German occupation with a strong national resistance movement. By the spring of 1945, some 30,000 armed men roamed the woods (see Table 4), although a unified command was not to emerge until 1946. In Latvia, indirect evidence suggests that 10,000–15,000 individuals were in the forests during the peak period; *The History of the Latvian SSR* reports over 1,000 surrenders in the Rēzekne district alone. In the Madona district, about 780 guerrilla fighters were reported killed or captured in 1945–7.[13] No unified command emerged. The situation was similar in Estonia, where the forest brotherhood may have at times reached a strength of 10,000.

13. Vietnam: *The Economist*, 16 August 1969, p. 26. Latvia: *Istoriia Latviiskoi SSR*, III (Riga, 1957), p. 596; Carson, p. 499.

Why was it now that people joined the forest brotherhood, although they had submitted peacefully to the Soviet invasion of 1940? Why did they decide to resist under the much less favorable postwar occupation conditions? Patriotic idealism was an important motive. In 1940 it had been tempered by the desire not to die, but by 1945 war and both occupations had engendered a feeling that one might die soon anyway. Life as a fugitive had become familiar to many, and scattered arms had become plentiful. However, the prime direct reason for resistance was the Soviet terror during the 1940–1 occupation, and its reintroduction after reoccupation. Terror affected many more than just the wealthy or the German collaborators. Anyone with democratic views, including Social Democratic workers, or who had voiced a preference for national independence instead of Russian or German domination was a target — as was anyone who complained of some aspect of Soviet bureaucracy or could not adjust to its demands (such as farm grain deliveries). The sloppy randomness of the MVD and MGB repression units, and lack of due process, in fact made almost everyone a potential target, the more so since the Soviets considered all who had survived the German occupation to be Nazi collaborators of sorts. People went to the forests mainly when they could no longer tolerate the insecurity of civilian life.

Different groups and individuals reached that point at different times, depending on their personal and social circumstances of the moment. The first wave consisted of willing and unwilling German collaborators and draftees, anti-German national underground members (chiefly in Lithuania) and ex-members of the Finnish army (in Estonia). Men avoiding the Soviet draft and Red Army deserters soon followed. Soviet land redistribution and other social restructuring measures produced new waves, as did Soviet screening and deportation campaigns. The last major wave was to come during the 1949 farm-collectivization process.

In Lithuania, religion added a particular facet to resistance. Catholic parishes represented a grassroots institution encompassing the majority of the population. The Soviet threat to their existence in itself fostered resistance. The Lutheran Church in Latvia and Estonia offered no comparable spiritual and national rallying-point due to its century-long association with Baltic Germans. This difference may explain the relative strength of the Lithuanian guerrillas. Some clergy and sacristans figured among guerrilla leaders in Lithuania, but there is only one claimed instance of their participation in the Latvian guerrilla effort[14] and none in Estonia.

While pushed by despair, people were also pulled into the forest brotherhood by expectation of an imminent Western-Soviet war. This was not an unreasonable prognosis if through bitter experience one had learned Stalin's attitudes toward the Western way of life and now observed a sharp increase in Soviet anti-Western propaganda. From such a viewpoint, it was only a matter of holding out for a few years, thus minimizing the risk of deportation and the harm done to the nation's social fabric. While such an outlook boosted morale, it also led the guerrillas to overstress the military aspect of the struggle and to neglect political education and planning. Even military action was to be directed only at the MVD units, their local auxiliary units and other real or perceived collaborators; regular Red Army units were not to be needlessly provoked any more than their German predecessors had been.

Russian deserters and escaped German POWs occasionally found their way into the Baltic forests. At times they were accepted into guerrilla groups, but they rarely played a leading role. There is also little documentation identifying any of the guerrilla leaders as previous German collaborators of any significance. Such people fled to Germany or switched to collaboration with the Soviets, often under new identities. Before their defeat in 1945, the Germans (who still held Courland) tried to make use of the Baltic guerrillas. In Lithuania an anti-German underground group called LLA (Lithuanian Freedom Army) reoriented itself in 1944 as the Soviet front reached Lithuania, and received limited amounts of German arms.[15] There is no evidence that such supplies bought the Germans any more influence than British supplies had achieved for Tito. Guerrilla groups also tend to attract adventurers, criminals and romantic rebels against any authority, but in the Baltic case there were factors reducing this component. The business was too deadly, dull and devoid of booty. Joining the Soviet-organized militia offered a greater feeling of power and importance, looting during arrests and deportations, and a feeling of rebellion against one's own society's established values.

14. *Cīņa*, 2 November 1966.

15. Thomas Remeikis, *Opposition to Soviet Rule in Lithuania, 1945–1980* (Chicago, 1980), p. 60. The Soviets published a series of former LLA member testimonies to Soviet interrogation authorities, in *Hitleriniai parašiutininkai* (Vilnius, 1966), pp. 63ff.

The underground ranged from forest brotherhood groups of 800 men down to individuals in bunkers near their home farms or even under their family homes. Many of the individual underground people were merely hiding, did not take any action against the Soviets and had little contact with others. Some married couples or small groups of friends would circulate from one acquaintance to another, never spending more than a few weeks in one spot. Many others joined larger armed groups. An even larger segment of the population supported and supplied individual fugitives and guerrilla groups while remaining in the cities and on farms. Some "forest brothers" would return to the cities with forged papers to carry out intelligence and passive resistance work, or to try to give up forest life for good. As terror temporarily relaxed, people would drift back to civilian life. As organized guerrilla units suffered casualties, some supporters would shift to an active role. Members of decimated guerrilla units might become individual fugitives. It is thus impossible to draw a firm line between guerrilla and non-guerrilla.

The average lifespan of a forest brotherhood career has been estimated at no more than two years, due to casualties, disease and return to civilian life. Thus over the eight years of intense guerrilla activity (1945–52), about 100,000 people may have been involved in Lithuania. This estimate is in line with estimates of guerrilla casualties as between 20,000 (Soviet estimate) and 50,000.[16] The Latvian and Estonian forest brotherhoods may have involved at one time or another respective totals of about 40,000 and 30,000 people.

Forest brotherhood living conditions were primitive. Housing tended to shift from the use of outlying haybarns in 1944 to above-ground huts in 1945 and underground bunkers later. The latter rarely accommodated more than three people, had poor ventilation, one entrance, and were suitable for hiding but unsuitable for self-defense when discovered. Bunkers were located in forests, farms and even under village roads. Humidity was the main enemy in the long run, and lack of medical aid made every disease and wound deadly. Food and clothing supplies from the population were adequate, especially before collectivization. After that time, attempts to build up forest reserves of grain and fat were made. Large quantities of arms had been

16. George Weller, *Chicago Daily News*, 17 August 1961, p. 21, based on an interview with Soviet Lithuanian official Romas Šarmaitis; Remeikis 1962, pp. 32. On lifespan: V. Stanley Vardys, "The Partisan Movement in Postwar Lithuania," in *Lithuania under the Soviets*, p. 95.

abandoned by the Germans, but ammunition soon ran out or rotted. By 1948 most guerrillas had shifted to Soviet arms obtained in battle or by raids, but ammunition remained a problem.[17]

Compared to the German occupation, the Soviet one confronted the national resistance with more difficult operating conditions. A Council for the Liberation of Lithuania formed in the fall of 1944 was broken up by arrests by May 1945, as were several subsequent centers. Consolidation was finally achieved from the bottom up, with individual groups of ten to several hundred men coordinated at the county level. Thus on 25 August 1945 all detachments in the Suvalkija region (south of the Nemunas River) merged into a Tauras guerrilla district. A central organization for Lithuania was finally restored in 1946, and was to last until 1951. The United Democratic Resistance Movement (*Bendras Demokratinio Pasipriešinimo Sajūdis*, or BDPS), formed on 10 June 1946, sought to coordinate armed units, passive resistance groups and political organizations. The armed forces were called Freedom Fighters. The declaration of the founding conference rejected narrow-minded nationalism, spoke of the need for far-reaching socio-economic reforms and a world government, and proposed the creation of an international democratic welfare state. The BDPS seemed to have the format of an underground government, with a President and a Council of the Republic.[18]

The guerrillas later split with the passive resistance and formed a separate Lithuanian Freedom Fight Movement (*Lietuvos Laisvės Kovų Sajūdis*, or LLKS) on February 1949. Nine separate guerrilla districts were fused into three military regions (Northeast, Northwest and the Nemunas area), with common military and political staff. Leadership of the guerrilla groups was as diverse as the membership. In June 1945 the staff of the Skardupiai unit (50 km. southwest of Kaunas) consisted of a carpenter, a church janitor, an education student, a farmer, a policeman and a priest. Leaders of primary groups were elected by the ranks, and they in turn elected higher commanders. Leadership gradually passed into the hands of former officers of the Lithuanian army, who tended to underestimate the importance of political struggle.[19]

17. Eerik Heine, "Metsavennad," in *Eesti saatusaastad*, II, pp. 68–70; Tauras, p. 40.
18. Remeikis 1962, p. 34; Vardys, "The Partisan Movement," p. 97; Tauras, p. 34; Stasys Žymantas, "Twenty Years of Resistance," *Lituanus*, VI/2 (September 1960), p. 44.
19. Remeikis 1962, pp. 31 and 35; also Vardys, "The Partisan Movement," pp. 100–1.

The underground press ranged from irregular mimeographed leaflets and posters to printed periodicals such as *Laisvės varpas* (*The Bell of Freedom*), consisting of 127 issues by 1947 and continuing at least until 1951. Apart from BDPS's *Kovas*, publication was decentralized to district level, with a distribution of about 1,000 copies. The press carried local and international information, using foreign-radio monitoring sites and "correspondents" in the administrative offices of the occupation regime. It warned, advised and encouraged the population. Articles were often written by civilians. Anti-Soviet posters in public places were sometimes used as mine triggers in order to discourage removal by collaborators. Manufacture of forged Soviet documents was another aspect of the guerrilla press.[20]

A countrywide 17-day officer training course was successfully carried out in the summer of 1947, with 72 graduates. The second course in September 1948 was interrupted on its last day by a random MVD or MGB search group, which lost half of its 70 men.[21]

External contacts of the Lithuanian guerrillas were limited, although there was some cooperation with Latvian guerrillas. Western agents apparently established contacts with Lithuanian guerrillas as early as 1945, and a prominent guerrilla leader, Juozas Lukša-Daumantas, reached the West in 1948 to request help and write a book on *Partisans behind the Iron Curtain*.[22] No material help was forthcoming, but American intelligence parachuted Lukša and several other guerrilla representatives back to Lithuania in 1949–51, where Lukša soon perished.

Guerrilla military activity largely consisted of surprise raids by small groups against the Soviet MVD repression units in order to keep them on the defensive. In summer 1946, the MVD office in Šiauliai was reportedly blown up. On occasions there were more ambitious enterprises. In February 1948 a 250-man MVD garrison in eastern Lithuania was unsuccessfully attacked by 120 guerrilla fighters. Major engagements took place when the MVD tried to penetrate the guerrilla territory. An underground report of 7 June 1946 lists six major battles within 13 months, with the following median figures: 2,000 MVD troops attacked 100 guerrillas; 174 Russians and 24 Lithuanians died.[23] While the absolute numbers favor the Lithuanians (and may

---

20. Tauras, pp. 43–6; Žymantas, pp. 44.
21. Tauras, p. 36.
22. Juozas (Lukša) Daumantas, *Partizanai už geležinės uždangos* (Chicago, 1950).
23. *Ibid.*, pp. 305–6; Žymantas, p. 43.

be exaggerated), the Lithuanians tended to lose one-quarter and the MVD only one-tenth of forces engaged.

Major guerrilla and passive-resistance efforts went into disrupting the administration and social structuring by the occupation forces. Local Soviet-appointed officials were intimidated, forced into being double agents, and — in case of excessive collaborationist zeal — murdered. From 1945 to 1952, an estimated 4,000 to 13,000 Soviet collaborators and suspects were executed.[24] The terror tactics of Soviet repression placed many uninvolved individuals into unbearable positions. The guerrillas and the occupation regime agreed on one point: no one must stay neutral. At the same time, the guerrillas did enjoy success in protecting the population against robberies committed or tolerated by Soviet officials. They also tried to warn of impending deportations as well as to liberate prisoners and deportees. However, the heavy MVD supplements brought in for deportations largely foiled such attempts. In the spring of 1946, an effort was also made in southern Lithuania to limit moonshining and drinking. Throughout the period 1944–6, Soviet land-redistribution measures were opposed with force.

The active opposition presented to the Soviet elections of 1946–7 forms a special chapter in the history of Lithuanian guerrilla activity. They countered Soviet propaganda and threats designed to achieve a total turnout by destruction of communications, attacks on armed guards at polling stations, and collection of passports (where proof of voting was to be entered) from among the rural population. The last measure both intimidated the prospective voter and provided him with an alibi for not voting.

Dogged Lithuanian efforts at establishing and maintaining unified command apparently had few parallels in the other two countries. A systematic account by a presumable participant (Eerik Heine) discusses arms, local intelligence, tactics, and group leaders, but the very idea of even district-wide cooperation is absent. There is no evidence of mimeographed guerrilla publications, of active contact attempts with the West, of organized officer training, of city intelligence activity, or of concerted campaigns against elections. A Soviet source reports destruction of an Estonian National Committee with numerous branches. In Latvia, a Soviet source names three regional guerrilla associations which had their own commanding staffs. Furthermore, a nationwide Latvian Partisans Communications Staff

24. Low estimate by Tauras, p. 52; Soviet estimates are on the higher side.

seems to have operated until 1947 in Riga itself, on Matiss Street.[25]

At the local level, fighting was as hard as in Lithuania. The forest brotherhood operated in almost every Latvian and Estonian county. Whole townships were for weeks outside Soviet control, and church towers flew national flags. However, it seems not to have occurred to the guerrillas to make positive use of this power-base to inform and organize the population. At night the guerrillas ruled wide stretches, with Soviet occupants and quislings ensconced in stone buildings or moving about in armed convoys. Offices and railroad bridges were blasted. In 1945 a 100-man group attacked the central prison in the city of Tartu, and an 800-man guerrilla unit allegedly fought it out with a Red Army division in Tartu district. In October 1946 the forest brotherhood occupied the small town of Kilingi-Nõmme in southwest Estonia. October Revolution celebrations in that area were blocked by guerrilla posters threatening to blow up the buildings. Collaborators were forced to turn in their Communist Party or Komsomol (Communist Youth) cards and to go easy in their jobs, or give them up in face of death-threats. Giving in to the guerrilla threats could mean arrest by the Soviets. The population faced double terror regardless of their personal preferences. *The History of the Estonian SSR* says that "several hundred Soviet people were killed" by the guerrillas in 1948 and early 1949, although "the backbone of banditism was broken by the end of 1946." Hence close to 1,000 collaborators must have been murdered in Estonia between 1944 and 1952.[26]

The Decline of the Guerrilla Movement. The occupation regime countered the national guerrilla movement with overwhelming brute force, coupled with sophisticated political measures to drive a wedge between the guerrillas and at least a part of the population. Defending themselves against this force kept the guerrillas so busy that they lost the political struggle through default without even noticing it.

The Kremlin's dispatch of top cadres to organize repression indicates how seriously it viewed the guerrilla challenge to the Soviet

25. Heine, pp. 66–75; Purre, "Teine punane," p. 37; J. Vēvers, *Indīgas saknes* (Riga, 1970); Ādolfs Šilde, *Važu rāvēji* (Stockholm, 1960), p. 102, and *Resistance Movement in Latvia* (Stockholm, 1972), p. 9; A Pork, "Na strane zavoevanii Oktiabria," *Kommunist Estonii*, 1967/12, p. 10. For further Soviet views, see Rein Taagepera, "Soviet Documentation on the Estonian Pro-Independence Guerrilla Movement, 1945–1952" (henceforth cited as "Guerrilla"), JBS X/2 (Summer 1979), pp. 91–106.

26. *Eesti NSV ajalugu*, III, pp. 588 and 592; Purre, "Teine punane," pp. 35–8.

occupation. Beria's deputy and successor, Sergei Kruglov, was placed in charge of NKVD operations in Lithuania, and in July 1944 was assigned the special troops which during the preceding month had carried out the deportation of the Crimean Tatars. In September, he urged them to abandon their "sentimental approach," to shoot unarmed people who tried to run, and to burn farms and villages where such people took refuge.[27]

The forces massed to break the Lithuanian guerrilla activity in 1948 included at least 70,000 MVD and MGB troops. The eight regular Red Army divisions stationed in Lithuania, as well as some air force units, were also sometimes used against the guerrillas. To these figures one must add the locally-formed militia, which often proved unreliable, as well as "special extermination squads" consisting of Lithuanian Komsomol members commanded by Russian MGB officers. In 1948, some 300 such groups involving about 7,000 individuals were active. The losses suffered by the forces of repression have been estimated at 20,000 by the Soviets and 80,000 by guerrilla sources.[28] During 1950–1, repression was handled by the MVD 2nd and 4th Special Task Divisions, from which many soldiers and officers deserted in disgust. On a smaller scale, the pattern was similar in Latvia and Estonia. During deportations, election campaigns and major forest searches, massive repression forces could be concentrated, including Russian units temporarily brought in from Russia and Poland, while guerrilla units had little mobility beyond the district level. Most casualties occurred in small-scale raids and searches.

Provocateurs were trained by a special MVD school in Vilnius to infiltrate the guerrilla groups and locate their civilian supporters. In 1946, whole pseudo-guerrilla bands were formed to plunder and murder civilians in an effort to prove that the guerrillas were bandits. Soviet sources confirm that fake guerrilla groups were used to catch the real ones. In response to such tactics, some guerrilla units assigned newcomers to execute local collaborators.[29]

Mass deportations of the civilian population in guerrilla-frequented areas severely affected guerrilla activity. The guerrillas lost not only

27. Testimony to the US Congress by former Soviet Border Guard Colonel Burlitski, in *Fourth Interim Report of the Select Committee on Communist Aggression* (1954); also reproduced in *Lituanus*, VIII/1–2 (1962), pp. 52–5.

28. Remeikis 1962, pp. 32–3; Tauras, pp. 50 and 77; Weller, *Chicago Daily News*, 17 August 1961.

29. Remeikis 1962, p. 38; Tauras, p. 79; *Noorte Hääl*, 30 March 1957 and following issues, as reported by Purre in "Teine punane," p. 37; Heine, p. 73.

potential recruits but also their all-important food-supply system, and the remaining population was scared away from supporting the forest brothers. Soviet Baltic literature contains description of entire grown-over villages where not a single farmhand remained after the "kulaks" had been deported for supplying the guerrillas, but, as has been mentioned, deportations also backfired by forcing people to flee to the forest.

Amnesties were repeatedly offered to guerrillas. In Estonia the offers in October 1944 and the spring of 1945 were followed by two more, but the Soviets destroyed their effect by deporting most returnees after a few months of showcasing. Only the fifth amnesty, in 1955, was largely genuine. In Lithuania the occupation forces invited the clergy to join the 1945 and 1946 surrender appeals, but spoiled the show by arresting bishops. The 1946 amnesty proclamation threatened to deport families of guerrillas and passive-resistance members, and announced that people who did not report guerrilla bunkers on their property would be tried as bandits.

The Soviet land redistribution (described in the next section) presented the forest brotherhood with its most sophisticated political challenge. Redistribution pitted those who lost land against those who received it. The latter now had an apparent economic stake in the continuation of the Soviet regime (as long as collectivization was soft-pedalled), in conflict with their national and, in Lithuania, religious feelings. Land-losers were motivated to join the guerrillas, and tilted the guerrilla policy, at least in Lithuania. "The resistance came out strongly against this land reform . . . This was exactly what the Soviet regime desired. First of all, the Soviet regime expected to create a 'class struggle' with the land reform, and partly succeeded."[30]

The power for positive action was in Soviet hands. Opposition to every Soviet measure may have looked supremely patriotic at first, but as the years went by, it became indistinguishable from social obstructionism. The Soviet viewpoint, spread comprehensively through schools, newspapers and meetings, may have been largely discounted, but even minor successes outweighed the meager information flow by the guerrillas. As the Soviet regime endured, more and more people came to believe that stable jobs and careers were better assured by collaboration. As more people collaborated, more become targets of guerrilla counterterror, with the result that victims' families became more pro-Soviet. More people joined the Komsomol and the Soviet

30. Remeikis 1962, p. 37.

militia. As victory for the guerrillas (with Western help) became ever more unlikely, their national-liberation aura was increasingly transformed into an image of rebels who hit and ran, leaving the civilian population to face the wrath of those in power. People were tired of living between two terrorisms.

The deportation and collectivization drive of 1949 (discussed in a later section) gave the guerrilla war its last Pyrrhic boost. A new wave of escapees flowed into the forest, but the guerrilla supply-system was wrecked. Even worse, their relations with the farm population received a new antagonistic turn. Voluntary donations by farmers were replaced by raids on collectivized cattle and grain which the guerrillas blithely regarded as Soviet property. The peasants, however, were still forced to meet the unrelenting state-delivery norms. By raiding stores, the guerrillas felt they robbed only the illegal Soviet state; but the civilian population were left without scarce consumer goods. Increasingly reduced to struggle for their personal subsistence, the Freedom Fighters started to fit the "bandit" label the occupation forces tried to pin on them.

By 1949, the Lithuanian guerrilla groups could no longer paralyze the functioning of local Soviets. In Latvia and Estonia this ability had been largely lost by the end of 1946. By the end of 1949 the Latvian guerrilla resistance was largely crushed, although even in February 1950 a battle near Okte in Courland is said to have involved some 50 guerrillas. In Estonia, fighting continued well into 1953.[31]

Lithuanian guerrilla numbers fell to 5,000 by the end of 1950 and to 700 by the end of 1952, when the unified command ended after calling for "demobilization" in favor of passive resistance. Most remaining guerrillas reentered civilian life with forged documents, and many made use of the 1955 amnesty. A 1956 amnesty offer indicated some continuing guerrilla existence.[32] Isolated arrests and executions continued into the late 1950s and even much later. A typewritten guerrilla prayerbook dated 1956 was on display at the Vilnius Museum of the History of Religion and Atheism in 1968. The unmasking of a partisan, J. Vaičulis, was reported in *Tiesa* in 1961, and as late as 1978 a guerrilla survivor, August Sabe, drowned rather than surrender in the south Estonian woods. The last leader

---

31. Jānis Rutkis (ed.), *Latvia: Country and People* (Stockholm, 1967), pp. 260 and 275; Šilde 1972, pp. 12–13. Armed underground activities in Estonia were, according to the ESSR KGB chief Ado Pork, largely crushed by early 1953; see Pork p. 11.

32. *Sovetskaia Litva*, 22 March 1956.

of the Lithuanian movement, Adolfas Ramanauskas-Vanagas, was arrested and murdered in 1956.[33]

It seems that Western interest in Baltic guerrilla activity rose during the Korean War, but it was too late. The forest brotherhood was disillusioned with the West, literally sick of living for years in the forest, facing a tired and decimated population, outwitted politically, and — above all — outgunned by vastly superior occupation forces.

Successful guerrilla fighting requires both extensive popular support and foreign supply and rest bases. In the 1970s, the world observed the sudden collapse of the rugged and widely popular Kurdish guerrilla effort in Iraq the moment that Iranian support was withdrawn. The Baltic guerrilla movement received from the West nothing beyond a few dozen liaison men and their handguns. It is pointless to ask why it failed in the face of such heavy odds. Its persistence for eight years, even with obviously extensive popular support, defies imagination.

Land Redistribution and Taxation. Land redistribution had high priority on the Soviet agenda. Given their overall shaky hold over the countryside after the war, the Soviets had to reassure owners of middle-sized farms that their property was safe. They also had to distribute the land of large farms among peasants with little or no land in order to build up a group with a vested interest in the new regime.

The 30-hectare upper limit on farm size imposed in 1941 was reasserted, with a new stipulation: this allotment could be reduced to 20 ha., "taking into account the quality of the soil and the situation of the land."[34] The farmsteads of "active supporters" of the German occupation were cut to 5–7 ha. As in many other areas of Soviet legislation, the definition allowed flexible interpretation. Even those who had fulfilled German requisition norms under threat of execution could, if it suited officials, fall into the collaborator cate-

---

33. Žymantas, p. 45; Tauras, p. 96; *Sõnumid*, no. 71 (March 1979), pp. 3–5; Remeikis 1962, p. 39. The guerrilla prayerbook was seen by R. Misiunas: *Tiesa*, 7 October 1961.

34. Pranas Zundė, "Lithuania's Economy: Introduction of the Soviet Pattern," in Vardys (ed.), *Lithuania under the Soviets*, p. 145; Jānis Labsvīrs, "A Case Study in the Sovietization of the Baltic States: Collectivization of Latvian Agriculture" (Ph.D. diss., University of Indiana, Bloomington, 1959), p. 64; Edgar Tõnurist (ed.), *Eesti NSV Põllumajanduse kollektiviseerimine* (Tallinn, 1978), p. 48.

gory. All refugees to the West were apparently declared "traitors to the fatherland," and their farms were redistributed. From mid-1945 on, similar treatment was applied to supporters of the guerrilla resistance.

The result of such measures was the creation of state-land funds which were considerably larger than those in 1940. The Latvian state-land fund increased from 875,252 ha. in 1940 to over 1,500,000 in 1944. According to 1948 statistics, the Lithuanian state-land fund consisted of 1,575,094 ha., and it included about one-third of the republic's farm assets: 33,400 horses, 55,600 cattle, 126,600 farm machines, 116,400 farm buildings and 47,200 farmsteads; 96,330 recipients received 688,466 ha. of land. In all, 17,133 horses, 24,238 cattle, 50,162 farm machines, 60,565 farm buildings and 26,095 farmsteads were given out to smallholders *and* to their cooperatives. Presumably, the rest went to state farms.[35]

In practice, however, the redistribution worked slowly because, for a variety of reasons, there were not at first many applicants among the landless and small farmers. Some plainly disliked Russian rule, felt that the Soviets had no legitimate authority to carry out land redistribution, and saw in it a device to divide-and-rule the countryside. Others knew that this was how the situation was perceived by the previous owners, who were ready to work retribution on those who accepted land from the conquerors. While expropriation was formally carried out in 1945, redistribution was slower. In Latvia, 42 per cent of the land fund remained undistributed by the end of 1945. In Estonia, 32 per cent remained so even by July 1947, when the program was declared complete. In Lithuania, the process continued into 1948, and 19 per cent remained undistributed.[36]

Implementation of the land-reform measures was also accompanied by the creation of a "socialist sector" in the countryside consisting of state farms, MTS (machine-tractor stations) and MKPP (machine-horse-renting points). Established on larger sequestered farms, these ostensibly sought both to serve as examples of large-scale mechanized cultivation and to provide traction power for the newly-established smallholder farms. During 1944–6, 41 state farms, 50 MTS and 445 MKPP appeared in Latvia. The figures for Lithuania were 101, 58 and 279, and for Estonia, 70, 24 and 240. Official complaints about the

35. *Istoriia Latviiskoi SSR*, III, pp. 503 and 594; *Tarybų Lietuvos valstietija*, p. 80.
36. Labsvīrs, p. 66; Tõnurist, p. 134; Pranas Zundė. "Die Kollektivierung der Landwirtschaft Sowjetlitauens," AB, II (1962), p. 99.

low profitability levels of the state farms and the poor functioning
of the MTS suggest that their impact on the countryside at this time
was minimal. The MTS were hampered by a lack of tractors; in 1946,
only 1.5 per cent of the total arable land in Estonia was worked by the
republic's MTS. At the end of 1945, the 48 Lithuanian MTS possessed
a mere 342 tractors, and the 50 stations in Latvia had 400 tractors.[37]

Equality of farmsteads was not among the Soviet goals. Later,
Soviet analysts were agreed that the express purpose of redistribution
was a parcelling out of the land in unviably small patches:

By redistributing land and other means of production . . . the ECP agrarian
policy, including land reform, did not aim at all at a blooming of individual
small farms . . . Already by 1947 the wide masses of the working peasantry
in the Estonian SSR could convince themselves through their own experience
that their individual farms would not enable them to reach a prosperous and
cultured life.[38]

The initial strategy for supplying such experience consisted of
gradually increasing taxes and obligatory deliveries. Nonetheless,
the farmers did relatively well in 1946–7. Obligatory farm-product
deliveries were not as sharply differentiated as they had been in 1941,
and were light compared to those in force toward the end of the
German occupation. The amounts represented about one-fifth of a
farmer's produce, and were generally delivered early and completely
in order to avoid further trouble with the authorities. Plenty remained
for farm consumption (including guerrilla needs) and for the free
market in the cities, where a sellers' market prevailed — especially in
Estonia, where local inhabitants had to compete with hundreds of
wholesale speculators from Leningrad. In addition to black market
industrial goods, many farmers with new land needed money to pay
high interest on state loans for construction and inventory purchases.
A major rural nuisance consisted of swarms of beggars from Russia
(called "the bagmen" in Estonia), who were inclined to steal anything
and at times even murdered whole farm families.

By 1947 Soviet land redistribution had cut many farms to economically inefficient size, and created new ones that were purposely so
small that they could not flourish. The "policy of restricting and

---

37. Mačiuika 1963, pp. 141–2; *Tarybų Lietuvos valstietija*, p. 85. There are some
minor discrepancies in the data presented in these works.

38. Ervin Kivimaa, "Eesti NSV Põllumajanduse kollektiviseerimine aastail 1947–
1950," in Edgar Tõnurist (ed.), *Sotsialistliku põllumajanduse areng Nõukogude Eestis*
(Tallinn, 1976), p. 71.

expelling the kulaks" made doubly sure that efficient private farming would become impossible. People somehow continued to belong to the wealthy "*kulak*" category even after their farms were cut in size and paid labor was prohibited. State credit (the only credit available) was denied to them. They were forced out of voluntary agricultural cooperatives, a heritage of the independence time which flourished, in contrast to western Belorussia and Ukraine, in the postwar Baltic republics. In late 1947,

an offensive through taxation policy . . . undermined prosperous farms and demonstrated to wide peasant masses, also including medium farmers, that the past traditional road to prosperity was permanently blocked, that the Soviet regime follows a firm course toward liquidation of exploitive households.[39]

For the average kulak, income tax was 40 per cent of his estimated income in 1947 and 75 per cent the following year. The income estimates tended to be on the high side, so that "the total taxes started to surpass the money income of the kulaks." Taxes on other farms also rose steeply — to about 35 per cent of estimated income in 1948 for larger farms, and close to 30 per cent even for the small ones.[40] For example, a 5-ha. farm in Lithuania was annually assessed 60 kilos of rye, 50 kilos of potatoes, 200 liters of milk, 20 kilos of meat, 70 eggs and 0.5 kilos of wool per hectare, at exceedingly low official government-delivery prices.[41]

Confiscatory taxation was accompanied by collectivization propaganda. Whereas during the first two years of reoccupation the Soviet authorities appeared reticent over collectivization, as they had been in 1940, by the end of 1946 the tone changed. Increasing space in the local press was devoted to discussion of collective farm operations elsewhere in the USSR, along with glorious depictions of collective rural wellbeing. "Fact-finding" visits by delegations of Baltic peasants to various havens of prosperity became increasingly frequent objects of news reporting. From 1948 on, various party directives and government decrees were aimed at facilitating "spontaneous" efforts by peasants to establish *kolkhozes* (collective farms). The results were

39. *Ibid.*, p. 72. The remainder of this section is based mainly on Rein Taagepera, "Soviet Collectivization of Estonian Agriculture: The Taxation Phase" (henceforth cited as "Taxation"), JBS, X/3 (Fall 1979), pp. 263–282.

40. Kulak taxes: Kivimaa, p. 83; other farmers: Zundė, "Die Kollektivierung," 1962, pp. 97 and 101; and Taagepera, "Taxation," p. 276.

41. Mačiuika 1963, p. 139.

not only meager but also disconcerting to the Soviets. Contrary to ideological presuppositions, some of the larger farmers were more willing than the smaller ones to join kolkhozes, hoping thereby to escape high taxes and the label of "kulak" which made one liable to deportation.

Collectivization of agriculture was carried out according to a unified pattern and timetable not only throughout the three Baltic republics, but also throughout all western areas annexed by the USSR in 1939–44. The percentage of Baltic, Moldavian and western Belorussian and Ukrainian farms collectivized grew in a similar way, with a very sharp increase in 1949. Policies visibly formulated in Moscow were hardy adjusted to local conditions and moods. The same periodization thus applies throughout this area:

— softening the ground for collectivization through taxation (1944–8);
— deportation-induced mass collectivization (1949–50);
— completion and consolidation (1951–3).

The first postwar kolkhozes were formed in Latvia in November 1946, in Lithuania by February 1947, and in Estonia in September. Meanwhile, Moscow issued a short decree on collectivization in the Baltic republics on 21 May 1947. It first told the Baltic lieutenants that "no hurry must be shown; no extensive plan must be made regarding this endeavor; the kolkhozes must be created on a completely voluntary basis." Then, in a masterful turnabout, it "recommended" that the Baltic lieutenants hand in detailed plans within 12 days. They did. Nonetheless, progress was slow. Published Soviet documentation shows extreme reluctance by most farmers. Even among the party members, 67 per cent in Estonia were not yet collectivized in January 1949. Most kolkhoz chairmen were appointed from outside the village, and the process was rigidly centralized and run from the cities.[42]

The advances made were achieved mainly through the confiscatory tax squeeze: the percentage of farms collectivized tended to be higher in districts where the normal (non-kulak) taxes were higher.

42. CPSU CC decree on the formation of kolkhozes in the Lithuanian, Latvian and Estonian SSRs, 21 May 1947. Full text in *Resheniia partii i pravitelstva po khoziaistvennym voprosam v piati tomakh*, III (Moscow, 1968), pp. 427–8;. also in Tõnurist 1978, p. 239. On party members' not joining kolkhozes: Evald Laasi, *Eestimaa Kommunistlik Partei ellu viimas V.I. Lenini kooperatsiooniplaani, 1944–1950* (Tallinn, 1980), p. 157.

Rich farmers' counterpropaganda — stressed in Soviet accounts — seemed to have no effect: if anything, collectivization advanced faster in districts with a larger percentage of farms classed as kulak. Thousands of farmers (medium and kulak) were unable to pay their taxes and saw their farm tools auctioned away. Thousands of others liquidated their households, abandoned the land and fled to the cities. Cattle were slaughtered on a massive scale, despite fines ten times the value of the cattle.

Farmers had accurate information about the miserable life on long-standing Russian kolkhozes, and most of them tried to postpone for as along as possible a capitulation which by that time must have looked inevitable in the long run. At the beginning of 1949, only 3.9 per cent of the Lithuanian and 5.8 per cent of the Estonian farms were collectivized; in Latvia the figure was around 8 per cent.[43] Due to tax pressures, the percentage was starting to rise relatively quickly (to 8.2 per cent in Estonia by 20 March), and collectivization could be expected to be fairly complete in a few years, with no new types of pressure needed. Nonetheless, more brutal methods were introduced.

Collectivization through Deportation. The decisive stage of Soviet rural rearrangement started at the end of March 1949 when, in the words of a Soviet scholar, Ervin Kivimaa,

The collectivization process acquired a massive character. Peasants joined by entire villages and townships. It coincided with the liquidation of the kulaks as a class, by methods . . . similar to those which had been used in the older Soviet republics: expropriation and deportation.[44]

In a few days after 20 March 1949, about 60,000 individuals were deported from Estonia and at least 50,000 from Latvia. In Lithuania, where 70,000 had been deported in late 1947 and another 70,000 on 22 May 1948, 40,000 joined the earlier groups on 24–27 March 1949 and another 40,000 in the summer. During the last ten days of March 1949, the Baltic nations lost about 3 per cent of their native populations.[45]

43. *Lietuvos TSR istorija*, IV, p. 206; Taagepera, "Taxation," p. 265; also calculations based on Carson, pp. 530–531, and Walter Hanchett, "The Communists and the Latvian Countryside, 1919–1949," in Adolf Sprudzs and Armins Rusis (eds), *Res Baltica* (Leiden, 1968), p. 109.

44. Kivimaa, p. 85.

45. Most of this section is based on detailed analysis of Soviet documentation, in Rein Taagepera, "Soviet Collectivization of Estonian Agriculture: The Deportation

Preparations had begun late in 1948. In December, numerous Communist Party and Komsomol members, many of them postwar immigrants, received special training in secret. In January 1949 they were sent throughout the countryside to "enlarge" kulak lists, prepare deportation schedules and find suitable candidates for kolkhoz chairmen. During the spring months of 1949, the number of Communists in the rural areas of Lithuania almost tripled. The Lithuanian CC and its district committees sent more than 1,050 party members into the countryside.[46] The actual deportations were carried out with the help of special MVD troops from Russia. As a Soviet Estonian newspaper put it: "When collectivization started in our country, the Russian working class gave tens of thousands of its best representatives, who helped to create a new happy life in our villages."[47]

Although a background of wealth was not an absolute requisite for inclusion in kulak lists, it helped. According to official definitions, only kulaks objected to any aspect of Soviet farm policy or practice; therefore, any farmer who displeased Soviet authorities was a kulak. Moreover, the criterion of wealth referred only to the past; land reform had reduced all farms to 30 ha. or less, and some kulaks now owned only 5–7 ha. Laws against hired labor were also applied retroactively, cutting a wide and arbitrary swathe into villages where even small farms occasionally used to employ some hired help. The Lithuanian CC definition of "kulak" issued on 12 December 1947 included seven categories of farms:

(1) those which employed agricultural workers or craftsmen for pay in either cash or goods,

---

Phase," *Soviet Studies*, XXXII/3 (July 1980), pp. 379–97. The number of Estonian deportees is based on a decrease in the number of inhabited farms (about 20,000, from 20 March to 5 April) which can be calculated from Soviet data, e.g., in Kivimaa, p. 87, or Tõnurist 1978, pp. 521 and 568. This number agrees with a figure of 80,000 people on the deportation list, as leaked from the Soviet Estonian Trade Union Council. Of these, about 20,000 escaped into the forests. The Latvian figure is a very conservative estimate reported in King, p. 83. It can be calculated from data in Carson, pp. 530–1, that the number of inhabited farms decreased by about 30,000. The Lithuanian estimates for 1949 are also based on a decrease in the number of farms; 12,000 from 1 January to 1 April, and another 12,000 from 1 July to 1 October, as can be calculated from *Lietuvos TSR istorija*, p. 206. The summer deportation seems to have occurred in July (Remeikis 1962, p. 38, even says June), and by 1 October many emptied farms would have found new occupants — see specific case in Taagepera, "Guerrilla," p. 101.

46. Mačiuika 1963, p. 154, based on A. Sniečkus in *Pravda*, 21 July 1949.

47. *Rahva Hääl*, 30 December 1952.

(2) those which had employed hired help during the German occupation,

(3) those which had taken in unpaid outsiders as "members of the family",

(4) those which systematically employed seasonal help,

(5) those which rented out animals or equipment,

(6) those which owned any complex machinery, and

(7) those which systematically purchased agricultural goods for resale.[48]

The categories were similar in Latvia and Estonia.

The first kulak lists were compiled in 1945, but under pressure from higher authority these were gradually expanded. The last drastic revision was made in early 1949 by outsiders, in preparation for the deportations — haphazardly, often on the spur of the moment, and with quotas to fill. In a letter to Stalin on 17 January, the ECP First Secretary, Karotamm, said that there were 5,500 kulak and German-collaborator farms in Estonia,[49] but nine weeks later the number of inhabited farms dropped by at least 19,000. Many people on the final deportation list cannot have fitted the official criteria for a kulak — otherwise they would have been found out and listed much earlier. Anyway, by 1949 all the formal criteria applied only to the past. The only "property" which was not confiscated was the kulaks' possibly higher education and spirit of initiative. In the case of younger children, the kulak label applied to the time before their birth. A regime which did not recognize hereditary wealth applied the criterion of hereditary guilt. An entire population category was destined to slow extinction in the Siberian woods. Whether this was genocide depends on how one defines the term.

A report by a township CP Secretary a week later described the deportation as follows:

Following the [party] meeting, the deportation of kulaks and of German collaborators in the Ruusmäe township was carried out. Altogether it was planned to send away 13 families. Sent away: 8 families, 31 persons in total. Five families who had been listed for deportation had fled from home. Most of those families of German collaborators who were not listed for deportation also had fled from home. Of these, Tigane and Minnat have not returned

48. Zundė 1965, pp. 148–9, based on Gregorauskas, p. 137; Tõnurist 1978, p. 231, has the text of a similar decree by the ESSR Council of Ministers, 30 August 1947.

49. ECP CC First Secretary's report to the Chairman of the USSR Council of Ministers, J. V. Stalin, 17 January 1949. Full text in Tõnurist 1978, pp. 489–94.

up to this time. The rest have returned. Four explanation meetings have been carried out.[50]

Typically the farmer and his family were only told, often in the middle of the night, that they were to "settle elsewhere." They had to pack their things in ten minutes to two hours, depending on how heavy the deporters' schedule happened to be. Trucks took them to railway stations where they were packed into cattle wagons with barred windows. The destination apparently was western Siberia (Novosibirsk) or northern Kazakhstan (Semipalatinsk). About a quarter of the people on the deportation list managed to avoid the dragnet by hiding in the forests until the chase was over.

After one-tenth of Latvian and Estonian farmers had been deported, the remainder decided voluntarily to collectivize. In Latvia, the percentage of farms collectivized jumped from about 11 per cent on 12 March to more than 50 per cent on 9 April. In Estonia, according to detailed Soviet data, it rose from 8 per cent to 64 per cent within a month (20 March to 20 April). By the end of the year, 93 per cent of the Latvian and 80 per cent of the Estonian farms were collectivized. This speed exceeded by far projections of the party and the rate of Soviet collectivization in 1929. In Lithuania the process went more slowly. By the end of June the figure was 34 per cent, and there were new deportations. Even by the end of 1949, a figure of only 62 per cent had been reached. It is possible to attribute the slower rate to guerrilla activity. In the Varėna district, for instance, only 3 per cent of all farms had been collectivized by 1950. The surrounding forests were guerrilla strongholds. There was a similar delay in the southeast Estonian guerrilla stronghold of Haanja, which had reached only 30 per cent collectivization by July 1950. However, it should be noted that western Belorussia also reached 60 per cent only by mid-1950, and there is no indication of extensive guerrilla activity in that region.[51]

Soviet and Western historians later seemed to agree that deportation began a stampede into kolhozes, but there is disagreement over the motives. Were farmers afraid of being deported unless they joined?

---

50. A report (31 March 1949) by Secretary Zhilkin of the Ruusmäe township party organization in Võru district, Estonia; partly reproduced by Tõnurist 1978, pp. 523–4.

51. Taagepera 1979, "Taxation," p. 265; Carson, pp. 530–1, and calculations based on it; *Lietuvos TSR istorija,* IV, p. 206; Kivimaa, p. 88. The Estonian figures are based on extensive documentation in Tõnurist 1978.

Or were they, as claimed by Soviet historians, eager to join kolkhozes
the moment they were freed from the threats and scare stories spread
by the "kulaks"? The very suddenness of the rush argues strongly
against the latter scenario. The strongest physical threats against collectivization would have come not from farmers still living on their
farms, but from the guerrillas, whose strength was affected by deportation only indirectly and slowly. As for scare stories regarding
kolkhozes, their effect could not have vanished within a few weeks
after the deportation of presumed propagators, especially since they
were supported by factual knowledge about "the difficult situation of
USSR agriculture as a whole and by the peasantry's fairly deep attachment to their small property."[52] Moreover, the previously wealthy
farmers were far from presenting a united front against collectivization: under the pressure of confiscatory taxes, many had sold out or
were willing to join kolkhozes. The deportations affected not only
those who retroactively fitted the "kulak" criteria, but also "other
elements hostile to the people." The sudden panic-speed rush into
kolkhozes can only be explained by fear of deportation.

After a slowdown in early 1950, collectivization of the remaining Latvian and Estonian farms speeded up in the fall when the
state deliveries and taxes became due. Taxes had been meanwhile
"regulated" to confiscatory levels even for small farms. By the end
of 1950, only 4 per cent of Latvian and 8 per cent of Estonian individual farms survived. In December 1951, 98.4 per cent of Latvian
farms were collectivized. Throughout the process, the smaller farmers
and recent land recipients showed the greatest reluctance to join, or
the greatest ability to avoid joining. In the words of a district super-
visor's report:

The greatest activity and rush into the kolkhozes is shown by the medium
peasants; the farmhand and the poor peasant are slower to join.[53]

This observation, which goes against conventional wisdom, is borne
out by statistical analysis: the average sown area of Estonian farms
remaining in private hands decreased from 6.2 ha. in 1948 to 4.4 ha.
in 1950 and 2.5 ha. in 1951.

52. Kivimaa, p. 73.
53. Control Brigade member M. Dorogov, report to N. Karotamm (October
1948), reproduced in Tõnurist 1978, pp. 411–12, translated in Taagepera, "Taxation," p. 277. Statistics in this paragraph are based on *Eesti NSV ajalugu*, III, pp. 583
and 586; Kivimaa, p. 87; and *25 aastat Nõukogude Eestit: statistiline kogumik* (Tallinn,
1965; henceforth cited as *25 aastat*), pp. 49–50.

In Lithuania, the collectivization process was appreciably slower than in Latvia or Estonia, and almost came to a halt in the spring of 1950. Even by July 1950, 27 per cent of farms were still private, but the figure dropped steeply to 11 per cent by the end of the year, possibly because of new deportations.[54]

Meanwhile, several hundred thousand deportees, who had left at short notice with scanty baggage, were cut off from their homelands and had to adapt to new surroundings and a new language. There were no native-language books, newspapers, or schools. Most often there was a dire lack of food and shelter and many, possibly more than half, died of cold and hunger. Families were systematically torn asunder. Typically men were sent to labor camps, ranging from coal mines in Karaganda (Kazakhstan) and Vorkuta (beyond the Arctic Circle) to lumber camps throughout Siberia, while women and children were brought to Siberian kolkhozes and left to fend for themselves: they would build cave-like earthen huts, and try to tear up the ground to grow food and survive somehow until this miserable crop ripened.[55]

Stalin's lieutenants in the Baltic area were concerned with nominating supervisors for the kolkhozes, establishing a system of political propaganda on the new units and reading reports. The pressing economic issues resulting from the switch to collective farming received little attention. Local farmers with some organizational experience had mostly been deported. The pre-war voluntary cooperatives which had operated successfully until 1949 had been totally dismantled instead of being utilized for gradually increasing cooperation. Terse orders from Moscow "paralyzed local initiative and creative attitudes toward building up the kolkhozes," and the official denial of the "principle of material interest" as an incentive for farmers made the situation "rather difficult."[56] Production decreased, and along with it the farmers' standard of living.

54. On 1 April 1950, 71.9 per cent of Lithuanian farms were collectivized, on 1 July the figure was 72.8 per cent and on 1 January 1950 it was 89.1 per cent, according to *Lietuvos TSR istorija*, IV, p. 208, and *Mažoji lietuviškoji tarybinė enciklopedija*, II (Vilnius, 1968), p. 177.

55. See, e.g., eyewitness descriptions by Maria Jürimäe, as written down by Johannes Kaup, *Hauatagune Siber* (New York, 1963); and by Barbara Armonas, as told to A. L. Nasvytis, *Leave Your Tears in Moscow* (Philadelphia, 1961). A condensed version of the Armonas experience appeared as "A Brave Woman's Ordeal in Siberia," *Life*, L (28 April 1961), pp. 84–8. Camps with Baltic prisoners have been described in some detail by Ādolfs Šilde, *The Profits of Slavery* (Stockholm, 1958).

56. Kivimaa, p. 90.

The human and economic costs of collectivization can only be estimated. A 1970 prize-winning Soviet Estonian novel *Tondiöömaja* (The Spook Hostel) by Heino Kiik provides a wealth of vivid detail from those years.[57] His description of wasteful management, poor organization and petty interference by Moscow can generally be said to typify conditions in all three republics. Prevented from farming individually, Baltic farmers were also not allowed to form a really functioning collective. They seem to have been kept in a halfway house gradually wrecked by order-spewing spooks from townships, district, *raion*, *oblast*, republic and Moscow offices. Some examples from Kiik's novel follow.

With masterful disregard for climate, Estonian kolkhozes in 1949 were ordered to start deliveries to the state before normal harvesting time, so as not to fall behind the more southerly Latvia. But in 1951 they were forbidden to harvest barley which had ripened before the planned date. They also wasted critical hay-making weather on cutting reeds for "silage," which became a gooey mess, and in 1954 they had to sow corn, which does not ripen so far north. In 1950 women were forced to pick potatoes from chilly flooded fields, in disregard of health and economics, because "the state cannot allow a single hectare to remain unharvested."

City-bred district officials and kolkhoz chairmen imposed grotesque orders, with ignorance and contempt for agricultural realities. Kolkhozes were ordered to deliver teenagers for work in oil-shale mines. "Making kulaks" continued: farmers who displeased the party or whose homes were coveted by the kolkhoz chairmen were expelled, in spite of votes to the contrary by the kolkhoz general meetings, and they vanished, presumably to Siberia. The farmers eventually learned to vote in favor of every mild suggestion from higher up. They even elected total strangers as kolkhoz chairmen at an hour's notice. Kolkhozes which still managed to cope which this *diabolus ex machina* show were in 1950 ordered to fuse with several failing ones, as if to ensure that failure be general.

While individual farmers paid 6,000 rubles in tax per year, the collective farmers paid only 600 rubles. But the daily pay for collective work in the kolkhoz amounted to 4 pounds of potatoes and 3 rubles

---

57. Heino Kiik, *Tondiöömaja* (Tallinn, 1970); review by Ilse Lehiste, "Where Hobgoblins Spend the Night," JBS, IV/4 (Winter 1973), pp. 321–6. Some similar, though not as extensive, descriptions of Lithuania can be found in J. Avyžius, *Kaimas kryžkelėje* (Vilnius, 1964), also available in Russian translation, *Derevnia na perepute* (Moscow, 1960); the bulk of the novel, however, concerns the later 1950s.

(the price of a pack of cigarettes) in 1952, and to 3 kopeks (0.03 rubles) in 1953. Obligatory state deliveries amounted to confiscation: farmers received 2 kopeks per liter of milk, and could not buy a bottle of state-sold vodka for the price of a bull. State deliveries left no grain for the kolkhozes, and farmers competed with city people in buying scarce but cheap bread from city stores. One state official threatened to fire a collective farm's agronomist for using substandard seed because another had seized seed-grain for state deliveries. People (including kolkhoz chairmen) started to compare their units to the despised nineteenth-century estates of the Baltic barons. By 1952 villages looked as if they had undergone three years of warfare. Some farmers avoided unpaid kolkhoz work, subsisting on their private patches and on work outside their farms, while others fled to the cities, abandoning their theoretical share of common ownership. Harvesting sometimes lasted until December; rotten grain was gathered. By the spring of 1954, cows had to be carried out of stables. Drinking moonshine had become rampant.

This is how the Soviet Estonian novel describes this period, and the truth of this picture is confirmed by reminiscences of participants and by statistics published later. In the words of a kolkhoz chairman:

In the spring of 1953 we gave one sturdy collective farmer the special job of lifting up cows blown over by the wind. The cows were so weak they could not get up by themselves. That man got his norm days calculated on the basis of this work. This story makes one laugh now, but then we were were far from laughing.[58]

As for statistics, Table 8 shows the drastic decrease in total agricultural output and in cereal-crop yields in all three countries from 1950 to 1955. The 1950 production itself was already well below that of 1940, and probably also below that of 1948 (a year on which the Soviets did not publish any data). The decrease extended to most aspects of agriculture, and took place gradually over the years. The sown area tended to decrease up to about 1958. Total grain pro-

58. *Sovetskaia Estoniia*, 26 October 1963. Prices of 0.58 to 1.64 kopeks per kilo of grain, 3.33 kopeks per liter of milk and 10 kopeks per kilo of live cattle can be calculated from M. Rubin, "Varumishinnad ja kolhooside rahalised sissetulekud Eesti NSVs aastail 1950–1960," *Eesti NSV Teaduste Akadeemia Toimetised — Ühiskonnateadused*, XXX/4 (1981), pp. 350–61. The price/production-cost ratio for the Estonian kolkhozes decreased from 0.55 in 1950 to 0.46 in 1952. Rubin comments: "The obligatory sale to the state effectively represented taxation in kind, since the state was paying the kolkhozes only a symbolic price."

duction in Latvia dropped from 1,372,000 tons in 1940 to 732,000 in 1950, and to 436,000 tons in 1956. In Lithuania dairy cattle dropped from a pre-war figure of 848,000 in 1939 to 504,000 in 1951 (after a major decrease during the preceding two years); not till 1957 was there a slight rise to 531,000. In Estonia, the total number of cows dropped from 294,000 in 1949 to 263,000 by 1953 and stayed at that level for many years. Milk production per collectivized cow kept steadily decreasing between 1950 and 1955, while that of privately owned cows increased by 38 per cent.[59]

Collective farm operations were further hampered by reorganizations. The original units had generally been small, involving at the end of 1949 an average of 48 households in Latvia, 38 in Lithuania and 34 in Estonia. In accordance with a Union-wide decree of 1950, the regime began a consolidation which hit the young Baltic kolkhozes at a particularly vulnerable stage. The number of Latvian kolkhozes decreased from a peak value of 4,169 in May to 1,792 by the end of 1950; Lithuania's decreased from 6,032 to 1,795 in 1950. The number of households per kolhhoz was multiplied accordingly, and so were problems of internal workforce management.

Improvements in some aspects were cancelled out by further setbacks and demoralization in others. In 1952, parents and adult children crowded under the same roof were declared to be a single household, thus reducing the total number of private cattle they could own; the excess cattle were confiscated. Calves and pigs were also collectivized, and yet every household was required to deliver 30 kilos of meat annually from their single privately owned cow.[60] A vicious circle formed between state demands and farmer productivity. Collective farmers who at times were not paid for their collective work for two years in a row lost almost all interest. They concentrated on their private patches, bringing collective farming almost to a complete standstill.

59. Andrivs Namsons, "Die Umgestaltung der Landwirtschaft in Sowjetlettland," AB, II (1962), p. 75; Zundė, "Die Kollektivierung," p. 105; and calculations based on: *Eesti NSV ajalugu*, III, p. 586; *25 aastat*, pp. 53–63; and *Nõukogude Eesti saavutusi 20 aasta jooksul: statistiline kogumik* (Tallinn, 1960; henceforth cited as *20 aasta*), pp. 41–52.

60. Labsvīrs, p. 96; Taagepera, "Taxation," p. 265; Carson, p. 531; Arnold Purre, "Kommunistlikus haardes," in *Eesti saatusaastad*, III, pp. 51–3. By law, farmers could own two cows, but in Soviet practice they were limited to one — see Tõnurist 1978, p. 89.

Economy and Culture

Immigration and Industrialization.   Reconstruction and expansion of industry were high on the Soviet priority list in the Baltic states for a series of economic and political reasons. From a pragmatic economic viewpoint, Latvia and Estonia represented a skilled-labor reserve unlike any other in the Soviet Union. They also had a substantial physical infrastructure which had not been destroyed during the war, or which could be reconstructed quite easily compared to, say, Belorussia's. The existing network of roads, factory buildings, housing and schools could, from the Soviet viewpoint, be used more intensively. New workers could be crammed into existing apartments, and night shifts could be added to existing factories. The infrastructure was also very attractive for placement of new plants. Precisely because there had been previous development during independence, further investment was, in a sense, encouraged.

There were also non-economic reasons. Ideologically, the industrial proletariat were considered superior to the peasantry and expected to be more supportive of the Soviet regime. From a colonial imperialist viewpoint, industrialization offered a path for settling large numbers of Russians among a reticent local population. At times such colonization seems to have become a goal in itself rather than a means of industrialization. In particular, it made little economic sense to deport Baltic farmers to Siberia and then import Russian labor to the Baltic cities.

By early 1945, most undestroyed industrial facilities were back in operation, and "socialist competitions" between plants had started. City streets were cleared of bombing rubble, largely with the help of unpaid "Sunday sessions" by the public. Such private industry (mostly small servicing enterprises) as had existed in 1945 was nationalized by 1947. For those not affected by the continuing sporadic arrests and deportations, city life continued on a course toward postwar normalization. Food rationing ceased at the end of 1947, but limited food supplies resulted in huge waiting lines. Also at the end of 1947, an all-Union currency reform depleted savings: 10 old rubles were exchanged for 1 new ruble, with prices remaining the same. Designed to hit speculators, the conversion hit hard at anyone with even modest savings.

By 1948, clothing and shoes seem to have become available in stores. Black markets flourished, fed by home industry, farms, thefts from state enterprises and leaks from special stores for party members and military officers. In early 1947 a kilo of sugar cost 250 to 300 rubles, while a schoolteacher's pay in Tallinn was 350 to 450 rubles per month. The flood of food-seeking "bagmen" from Russia decreased around 1948, and by 1951 street robberies, which had been a nightly occurrence, had become rare. Fuel supplies also improved, but firewood was still rationed, and remained scarce at least until 1954. In the store waiting lines, Russian-Baltic conflict flared frequently.[61]

Reconstruction of war-damaged cities was largely completed by 1950, but insufficient allowance was made for the influx from the countryside as well as for immigration from Russia. Private construction of single-family dwellings was officially encouraged, but few construction materials were available through legal channels.

Despite the local shortage of labor, industrialization plans and investments in Latvia exceeded the average for the USSR as a whole. Emphasis was placed on machine-building and metalworking, and major factories were created or expanded, mostly in Riga. The Riga Electrical Machine Plant started operations in 1947 and the Riga Diesel Plant in 1949. Products included electric motors (especially for locomotives), electrical apparatus for cars, various control instruments and diesel engines. Textile fibers were expanded in Daugavpils. Lumber-cutting in 1950 surpassed its 1938 level by 55 per cent, resulting in serious depletion of Latvia's forest reserves. Production of textile fabrics was up by 27 per cent and of paper by 77 per cent. Shoe production had reportedly increased sixfold. There is no information on quality and destination; the local market continued to be short of consumer goods. By 1947, total industrial production had reportedly surpassed that of Soviet Latvia in 1940 by 28 per cent. However, judging from data in natural production units, the 1937 level had not yet been reached by 1947. The explanation of this discrepancy may lie in the fact that the 1940 comparison figures refer, literally, to *Soviet* Latvia, and Latvia did not become a Soviet republic until August that year. Thus "Soviet Latvia" existed in 1940 for less than five months. An index pegged to the production of the whole calendar year 1940 would be five-twelfths or roughly 40 per cent of the index pegged to the Soviet Latvia of 1940. The same observation applies to Lithuania, which for 1950 claimed a 91 per cent increase over the 1940 figures, as well as to

61. Purre, "Teine punane," pp. 26–7; Endel Kareda, *Estonia in the Soviet Grip* (London, 1949), pp. 59–65 and 74–80.

Estonia.[62] But regardless of such index games, Baltic industry quickly surpassed its pre-war level by a wide margin (see Table 7).

In Lithuania, heavy industry was also emphasised. However, although industrialization was conducted at twice the all-Union rate in Latvia and Estonia, in postwar Lithuania it remained below the all-Union level in terms of capital investment. The intense resistance and extent of guerrilla opposition may have been partly responsible. Lithuania's weaker industrial base may also have led industrial planners to favor Latvia and Estonia, where investment would yield tangible results more quickly. Light industry and food processing continued to predominate in Lithuanian industrial production. Food processing retained the preeminence it had held in 1940. However, while most other areas indicated growth compared with pre-war figures, Lithuania's 1950 indicators show a considerable decline. The emphasis on heavy industry meant that the food industry was not given adequate support in terms of machinery and equipment.[63]

In Estonia, the industrial workforce in late 1944 was down to 52 per cent of its pre-war total of 89,000. The gap was partly filled by Estonian Labor Battalions of the Red Army and by German prisoners of war, of whom there may have been 40,000 in Estonia, half of them in the Kohtla-Järve oil-shale region and a quarter in Tallinn. There were also civilian prisoners, including women from the Baltics, Russia, Poland and, after 1948, Czechoslovakia. In the postwar years up till 1949, *per capita* investment in Estonia exceeded the Soviet average by 54 per cent, imports exceeded exports by 70 per cent, and industrial production grew by more than 35 per cent. Much of the equipment initially came from dismantled plants in Germany.[64]

In Estonia, development of oil-shale products overshadowed machine-building. While oil-bearing shale occurs throughout the world, it has been neglected because its energy content is less than that of coal, and its burning produces large amounts of ash. Motivated by a desire to reduce dependence on imported coal, independent

62. Production data from Jānis Bokalders, "Die Industrialisierung Lettlands nach 1940," AB, II (1962), pp. 146–75. For the five-month year, see King, p. 19; Zundē 1965, p. 156; and Elmar Järvesoo, "The Postwar Economic Transformations," in Parming and Järvesoo, p. 136.

63. Zundē 1965, p. 157; Thomas Remeikis, "Modernization and National Identity in the Baltic Republics," in Ihor Kamenetsky (ed.), *Nationalism and Human Rights: Processes of Modernization in the USSR* (Littleton, Colo., 1977), p. 116.

64. *Eesti NSV ajalugu*, III, p. 569–71; Purre, "Teine punane," pp. 40–3.

Estonia had become the world pioneer in oil-shale development. The Soviet regime continued and expanded this effort in order to supply Leningrad, with transport costs being reduced by gasifying the oil in the shale on the spot. The world's first shale-gas facility became partly operational in 1948, and oil-shale mining was increased at a rapid rate, largely with labor imported from Russia.

The continuing labor shortage was only temporarily eased by returning evacuees, men demobilized from the armed forces and prisoners. Local artisans, women and youths were pressed into "social production," including mining and lumber work. Collectivization of agriculture in 1949 opened up another local labor pool. But the largest increase came from an influx of outsiders, mainly Russians. Some came on their own initiative, attracted by the relative wealth and wellbeing in the Baltic states compared to areas long under Soviet control. But others were actively recruited. In the Soviet view:

During the years of building socialism, the specific weight of other nationalities increased within the Estonian working class, but the identical interests and goals and common work linked the settlers from fraternal republics to the local workers. Both were formed into a single Soviet Estonian working class. . . . Political educational work was used in trying to help workers to free themselves from the influence of the bourgeois-nationalist propaganda.[65]

In other words, the Baltic workers themselves did not perceive those "identical interests and goals." It was an industry based on Russian investment and Russian labor, managed by Russians according to goals set by Russians, importing a large part of the raw materials from Russia and exporting most of its product. The whole show was called "Baltic" industrial growth because the Soviets decided to run it on Baltic soil.

While the native population was decimated by deportations and guerrilla-war losses, large contingents of Russians and other non-Balts were brought in, along with Russianized Latvians and Estonians whose families had settled in Russia in Tsarist times. The most influential segment of Russians consisted of thousands of officials assigned to direct and supervise social and economic changes at republic, district and commune levels. Numerically the largest segment consisted of unskilled industrial labor. Some of them were voluntary immigrants, while others were forced labor deported from other Soviet

65. *Eesti NSV ajalugu*, III, p. 577.

areas; many of the latter were non-Russians forced to play a Russianizing role, since they tended to know some Russian but not the local national language. Armed forces, ranging from Red Army units facing Scandinavia to MVD repression units designed for internal use only, were also numerous.

The peak influx period may have been 1945–7, but immigration continued later, and its denationalizing effect was aggravated by depletion of the native farm population through the deportations of 1949. Collectivization pushed farmers into cities and thus reduced the need for immigration in the short run. In the long run, however, the deportations reduced the local rural labor pool. Expansion of Soviet industry in the Baltic states continued. At best, this was in disregard of its denationalizing effect, and quite possibly it was done with the express intention of imperial colonization.

About 400,000 Russians and 100,000 people of other nationalities migrated into Latvia from 1945 to 1959, most of them probably before 1953. This amounted to 25 per cent of the pre-war population. Riga's population in 1951 was 149,000 or 43 per cent higher than it had been in 1939 (see Table 11), despite heavy war losses, including flight to the West, and only minor influx from the Latvian countryside. (The rural population decreased by 185,000, but war and deportation losses accounted for most of that) The Latvians' share of their country's population was probably around 83 per cent in 1945, but dropped to about 60 per cent by 1953, due to immigration and deportations (see Tables 1 and 5).

Approximately 180,000 non-Estonians arrived in Estonia in 1945–7 and at least 33,000 more immigrants came in 1950–3, adding up to an increase of 19 per cent over the pre-war population, or 25 per cent of the reduced population of 1945. The share of Estonians in their country's population decreased from about 94 per cent in early 1945 to 80 per cent in early 1949; this plunged to 77 per cent during the 1949 deportations, and continued to slide to about 72 per cent by 1953.

In more agricultural Lithuania, the local rural labor pool seemed to supply most of the relatively modest increase in the industrial workforce. New immigrants could hardly be attracted to the countryside, especially under the conditions of continuing guerrilla resistence. Influx was thus largely limited to functionaries and the armed forces. Due to heavy guerrilla and deportation losses, Lithuania's population probably decreased from about 3.1 million in 1940 (within the postwar borders) to 2.6 million in 1953, about 75 per cent of whom were Lithuanians.[66]

Given Soviet policies of massive labor transfer, a drastic increase in Soviet industrial production on Baltic soil was not surprising. The degree to which such output surpassed the pre-war Baltic output is unclear. The proper point of comparison would be a year preceding major war distrubances, i.e. 1939 or even 1938, or an average of 1937–9. However, Soviet statistics invariably start with 1940, and, as mentioned before, may apparently take into account only the last five months of that year, during which the Baltic states were technically part of the USSR. Both baselines are shown in Table 7, which compares production between 1940 and 1980. Since the product-mix and relative prices were changing, the comparisons are perforce approximate. Furthermore, the 1940 baseline may not include production by small private shops. The median ratio of physical outputs in 1955 and 1940 in Estonia is around 3.7. The pre-war level of industrial production was certainly reached by 1949 in Latvia and Estonia, and by 1952 in Lithuania. By 1953 Baltic industrial employment was double the pre-war level, and industrial production showed at least as great an increase (see Table 7).

Aggregate industrial-production efficiency per worker was shown by the Soviets to have increased well beyond the pre-war level in terms of non-market-determined prices. However, data on physical quantities tell a different story. For instance, Estonian oil-shale production per worker was 494 tons per year in 1939 and 482 in 1950.[67]

Education and Culture. The flight to the West had particularly affected the educated Baltic élite. Close to half of those who had received a higher education may have left.[68] In the short run, the

---

66. For all three countries, see Rein Taagepera, "Baltic Population Changes, 1950–1980," JBS, XII/I (Spring 1981), pp. 35–57. See also King, p. 92; Carson, pp. 174–5; *Narodnoe khoziaistvo Latviiskoi SSR v 1977 godu* (Riga, 1978; henceforth cited as *Nar. khoz. LaSSR 1977*), pp. 6–8; Parming 1972, pp. 56–65; *Narodnoe khoziaistvo Estonskoi SSR v 1977 godu* (Tallinn, 1978; henceforth cited as *Nar. khoz. ESSR v 1977*), pp. 12–16; Zundé 1965, pp. 155–69.

67. ESSR Academy of Sciences, *Tööstuse ja ehituse ökonoomika küsimusi*, I (Tallinn, 1959), p. 6.

68. The percentages appear to have varied considerably, depending on the particular country and the particular profession. More writers than artists tended to leave. In Lithuania, 637 physicians and 221 dentists remained in 1946, out of a pre-war total

losses weakened Baltic society, but they also brought an unusual surge of upward mobility and thus brought about, in the long run, a rejuvenation of the élite. This effect was most pronounced in education and cultural fields, where the need to know the national language prevented an injection of Russians, and where even the Russianized Balts from the pre-war USSR, who were prominent in Latvia and Estonia, were at a disadvantage. In economic and technological fields, the gap left by the refugees offered Moscow a welcome opportunity to introduce outsiders.

Schools started to reopen in October 1944, largely using the existing non-Soviet-trained teachers. Some textbooks printed during the German occupation were temporarily accepted. Those published during Baltic independence were banned immediately, though some nevertheless had to be used initially. By the beginning of 1945, most grade schools had reopened (although heating remained a problem), and new textbooks had been printed. But one-third of the teaching staff were not trained teachers. Of those teachers who had not fled, "many were scared and took an apolitical, sometimes even an hostile attitude toward the Soviet regime."[69] The Soviet response was reeducation of existing teachers, bringing in teachers from other parts of the USSR, and a gradual introduction of new local teachers, trained according to the Soviet pattern. By its very nature, such a process had to be gradual in all three republics.

The Komsomol and the Pioneers (Communist youth organizations) became an integral part of the school system. In at least some schools, youngsters were forced to attend classes preparing them for the Pioneer oath. Strong-arm tactics were sometimes used to make them take that oath, but initial results were meager. At times, children's clothing, which was extremely scarce, was made available through the Komsomol. By the summer of 1946, about 15 per cent of Estonia's students had joined the Komsomol or the Pioneers. The figures were hardly higher in the other two republics. However, by 1950, 28 per cent of Lithuanian and 44 per cent of Estonian students had joined.[70]

---

of 1,446 and 686, respectively, according to Mačiuika 1963, p. 90; this decrease may involve an appreciable number of Jews murdered by the Nazis.

69. *Eesti NSV ajalugu*, III, p. 617.

70. *Ibid.*, p. 622; A. Bendžius, *Bendrojo lavinimo ir aukštoji mokykla Lietuvoje, 1940–1970 m.* (Kaunas, 1973), p. 228; Manivald Rästas, *Tulin kodumaalt* (Lund, 1955), pp. 20–30; Jaak Survel [Evald Uustalu], *Estonia Today* (London, 1947), p. 36.

Higher education suffered most from the flight of faculty to the West.[71] Vacant posts had to be filled by assistants and high school teachers. The effect on quality was only temporary; the new incumbents were well prepared and adjusted rapidly. But posts won by default rather than through competition left some with a persistent feeling of inadequacy. As might be expected, scholarly activities recovered more rapidly in the natural sciences than in the humanities.[72]

The Soviet system identified the goals of ideological penetration with educational training. Mass education was accordingly expanded rapidly, and the sheer number of students in general secondary, special secondary and higher educational institutions grew rapidly. A concerted attempt was made to offer crash education and more significant roles in society to those who could never have dreamed of such a thing within the traditional social structure. "*Rabfaks*," where eight years of schooling could be had in three years, appeared for adults who had not been able to continue their education above the primary level. Such recruitment of a fraction of the underprivileged served both to intimidate the traditional establishment and to set up a new "élite" of faithful adherents to the new order, who were inclined to see the new and unexpected opportunities before them as an embodiment of social justice. Although this process began before the German attack, it could not have had any significant effect until after the war.[73]

Mass culture was both developed and regimented through "culture houses," and indoctrination courses were soon organized on a vast scale for their directors and inspectors. By 1948, hundreds of political, agricultural and literary study groups had been formed. Massive song and folk-dance festivals began to be held, which included an increasing number of Russian songs and dances as well as those of other republics. Sports were also encouraged. During the late 1940s, the Soviet basketball team was largely Baltic.

Literary activity revived, but remained low. Half to two-thirds of the recognized writers of the pre-war period in all three republics had

71. At most, 35 per cent of Tartu University's faculty remained; see tabulation in Survel, p. 38.
72. For a detailed picture of the immediate postwar situation at the University of Vilnius, see Tomas Venclova, "The Years of Persistence," *Lituanus*, XXVII/2 (1981), pp. 101–8.
73. Aleksandras Shtromas, "The Official Soviet Ideology and the Lithuanian People," in Rimvydas Šilbajoris (ed.), *Mind against the Wall* (Chicago, 1983), pp. 61–2.

fled to the West.[74] Those who stayed tended to remain silent. Others tried to adjust to the new demands with pitiful results, sacrificing literary quality, yet still failing to satisfy the authorities. Most of the Communist-oriented writers who had been evacuated returned after the war, but their productivity was also kept low by increasing ideological demands.

The immediate postwar period actually proved to be one of relative relaxation. From mid-1946 on, a "struggle against apolitical culture" engulfed the Soviet Union. This first wave of the so-called *Zhdanovshchina* was followed in mid-1947 by a second one "against cosmopolitanism," aimed primarily against Jews. Already on 31 August 1946, the Chairman of the Latvian Council of Ministers charged that the editorial boards of the literary periodicals *Karogs* and *Literatūra un māksla* were poisoning the minds of Latvian youth: "On the pages of *Karogs* there prevails nothing but rotten and nonsensical liberalism." Lācis attacked a dozen writers by name; charges included depicting only the past, work filled with grief or sadness, and daring to exclaim that "nothing is more beautiful than love." It could have sounded funny, except that such attacks could end with deportation. In late 1949 and early 1950, the Soviet Latvian Artists' Association expelled 50 members. One wave of criticism followed another, until even the work of Lācis himself was taken to task in *Pravda* in late 1951. This overeagerness was dampened, however, and Lācis received his second Stalin Prize in five years.[75]

Much of the scarce paper was assigned to socio-political publications, and ideological requirements strangled art. Social-realist optimism became obligatory. A typical description of a writer's function was given in an editorial of the Lithuanian cultural weekly *Literatūra ir menas* of 24 April 1947:

The struggle against the bourgeois nationalists, against the bourgeois nationalist ideology and its influence, struggle against the villainous kulak bandits, against the reaction of clericalism, which is doing everything it can to poison the consciousness of youth and to insinuate itself into its spirit, sharp class struggle, the rise of a new, brave, and energetic working-man, all this is a fine ideological weapon which must be given first of all to the young people by the writer.[76]

74. Rolfs Ekmanis, *Latvian Literature under the Soviets, 1940–1975* (Belmont, Mass., 1978), p. 53. This is the major English-language source for this section.

75. Ekmanis 1978, pp. 119–22, 151 and 384; Rutkis, p. 534; *Pravda*, 14 December 1951 and 25 February 1952.

76. Cited in Rimvydas Šilbajoris, "Socialist Realism and the Politics of Literature in Occupied Lithuania," in *Mind against the Wall, op. cit.*, p. 77.

In Latvia, Jānis Plaudis was reproached for having written the poem "The Scent of Soil" without specifying that it was Soviet soil that he had in mind. When describing love between two people, authors were enjoined to make it clear to the reader that love for a person did not mean an end of love for the whole working class. Sycophantic praise of Stalin continued:

> Your name glows for us like the flaming sun,
> Like an eternal flame that calls to battle,
> To all of us you are the dearest friend,
> You, our conscience and our honor.[77]

As one Soviet observer later noted, while writers around 1950 supposedly sought a complete description of Soviet man,

a tendency to smooth out many of the contradictions which life presents also occurred. Many superficial works were also published, where real conflicts were replaced by apparent and superficial ones, and where positive figures often suffered from grayness and stereotype. Vulgar sociological tendencies exerted an inhibitive influence.[78]

In 1949–52, literature, language and theatrical arts faced the pressure of increased Russification. As one apologist for the trend observed, continuing technological development and the changing socio-political scene required new terminology. In the past, new words had been derived from native word-roots or borrowed from international usage. Now Russian became the source:

When a new term is needed which the given language does not have, then it must not be created anew but must be boldly taken from the Russian, which is the richest of languages and which in the Soviet Union is the international language. Enrichment of the vocabulary of the languages of Soviet nations with Russian words is perfectly natural. The influence of the Russian progressive culture and language enriches and develops the culture and languages of the other nations.[79]

Baltic writers were made to praise the master-nation's tongue. In a poem titled "People's Friendship," the roles of different nations were strikingly disparate:

77. Anna Brodele, in *Latviešu padomju dzeja* (Riga, 1952), pp. 269–70, as translated in Ekmanis 1978, p. 164. For soil and love, see *ibid.*, pp. 122–4.
78. *Eesti NSV ajalugu*, III, p. 642.
79. *Bolševik*, no. 8 (1952); as reported in Purre, "Teine punane," p. 52.

The Russian language seems to me like a huge bridge of sunbeams
Over which the Latvian heart will climb to high horizons.[80]

Literature, long purged of anything critical of the Soviet occupation, was now purged of anything politically neutral or lukewarm.
Even within the range of political orthodoxy, any literary techniques
unfamiliar to the Stalinist leadership were denounced as Western
capitalist-formalist and bourgeois-nationalist. A look at book covers
is striking: from the contemporary European style practised in the
1930s, Baltic book covers of the 1950s seem to be set back into the
nineteenth century. The same was true of the level of sophistication
of the contents. No Western literature could be published, not even
leftists like Brecht or Neruda, and nearly all native literary groupings
and trends of the twentieth century were declared decadent. Such
books were removed from circulation, and any defense or imitation
of them became punishable. The few classics which were republished
suffered deletions and even additions.[81] The same methods applied to
the theatrical and figurative arts. The Latvian cultural monthly *Karogs*
and the Estonian daily *Rahva Hääl*, replete by now with attacks on
national culture, were still severely admonished in *Pravda* for being
nationalist:

Rahva Hääl acquaints its readers extremely poorly with the friendship of
peoples and with Soviet patriotism. . . . Instead of unmasking the attempt
of the Estonian bourgeois literature in the past to drug its readers' awareness,
it focuses its attention on the personal life of bourgeois Estonian writers. . . .
Rahva Hääl does not unmask the rotten bourgeois culture of the West.[82]

The newly-created or recreated Academies of Sciences for the Baltic
republics were also hampered by the "conditions of a sharply intense
ideological struggle" where young ideologists were telling older specialists how to run their business.

Cultural Russification was reflected especially in the rewriting of
history through the pretense that intense and friendly relations had
existed through the ages with the Russians, who were always presented as superior to the Balts. LaCP First Secretary Kalnbērziņš maintained that the ancient Latvian tribes had grown and developed "only

80. Jānis Grots, in *Latviešu padomju dzeja*, pp. 97–8; translated in Ekmanis 1978,
p. 162.

81. For a detailed exposition of the process in Lithuania, see Tomas Venclova,
"Translations of World Literature and Political Censorship in Contemporary
Lithuania," *Lituanus*, XXV/2 (Summer 1979), pp. 10–15.

82. On Estonia: *Pravda*, 6 July 1951; on Latvia: *ibid.*, 4 February 1952.

thanks to their organic connection with the Russian principalities, to the extremely powerful influence of Russian culture."[83] It was like Nazi propaganda, with the term "Russian" substituted for "German." It was irrelevant to Marxism, and contrary even to Lenin's views about Russian imperialism. Baltic struggles against German aggression in the thirteenth century were given full coverage; temporary alliances with Russians or East Slavs were emphasized, while wars against them, sometimes waged by the same Baltic leaders as fought the Germans, had to be ignored.

The expected behavior of the Balts toward the Russians is well expressed by a much-reproduced bronze statue by Olav Männi (1950), with the detailed title "Prince Viachko of Polotsk and Lembitu's son Meelis defending Tartu in 1224" (see Plate IV). The statue shows a sophisticated Russian feudal prince pointing something out to an eager but not too bright peasant boy. The boy is supposed to be the son of Lembitu, the chief leader of Estonian resistance to the Germans, who in his spare time pillaged the Russian city of Pskov — a fact ignored by Stalinist history.

It was claimed that, as if by magic (and without any presentation of proof), commerce had flourished whenever an area was taken over by Russian rulers, and wilted if they had to withdraw. The Lithuanian expansion in Belorussia and the Ukraine in the fourteenth century was labelled "feudal aggression," while subsequent comparable Russian expansion was not. Swedish rule (1600–1700) in Estonia and northern Latvia, which had been somewhat excessively praised by Baltic historians reacting to German as well as Russian views of their history, was now excessively vilified. The Russian conquest of this area at the beginning of the eighteenth century became "progressive," even though it resulted in enormous population losses in both Latvia and Estonia as well as a tightening of the grip of German estate-owners over their peasants. Likewise, the late-eighteenth-century partitions of the Polish-Lithuanian Commonwealth — which brought Lithuania and Courland, among other areas, into the Russian Empire — also became "progressive," since this foreshadowed their eventual inclusion in the USSR.

This reinterpretation of the past extended from the press to school textbooks; few scholarly studies were written in the short time available, but those which did appear were soon denounced for being over-

---

83. Jānis Kalnbērziņš, *Ten Years of Soviet Rule* (Moscow, 1951), p. 21; as reported in Ekmanis 1978, p. 118.

modest. It overflowed into operas and films about medieval and recent history, with the Marxist form continously overridden by the Russianizing content.

The Russification of history also affected the past of the Communist movement. Many Balts, especially Latvians, had been prominent activists within the Bolshevik ranks, among them Jukums Vācietis, the first Commander of the Red Army; Pēteris Stučka, the creator of the Soviet legal system; and Jānis Rudzutaks, a long-time Politburo member. While a Marxist approach to Baltic history would have been expected to emphasize such native initiatives, the reverse was true under Stalin. Most of these Baltic Bolsheviks were purged during the 1930s, and their names had thus become unmentionable. But even more generally, the Russian imperialist view of history denied any initiative by the Balts, even one of Marxist character. The Baltic masses were depicted as enthusiastic albeit passive followers of Russian Marxist leadership.

Even the events of 1940, which in Soviet historiography were depicted as "native revolutions" against fascist regimes, came — at least in one instance — to be partly credited to Soviet action. A 1949 Lithuanian booklet, *The Aid of the Soviet Union to the Lithuanian Nation in its Defense of Liberty and Independence in 1939 and 1940*, appeared under peculiar circumstances.[84] In 1948, the Soviet Information Bureau responded to the American publication of *Nazi-Soviet Relations*, a collection of diplomatic documents captured during the war, with a pamphlet entitled *Falsifiers of History*. Claiming that the West had contrived to deflect German aggression eastward, the brochure interpreted Soviet actions in the Baltic states mainly as having been dictated by the need to prepare for eventual Nazi aggression. They were likened to the stationing of British troops in Egypt and the American landings at Casablanca. The Lithuanian author's task became one of reconciling this new line with the "spontaneous" Baltic revolutions. He did this by pointing out that the class struggle in Lithuania had reached a revolutionary level in 1939–40 which forced the regime to accept the Mutual Assistance Pacts offered by Moscow. This was a success which had inspired the masses to greater revolutionary activity. Lithuania should thus be grateful to the USSR and its party as well as to Stalin for its 1940 "revolution."

---

84. Juozas Žiugžda, *Tarybų Sąjungos pagalba lietuvių tautai apginant savo laisvę ir nepriklausomybę 1939 ir 1940 metais* (Vilnius, 1949). This work is extremely rare in the West; insofar as we can ascertain, no major library in the US shows it in its holdings.

Even historians who had gone over to the Soviet side found no mercy. Professor Hans Kruus had become Soviet Estonia's first puppet Vice-Premier in 1940, and after the war, as Foreign Affairs Minister, he attended international meetings requesting UN membership for Soviet Estonia. Yet in 1950 he was thrown out of the party. As Soviet Estonia's main daily explained it, the reason lay in his pre-war writings on thirteenth-century history:

Kruus adjusted his step to that of his fascist colleagues and complemented his friends' slander theory with his own contribution: Estonians supposedly defended their country against the Russians. . . . Reversing the facts, Kruus wrote that, in the eastern Baltic areas, before the thirteenth century, "Russians were the nearest and the most active adversaries." . . . Facts show, on the contrary, that in the fight with the "dog-knights," the Russians from the very beginning acted as the protectors and helpers of the Estonians.[85]

The Baltic cultural élite reacted to this straitjacketing in various ways. Some retired or withdrew into manual occupations and minor office work. Certain writers switched to translating Russian classics, and if they wrote original work it would be only "for the drawer," i.e not for publication but for safe-keeping in the hope of better times. Sometimes such passivity was accepted by the regime, at other times not. Some cultural figures tried to cooperate with the regime's demands in order either to remain culturally active, to avoid the possible appearance of hostility, to make a career, or because somewhere between 1940 and 1944 the zigzag course of history had carried them into partial collaboration with the Soviets, and there was no quiet let-out for anyone whom the Soviets had identified as activists on their behalf. During 1949–51, 16 members were excluded from the Lithuanian Writers' Union, nine for inactivity.

In retrospect, collaboration proved no safer than passivity, since collaborators risked unwittingly committing ideological errors and being charged with subversion. Criticism was dished out erratically, and penalties could range from public admonition, to demotion, to effective house arrest and actual arrest, questioning under torture and deportation. In Latvia, the prominent lyrical poet Jānis Medenis was caught in 1945 as he was trying to go to Sweden in a fishing boat. He was jailed until the late 1940s, and then sent to the Kolyma forced-labor camp in northern Siberia. Also deported were Elza Stērste, Valdis Grēviņš and Vilis Cedriņš (who died in 1946), to mention just

85. Artur Vassar, in *Rahva Hääl*, 21 October 1951.

some of the best-known Latvian poets. The Estonian poet Heiti Talvik was arrested and died in 1947. Deported and imprisoned Lithuanian writers included Juozas Keliuotis, Kazys Inčiūra, Antanas Miškinis, Kazys Boruta and Valys Drazdauskas, individuals covering the whole spectrum of pre-war political views. Others became "non-persons" whose names could not be mentioned in the press.[86]

Balys Sruoga, a veteran of the Stutthof concentration camp, was attacked on ideological grounds. The immediate catalyst for the attack was provided by his camp reminiscences, *The Forest of the Gods*, which proved unsuitable for publication. As LiCP Secretary, Kazys Preikšas put it in his speech to the Lithuanian Writers' Congress, 1–2 October 1946 (one year before Sruoga's death):

As a concentration camp inmate, [Sruoga] had a good opportunity to acquaint himself with the other inmates. He saw fighters against German aggression. But the description of the camps in his book is essentially a mockery of them, cynical banter at the expense of victims of German aggression. . . . It appears as if the inmates themselves bear the guilt for their travail, and the German fascist goons are innocent.

What did Sruoga see in this giant tragedy called the German camps? He only saw petty people concerned with some of their physiological functions. . . . If Sruoga's book had appeared, our enemies would be perfectly justified in claiming that the Germans were right in holding such dregs of humanity in concentration camps.

However, as Preikšas elaborated, it was not only this work which evoked condemnation. Sruoga seemed to be intrinsically unacceptable to the new masters.

In talking about Sruoga, one cannot ignore his earlier two-volume *History of Russian Literature*, slandering the Russian nation and the Soviet state system.[87]

Following a somewhat similar pattern, the prominent Latvian poet Aleksandrs Čaks, who drank himself to death in 1950, was viciously criticized in 1951, and publication of his works ceased.

---

86. Ekmanis 1978, pp. 215–17 and 384; *Eesti kirjanduse biograafiline leksikon* (Tallinn, 1975), p. 387; Jonas Grinius, "Literature and the Arts in Captive Lithuania," in Vardys (ed.), *Lithuania under the Soviets*, p. 199.

87. *Už tarybinę lietuvių literatūrą* (Vilnius, 1948), pp. 22–3. Ten years after Sruoga's death, his *Forest of the Gods* was published in Lithuania. It subsequently saw considerably abbreviated Russian (1958), Polish (1965), French (1967), and Latvian (1968) translations.

In Estonia, massive personal reprisals against prominent figures on the cultural scene, starting in 1949, accompanied the purge of native Communists in 1950. In July 1949, an article appeared in the cultural monthly *Looming* which charged several passive and collaborationist writers and artists with formalism and bourgeois nationalism. Even before, people were forced to condemn themselves publicly and in writing for formalism (e.g. the composer Lydia Auster in 1948). Now people would be required to launch surprise attacks on their colleagues, or be themselves doomed. One such attack was later described by Soviet Estonian writer Enn Vetemaa: a professor's favorite student is asked to denounce him, supposedly to spare the professor from worse attacks by others. The professor soon dies during a police interrogation.[88]

Among major neutral cultural figures, writer Friedebert Tuglas was drenched with invective ("He tried to cover up the stench of putrefaction of the bourgeoisie's corpse")[89] and banned from public life, to become a non-person. This fate was shared by hundreds of writers, artists and teachers. The popular playwright Hugo Raudsepp was deported in 1951 and died a year later. The collaborationist Chairman of the Writers' Union, Johannes Semper, was suddenly found to be "the meanest enemy of the Soviet people and literature." Soviet Estonia's pro-Russian anthem, of which he was the author, could no longer be sung, but only played. The Marxist literary critic Nigol Andresen, a left-wing Socialist parliamentarian during Estonia's independence, had become the quisling government's Foreign Minister after the Soviet occupation in 1940 and later (1946–9) the equivalent of Vice-President. In 1950 he was deported as a "venomous bourgeois nationalist" who "tried to poison our adolescent youth." The most ironic casualty was Soviet Estonia's formal head of state Eduard Päll, an Estonian who grew up in Russia and was to remain an unreconstructed Stalinist well into the 1970s. In 1950 he was demoted to faculty member of the Pedogogical Institute, due to the following charges:

Andresen's group directed our literature not toward the Russian and Soviet classics but toward the rotting bourgeois literature of the West. Andresen, and with him Päll too, glorified the reactionary bourgeois nationalist ideas

---

88. Lydia Auster, in *Looming*, no. 10 (October 1948), p. 1256; Enn Vetemaa, *Pillimees* (Tallinn, 1967); see review by Rein Taagepera, "The Problem of Political Collaboration in Soviet Estonian Literature," JBS, VI/1 (Spring 1975), pp. 30–40.

89. Lembit Remmelgas, *Rahva Hääl*, 7 July 1951.

of "Young Estonia." "Young Estonia" was created as early as 1904, and since then it has never tired of exhorting everyone to acquire a Western orientation.[90]

The notion of a "historical gap" in the development of Baltic culture around 1950 had wide currency among the Soviet Estonian intelligentsia, although its existence was denied in official Soviet announcements. However, the major post-Stalin Soviet Estonian anthology (1967) selected fewer poems from 1949–51 than from any other three-year period during this century (if one excludes poems by refugees in the West). There is a similar pattern with literary works mentioned in the major English-language survey of Estonian literature (1970); the average number for 1949–53 is only a quarter of the average of the last five years of independence. Even according to the Soviet criteria 20 years later, the last five years under Stalin were less creative and productive than the war years or the early postwar reconstruction period, not to mention the years of independence.[91] This historical gap of 1949–53 is likely to be found in most areas of cultural creativity in all three Baltic countries. It does not, however, seem to have become a question specifically discussed by the Lithuanian intelligentsia, although there seems to have been some official admonition against needless denigration of the postwar period.

Religion.   After the war, foreign-policy considerations induced the Soviets to take a softer line with the churches in the Baltic states, to use them for peace campaigns abroad, and to try and reduce their domestic influence by means of atheistic lectures, coupled with taxation, regulation and infiltration. Their degree of success varied according to the historical background of the various churches.

In Lithuania, the dominant Catholic Church had deep native roots. As in Ireland, nationalism and religion were closely interconnected, and some priests participated in the guerrilla resistance. This nationalism made the Church a prime target of the Soviet campaign against Lithuanian national culture, but the concomitant broad popular support also made it resilient. The first step, which the Soviets started in 1944, was to try to create a "national church" that would be forbidden

90. Ivan Kebin (Johannes Käbin), *Pravda*, 13 May 1950.
91. Rein Taagepera, "A Portrait of the 'Historical Gap' in Estonian Literature," *Lituanus*, XXVI/3 (Fall 1980), pp. 73–86, based on analysis of Paul Rummo (ed.), *Eesti luule* (Tallinn, 1967), and Endel Nirk, *Estonian Literature* (Tallinn, 1970), biographical appendix.

to have any ties with the Vatican. Bishops who refused to condemn guerrilla violence without mentioning Soviet violence were arrested. Mečislovas Reinys, Archbishop of Vilnius and a former Foreign Minister and scholar with an anti-totalitarian record, was arrested in 1947 and died in 1953 in the prison of Vladimir, Russia. Three other bishops were deported or executed in 1946, three others fled to the West and one died. By 1948, only one bishop was left in Lithuania — the ageing Kazimiras Paltarokas — but he still refused to denounce the Pope or accept lectures on Marxism in the sole remaining seminary.[92]

The Soviets assumed that the clergy had taken up their profession for the sake of profit. Yet most of them continued to serve even when Church property was confiscated, their regular salaries were discontinued and income received from their congregations was subjected to heavy special taxes. Sermons were recorded, hospital and school visits were prohibited, and visitors to the priests were blacklisted. From 1946 to 1949, about 350 priests were deported, especially when the Soviets failed in their attempts to induce younger clergy to form a collaborationist church. By 1954, the number of priests was 741 (compared to 1,451 in 1940), and 688 churches were open (1,202 in 1939); the appointment of priests was subject to approval by the regime's Director for Religious Affairs. The number of seminaries was reduced from four in 1944 to one by 1946, and over the same short time-span the allowed number of seminarians was reduced from 300 to 150. It had fallen to 75 by 1954. No Catholic literature was legally published until 1956, whereas atheistic literature and oral propaganda expanded, but the success was limited due to a simplistic heavy-handed approach and the stigma of their connection with foreign occupation.

In Latvia and Estonia, the prevalent Lutheran Church never had become very popular because of its association with the Baltic German oppression. Even during independence, the percentage of children christened in Estonia decreased steeply — from 92 per cent in 1922 to 77 per cent in 1933, a drop of almost 2 per cent per year. The further decrease to 56 per cent by 1957 — much slower, at less than 1 per cent per year — suggests that Stalinist persecution of the Church may have slowed down secularization rather than speeded it up. There had been about 250 Latvian Lutheran clergy in 1940 but only 95 were

92. V. Stanley Vardys, *The Catholic Church, Dissent, and Nationality in Soviet Lithuania* (Boulder, Colo., 1978), pp. 62–82.

left by late 1944 (most had fled to the West); the Estonian figures were 191 and 79. Before his deportation to Germany in October 1944, the Latvian Archbishop Teodors Grünbergs had appointed Dean Kārlis Irbe to act in his place, but the Soviets deported Irbe to Siberia. Two successive bishops in Estonia, Anton Eilart and August Pähn, met the same fate in 1945. Of the remaining 95 Latvian clergy, five had been killed and 35 imprisoned or deported by 1950. A new Soviet-sponsored Archbishop, Gustavs Tūrs, was finally accepted in 1948. In Estonia, a bishop was appointed in 1949 as part of an accommodation which gave a Soviet agent the post of Chief Secretary of the Church Consistory. Latvia's Catholic Metropolitan Antonijs Springovičs managed to maintain his post, but one of his two auxiliary bishops, Kazimirs Dulbinskis, was deported soon after being appointed in 1947. The Baltic Orthodox Churches were attached to the Russian Patriarchate of Moscow in 1946, and a non-Estonian-speaking bishop was appointed for Estonia. The Jewish synagogues destroyed by the Nazis were apparently not rebuilt. The Free Churches were ordered in 1945 to join a single Baptist League for the entire USSR: traditionally militant minorities, these congregations flourished until 1950 and held their own thereafter.[93]

Interaction with the World. The Soviet annexation of the Baltic states in 1939 was immediately recognized by Nazi Germany and Sweden, but after the war, Baltic diplomatic representatives continued to be accredited in countries such as Britain, the United States, Canada and Australia.[94] France, under pressure from Nazi Germany to recognize the annexation, reestablished limited accreditation after the war. The Soviet Union brought the puppet Foreign Affairs Ministers of the Soviet Baltic republics to the Paris Conference of 1946, trying to make them part of the peace settlement and to obtain United Nations seats for the republics, but the attempts failed. The activities of Baltic diplomatic representatives and pre-war emigrants probably played a role. As Baltic refugees started to acquire citizenship in the countries

---

93. Vello Salo, "The Struggle Between the State and the Churches," in Parming and Järvesoo, pp. 198–204; Ernst Staffa, "Religion im historichen Materialismus in Sowjetrussland und in den baltischen Ländern," AB, X (1970), p. 82; Rutkis, pp. 624–5.

94. See Romuald J. Misiunas, "Sovereignty without Government: Baltic Diplomatic and Consular Representation, 1940–1990," in Yossi Shain (ed.), Governments in Exile in Contemporary World Politics (London, 1991), pp. 134–44.

where they now resided, their opposition to recognition of Soviet annexation acquired electoral weight in those countries.

Of the total pre-war ethnic Baltic population, these refugees constituted 6 per cent of Estonians, 8 per cent of Latvians and 3 per cent of Lithuanians; they formed an even larger proportion of the educated élite. The numerical basis for an émigré culture was there, and the need for such a culture was felt more acutely the more a historical-gap syndrome developed in the Baltic states. In the first postwar decade, émigré activities played a prominent and possibly indispensable role in keeping the national cultures alive. Their very existence influenced developments back home, and probably speeded up the post-Stalin cultural recovery.

The Soviet reaction to émigré culture was a mixture of clumsy repatriation propaganda and thorough isolationism. The threat of Soviet reprisals against those with foreign ties cut even private correspondence between émigrés and their relatives back home almost to zero. Practically no printed émigré literary works reached the Baltic republics. Listening to foreign radio information was restricted and punishable. Little mention of émigrés was made in the Soviet Baltic press and literature, except in negative generalities. However, general awareness of fellow-countrymen abroad persisted among the Baltic population and indeed, in the absence of specific information, their activity was often overestimated. The ideological content of Soviet policies in the Baltic republics may have been hardened by the awareness of competition from abroad, but the existence of the émigré culture also made it harder for Stalin to toy with the idea of strangling Baltic cultural life altogether. The émigré component meant that even the most drastic acts within the Baltic states could not obliterate their culture altogether.

Surprising as it may seem, the Baltic deportees may also have had some cultural-political impact on the Soviet Union. Forced to live in camps with Russians and other nationalities, they sometimes managed to transmit to the latter some utterly novel ideas about Western democracy and practices. The best-documented case is the interaction of Aleksandr Solzhenitsyn with Arnold Susi, a member of the briefly reconstructed government of Estonia of September 1944. In his *Gulag Archipelago*, Solzhenitsyn repeatedly stressed the impact that Susi's long talks made on his incredulous mind:

To understand the Revolution I had long since required nothing beyond Marxism. . . . And now fate brought me together with Susi. He breathed a completely different sort of air. . . . I listened to the principles of the Estonian Constitution, which had been borrowed from the best of European experience, and to how their hundred-member one-house Parliament had worked. And, though the *why* of it was not clear, I began to like it all and store it all away in my experience.[95]

There were limits to such impacts, and one cannot evaluate the total effect of Baltic inmates on other Soviet prisoners. After 1955 most of the surviving deportees returned to the Baltic republics, often broken in health, but often also with steeled spirit: they could no longer be threatened with an unknown land called Siberia.

Normalization under New Norms, 1952–1953

In 1952 the Baltic scene changed. The period since 1944 had seen an unending succession of shattered hopes and social upheavals. Nationally the guerrilla resistance was broken, and hopes of Western support had to be abandoned, and personally one had to give up hope of finding any formula for escaping terror, even if one was not a German collaborator, an outspoken patriot, a private farmer, an intellectual or a native Communist. All of these groups had been reached by the terror, one after another. Which one would be the next group to suffer? The answer was "none," but at the time no one knew that. Terror had become an expected norm, so in this sense things had normalized.

Every year since 1944 (and indeed since 1939) had brought major social changes, but in 1952, for the first time, nothing changed much. The same slogans and the same repression continued, with occasional arrests, and toward the end of the year there were rumors of new mass arrests, deportations of Jews (in the wake of the alleged "doctors' plot" in Moscow), new deportations from the badly functioning kolkhozes, and purges of the remaining intellectuals. But Stalin died in March 1953, and small things that had been unthinkable a year earlier began to happen.

Newspapers reduced threats and started to write about socialist legality. At the Estonian trade union conference, a delegate dared to declare: "Regarding improvement of workers' welfare, only promises are made. That doesn't take us very far." Such unheard-of criticism now was even reported in the press.[96]

95. A. I. Solzhenitsyn, *The Gulag Archipelago, 1918–1956* (New York, 1974), pp. 213–14.
96. *Rahva Hääl*, 20 February 1954.

None of the Stalinist decrees was rescinded, and some practices were even tightened. Social norms remained harsh, but at least they did not change any more. Adjustment to them became possible, and was something people actually desired. The sense of irony and resistance that met the first Soviet measures in 1940 and even after 1944 had dissipated long before. Terror had outlasted any rationale for it, and the Baltic populations were numb. Having stable harsh rules and getting hit only when overstepping known bounds — that sounded like a happy dream after years of erratic terror and shifting demands.

Some resistance still continued in 1953 and later, but this seems to have been an exception. People who felt that they might be deported anyway could as well die fighting when it looked like a choice between death and Siberia. With terror subsiding, the choice was between death and collaboration, and few chose death.

By 1953, Soviet rule had come to be considered more than a momentary and superficial occupation. In this sense it had become "legitimate" — if the Soviets were not considered morally entitled to proclaim and enforce laws, at least it was accepted that they were able to enforce their laws fully, and that one had better act as if Soviet rule were legitimate. The habit of mentally challenging every Soviet law gradually shifted to the less stressful habit of submission. There seems to have been a significant change of attitude — from struggle against foreign "occupation" to working for one's own interest within a framework of foreign "rule."

Like the war period, the postwar years were ones of tremendous population loss for all three Baltic peoples — accompanied by an influx of colonists. Latvia lost at least 150,000 natives through deportations, executions and guerrilla warfare, and Estonia about 100,000. Over the period of a decade, births only compensated for less than half of these. The wartime and postwar losses amounted to about 30 per cent of the pre-war population through death, deportation and flight (see Table 5). Colonization added an equal number of newcomers. Predominantly Russians, they represented an alien class of colonial overlords unable and unwilling to integrate with the existing national language and culture. On the contrary, they largely expected the national population to assimilate with them. In Lithuania, guerrilla warfare resulted in proportionately higher losses, with a total of about 450,000. This was partly compensated by higher birthrates; also, the lower level of industrialization kept down Russian immigration.

In 1953 the future of the Baltic nations looked grim. A few years earlier, terror had proceeded at a genocidal rate. The only hope had been the dictator's death; this had now come, but the system had survived. Terror had subsided, but the machinery that had wielded it was still intact, and the new leaders could reactivate it once the power-struggle was over. Hopeful signs appeared. One wanted to hope, but one was afraid to hope — hope had already been crushed too many times.

The countryside was not recovering from collectivization. City life showed hardly any improvement. Culture was at a standstill. National survival had stopped being a prime concern when common resistance had been smashed and everyone's personal survival was at stake. Society was atomized. All the gains of the period of independence had been undone — political, cultural and even economic.

It could have been worse: Russian-language schooling could have been introduced, as it had been around 1900, and even total deportation, like that of the Crimean Tatars, would not have been an impossibility. But the situation was already bad beyond the worst expectations of 1940. Major improvements were around the corner, but they could not be foreseen. In 1953 the future of the Baltic nations appeared more grim than it actually turned out to be.

4

THE RE-EMERGENCE OF NATIONAL
CULTURES, 1954–1968

The Vain Struggle for Political Autonomy

The Thaw. The general relaxation ("Thaw") in Soviet life which followed the death of Stalin affected the three Baltic republics perhaps somewhat more than most other regions of the USSR, though not as much as the East European satellite countries. As elsewhere in Eastern Europe, the psychological impact of de-Stalinization served as a catalyst for reassertions by the local leaderships of their prerogatives within the system as well as for trends toward fundamental change which questioned the social order itself.

The struggle for succession in the Kremlin allowed a slight and gradual extension of the functions and privileges of the republics' administrations. Among the contenders for supreme power, Nikita Khrushchev proved particularly adept at exploiting such local sentiment in his advance to power. The republics' leaderships tried to use the situation to expand their local political machines, perhaps in the hope of securing some indigenous approbation of their existence. During the 15 years after Stalin's death, the Lithuanian regime was most successful in weathering reactions and in exploiting the situation to nativize its administrative apparatus and secure a grudging indigenous acceptance as being perhaps the lesser evil under the circumstances. In this the Latvian regime proved least successful, with that of Estonia falling somewhere in between.

One of the earliest reflections of the new tendency appeared in party membership, which in 1953 reached its all-time peak throughout the USSR, including the Baltic republics. The number of candidates (new probationary members) in particular dropped drastically after Stalin's death, as people adopted a wait-and-see attitude. In Estonia, the number of candidates fell from 1,903 in 1952 to 578 in 1953; the earlier figure was not reached again till 1956. The remarkably high

Lithuanian figure of 9,224 candidates in 1952 was not equalled during the subsequent decade.[1]

Since the war, the three Baltic parties had remained small by Soviet standards and suffered from a lack of indigenous participation. Necessarily, all three parties as well as the administrative apparatus in the three republics had to be disproportionately staffed by imported cadres, although the existence in Russia of small bodies of pre-war Estonian and Latvian Communist expatriates who could be transferred back to their former homelands mitigated this situation somewhat in those two republics. The "foreignness" of the party was particularly acute in Lithuania, for which even such a limited pool had been almost nonexistent. Moreover, having recently been areas of rampant opposition to Sovietization, the three republics had been inundated with heavy concentrations of Soviet security forces and personnel who swelled the non-indigenous ranks of the party membership. By 1953 the new Soviet leadership may have decided that because of the number and growing seniority (and trustworthiness) of home-grown members, a moderate renationalization was desirable in order to reduce the most glaring signs of external control. In the summer of 1953, the Russian Second Secretaries of the Baltic party organizations were all replaced by ethnic Balts. However, Russians were soon reintroduced in Lithuania (1955) and Latvia (1956), while in Estonia a "Yestonian" held office till 1964 (see Appendix A).

The Lithuanian party leadership took advantage of the new moods in the Soviet Politburo to emancipate itself from much of the direct control by *apparatchiks* (full-time party officials) which had been exercised by Moscow. Rapid and evident nativization of party as well as non-party personnel seems to have taken place immediately after Stalin's death, probably in connection with an effort by Beria to curry favor among the national republic leaderships. The Fourth Plenum of the Lithuanian CC in June 1953 sanctioned such nativization, although this was not mentioned in the press at the time. Widespread dismissals of non-natives who had not learned the Lithuanian language followed. Popular expression of anti-Russian sentiment led, in some cases of overexuberance, to arrests; after the fall of Beria these cases were generally de-politicized through reclassification as distur-

1. For more details on administration and party affairs in 1955–68, see Thomas Remeikis, "The Administration of Power: The Communist Party and the Soviet Goverment," in Vardys (ed.), *Lithuania under the Soviets*, 1965, pp. 111–40; King, pp. 170–206; Pennar 1978, pp. 105–27; Remeikis 1970, pp. 112–56; Aleksander Kaelas, *Das Sowjetisch besetzte Estland* (Stockholm, 1958).

The fate of the Baltic states was decided on the night of 23–24 August 1939 with the conclusion of the Treaty of Non-Aggression between Germany and the USSR. The above pictures of Stalin and the German Foreign Minister, Ribbentrop, were taken during the signing ceremony in the Kremlin in the early hours of 24 August. (*Photos*: Hoover Institution.)

Two facets of Soviet-Estonian relations. *Above*: In 1937, the Soviet Chief of Staff, Marshal A. I. Egorov, being welcomed on a visit to Tallinn by the Estonian President, Konstantin Päts. Egorov was purged in February 1938 and shot on 2 February 1939. Päts was deported from Estonia to Ufa in July 1940. *Below*: The Soviet armored car which appeared in front of the Tallinn central prison on 21 June 1940 during what was described in Soviet sources as an internal uprising.

The drama of the incorporation of the Baltic states into the USSR included staged mass demonstrations to convey the popular approval of the moves. The Soviet-organized demonstration in Tallinn on 21 June 1940, *above*, is claimed to have drawn 30,000–40,000 participants, although this officially promulgated picture suggests a much smaller number.

Postwar guerrilla resistance appeared in all three republics but proved most marked and prolonged in Lithuania. This photograph from 1947 shows a group of partisans from the Kęstutis Unit (named after a fourteenth-century Lithuanian ruler) in the Tauras Guerrilla District which covered southwest Lithuania. The men are wearing the uniform of the army of the prewar republic. Their weapons appear to be of diverse origins.

The bronze statue "Prince Viachko of Polotsk and Lembitu's son Meelis at the Defense of Tartu in 1224" by the Estonian sculptor O. Männi is a prominent example of the Stalinist historical canon expressed in a work of art. The Russian elder brother is helping the younger Estonian to resist German invaders.

The long-serving Lithuanian CP First Secretary, Antanas Sniečkus, at the dedication ceremony in 1972 of the massive outdoor war memorial at Kryžkalnis near Raseiniai to "The Red Army, the Liberator."

Despite a complaint from N. S. Khrushchev in 1961, restoration work continued on the island fortress of Trakai, one of the capitals of the medieval Lithuanian state which had been in ruins since the early eighteenth century. The photograph, taken in 1980, shows the restored central building.

Two facets of monumental modernist architecture in the Baltic republics. The Stalin-Gothic building in Riga, *above*, is the only one of its kind in the area. Begun in the post-war years as a "House of Collective Farmers," it became the Academy of Sciences of the Latvian SSR on completion in 1957. *Below*: the Vilnius opera house, completed in 1974. Both buildings are prominent in the centers of the two cities.

Housing developments accompanied the rapid post-war urbanization and immigration. Above is a panoramic view of Lazdynai, a residential suburb of Vilnius, where construction began in the late 1960s and continued into the mid-1970s.

According to a 1956 Soviet geography book, "enormous ash mounds up to 100 meters in height" were a typical panorama of the oil-shale region along Estonia's north coast. Such trumpeting of pollution in a positive vein had abated by the early 1980s, but the mounds continued to grow, as is seen here.

Left, the Estonian dissident Jüri Kukk, a lecturer in chemistry at the University of Tartu, who died in a north Russian prison in 1981, apparently after attempted forcefeeding during a hunger strike. *Right*, Romas Kalanta, a nineteen-year-old student of Kaunas, Lithuania, who, on 14 May 1972, poured gasoline over himself and struck a match. He died later in hospital. The act took place in front of the theater where in 1940 the People's Assembly staged its session to vote on incorporation into the USSR. Kalanta's funeral sparked riots involving several thousand students.

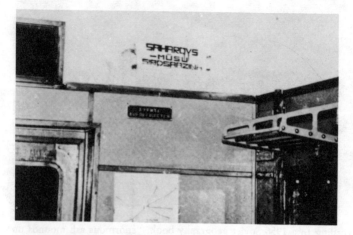

Outward manifestations of dissent were endemic in the three republics under Soviet occupation. The above example dates from the spring of 1976 when the words "Sakharov — our conscience" appeared stencilled in paint on Riga suburban trains.

bances of the peace or hooliganism, and the policies of the late Security Chief were blamed for provoking such unacceptable behavior.[2] On the whole, however, Beria's death did not result in a change in the nativization policy, although it came to be pursued at a gentler pace.

Numerous transfers of non-native party cadres out of Lithuania are suggested by the extremely slow growth between 1953 and 1956 of the total LiCP membership, at a time when it was claimed that significant numbers of recruits were being accepted. The post-Stalin uncertainty also made some Russian party members leave Latvia and Estonia. Between 1952 and 1956, the number of non-Estonian members of the ECP decreased by over 1,000, from 13,374 to 12,138 — the first such decrease since 1945. A purge of Beria supporters may have affected Baltic Russian party members more than home-grown ones.

Khrushchev's denunciation of Stalin at the February 1956 CPSU Congress released a shock-wave which furthered the trend toward an increased stature for the republics within the Soviet system. The condemnation of the "cult of personality" implicitly reaffirmed the need to observe the law, and the "sovereignty" of the republics was a constitutional principle.

2. Based on a conversation with Aleksandras Shtromas, who at the time worked as a defense lawyer in Lithuania and had close family connections with then First Secretary Sniečkus. For the LiCP plenum as well as an analogous plenum in Latvia, see Borys Lewytzkyj, *Die sowjetische Nationalitätenpolitik nach Stalins Tod (1953–1970)* (Munich, 1970), pp. 25–6. Perhaps the most dramatic case of this Beria nativization in Lithuania occurred within Beria's own domain, the Security Service. Since 1945, a Russian, Dmitrii Ardalionovich Efimov, had been Minister of State Security in the Lithuanian SSR. His ministry was now merged with that of the Interior and placed under an old native Communist, Jonas Vildžiūnas. Efimov, who under normal circumstances could have been expected to head the new unit, became Vildžiūnas' deputy. Vildžiūnas had briefly worked for the Security Police after the Soviet occupation in 1940; however, since he had a brother resident in the US, he was not, according to Stalinist canons of eligibility, considered suitable for such service and had been sidetracked into other posts, most recently that of Chairman of the Kaunas City Executive Committee. His interview with Beria on his new appointment forms part of the lore among high Lithuanian party personnel. In a thick Georgian accent, Beria is supposed to have answered Vildžiūnas' mention of his American brother with: "We will discuss that when we decide to appoint him minister." After Beria's fall, Vildžiūnas returned to apparently more normal preoccupations of urban management. In 1954, he was demoted to Chairman of the Vilnius City Executive Committee. For a biography of Jonas Vildžiūnas, see *Mažoji lietuviškoji tarybinė enciklopedija*, III, p. 751.

A series of administrative reorganizations conducive to the expansion of local prerogative were carried out; these were all part of the psychological atmosphere surrounding de-Stalinization. Abolition of the USSR Ministry of Justice made the important state procurators subordinate to local ministries of justice. The republics were given the right to draft their own legal codes within a general all-Union framework. Police functions were separated from the organs of state security.

Even though the precise implications of the move remained vague for some time, establishment of the *sovnarkhozy* (regional economic councils) in 1957 appeared to be a tangible expansion of the role of the republics. The discussions preceding their appearance served as a forum for the expression of local interests. In an *Izvestiia* article of 22 September 1956, Aleksei Müürisepp, Chairman of the Council of Ministers of the ESSR, criticized the policy of economic interdependence for having prevented Estonian industry from using local raw materials, for having mandated export of output before the republic's own needs had been met, and for the dispersal of Estonian specialists throughout the USSR and the influx of Russians to replace them. Similar critiques also appeared in the press of the three republics.

Müürisepp's last point touched on an extremely sore issue among the Baltic population. The large influx of Russians was rationalized in Estonia by presenting it as having been inevitable to cover the loss of so many specialists who had left during the war.[3] Open concern also appeared in Latvia over an indigenous brain-drain. The shortage of engineers in the republic was blamed on the annual dispatch of about half of the graduating specialists to the Soviet Union outside the republic.[4] Another complaint was that Latvians studying in Moscow, Leningrad and other cities were not being sent back to their own country after graduation.[5] While the temporary harvest work performed by students in the Virgin Lands of Kazakhstan was extensively publicized in 1956, publicity accompanying such "volunteer" labor lessened considerably in Lithuania during the following year.

According to the new system, each republic was to become a separate unit for the purposes of economic planning. As one observer noted in the Latvian party journal:

3. "V bratskoi seme sovetskikh narodov," *Kommunist Estonii*, 1957/7 p. 10.
4. *Cīņa*, 5 June 1957.
5. *Ibid.*, 21 April 1957.

The establishment of the Economic Districts and the *Sovnarkhozy* in the republics will contribute widely to an extension of their rights. The republics' organs will work out plans for the development of their economies and will carry out organizational work.[6]

The stature of local managers and planners was thus enhanced. Moreover, the reorganization necessitated some expansion in the political and administrative bureaucracies. Some officials were doubtless made available by the consolidation of local government districts between 1954 and 1967, with most rapid change in 1959 (see Table 9).[7] The expansion of the pools of economic administrators and managers provided an added rationale for increasing native cadres.

De-Stalinization and economic reorganization combined to nurture the mood that considerable change was necessary and would be beneficial. Visible expressions of native patriotism appeared which would not have been tolerated earlier. The officially sanctioned moves all fell into the pattern of a search by the local regimes for symbolic legitimation. Prizes were instituted in the different republics for promotion of science and the arts among native cultural circles. In May 1957, a three-colored university student cap based on the pre-war student fraternity tradition appeared in Estonia. In 1957 Estonian athletes began sporting "EESTI" (Estonia) on their uniforms, instead of "EESTI NSV" (Estonian SSR). In Latvia and Lithuania such shifts had already taken place in 1956.

A sense of communality made its appearance among the three Baltic republics, distinct from their membership in the USSR. In 1958 the first postwar Baltic soccer games were held. With time, an attempt was made to water down this growing sense of regional identity by artificially including Belorussia, the Kaliningrad *Oblast* and/or the Leningrad *Oblast* in "Baltic" events.

Efforts were made at times to subsume focal points of native patriotism into Soviet tradition. The Brethren Cemetery in Riga, an elegant pre-war memorial to those who fell on both sides during the 1918–20 Latvian War of Independence, had been privately cared for in the postwar years. Now the authorities took over maintenance of the shrine, but in July 1958 added the graves of 22 Red Army soldiers and partisans of the Second World War.

---

6. "Novyi etap v ekonomicheskom razvitii strany," *Kommunist sovetskoi Latvii*, 1957/6, p. 6.

7. Gottlieb Ney, "Administrative Gliederung und Verwaltungsorgane der sowjetisierten baltischen Staaten," AB, II (1962), pp. 9–34; *Eesti nõukogude entsüklopeedia* (Tallinn, 1968–76), II, p. 85, and IV pp. 381 and 541.

Rising Expectations.   The impatience for change was particularly strong among the youth, where it proved difficult to contain de-Stalinization within officially approved channels. In 1956, for instance, the students of the Tallinn Polytechnic Institute sought to form a new student organization. Their cardinal sin was not so much this move in itself as the apolitical nature of their organization, which was not intended to be a part of the Komsomol or trade union organizations.

The psychology of rising expectations fanned incidents. In Lithuania on 2 November 1956, the All Souls' Day tradition of lighting candles by the graves of loved ones turned into a massive demonstration. It was a work day, and the custom had not been sanctioned by the regime. Student riots also broke out in Vilnius concurrently with the Hungarian uprising.[8] Likewise, thousands of candles appeared that year on 25 November, the pre-war Latvian Memorial Day, by the statue of mourning Mother Latvia in Riga.

The rise in open dissatisfaction alarmed official circles, especially coming on top of the events in Poland and Hungary. A hardening attitude, accompanied by searches for new culprits, began to appear in the media in late 1956. Three offenses were particularly singled out for castigation: propaganda by hostile elements abroad; bourgeois nationalism; and corruption, as well as bureaucratic inefficiency, at home. Attacks on "undue" fascination with the West and growing attention to nationalist propaganda by émigré organizations increased. Arvīds Pelše, Secretary of the Latvian CC, declared in a radio broadcast on 20 July 1957:

Bourgeois nationalists abroad croak like crows that the unfortunate Latvian nation and her future are endangered because the people are subjected to Russification. In telling these and similar fairy tales, our enemies seek to touch the national spirit and to influence hesitating elements in our republic. . . . Maybe, and quite obviously . . . we committed some mistakes, and some failures have been evident. For example, not always and not everywhere have equal rights been given to languages. Not every sign or name of a street is written in both Latvian and Russian. Not every salesman or militiaman speaks both languages.[9]

8. Thomas Remeikis, "Acquiescence and Resistance," *Lituanus*, VI/2 (1960), p. 65.

9. Assembly of Captive European Nations, *A Survey of Developments in Nine Captive Countries* (New York, 1957; henceforth cited as ACEN), III, p. 5, based on a Radio Riga broadcast of 20 July 1957.

Pelše's need to make fun of national sensitivities, highlighting the language question, indicated their relevance. The continuing nativization of the party cadres in all three republics had evidently begun to raise a question of the possibility of "national Communism," as attested by the frequent appearance of press attacks during the summer of 1957. The Latvian party organ *Cīņa* likened national Communism to "sophisticated bourgeois nationalism":

The aim of the slogans of national Communism is to smash the indestructible foundations of proletarian internationalism, to split it and to make people of socialist countries fight each other in order to destroy the foundations of socialism. National Communism is nothing but sophisticated bourgeois nationalism.[10]

The most forceful statement came a year later from the Lithuanian First Secretary Sniečkus in his speech to the Tenth Congress of the LiCP:

It is important for every member of the working class to know that anyone who would stir up antagonism toward the Russian nation, anyone who would tear the Lithuanian people away from the Russian people, would be digging a grave for the Lithuanian nation.[11]

The third villain, corruption and bureaucratic inefficiency, was also blamed for contributing to a loss of faith in Communism and receptivity to enemy blandishments. This was clearly enunciated by Pēteris Plēsums of the Latvian CC in his article "On the Moral Attitude of a Communist." He catalogued a whole series of negative phenomena in the party ranks:

There are cases where particular persons who strongly believe in remnants of capitalism try to join the party, not because they believe the party is right or because they want to help, but only in search of some material benefit. Because of such "Communists," it happens that good people, people doing decent work who deserve to be members, avoid the party . . . What kind of example can a Communist show who till now has not freed himself from religious prejudices? But such Communists — admittedly not many — are still to be found in our party. There are cases where Communists baptize their children, ask ministers to attend funerals of their family members etc. . . . Among those in the republic expelled from the party in 1956 were 39 candidate-members whose faults were mostly drinking, hooliganism and

10. *Cīņa*, 11 July 1957.
11. *Literatūra ir menas*, 15 February 1958.

misbehavior. . . . The largest group was expelled because of appropriations of state and private property.[12]

Widespread corruption was thus held responsible for the evident lack of ideological fervor. While it is difficult to judge how fervent belief in Communism had been among the Baltic Communists, of whom there had only been few to begin with, it is probable that Khrushchev's revelation of the crimes of Stalin also contributed significantly to the undermining of faith in the ideology.

Such concern over the effects of a light-hearted attitude to ideology was also used to rationalize manifestations of real dissatisfaction among the workers, which was usually caused by chronic economic weaknesses. A wave of dissatisfaction apparently swept the 250-worker Parkett *artel* in Tallinn during 1957. Ivan Kebin of the Estonian CC offered the following explanation:

No one acquainted himself with the interests of workers and personnel at the artel. . . . Hostile elements made use of this situation, misinterpreting the meaning of current events, trying to create an unhealthy attitude and dissatisfaction among people who were not firm enough in their beliefs.[13]

Discussions of the *sovnarkhozy*, which had initially emphasized local initiative, now came to be accompanied by a marked stress on the growing unity and interrelationship of the Soviet nations. The Union was presented as a giant melting-pot in which the national groups were "freely" abandoning their identities to blend into a homogeneous Soviet people with the coming of Communism — which, according to one ebullient pronouncement of Khrushchev, was barely 20 years away. Attacks on impediments to its achievement, such as nationalism and religion, were stepped up. While the terror of the Stalin years could not be brought back — the regime had locked itself into condemnation of such a system — attempts set in to repress the national self-assertion which had been permitted by the Thaw.

The effect of the Thaw on the economy was slow, as there was gradual reorganization and the difficulties of transition were overcome. The change was slowest in agriculture. While Stalin's death may have saved Baltic farmers from further deportations, it did not immediately reverse the "spook hostel" syndrome; indeed, it was even

12. P. Plesum(s), "O moralnom oblike kommunista," *Kommunist sovetskoi Latvii*, 1957/7, pp. 51–2.
13. Ivan Kebin (Johannes Käbin), "Politicheskaia robota v massakh," *Kommunist Estonii*, 1957/3, p. 22.

deepened by Khrushchev's drive to grow maize everywhere. However, the new emphasis on collective leadership did not extend down to the collective farms. Chairmen were appointed without any say by the collective owners and, worst of all, the farms were not allowed to own their own tractors; they remained at the mercy of the state machine-tractor stations (MTS), which faced no produce-delivery pressures and which the kolkhozes had to pay in kind. Meddling by "plenipotentiaries" dispatched from district headquarters continued to erode initiative. The first major reprieve came in June 1955, when Khrushchev declared, at an agricultural conference in Riga, that the implementation of his *agrogorod* ("agricultural cities") idea had been pursued too fast and with too many errors. Some of the largest kolkhozes were subdivided, and kolkhoz chairmen started to feel that they could ignore the most senseless instructions from above and address the real problems.

The real breakthrough in agriculture came only in 1958, when the MTS were dismantled throughout the Soviet Union. Collective farms were now able to buy and maintain their own machinery. Baltic farmers had cooperated in the use of machinery since the period of independence, and they eagerly bought the equipment from the MTS (mostly on credit, with state support). This was not always how it was done elsewhere in the USSR. The complicated system for disposal of farm produce (compulsory deliveries below cost, low-price payments in kind to the MTS and voluntary sales at higher rates) was simplified. Compulsory delivery was abolished; prices were raised so that they would no longer be confiscatory; and price differentials were eliminated. High taxes and compulsory deliveries from private plots were also ended in 1958–9.

The demographic pattern was markedly changed by the Thaw. The immigration of non-Balts largely stopped around 1953, as people and officials adopted a wait-and-see attitude. People brought to the Baltic republics as forced labor started to leave, and so did some functionaries who were uneasy about the native popular mood. Indeed, the ouflow surpassed the inflow in some years. In 1956–9 many Baltic deportees returned, possibly the majority of those who had survived. As a result, the percentages of ethnic Latvians and Estonians in the countries' populations increased, recouping some of the losses inflicted by Stalin, and probably reached a peak of 62.0 and 74.6 per cent respectively around the 1959 census (see Table 1). Many of the returnees stayed in the cities, and scarcity of living space became more acute than at any other time during the whole postwar period around 1955–6 (see Table 10). Latvia saw a sharp upsurge of immigration in 1956, for unknown reasons — a net influx surpassing that of the six preceding years combined.[14] This surge may have been a major motive for a nativist reaction which, in turn, brought on a severe purge.

The Latvian Purge of 1959.   Khrushchev's successful purge of the "Anti-Party Group" in June 1957 marked an end to the expansion of the republics' prerogatives. Khrushchev no longer needed to court political support in this quarter. The shift proved most traumatic in Latvia,[15] where it coincided with difficulties in the LaCP which emerged at the Fifteenth Congress in January 1958. During the preceding two years, the number of party members and candidates had considerably decreased. It is unclear whether this was the result of a massive transfer of Russian party members out of the republic, as in Lithuania, but it is clear that a trend toward "national Communism" had emerged in the Latvian party organization. Its main goal seems to have been to reduce the unpopularity of the Soviet regime and of the CP by expanding the republic's autonomy and by eliminating the Russifying aspects of the regime.[16] Some speeches favored strengthening the party through admission of native Latvians, increasing the use of the Latvian language within the party and devoting more attention to the Latvian intelligentsia and youth.

The decisions concerning personnel announced during the Congress reflected a slight "Latvianization" of the leadership. While the percentage of Russians in the CC did not decrease, the composition of its Bureau (executive body) became markedly more Latvian. A trend toward "Latvianization" could be noted in other bodies as well. At the Twelfth Congress of the Latvian Komsomol in March 1958, Vladislavs Ruskulis, a native, replaced an immigrant Latvian from Russia in the post of First Secretary. The Council of Trade Unions elected in May 1958 contained 21 Russians out of 71 members; the previous Council had had 24 Russians out of 47. The Council's

14. The outflow was massive in the case of Lithuania (see Table 14). In Latvia and Estonia, the net outflow was close to 2,000 each in 1955. However, in 1956 the net influx into Latvia suddenly surged to 26,800. See Taagepera, "Baltic Population Changes," p. 36.

15. For a detailed study of the Latvian purge, see Widmer, pp. 196–217. A more concise overview is presented by Juris Dreifelds, "Latvian National Demands and Group Consciousness since 1959," in George W. Simmonds (ed.), *Nationalism in the USSR and Eastern Europe in the Era of Brezhnev and Kosygin* (Detroit, 1976), pp. 138ff.

16. King, pp. 193–5.

perennial Chairman, Kārlis Voltmanis, an old Stalinist, was replaced by Indriks Pinksis, First Secretary of the Liepāja Municipal Committee, a partisan commander during the war who had been active in the extreme left trade union movement of independent Latvia.

In August 1958, a Second Plenum of the LaCP was held, at which the most significant development was the return of Vilis Krūmiņš as Second Secretary, the post he had lost in 1956 to a Russian.[17] At that time, however, he had retained his membership of the Bureau while also becoming Deputy Chairman of the Council of Ministers. In mid-1958, Colonel-General Aleksandr Gorbatov, Commander-in-Chief of the Baltic Military District, was also dropped from the Bureau and soon transferred out of Latvia. His successor, General Pavel Batov, was apparently not coopted into the Bureau *ex officio*, as had been the practice hitherto. As a result of these and other changes, only one Russian, Aleksandr Nikonov, remained as a full member of the Bureau, and he had been a resident of Latvia between the wars when it had been independent. Moreover, only two of the full members of the Bureau were post-1940 immigrants. The return of Krūmiņš to the position of Second Secretary left a vacancy in the Council of Ministers, and his old position there as Deputy Chairman was filled by Eduards Berklāvs, who since January 1956 had been First Secretary of the Riga City Committee. Like Krūmiņš, Berklāvs was a younger native Communist.

Continuing ferment in Latvian party circles was reflected in a series of articles attacking irresponsible statements at party meetings as well as corruption. At some conferences the party leadership came under heavy fire:

17. Many sources indicate Pelše as Second Secretary in 1958–9. However, his biography in the *Bolshaia Sovetskaia Entsiklopediia*, XIX (1975), clearly says: "March 1941 to 1959, LaCP Secretary for propaganda and agitation." King, p. 190, says an autonomist was elected, and Krūmiņš is specified as the Second Secretary by Vilis Hazners, "Who is in Power in Latvia?" *Baltic Review*, no. 24 (March 1962), p. 10. On the other hand, Pelše is listed as such for July 1958 by Andris Trapans, "A Note on Latvian Communist Party Membership, 1941–1961," *Baltic Review*, no. 26 (April 1963), p. 28. A possible explanation of the confusion may be that Pelše became Second Secretary during the January 1958 congress, but was replaced by Krūmiņš during the August 1958 plenum. See Appendix A for chronological list of LaCP Second Secretaries. Ādolfs Šilde, *Bez tiezībām un brīvības* (Copenhagen, 1965), p. 61, lists Filipp Kashnikov from January 1956 to April 1958 and Krūmiņš from April 1958 on. *Latvijas PSR maza enciklopēdija*, vol. III (Riga, 1970), for which Krūmiņš is a "non-person," says nothing on 1958–9. An unpublished draft study by Professor Grey Hodnett (no date) says Kashnikov was not reappointed in January 1958 and the post remained empty until April.

At the party conferences at Dobele, Daugavpils and Ogre, some faultfinders even produced irresponsible and demagogic speeches. . . . It is no secret that there are also among us Communists who do not play any advance-guard role. Some are passive, but others transgress party and state discipline, and there are those who transform themselves into petty bourgeois, drink heavily, and do not behave properly.[18]

Much of this criticism should be seen in the context of an effort to "Latvianize" the party. Since it has been established that two-thirds of the LaCP members at the time were Russians, such criticism may well have been aimed at non-Latvian-speaking Communists.

The autonomists' goal of making Communism more palatable to the Latvian population required an increase in living standards. Medical services, housing, construction, pensions and the distribution of consumer goods in the rural areas were expanded in 1957–8. More generally, the autonomists offered Moscow increased deliveries of commodities in exchange for more autonomy in the organizing of the local economy.[19] In the words of Pauls Dzērve, Director of the Latvian Institute of Economics, the goal was

to develop Latvia's industrial structure and specialization so that the most rational and economic use of *all* Latvian natural and labor resources would *maximize* the Latvian contribution to the development of the Soviet Union's economy as well as the living standard in Latvia.[20]

Matters came to a head during the summer of 1959. In mid-July the Latvian mass media announced laconically that the Presidium of the Supreme Soviet of the Latvian SSR had, by its decree of 15 July 1959, dismissed Berklāvs from his duties as Deputy Chairman of the Council of Ministers. On 5 August, it was further announced that the Plenum of the Latvian Council of Trade Unions had discharged Pinksis from his duties as Chairman and had removed him from its Presidium as well. Both were expelled from the party. This was the start of an extensive purge which continued for several years.

The ostensible reason for dismissing Berklāvs was provided by Vilis Lācis, Chairman of the Council of Ministers of the Latvian SSR. In a discussion of Latvia's contribution to the Seven-Year Plan, Berklāvs had supposedly expressed open opposition to the general party line

18. "Usilit vnimanie k vnutripartiinoi robote," *Kommunist sovetskoi Latvii*, 1959/2, p. 61.

19. King, pp. 195 and 200–3.

20. Summarized by King, p. 201, from Dzērve's statement in *Karogs*, no. 1 (January 1959), p. 103.

on the development of heavy industry. He had favored industries for which Latvia had raw materials and could supply labor, arguing that Latvian products should first satisfy the local demand before being poured into the general Soviet pool of production. Berklāvs was also one among "some leading workers who attempted to turn the development of the republic from the correct path to one which would have led it in the direction of nationalistic limitations and seclusion."[21]

No specific rationale was provided for the dismissal of Pinksis. He was known, however, to have objected to the transfer of workers, especially skilled ones, to other republics while a labor shortage existed in Latvia, and he had openly doubted the possibility of finding the 10,000–12,000 workers from rural districts for the construction projects of the Seven-Year Plan. In effect, he was implicitly criticizing the plan to bring non-Latvian immigrants into the republic, which would become necessary to carry out these projects. Pinksis had had a feud with Lācis back in Stalin's time, after criticizing Lācis' novel *Towards New Shores*, and had received a rebuke in *Pravda*. Lācis had been awarded the Stalin Prize.

Initially, the majority of the Latvian CC apparently opposed the measures. Lācis supposedly declared that Berklāvs' policy had also been his own. Only repeated pressure, including personal intervention by Khrushchev, carried the day. As a result, Lācis, Chairman of the Council of Ministers, and Jānis Kalnbērziņš, First Secretary of the LaCP, both of whom had occupied their positions since 1940, were forced to resign soon after they had agreed to Berklāvs' dismissal.

While it is impossible to be sure that the whole of the preceding account is accurate, both Kalnbērziņš and Lācis were replaced in late 1959. On 25 November, Kalnbērziņš was "released from his post at his own request" during a plenum of the CC. The speech of his successor, Arvīds Pelše, indicated that the stated reason for his ouster was an inability to educate youth in the proper spirit of internationalism (codeword for subservience to things Russian). Perhaps because of his long service, Kalnbērziņš remained a member of the Latvian CC and its Bureau. Furthermore, he was appointed Chairman of the Presidium of the republic's Supreme Soviet, i.e. titular head of state. Pelše, his replacement as First Secretary, came from a prosperous farmer's family. He had joined the party in 1915 while studying in Petrograd,

21. V. Latsis (Lācis), "Blagotvornye preobrazovanie," *Partiinaia zhizn*, 1959/16, p. 15.

returned to Latvia only in 1940, and then quickly become one of the LaCP Secretaries (1941–59). He was known as a prominent opponent of "localism and nationalism."

The following day, Lācis was released from his position as Chairman of the Council of Ministers "for reasons of health". Like Kalnbērziņš, he retained his position in the Latvian CC. As a writer, he continued publishing and participating in cultural events. His successor, a prominent agricultural chemist Jānis Peive, had been born in Russia and resided in Latvia only since 1944, becoming Rector of the Latvian Agricultural Academy (1944–50) and President of the republic's Academy of Sciences (1951–9). Although he was Chairman of the USSR Soviet of Nationalities (1958–66), Peive became a member of the Latvian CC and of its Bureau only with his appointment as Chairman of the Council of Ministers, which was to last till 1962 (see Appendix A).

The purge rapidly encompassed the Latvian party and government. While some of the changes may have been planned in advance and cannot be directly ascribed to the purge, others showed an unmistakable connection. In November 1959, the ministries of Justice and of Communal Economy were abolished, but their incumbent heads were appointed to newly-created successor-bodies.

Widespread changes were revealed during the Seventeenth Congress of the party in February 1960. Second Secretary Krūmiņš was again replaced by a Russian. Another CC Secretary, Nikolajs Bisenieks, was discharged. The Commander-in-Chief of the Baltic Military District, Iosif Gusakovskii, was coopted into the Bureau. Only three members of the outgoing Bureau — Pelše, Kalnbērziņš and Ādolfs Migliniks — remained; and Migliniks resigned a year later, ostensibly for health reasons. Only 57 of the 91 members of the outgoing CC remained in the new body. The number of Russians increased from 33 to 35, but the body as a whole was also enlarged to 93. The number of CC members openly connected with the security apparatus increased from two to 11.

The purge in the Latvian Komsomol can be said to have preceded that of the party as a whole. On 22 September 1959, both the First and Second Secretaries were removed, and at the March 1960 Congress an entirely new leadership was installed, now headed by a Latvian from Russia as First Secretary and a Russian as Second Secretary. The speech of the recently-appointed head of the LaCP, Arvīds Pelše, to the Komsomol indicated clearly the tenor of the pervasive purgative mood. Attacking nationalism, it was laced with phrases like "serious

defects," "it is bad" and "it is not tolerable." Pelše found fault with
the youth for their insufficiently vigorous struggle against bourgeois
ideals:

Anti-Soviet rumors and fiction are not being sufficiently unmasked, and no
counterattack is being launched against the manifestations of bourgeois
nationalism and the chauvinism of the great powers. Young people are being
inadequately educated in the spirit of international proletarianism and friendship among the peoples. The friendship of the Latvian people with the other
nationalities of our country, and primarily with the great Russian nation, is
the object of national pride and one of the great sources of happiness for the
Latvian people.[22]

The mass media were accused of a lack of political vigilance, and many
serious "mistakes" were found in the work of the State Publishing
House. Not long thereafter, almost all the editors of the major newspapers were replaced.

The purge continued through 1960. At the April Plenum, Pēteris
Plēsums, Chairman of the Party Commission, was among those dis-
missed. No native Latvians were left as heads of CC departments. In
June, Jānis Auškāps, Deputy Director of the Latvian *sovnarkhoz*, was
replaced. Although he was given a pension, it was an open secret that
he had belonged to the Berklāvs group. His successor was not a native
Latvian. Later in the year, the Office Director of the Council of
Ministers, the Senior Editor of the State Publishing House and the
Senior Engineer of the State Geological and Mineral Department were
all expelled from the party. They had previously been reproached for
bourgeois "narrow-mindedness." Likewise, two prominent economists, Pauls Dzērve, Director of the Institute of Economics, and his
deputy, Benjamins Treijs, were forced to resign. Both had been drafting plans for the Latvian *sovnarkhoz*, which presumably favored local
interests.

The removals extended to municipal and rural self-government
bodies. It seems that several thousand party members were expelled
within less than two years. In 1961, the party membership represented
about 3.5 per cent of the population of Latvia. However, since this
included 33,000 members of the armed forces and security apparatus
stationed in Latvia, the actual figure was just under 2 per cent of the
population. Latvians may have made up about half of the resident
party membership.

22. ACEN, VIII, p. 119, based on a Radio Riga broadcast of 3–4 March 1960.

Nativization of the LaCP received a considerable setback through the purge. The leadership of the party would remain dominated by Latvians from Russia. When Pelše was promoted to the all-Union Politburo in 1966, he was replaced by Augusts Voss, another immigrant (in 1945) of the period after the imposition of Soviet power. The percentage of indigenous party members continued to be lower than in the other two Baltic republics: in 1967 it was 45 per cent (including Latvians from Russia), compared to 52 and 66 per cent for Estonia and Lithuania respectively.[23]

In 1963, Peive left Latvia again for his native Russia. The new LaSSR Premier (1962–70), Vitālijs Rubenis, was also a Russian Latvian. The pattern of disproportionately low representation of native-born Latvians in leadership positions was paralleled at lower levels. A 1967–8 study for Riga showed that while the local-born population of the city was 51 per cent and made up 39 per cent of the workforce, only 27 per cent of the leadership positions were held by members of this group. On the other hand, immigrants, making up 25 per cent of the population and 32 per cent of the workforce, held 48 per cent of the leadership positions.[24]

The Reaction in Lithuania and Estonia.   The shift in Kremlin policy passed much less eventfully for the Lithuanian and Estonian Communist leaderships. In Lithuania, this was largely due to the adroitness of Antanas Sniečkus, a member of the LiCP CC since 1926 and its First Secretary since 1936, in adapting to changes in Moscow. While he had been prompt in condemning Beria in 1953, he seems to have adopted a cautious wait-and-see attitude after the Twentieth Party Congress. In February 1956, the Lithuanian party organ *Tiesa* carried a mere *pro forma* condemnation of the cult of personality; only on 29 March, in a reprint from *Pravda*, did it specify that the cult referred to was that of Stalin. The stability of the top party and government personnel appears remarkable by Soviet standards. The only change

23. *Estonian Events* and *Baltic Events* (henceforth cited as EE/BE), no. 37, p. 8 (1973). The Latvian figure of 45 per cent comes from Jānis Sapiets, "The Baltic Republics," in George Schöpflin (ed.), *The Soviet Union and Eastern Europe* (New York, 1970), p. 224. A similar figure of 46.3 per cent for 1965 is given by Widmer, p. 144. The ethnic composition of the LaCP has never been published, so these are likely to be estimates. Another calculation based on 1973 figures for the total LaCP membership concludes that the native composition of the LaCP in that year could not have been higher than 43 per cent: V. Stanley Vardys, "Modernization and Baltic Nationalism," *Problems of Communism*, XXIV/5 (1975), p. 40.
24. Dreifelds 1976, p. 144.

came in 1956 with the replacement of the Chairman of the Council of Ministers, Mečys Gedvilas, by Motiejus Šumauskas. It appears that the move was prompted more by problems in agriculture than by shifts in the Kremlin. At any rate Gedvilas, one of Sniečkus' old-time colleagues, was merely demoted to the position of Minister of Education.

Sniečkus faithfully echoed the shift toward a reassertion of centralization. At the time of the expulsion of the "Anti-Party Group" in Moscow, he deemed it wise to warn the LiCP of the dangers of decentralization, as in a speech to the Lithuanian Supreme Soviet in June 1957:

Separate tendencies toward *localism*, attempts to create a closed economy and to solve economic problems on the basis of limited local tasks, may become evident. Such tendencies must be combatted from the very beginning.[25]

Soon afterwards, he launched a purge of the Lithuanian cultural establishment (see sections below on the Thaw in culture).

Nevertheless, a quiet "Lithuanization" of party cadres, which had begun after the death of Stalin, continued. While membership of the CPSU increased by about 26 per cent in 1956–60, that of the LiCP did so by over 40 per cent.[26] The "Lithuanization" of the party continued through the anti-nationalism campaign of the early 1960s, in spite of a slight increase in the number of Russians in leadership positions. Its CC became only slightly more Russian — 28.4 per cent in 1961, as compared to 22.7 per cent in 1960 and 21.7 per cent in 1958; in 1952, this figure had stood at 33.3 per cent. Its Presidium had only one non-Lithuanian, whereas in 1949 there had been five. The only marked increase of Russians, perhaps for show, came in the 1962 Lithuanian delegation to the USSR Supreme Soviet — 23 per cent, up from 11.5 per cent in 1958. Three members of the 35-member delegation were not even residents of the republic and had no ostensible connection with it. This ratio seems to have been maintained in subsequent years; in 1966 the delegation was 24 per cent Russian.

The tendency for the party as a whole to become more Lithuanian continued. Its younger members with technical competence began to replace older revolutionaries who, in view of their pre-war experiences, apparently found it more difficult to be nationalists than

25. *Tiesa*, 8 June 1957.
26. Remeikis 1965, p. 116.

the younger group, who were more attuned to the population from which they stemmed. While some friction seems to have developed between them and the old revolutionaries, Sniečkus managed to keep the peace and to prevent the situation from boiling over as it had in Latvia. In 1964, the Lithuanian party (2.5 per cent of the republic's population) was still smaller than the Soviet average. However, its indigenous element stood at around 60 per cent. The notable "Lithuanization" of the party can also be seen in the republic's Komsomol. Despite the anti-nationalism campaign, its membership rose rapidly. By 1964, it stood at 209,000, double that of 1957, and included 40 per cent of the Komsomol-age youth of the republic. As Lithuania was still predominantly populated by Lithuanians, this pool of prospective party members was likewise predominantly indigenous. In 1965 Lithuanians made up 61.5 per cent of the LiCP, in 1968 66.2 per cent.[27]

In Estonia the possibility of a purge of top native administrators could not even arise, since they had already been purged almost out of existence in 1949–52. Ever since 1951, Estonia had been ruled through people of the type of Pelše and Peive: the First ECP Secretary, Käbin, had been in Russia from 1910 to 1941, and the Chairman of the Council of Ministers, Aleksei Müürisepp, had been in Russia from 1908 to 1944. The only remaining home-grown figure was August Jakobson, like Lācis a writer, who joined the CP only in 1942 and was Chairman of the Estonian Supreme Soviet Presidium from 1950 to 1958. He was replaced for health reasons by a polar biologist, Johan Eichfeld, who had been in Russia from about 1915 to 1950 and, remarkably, become a party member only in 1961, the year he ceded the chairmanship to the ailing Müürisepp. The new Chairman of the Council of Ministers (from 1961) was another "Yestonian," Valter Klauson.

Starting from such a baseline, the degree of nativization of top administration could only rise, or at least stay the same. It did increase somewhat. Some ranking native Communists purged around 1950 partly recovered their rank. The former Chairman of the Council of Ministers, Arnold Veimer, became its Vice-Chairman and head of the Estonian *sovnarkhoz* in 1957, and was even readmitted to the ECP Bureau in 1961 — a pale reflection of Gomułka's comeback in Poland. The former Vice-Chairman of the Council of Ministers (1943–50), Hendrik Allik, returned from forced labor in 1956 and, through

27. *Mažoji lietuviškoji tarybinė enciklopedija*, II, p. 386.

smaller jobs, worked his way back to the same post (1965–73). Rehabilitation and nativization were more extensive at lower levels, where incompetent outsiders were often replaced by more competent natives. There was also some re-acculturation of Yestonians. In particular, Ivan Kebin gradually re-Estonianized his first name to Johannes, and considerably improved his poor command of Estonian (nonetheless his language gaffes always remained a butt for popular jokes). Many other Yestonians remained Russian in their language and culture.

The ECP remained largely an alien organization in which home-grown Estonians formed about one-third of the total membership. The total Estonian share (including "Yestonian" immigrants from Russia) gradually rose from a low point of 41.5 per cent in 1952 to 44.6 per cent in 1956 and 49.1 per cent in 1961. After 1966, it levelled off at around 52 per cent — well below the Estonian share of the population (74 per cent in 1959, 68 per cent in 1970) and of specialists with higher or special secondary education (76 per cent in 1970).[28] The latter figure implies that Estonians were overrepresented in most jobs where skills were needed, but grossly underrepresented in the power structure. The hopes for more national autonomy within a Communist framework made many young Estonians join the party around 1956 — an act they would have considered treasonable only a few years earlier. Such hopes did not last. It would be hard to sort out to what extent the party discouraged Estonian membership, and to what extent Estonians chose not to join. In fact, desisting from joining under colonialist conditions could be interpreted in both ways, but either way Estonians were underrepresented in the ECP, and remained so.

In the rubber-stamp assemblies, on the other hand, Estonians were generously overrepresented. The ESSR Supreme Soviet was 86 per cent Estonian (or Yestonian) in 1959, and 85 per cent in 1966. In the local soviets (councils), the figures were 88 and 89 per cent, respectively. The 1966 ESSR delegation to the USSR Supreme Soviet was 80 per cent Estonian. In the same year, the more powerful ECP CC included 26 Russians, 45 Yestonians and only 26 home-grown Estonians.[29]

28. Pennar 1978, p. 118; EE/BE, April 1973, p. 8; ECP Party History Institute, *Nekotorye voprosy organizatsionno-partiinoi roboty* (1971); *Nõukogude Õpetaja*, 22 July 1972, p. 2.

29. Pennar 1978, p. 119; Uustalu 1970, p. 358.

The Fall of Khrushchev. During the early 1960s, the Soviet reactions of the preceding years continued as a full-fledged campaign affecting many aspects of Baltic national life. However, the purge in Latvia and the general hardening in all three republics did not affect the de-Stalinization which followed the Twenty-Second Congress of the CPSU in 1961. In its aftermath, six Latvian old Bolsheviks, members of the party since 1906–13, published an article "That is Correct!" expressing their approval of the decision to remove Stalin from the mausoleum on Red Square.[30] In general, not much needed to be done to eradicate his presence in the Baltic republics. In Latvia one monument in Cēsis and one publicly displayed bust in Riga were removed, along with more numerous framed portraits, and in Lithuania 42 collective farms had to be renamed.

The fall of Khrushchev in 1964 seems to have come as a surprise to the leading Baltic administrators. On 13 October, during the celebration of the twentieth anniversary of liberation from the Germans, the Latvian First Secretary, Pelše, repeatedly alluded to Khrushchev and his Leninist wisdom. The next day, Khrushchev was toppled. The Riga papers only included a short note on 18 October and made no comment until 30 November. Pelše, however, hastened to render homage to the new leadership with a *Pravda* article entitled "The Strength of the USSR Lies in Loyalty to Lenin's Heritage" (6 November), praising Lenin's supposed supreme desire to lead the party according to the principles of collective leadership. Public reactions in the other two republics were similarly delayed.

As could be expected, the ascendancy of a collective leadership meant a slackening of the policies pursued by its predecessor. In his last years of power, Khrushchev had begun to take a rather strong assimilationist course: the 1961 party program had adumbrated the eventual disappearance of republic boundaries and the organization of the state along regional economic lines. The concept of merging the three nations made its appearance, and the creation of regional *sovnarkhozy* in 1962 seemed to point toward further changes which could even threaten the existence of the "sovereign" republics. The uncertainty of the future of regional *sovnarkhozy*, as well as of other issues in a situation of collective leadership, led to a relaxation of the anti-nationalist campaign and a distinct downgrading of the "growing together" theme. This tendency favored the continuing assertion of the national cultures.

---

30. *Padomju jaunatne*, 1 November 1961.

Even some modest expansion of efforts to stress the "sovereignty" of the republics could be noted (the contrary trend toward economic recentralization will be discussed later). Prominent Baltic figures were included in symbolic Soviet delegations. The Chairman of the Presidium of the Lithuanian SSR, Justas Paleckis, frequently represented the USSR at the Interparliamentary Union; in 1966 he became Chairman of the all-Union Soviet of Nationalities, replacing Peive. The Soviet delegation to the UN General Assembly occasionally included such individuals as Juozas Matulis, President of the Lithuanian Academy of Sciences, and the ESSR Foreign Affairs Minister, Arnold Green. At times, prominence was given to the republics' "trade negotiations" with other countries, which were in reality little more than discussions of implementation of the provisions of USSR trade treaties with those countries.

The Successful Struggle for Cultural Autonomy

The Thaw in Culture.   The Thaw raised high hopes in cultural circles. Artistic and literary production increased rapidly in quantity and, more important, in quality. Cultural rebirth was the major development of the late 1950s and early 1960s. Therefore the cultural scene for this period is described here in more detail than for the previous period, when cultural achievement was dismal, and the period from 1968 onwards, when it was again taken for granted.[31]

The Thaw removed the obligatory models and simplistic declarations of formulae which had been dominant in the arts during the Stalin years. More personal introspection appeared, along with some stylistic and structural interpretation based on Western trends. Literature began to include such earlier taboos as stream-of-consciousness,

31. For more details on cultural affairs in 1955–68; see: Ekmanis 1978, pp. 181–235; Šilbajoris; Grinius, pp. 197–213; Jonas Vėlaikis, "Lithuanian Literature under the Soviets," *Lituanus*, XII/3 (Fall 1966), pp. 25–43; Arvo Mägi, *Estonian Literature* (Stockholm, 1968); Ivar Ivask, "Recent Trends in Estonian Poetry," BA, XLII/3 (Autumn 1968), pp. 517–20; Ivask (ed.), "A Look at Baltic Letters Today" — a special theme issue with articles by 12 authors, BA, XLVII/3 (Autumn 1973), pp. 623–716; Nirk; Rolfs Ekmanis, "Soviet Attitudes toward Pre-Soviet Latvian Writers," JBS, III/1 (Spring 1972) pp. 44–70; George Kurman, "Estonian Literature," in Parming and Järvesoo, pp. 247–80; Mardi Valgemäe, "Drama and the Theater Arts," *ibid.*, pp. 281–317; Ilmar Mikiver, "The Great Breakthrough of Youth in Soviet Estonian Literature," Seventh Conference on Baltic Studies (Washington, 1980); Marite Sapiets, "Lithuania's Unofficial Press," *Index on Censorship*, IX/4 (1980), pp. 35–38.

non-chronological narrative forms and psychological introspection. In general, three tendencies were seen in literary output. The first was an attempt to formulate a more modern and updated version of the standard socialist-realist form. A second group went even further and tried to update the socialist-realist content. It sought to introduce a considerably wider dimension to the earlier stereotyped characters, and themes such as collectivization, guerrilla warfare or the impact of industrialization on personal lives were no longer treated as simple elements in a Communist propaganda scheme. The heroes of works in this category became genuine human individuals who were seriously considering the changes facing them and honestly struggling with those changes in their attempt to find genuine meaning in the new scheme of things. While the essence of socialist realism was still there, its form had entirely vanished. A third category eschewed any of the questions that were central to socialist realism and still of concern to writers in the first two groups. For writers in the third group, modernism, embracing all the latest literary techniques, was representative of matters far more complex than those which could be treated within the official ideological structure.[32] While the official cultural establishments were not always pleased with writers in this category, some of their work began to be published.

Several deported Latvian writers returned from Siberia — Harijs Heislers in 1954, and Jānis Medenis and Andrejs Kurcijs in 1955. In 1955, most of the Estonian poets who had been publicly denounced for ideological crimes were readmitted to the Writers' Union. The works of pre-war writers who had become unmentionable were reissued. One of the earliest seemed to be Jānis Ezeriņš (1891–1924), whose selected short stories were published in Latvia in 1955. In Lithuania, Vincas Krėvė-Mickevičius, who had been the first Acting Prime Minister of the Soviet occupation regime in 1940 and died in the United States in 1954, was rehabilitated, and his works began to appear in 1956. Six volumes of the writings of Balys Sruoga, who died in 1947 after returning from wartime internment in the Stutthof concentration camp, began to appear in 1957. The prominent pre-war writer Ieva Simonaitytė, who had almost become silent in spite of the eminently acceptable flavor of her works — social critiques of her native Klaipėda area — resumed publication. Another suppressed pre-war writer, the left-wing Kazys Boruta, was reintegrated into

32. Rimvydas Šilbajoris, "Socialist Realism and the Politics of Literature in Occupied Lithuania," in Rimvydas Šilbajoris (ed.), *Mind against the Wall* (Chicago, 1983), pp. 81–4.

Lithuanian cultural life, and several pre-war writers — Antanas Miškinis, Kazys Inčiūra, Petras Juodelis and Juozas Keliuotis — returned from Siberian exile in the late 1950s. In December 1956, publication in the popular Latvian magazine *Zvaigzne* of the long autobiographical poem *Unfinished Song* by the returned deportee Harijs Heislers caused a literary sensation; it was one of the first Soviet works dealing with the theme of the Gulag. In another work, Heislers did not mince words in his criticism of Stalinist literature:

We still remember too well the infamous epoch in our poetry when the lyric hero loved only because his betrothed fulfilled the plan, when kisses were exchanged only on the scaffolding of newly-erected buildings. . . .[33]

Another returnee, Andrejs Kurcijs, succeeded in publishing a novel on the 1905 Revolution which had displeased several authoritarian regimes. On its publication in 1938 *Gates of Life* had been banned by Ulmanis' censors, and it was not republished under Stalin. It finally was in 1956, but in a revised form. In Estonia Rudolf Sirge's novel *The Land and the People* (1956) created a sensation with its realistic description of the 1941 deportations.

De-Stalinization made possible the resurrection of several Latvian writers like Fricis Bārda (1880–1919) and the poet Aspāzija (1868–1943); their works were published in 1956. The former practice of publishing classical works with new "proletarian" characters slipped in started to be condemned.

Several writers like the Lithuanian Vincas Mykolaitis-Putinas, who had been prominent in the salon-liberal sector of pre-war society and who had become silent, even if not formally suppressed, now resumed their literary activity. Estonia's Friedebert Tuglas, a non-person since 1951, saw eight volumes of his selected works published in 1957–62. The pervasive thirst for classics was demonstrated when, within a few months in 1956, a 25,000-copy edition of the poems of Jonas Maironis, a Lithuanian cleric who was the bard of the national renaissance at the turn of the century, sold out. None of his religious poems was included, however. The emergence of new Baltic talent, which began slowly in 1956, is discussed in the next sections.

A greater variety and substance were tolerated in the visual arts, and the creative legacy of some artists who had been unmentionable in Stalin's time was restored. The most prominent example was Mikalojus Konstantinas Čiurlionis (1875–1911), whose works had

---

33. *Literatūra un māksla*, no. 23 (1956), as translated by Ekmanis 1978, p. 198.

been considered expressions of individualism and symbolism and been removed from public exhibition in the pre-war Kaunas museum which had been built specifically as a home for his work. His *de facto* position as Lithuania's national painter reemerged with the publication of a collection of reproductions, accompanied by a reopened exhibition of his works. Preparation of the edition of reproductions came after considerable debate among the party's cultural authorities. Its appearance after lengthy wrangles and procrastinations was generally seen as a milestone in the official acceptance of Lithuania's cultural heritage.

A greater latitude of themes, styles and outside contacts appeared in the theater. In 1956, theaters in the three republics began to cooperate, and Lithuanian performers began to tour Poland. In music there was a beginning of modern experimentation.

In Latvia there was toleration of an effort to revive Latgalian culture. The Latgalian dialect had lost its official status as a language in Soviet times. In 1957 two small newspapers were started, each with a circulation of 1,000. They were closed the following year, and it is not clear whether this was due to a change in policy or to the effort proving unviable for other reasons. The summer solstice celebration, a major national holiday in Latvia (as also in Estonia), was allowed again in 1956 after being banned for many years.

In 1957, even the Stalin Prize winner Andreijs Upīts joined in condemning a style of which he had been a most successful practitioner. In a large volume entitled *Problems of Socialist Realism in Literature*, he ridiculed stories full of "extremely stupid and repulsive half-wits, instead of quite normal bourgeois professors," and of kulak villains "who force rusty nails and pieces of glass down the throats of Soviet cows."[34]

In 1957 *Neierastā Amerika* (Strange America), by the Latvian émigré Anšlāvs Eglītis, began to be serialized in the popular magazine *Zvaigzne*, but this "import of bourgeois nationalism" was attacked and discontinued after the first instalment. However, several plays by the eminent playwright Mārtiņš Ziverts, who was living in Sweden, were staged. Five books by another Latvian émigré, Jānis Jaunsudrabiņš, were published in 1957–9, and one of them was even filmed. The republication of Latvian Communist writers purged in the pre-war Soviet Union came more slowly. As persons they were "posthumously rehabilitated", starting from 1956, but publication of the

34. Ekmanis 1978, pp. 204–5.

first works only began in 1958 (selected works by Red Army General Roberts Eidemanis).

Expressions of the need to strengthen the role of the national languages in the Baltic republics appeared. One Estonian commentator felt that Russians in Estonia should be obliged to learn the local language:

The party organizations have to deal more seriously with teaching the Estonian language to those comrades who do not speak it, and more resolutely to require it from reponsible workers who have lived for many years in the country and whose success in learning it is insignificant.[35]

The ideological hardening noted at the end of 1956 slowed the Thaw in cultural life. The reaction was most marked in Lithuania, where a series of dismissals of cultural functionaries in 1957–8 can be said to have amounted to a purge. Juozas Bulavas, Rector of the University of Vilnius, was relieved of his post, dismissed from the CC and excluded from the party for "political mistakes." Somewhat later his successor, the mathematician Jonas Kubilius, provided a detailed exposé of the problems at the institution:

Quite recently some instructors at the university committed grave ideological errors; certain nationalist tendencies were intensified. Leninist principles for the selection of cadres were violated. No attention was paid to the multi-national composition of the population of the republic. . . . Some instructors in Lithuanian literature began to deny analysis and evaluation of literature based on a viewpoint of the class struggle. . . . The value of proletarian writers was minimized. . . . Shortcomings . . . were also reflected in the activity of various circles — young writers, folklore and ethnographic studies.[36]

Bulavas had been a pre-war member of the party in the underground, and his past services may now have secured him employment in the Academy of Sciences. His removal from the University was accompanied by a purge of the faculty. The dismissal of several prominent Lithuanian literary and linguistic scholars altered the whole tenor of study of these subjects in the Academy. The Deputy Rector of the Vilnius Pedagogical Institute and the Minister of Culture were also among those dismissed. Others engaged in the administration of scholarly work received public reprimands for the defense of religion, "apolitical thinking" and "objectivist research."

35. "V bratskoi seme sovetskikh narodov," *Kommunist Estonii*, 1957/5, p. 15.
36. *Tiesa*, 2 October 1960.

The changed climate was reflected in other cultural areas as well. A new Lithuanian opera, based on a recent novel about the 1863 uprising (Vincas Mykolaitis-Putinas, *The Rebels*, 1957), was scheduled to have its première in 1958, but apart from the announcement in 1960 of a revised version, nothing ever came of it. Perhaps the social and national elements in the 1863 revolt simply could not credibly be separated.

It is difficult to explain this reaction regarding culture in Lithuania. One possible hypothesis is that Snieckus, sensing the prevailing mood in the Kremlin, sought to deflect the coming anti-nationalist reaction away from the nativization of his political machine, the LiCP, by overtly cracking down in the cultural sphere.

By 1959 the cultural atmosphere in the Baltic republics had changed almost beyond recognition, compared to what it had been only six years earlier — while apparently remaining very much the same. Compared with the continuing gap between the Western and Baltic degrees of cultural freedom there was indeed very little change, but anyone comparing the foul air of 1959 to the suffocation of 1953 saw the difference between cultural survival and death. There was new hope, and the coming decade saw a veritable resurgence of Baltic cultures. The fact that it did not come about easily only added to its significance.

The Re-emergence of Estonian Culture.   Around 1960, more than one whole new generation of writers and artists made their appearance on the Estonian scene. The new wave included not only the generation whose time had come, but also the one whose time had been overdue ever since 1945, and those whose start had been stopped short after 1940. One might distinguish the following phases: the Thaw (1955–9); the "remarkable fluorescence of new, vital, and aesthetically satisfying verse"[37] and other cultural achievements in 1960–8; and a period of consolidation which began around 1968.

In poetry, the first major debut was *The Coal Concentrator* (1958) by Jaan Kross, already 38: a collection based on the former law teacher's personal experience in the coal mines.

Fresh, polemical, erudite, witty, and controversial, this volume, the publication of which had been delayed for years, opened new vistas in subject matter and technique. . . . The fresh breezes loosed upon the literary landscape by Kross . . . draw in their wake those who earlier had meekly submitted, those

37. Kurman 1978, pp. 251–2.

who had maintained silence, and those who were about to launch their first verses.[38]

Almost every year produced a new landmark. A group of young nature-sensitive women poets who began to publish in the late 1950s (Helvi Jürisson, Ellen Niit, Lehte Hainsalu) were dubbed "the Spring Maidens" — they had helped to turn the Thaw into Spring. The delayed generation who had been involved in the war produced the intellectual strophes of Ain Kaalep and Kaljo Kangur. Among those who had remained silent for almost two decades, August Sang and Betti Alver again started publishing powerful work. Even half-a-dozen former party bards freed themselves from declaratory, prepackaged rhetoric and produced non-preprogrammed poetry.

In 1962, a poetry "cassette" of five new slim collections was an instant hit among the young both at home and in exile. Almost unbelievably, it later proved to have introduced three writers who were to loom large in Estonian poetry, prose and drama for the next two decades: Paul-Eerik Rummo, Mats Traat and Enn Vetemaa. Rummo's brief introductory poem "The First Calf" aptly characterized the new period's mix of humor and quiet determination, as he contradicted the Estonian proverb that a cow's "first calf always will perish." In non-rhyme translation:

> I stand with straddled legs
> and wonder at the world.
> I have a funny tail
> and two big eyes.
> And I don't want
> to be a goner.[39]

Among the continuing flood of talent after the Thaw we should mention Artur Alliksaar's surrealism (first allowed into print in 1968, two years after his death) and Jaan Kaplinski's resonance with nature, religion and the fate of Vercingetorix and the American Indians:

> . . . There are no witnesses. The dead
> are good Indians. Marry.
> Get children. Kill. Try to be happy.
> Try to be happy if you can.[40]

38. *Ibid.*, p. 252.

39. Translated from Paul-Eerik Rummo, *Ankruhiivaja* (Tallinn, 1962), p. 5.

40. Jaan Kaplinski, "Meie peame ju väga tasa käima," *Tolmust ja värvidest* (Tallinn, 1967), p. 13; full translation by Rein Taagepera in *Akwesasne Notes*, IX/1 (Spring 1977).

As for prose writing, Arvo Valton (who had attended high school in Siberia after the war) emerged with allegorical and grotesque stories and miniatures in the style of Sławomir Mrożek. Mati Unt, a teenager writing about teenagers, broke new ground in sex and politics, responding to the protest of one of his own characters:

Our books have a damnably small vocabulary for that kind of thing: "He stayed for the night"; "She spent the night with him"; "He turned off the nightlamp." Don't you sometimes have the feeling that most Estonian writers are eunuchs?[41]

Problems of personal conscience during the Stalinist years were tackled in Vetemaa's short novels *The Monument* (1965) and *The Musician* (1967).[42] Touches of realism started to penetrate novels on war and postwar topics by old-guard writers such as Paul Kuusberg, Lilli Promet and Raimond Kaugver, whose *Forty Candles* (written by 1959, published in 1966) provoked official displeasure by having its narrator serve in the German and Finnish armies, lose his last shreds of decency in Stalin's labor camps, and end up a venal, respected and wealthy Soviet industrial executive. Since it received the Lenin Prize, Juhan Smuul's colorless Antarctic travelogue, *The Icy Book* (1959), should probably be mentioned. While poetry had stabilized by 1968, prose was still rapidly developing. Longer works not only took longer to write after the Thaw had given the signal, but they were also hit harder by censorship.

Poetic symbolism might escape the censor's attention, or a single controversial poem might be slipped into a journal, although it could be omitted from a later collection. So it was with a poem by Arvi Siig (1967) about a kindergarten teacher, Masha (a Russian name), who was good at heart but ineptly bossed the children (all with Estonian names, whose initials formed the Estonian word for "nation"). Also, Estonia's main cultural monthly commemorated the fiftieth anniversary of the October Revolution with a poem by Hando Runnel that began: "And yet I keep thinking about a small country," discussed at length Estonia's world role, and only in the last few lines remem-

41. Mati Unt, *Võlg* (Tallinn, 1964); translation in Kurman 1978, p. 261; full translation by Ritva Poom: "The Debt," *Literary Review*, XXIV/4 (Summer 1981), pp. 461–513.

42. *The Monument* was published in English in Enn Vetemaa, *Three Small Novels* (Moscow, 1977). For brief analyses of various Soviet Estonian works up to 1968, see also BA, XLII (1968), pp. 310, 472 and 621; XLIII (1969), pp. 289–90 and 446–8; and XLIV (1970), pp. 157–8.

bered to add that the country was now "tacking" with the "October wind." Both poets later published a number of books of poetry, but without those poems.[43] With novels, the prepublication of parts was usually impossible, and any cuts by the censors affected the balance of the whole, leading to protracted struggles. As an example, Heino Kiik's *Spook Hostel* on the miseries of collectivization (see above, pp. 105–6), received the first prize at the republic-level contest for novel manuscripts in 1967. Typesetting was started on 4 July 1968, but printing was only authorized 18 months later, on 29 December 1969. Meanwhile, a major negative character had his Russian name Estonianized, along with numerous other changes and cuts.[44] The book was published in 1970.

In drama, socialist realism was supplemented by the rise of a theater of the absurd influenced by similar trends in Western Europe, Poland and Czechoslovakia. In late 1966 and 1967, three of Sławomir Mrożek's short plays were performed on Estonian television, and a translation of Eugene Ionesco's *Rhinoceros* appeared in print in 1967. However, already in 1966 the first original absurdist play was published — *The Nameless Island* by Artur Alliksaar. Another play in the same vein by Ain Kaalep was performed in 1967, but apparently was never published except abroad. As with prose writing, the emancipation was still continuing in 1968. Both in the performing arts and in publishing, Estonia was leading (and possibly influencing and conditioning) Russia, ever since the first postwar Brecht production in the Soviet Union took place in Tallinn (in 1957–8).[45]

Western literary works continued (following the Thaw) to be translated into Estonian in great numbers, and often earlier than into Russian (e.g. Kafka's *Trial*, 1966). Even Fedor Dostoevskii, still officially shunned in Russia, was more easily available in Estonian. Moreover, some works by Estonian refugee authors were reprinted in Soviet Estonia, starting with the poetry of Marie Under (1958) and Gustav Suits (1964) and continuing with Karl Ristikivi's novel *The Island of Wonders* (1966). The struggle for the recovery of the nation's literary heritage was largely completed by the republication of Jaan Oks (1967) and Karl-August Hindrey (1968). One major voice

43. Rein Taagepera, "Nationalism, Collaborationism, and New-Leftism," in Parming and Järvesoo, pp. 75–103; full translation of Runnel's poem in *EE/BE*, no. 2, p. 2 (1967).

44. The source of this private communication to one of the authors preferred to remain anonymous.

45. Valgemäe, p. 291.

continued to be silenced — that of the former deportee Uku Masing, a theologian and orientalist. In 1965 his *Jungle Songs* were smuggled out and published in Sweden. No visible repression followed.

In the figurative arts, Tallinn rapidly emerged as the third Soviet center for abstract art, along with Moscow and Leningrad. In contrast to Russia, the avant-garde movement operated in Estonia with strong support from the general population and was tolerated by local party officials. From its definitely "unofficial" status in the early 1960s, it was inching toward a "semi-official" status. While the Russian avant-garde continued to exhibit in private apartments, in Estonia they moved into the galleries of the Union of Artists and Tartu University as early as 1964. That which was banned when called abstract art became acceptable when called "geometric art" or "experimental art." "I don't understand them at all," Käbin, the ECP First Secretary, reportedly said at an "experimental sculpture" exhibition at the library of the Academy of Sciences in 1967. ". . . No, you don't have to remove them. I am no art specialist."[46] Artists like Ülo Sooster (died 1970) were reestablishing links with the pre-war experimental tradition, and prepared the ground for a new generation which was to emerge around 1970. In the graphic arts, Vive Tolli gained wide recognition with her semi-abstract style. Applied and decorative arts rapidly returned to the way they had been in pre-war Scandinavia, helped by widening contacts with Finland.

The new music showed a deepened understanding and revival of Estonia's 1,000-year-old folksong tradition, alongside (and sometimes combined with) modern dodecaphonic experimentation. In the latter line, Arvo Pärt's "Perpetuum Mobile" gained early recognition at the Ninth Autumn Festival of Music in Warsaw (1965) while still under attack in Moscow. Veljo Tormis became the leading proponent of folksong inspiration.[47] The first Soviet jazz festival was held in Tartu around 1964. Film production, however, remained mired in clichés.[48] Architecture was often innovative as long as it remained on the drawing-board, but construction was restricted to more conservative approaches, due to bureaucratic attitudes combined with limitations on construction materials.

46. Stephen C. Feinstein, "The Avant-Garde in Soviet Estonia," in Norton Dodge and Alison Hill (eds), *New Art from the Soviet Union* (Washington, 1977), pp. 31–4; EE/BE, no. 3, p. 2 (1968), and no. 4, p. 1 (1968).

47. Harry Olt, *Modern Estonian Composers* (Tallinn, 1972).

48. *Eesti nõukogude entsüklopeedia*, II, p. 152.

As the national culture reemerged, each step forward was achieved after an uphill struggle against reactionary and imperialist forces within the republic and outside it. In literature, attacks against innovation went on throughout 1959; it was branded as revisionist, subjectivist, abstract humanist and pacifist, narrowly personal, and nihilistic. There was a concerted attack on Jaan Kross, Ain Kaalep and Ellen Niit. Free verse was condemned. In 1962 the fighting words were symbolism, impressionism, futurism, expressionism, surrealism and existentialism, all of which were declared to be decadent in an ill-disguised neo-Stalinist attack. The waves of reactionary criticism arose and then spent themselves, but they had to be taken seriously, and at times such harassment caused considerable personal harm. Publishing remained under full Soviet state control, and any work could reach the page-proof stage and then be prohibited without explanation. Works of popular authors could sell out, but then they would not be reprinted. Meanwhile, stores would be full of second-rate works approved by the party censors and issued in new editions regardless of the limited demand.

The Reemergence of Latvian Culture.   While the general pattern in Latvia was similar to that in Estonia, the purges of 1959 cast a long shadow over the whole decade of the 1960s. The start before 1959 was promising. Although remaining well within the framework of socialist realism, short stories by Jēzups Laganovskis (*When the Winds Rustle*, 1956) represented a landmark by their rather realistic depiction of the sad state of the collectivized Latgalian countryside. Ojārs Vācietis (*The Wind of the Distant Roads*, 1956) emerged as a promising poet.

In 1957–8 stimulating new prose writing tended to be published in the monthly journal *Karogs*, but republication in book form usually required conformist alterations, and often never occurred. In a short story by Dagnija Cielava-Zigmonte (*Golden Dust*), a college student is sleeping around, especially with her father's chauffeur, but as the daughter of a Stalin Prize-winning biologist, she would never consider marrying her lower-class lover. Angry establishment critics paid Cielava the compliment of comparing her story to Françoise Sagan's recent *Un certain sourire*. A novel by Laimonis Purs (*Have I Mused on It?*) extended the description of the pleasure-seeking children of the new managerial class. Zigmunds Skujiņš provoked a heated controversy with a story on the postwar guerrilla struggle (*One Night's Chronicle*).

As mentioned earlier, establishment attacks became a serious threat in 1958. Laganovskis, Cielava and even the ex-deportee Heislers were forced to repent publicly. However, by late 1958 a relatively liberal climate had returned. A strong demand for aesthetic criteria in literature and the arts was spearheaded by poet Ojārs Vācietis, whose first novel *Through the Eyes of Those Days* (originally published in *Karogs* 1958, issued in book form 1959 with alterations) depicted the hypocrisy and inhumanity of the collectivization and deportations of 1948–9. The peak of artistic achievement in post-Thaw novels may have been reached with *The Water Lily* (1958) by Visvaldis Eglons-Lāms, where the disappointments of the modern "superfluous man" are compounded by past and present Soviet practices.[49]

The political purge of 1959 thoroughly changed the cultural atmosphere. Starting in November 1959, it felt as if a new *Zhdanovshchina* (cultural purge) was blowing over Latvia, and the chill was to continue for many years. As late as 1967, an ex-Stalinist critic considered the stagnation in Latvian literature to be worse, in some aspects, than under Stalin. As one reason, he mentioned

the distrust that reigned some time ago and hindered development of free thought. Many writers suffered from severe and unmerited accusations. Latvian literary critics did not know how to protect the autonomy of literature during those times when literature was subjugated to rigid canons which turned young immature writers into obedient conjecture literati instead of artists and searchers for new truths.[50]

In 1968, the cultural weekly *Literatūra un māksla* published a complaint that, compared to their colleagues in some other Soviet republics, the overseers of Latvian cultural affairs were excessively insensitive to their nation's cultural values.[51] The very fact that such a criticism could be published suggested some improvement, but the struggle was hard.

The pressures of the early 1960s reinforced the "literature of compromise," although that of protest and exposure did not vanish altogether. A novel about Russian Latvians caught up in the pre-war purges, *My Greetings to Daugava* by Mārtiņš Krieviņš (in *Karogs* 1959), was published in book form 1961 with alterations. Eglons' *Smoke is Rising* (1960) painted a realistically drab picture of day-to-day

49. For details of the 1957–60 period, see Ekmanis 1978, pp. 235–88.
50. Edgars Damburs, in *Karogs*, 1967/6, as reported through *Looming*, 1967/11, in EE/BE, no. 4, p. 1 (1968).
51. Rasma Lāce, *Literatūra un māksla*, 30 March 1968; see Ekmanis 1972, p. 61.

working-class life, contrasting it with the lifestyle of the ruling class. Its condemnation by the LaCP Secretary, Augusts Voss, meant that Eglons did not get into print again until 1968. His fate seemed to reflect that of Latvian culture as a whole.[52]

National classics such as Bārda and Aspāzija, republished during the Thaw, were banned again in the early 1960s after attacks against an uncleansed literary heritage in the local press and even in *Pravda* (Moscow, 3 January 1960). Only in 1968, a half-dozen literary critics managed to publish articles protesting against the gross mistreatment of Bārda's and Aspāzija's work, and opened the way to gradual republication. In Estonia such struggles were fought more quietly, and were essentially won by 1968.

Poetry recovered first. Among the generation born in the 1930s, Ojārs Vācietis continued to publish. Always careful not to overstretch the regime's patience, his elliptic and penetrating *Time of the Cuckoo* (1968) was praised in Latvia and in the exile community. In clear protest against the merciless religion of progress, Vācietis claimed that:

> This century has a metallic voice
> And a steely hand
> And talks too much of: dominating
>   conquering
>   forcing
> And too little of protecting and preserving.[53]

Vācietis was joined by the impatient, impulsive Imants Ziedonis with *Sand of Land and Dreams* (1961), Vitauts Ļudēns, Māris Čaklais, Jānis Plotnieks, Vizma Belševica and Imants Auziņš. Among the silenced pre-war poets, Mirdza Bendrupe reappeared. In her "Voice Unceasing" (1969), she told people beyond the seas:

> Between us stand space and time.
> Oceans. Years.
> But we are one breath.
> We're kin.[54]

---

52. The extensive overview by Ekmanis 1978 mentions and describes numerous works from 1956 to 1960, but almost none from 1962 to 1966.

53. Ojārs Vācietis, "Naktsmājas," *Dzeguzlaiks* (Riga, 1968); translation by Vaira Vīķis-Freibergs, "Echoes of the Dainas and the Search for Identity in Contemporary Latvian Poetry," JBS, VI/I (Spring 1975), pp. 17–29.

54. Mirdza Bendrupe, in *Nerimas balss* (Riga, 1969); translation by Vīķis-Freibergs, p. 28.

The nation was repairing the broken ties with itself and with the world. Another major pre-war poet and deportee, Elza Stērste, also emerged from a long silence. A selection of her pre-war poems, announced in 1960, was finally published with some new poems in 1967.[55] The delayed generation (those born in the 1920s) which so powerfully boosted the early post-Thaw phase in Estonian poetry, was less conspicuous in Latvia.

Prose and drama needed a longer period than poetry in which to recover. However, by 1967 *The Investigator*, a short novel, immediately established Alberts Bels as a major writer acclaimed by émigré and (after a short hesitation) Soviet critics. The novel's main character, a 29-year-old sculptor, has a family which mirrors the recent fate of the whole nation: an Old Bolshevik grandfather shot by Stalin, a father bending before every political wind, one brother killed in the German army and another wounded fighting on the Soviet side. Many of his classmates were deported around 1947, but one of them, whose father was now declared to have been condemned in error, survived and returned, a toothless "old man at twenty".

He clasps me with both hands, and starts crying. "I hate, hate all of those who did the beating — hate them!" "Did they beat you, then?" I asked. I am a naive child, compared to Ivanovs, I do not know much yet. I thought that only the Gestapo beat people. "Not me," Ivanovs replies. "They beat my father, and it comes to the same!"[56]

The sculptor has decided to be optimistic about the future and avoid getting entangled in the past, while at the same time not forgetting it. But the past keeps resurfacing in his mind. He half-despises his weathervane father, without suspecting how much he and his father resemble each other. It's just that the circumstances are different. The importance of "picking the right birthdate" keeps coming up, just as it does in Vetemaa's *Musician*, also published in 1967 in Estonia. Bels' writings could make one believe "that not all the ideas of socialist realism must be discarded in order to write good literature." Among other prose writers who emerged in the late 1960s were Ija Meldere-

55. See Astrid Ivask, short review, BA, XLII/3 (Autumn 1968), p. 629; Ekmanis 1978, p. 217.

56. Alberts Bels, *Izmeklētājs* (Riga, 1967); translated from the Estonian translation (Tallinn, 1969), p. 73. See also Juris Silenieks, "Alberts Bels: In Search of Man," JBS, V/1 (Spring 1974), pp. 34–9; Ojārs Krātiņš, "Society and the Self in the Novels of Ilze Skipsna and Alberts Bels," BA, XLVII/3 (Autumn 1973), pp. 675–82, and short review, BA, XLII/3 (Autumn 1968), p. 628.

Dzērve, who interpreted the life of a Soviet manager in terms of the Daedalus myth (*Wax Wings*, 1967), and Andris Jakubāns whose very short stories form a mosaic of everyday life (*My White Guitar*, 1968).[57]

The most prominent dramatist of the period was Gunārs Priede. He first emerged before the Thaw in the officially prescribed style, but gradually evolved toward more varied techniques and a wider range of subject matter. Nonetheless, even by 1968, Latvian drama remained at what one critic abroad called "one of its lowest ebbs."[58]

In figurative art, a monumental straight-line painting style was developed in the late 1950s, and in the early 1960s this influenced all official art in the USSR. "Masters of the Land" (1960) by Edgars Iltners became one of the best-known examples of this style, combining Stalinist traditions with moderate modernization in the portrayal of marching men with clenched fists, who were presumably meant to represent collective farmers. More modern and politically disengaged approaches also came to be accepted gradually, especially in the graphic arts of the generation born in the 1930s (Gunārs Krollis, Semjons Šegelmans).

The Reemergence of Lithuanian Culture.   Developments in Lithuania ran parallel to those in Estonia, and in prose writing even preceded them. Furthermore, Lithuanian graphic arts, film and urban architecture achieved wide recognition by the late 1960s.[59]

As in Estonia and Latvia, poets were among the first to react to the Thaw. Seeking to update the socialist-realist form, some established figures began to shift from Stalinist rigidity to individual themes and a more experimental style. Justinas Marcinkevičius, a talented and unorthodox poet, attempted in his *Twentieth Spring* (1956) to present real social problems and their resolutions in the spirit of faith in the official progressive force of history, and to supplement clichés with subtle lyricism and a lively, easy-flowing prosody. *Devil's Bridge*

---

57. See Gunārs Irbe, short reviews in BA, XLII/2 (Summer, 1968), pp. 477–8, and XLIII/3 (Autumn 1969), p. 635. For other brief analyses of various Soviet Latvian works up to 1968, see also BA, XLII (1968), pp. 162, 316, 478 and 627; XLIII (1969), pp. 269 and 458; and XLIV (1970), p. 164.

58. Juris Silenieks, short review in BA, XLIII/2 (Summer 1969), p. 458.

59. A comprehensive overview of Lithuanian literature in 1956–66 is given by Vélaikis. A Soviet view can be found in *Istoriia litovskoi literatury* (Vilnius, 1977) and Algimantas Buchis (Bučys), *Roman i sovremennost: stanovlenie i razvitie litovskogo sovetskogo romana* (Moscow, 1977).

(1957) by Algimantas Baltakis added a new youthful flair, but retained a rather traditional declamatory style. However, the only Lenin Prize of the period went to Eduardas Mieželaitis for his skillful and expressive, though at times somewhat contrived, improvisations in *Man* (1962). This product of his implicit belief that Soviet poetry could become "modernistic" without losing its basic function as a vehicle of propaganda received wide acclaim throughout the Soviet world.

While Marcinkevičius, Baltakis and Mieželaitis can be clearly placed in the first and second general categories of literary reactions to the Thaw mentioned above (changes in form and in the content of socialist realism), some younger poets like Alfonsas Maldonis began to emancipate themselves entirely from socialist realism. In particular, Janina Degutytė in her first collection *Days are Presents* (1960) related her feelings and moods to nature and landscape. Judita Vaičiūnaitė displayed a fresh childlike outlook toward life in *As Green Wine* (1963). By the end of decade, some had clearly abandoned any attempt to resolve the dichotomy between art and politics. The first edition of Sigitas Geda's *Steps* (1966) is a curious hybrid including poetic homage to Lenin and Castro:

> The continents fall into Lenin's step,
> The world will fit into his straight finger!
> Fidel is strolling through Cuba's countryside,
> The laced shoes of the bearded one squeak![60]

However, most of the slender volume is devoted to a paean to continuity with the past, a notion which is hard to politicize:

> The steep eyes of the little wooden gods —
> Are they not my eyes,
> Not yours?
>
> How close you are,
> My ancestors![61]

New trends in prose writing appeared in the early 1960s, although political relaxation had already been marked in 1957 by Vytautas Rimkevičius' *The Students*, which even described the huge pro-independence demonstration on All Souls' Eve, 1956.[62] At first,

60. Sigitas Geda, *Pėdos* (Vilnius, 1966), p. 5.
61. *Ibid.*, p. 13.
62. Excerpts from Vytautas Rimkevičius' *Studentai* (Vilnius, 1957), with comments by Thomas Remeikis and Rimvydas Šilbajoris, in *Lituanus*, VI/2 (September 1960), pp. 68–74. For the 1960s, see Vélaikis, pp. 30–40; Bronius B. Vaškelis, "The

prose works seemed to be intent on discovering a more modern form of socialist realism, and the indifferently successful *Red Roses Bloom* (1959) by Alfonsas Bieliauskas and some of the early descriptions of war and guerrilla resistance by Mykolas Sluckis (1958) fit into this category. By the mid-1960s both writers were seeking to fuse modern forms with a socialist-realist essence. In his novel *Steps to the Sky* (1963), set in the turbulent countryside of postwar collectivization, Sluckis uses the Indriūnas family as the archetype of Lithuania's peasantry. The story unfolds through the perspective of an idealistic member of the intelligentsia, perhaps a self-portrait of the author. Although the hero is idealized for his faith in humanity and a socially better future, he discovers that social realities in the village are much more complex than the simplistic officially sanctioned version would have it. The peasantry's attachment to the land is pervasive and insurmountable. The head of the smallholder family sacrifices his loved ones to his perception of what is necessary to maintain land ownership, and tragedy is inevitable. One of the novel's most surprising facets was its portrayal, perhaps for the first time in Soviet Lithuanian literature, of the postwar partisans as human beings, albeit ones motivated by an alien ideology.

Sluckis subsequently pioneered the introduction of stream-of-consciousness narration into the Lithuanian novel in *Adam's Apple* (1966) and *My Harbor is Turbulent* (1968). Both bring a critical focus on problems among the contemporary intelligentsia, delving into the bureaucratic mentality and various facets of urban life.[63] Bieliauskas subsequently applied a stream-of-consciousness technique in *Romance in Kaunas* (1966), which treats the new Soviet bureaucracy, including its seamy side. While apparently bold and daring in its contention that truth — even Soviet truth — has more facets than could be inferred from official ideology, his novel also presented a "correct" historical viewpoint, suggesting to the reader that present shortcomings are merely a passing phase in the development of Soviet morality.

The most notable Lithuanian prose work which sought to fuse a socialist-realist essence with the complexities of the real world and to

---

Short Stories of Romualdas Lankauskas," in Arvids Ziedonis *et al.* (eds), *Baltic Literature and Linguistics* (Columbus, Ohio, 1973); Ilona Gražytė-Maziliauskienė, "Variations on the Theme of Dehumanization in the Short Stories of Juozas Aputis," BA, XL VII/3 (Autumn 1973), pp. 695–701.

63. For a study of the work of Sluckis, see L. A. Terakopian, *Mikolas Slutskis* [Mykolas Sluckis] — *Ocherk tvorchestva* (Moscow, 1976).

present them in contemporary form was Jonas Avyžius' *The Village at the Crossroads* (1964), which attempted seriously to portray the shortcomings of collective farms and the full moral as well as social chaos brought by collectivization into the lives of the peasants. It gives an appearance of moral courage through raising tough questions. However, its point — the ultimate resolution of the problems raised — is not unacceptable to official orthodoxy. An individual needs to make a conscious decision to join in the new order of things — continued resistance will yield only more bloodshed, which is unjustifiable historically. Perhaps as a good example of this new type of socialist realism, the novel received considerable all-Union publicity, and Avyžius' subsequent novel, *The Time of the Emptying of Homesteads* (1970), set in the time of the German wartime occupation, likewise received official attention and praise. Not long after its appearance, Avyžius was awarded the Lenin Prize.

A similar approach appeared also in the novels of Vytautas Bubnys. His guerrillas are portrayed as human beings — idealistic in their own nationalist way, but they also come to realize that continued opposition will only result in more misery without any historical justification.

Some Lithuanian prose works also clearly passed beyond the realm of socialist realism. Jonas Mikelinskas made his debut in 1960 with *The Old Man under the Clock*, which tried to analyze psychological crises and subtle conflicts with a somewhat detached curiosity. With *Wandering Sands* (1960), Romualdas Lankauskas introduced into Lithuanian literature a melancholy, disillusioned and alienated individual. This was followed in 1963 by two novels, *In the Middle of a Wide Field*, an objective depiction of the senseless horror of a war where Germans as well as Soviets die without knowing why, and *A Bridge into the Sea*, which viewed childhood reminiscences as "our only inviolable possession." The latter was severely criticized, and not published in book form.[64] Two works of Juozas Aputis (*The Flowering Bread of the Bees*, 1963, and *September Birds*, 1967) were only reluctantly published, because of alleged subjectivism and pessimism. Another far-reaching departure from socialist realism in both style and content was Icchokas Meras' *A Tie Lasts a Wink* (1963), in which a flashback technique is applied to describe the thoughts of a Jewish prisoner playing a fatal chess game with a Nazi guard.

64. Vėlaikis, p. 35; R. Lankauskas, "Tiltas į jūrą," *Pergalė*, 1963/3, p. 22.

The only notable exception to such trends appears in the work of Juozas Baltušis, whose literary career began before the war. Although his populist approach had never fallen foul of the dictates of socialist realism and his loyalty to the party was never questioned, his literary output became less during the Stalin years. His most notable work during the Thaw was the novel *Sold Summers* (two parts, 1957 and 1969), a realistic view of social conditions among the pre-war peasantry, depicted through the consciousness of a child of poor parents. Although the novel can be said to be eminently acceptable to the classical canons of socialist realism, it also became genuinely popular through its masterly recreation of peasant speech. His subsequent work continued in a similar vein, though he fell into some disfavor with the ideological establishment for the favorable impression of the United States, after he had made a trip there, conveyed by *In the Paths of Fathers and Brothers* (1967).

The ferment among the Lithuanian intelligentsia during the early 1960s comes through in the work of Justinas Marcinkevičius, *The Pine Tree that Laughed* (1961), and in the circumstances of its appearance.[65] It has been claimed that the book was written at the request of the KGB, which recognized the talent of Marcinkevičius for seeming to the intelligentsia to be "one of the boys" while actually always selling himself out to the party ideologues. Several of the protagonists were readily identifiable as prominent younger members of the intelligentsia. One of them, an émigré at the time, claimed that entire passages, set in dialogue, were taken verbatim from the record of his interrogation by the KGB, which he signed. The interrogation followed an abortive attempt by some members of the intelligentsia to assemble a Lithuanian issue of Aleksandr Ginzburg's *samizdat* publication *Sintaksis* in Moscow. Marcinkevičius' book appeared in the aftermath, was widely discussed, and quickly sold out. By 1963 it had been translated into Russian, Latvian and Estonian, and achieved some attention throughout the USSR and Eastern Europe. Its format may have inspired the pioneering short novels of Vetemaa in Estonia and Bels in Latvia, in 1965–7. While a main object of interest to younger readers, and a target of subsequent attack, in the novel was German existentialism, there were interesting parallels with an earlier official attack on student interest in living Marxism:

65. Justinas Marcinkevičius, in *Pergalė*, 1961/8, p. 38; also published in book form the same year.

Some students, with the help of dictionaries, are reading the works of Western aesthetes. . . . They are interested in the writings of the Hungarian revisionist G. Lukacs, whose works have reached our republic in German translation [sic]. In the mean time, we have not produced any works for our youth in their native language which reveal the nature of such bourgeois aestheticism.[66]

Socialism, Communism or the party never received a mention in *The Pine Tree* — the lines of attack were reactionary rather than Marxist.

History was used in drama to reflect the current Soviet dilemma between art and politics. Perhaps hoping that the issues of the present would attain a timeless immortality when expressed on stage by prominent figures from the past, Marcinkevičius wrote the play *Mindaugas* (1968), a study of the philosophy of history set in a recreation of the harsh rule of the founder of the medieval Lithuanian state. It clearly falls into the second category of literary works of the period, attempting to reconcile contemporary social problems and even personally reprehensible actions with long-term positive benefits. On one level, Mindaugas can be said to have been a murderer and adulterer; on another, he is a national hero. Juozas Grušas, a pre-war Catholic novelist, broke a long silence with a comedy in 1955, and continued with romanticized historical dramas such as *Herkus Mantas* (1957), a dramatization of a thirteenth-century revolt by the Old Prussians against the invading Teutonic Knights. He reached psychological realism with the landmark *Love, Jazz and the Devil* (1967).

Moving even further away from didactic realism toward the theater of fantasy and the grotesque, Kazys Saja reached a peak in "socialist allegory of the absurd" with *The Maniac* (1966), *The Orator* (1966) and *The Prophet Jonah* (1968).[67] In the first, a maniac commandeers a train because he is seeking to unmask a maniac who is planning to take over the train — a transparent parody of Stalin's takeover of the Revolution.

66. Kostas Korsakas, Third Congress of Soviet Lithuanian writers (21–23 January 1959), as reported in ACEN VI, 112.

67. Mardi Valgemäe, "Death of a Sea Gull: The Absurd in Finno-Baltic Drama," BA, XLVI/2 (Summer 1972), pp. 374–9; Tomas Venclova, "Echoes of the Theater of the Absurd and of the 'Theater of Cruelty' in Modern Lithuania (K. Saja, J. Glinskis)," in H. Birnbaum and T. Eekman (eds), *Fiction and Drama in Eastern and Southeastern Europe* (Los Angeles, 1980), pp. 429–41. English translations of Kazys Saja's *The Orator* and *The Maniac* in *Lituanus* XIII/3 (Fall 1967), pp. 29–71, and XIV/4 (Winter 1968), pp. 73–94, respectively.

Do you know how many people have already been locked up in the other cars? Five in some, seven in some. And how many do *we* have? A mere one-and-a-half. . . .

— But after all, there is only one maniac!

— However, we do not know who he is. Everyone looks the same. Even so, we are all quite humane, aren't we?[68]

On the whole, the emergence of a national theatrical tradition as a key element in the country's cultural life proved to be a significant and lasting development of the Thaw. The theater in the provincial center of Panevėžys, headed by the veteran director Juozas Miltinis who had received his training in pre-war France, achieved considerable renown and became a sort of cultural mecca whose performances attracted a wide audience from all over the country. The official cultural establishment rewarded this popularity with a modern building to house the company in 1968.

Along with the other Baltic republics, Lithuania became a leading center of the rebirth of graphic arts in the Soviet Union. The tradition of stained glass, which had been banned because of its obvious connections with the Church, was revived. In architecture, the Žirmūnai residential district in Vilnius was the first in the USSR to apply Finnish and Scandinavian city-planning concepts. The achievement was twofold: the concepts were approved, and the actual construction was carried out with Soviet materials.

The Lithuanian film industry, which up to that time had hardly produced anything of note, began to explore relevant themes. In 1966, two rather surprising films by Soviet standards, *No One Wanted to Die* by Vytautas Žalakevičius and *Steps to the Sky* by Raimondas Vabalas, treated the extremely sensitive issue of the postwar guerrilla resistance. Although reviews stressed their ideological correctness, the films did not lack artistic merit. It was also possible to reach interpretations which could be ideologically questionable. While *Steps to the Sky* received somewhat less praise, perhaps because of a greater subtlety in political differentiation, both won Soviet cinematographic prizes.[69] Another Lithuanian film, *The Last Day of Vacation*

68. Kazys Saja, *Mažosios pjesės* (Vilnius, 1968), p. 152. For brief analyses of various Soviet Lithuanian works up to 1968, see also BA, XLII (1968), pp. 479–80 and 629–31; XLIII (1969), pp. 297 and 636; and XLIV (1970), pp. 166–7 and 347.

69. M. Maltsene (Malcienė), *Kino sovetskoi Litvy* (Leningrad, 1980), pp. 67–74 and 112–16.

by Arūnas Žebriūnas, was awarded the Grand Prix at the 1966 Youth
Film Festival at Cannes.

Soviet Socio-Cultural Pressure. A renewed Soviet anti-nationalism
campaign in the early 1960s sought to replace the generally perceived
feelings of national distinctiveness with an all-Union identification.[70]
Accordingly, efforts to stress the community of the Baltic peoples
with the rest of the USSR once again increased. Grandiose all-Union
development projects in Central Asia or Siberia again assumed prominence in the mass media. An earlier Virgin Lands campaign had died
down, perhaps because it had been badly received. Now populariza-
tions of such projects reappeared. In June 1962, it was reported that
10,000 youths from Lithuania were helping in Kazakhstan with the
harvest, and large numbers had gone to other places.[71] In March the
same year, Latvian youths took part in road-building projects at
Kuibyshev, and Komsomol members from Liepāja worked as construction laborers in Saratov on the Volga. Recruitment articles with
titles such as "Siberia is Romantic," "Siberia and I" or "The North
Awaits Strong Men" proliferated.

Although its facilities were still quite underdeveloped, internal
Soviet tourism started to serve as a vehicle for the mingling of Soviet
peoples. The Baltic republics, endowed with attractive beaches, wood-
lands and lakes, began to be flooded with seasonal visitors, mainly
from the Russian republic. By 1968 it was reported that about a
million summer vacationers from the RSFSR had visited Lithuania[72]
(which has the least extensive beaches of the three republics).

Glorification of Russia and of things Russian continued as an intrinsic element of the stress on internationalism. As the Latvian party journal *Padomju Latvijas komunists* stressed in August 1960:

One should explain the force that stands behind the friendship of nations,
the extent of the assistance rendered by the brotherly Soviet republics, and
principally by the trusted friend of the Latvians — the Russian nation — in
reconstructing the Latvian economy and culture.

The campaign also involved a limited return to a Stalinist use of
history in stressing the alleged age-old affinity of the Baltic peoples
for Russia. As Vasilii Savchenko, a Russian historian at the Latvian

70. Cf. M. Suslov, *Pravda*, 18 July 1960.
71. *Komjaunimo tiesa*, 9 January 1962.
72. *Tiesa*, 10 December 1968.

Academy of Sciences, asserted, "Many times, Russians were assigned by history the role of being other people's saviors." Similar themes appeared in Lithuania. The Chairman of the Presidium of the Supreme Soviet, Justas Paleckis, perhaps mixed his metaphors in *Thoughts about the Elder Brother* (1959) when he compared Russia "to a wise and good mother who unceasingly cares about her children."[73] The historian Kostas Navickas produced a booklet on *The Historical Significance of the Leninist Nationalities Policy to the Lithuanian Nation* (1960), and somewhat later, the doyen of official Lithuanian historiography, Juozas Žiugžda, published a survey of Lithuanian ties with its "historical" ally, the Great Russian Nation. Considerable factual contortions were necessary in view of the long medieval rivalry between Moscow and Lithuania, as well as the role of Imperial Russia in the eighteenth-century partitions of Poland-Lithuania and its suppression of the nineteenth-century national uprisings. A new aspect of the integration of Baltic history into a tighter all-Union pattern was the glorification of the abortive Soviet Baltic republics of 1918–19 as precursors of the 1940 variety. This had been avoided in Stalin's time, as it might have required mention of some leading Baltic Communists like Jānis Rudzutaks and Roberts Eidemanis (Latvia), Zigmas Angarietis and General Vytautas Putna (Lithuania), and Jaan Anvelt and Hans Pöögelmann (Estonia), who had been victims of the Great Purge.

In 1961, Khrushchev in person complained (at the January Plenum of the CPSU CC) about the planned restoration work in Lithuania of castles which even the feudal lords themselves had abandoned, and pointed to ideological mistakes in appraising the traditions of Lithuania's past. He was particularly incensed when restoration of Trakai Castle, the capital of the medieval Lithuanian state (20 km. southwest of Vilnius), which had been in ruins since early modern times, was started.[74]

Three years later, the writings of the historian Juozas Jurginis were attacked for the minimal importance they accorded to the historical interaction with Russia and the faulty application of Marxist periodization, which had been set up on the basis of the Russian past. However, the full canon of Stalinist historiography was not restored.

Glorification of the military, which intensified in the 1960s, could be seen as another element in the stress on all-Union ties. The Red

---

73. Justas Paleckis, *Mintys apie vyresniji̧ broli̧* (Vilnius, 1959), p. 8.
74. *Pravda*, 22 January 1961. Speech of N.S. Khrushchev to plenum of CPSU CC, 17 January 1961.

Army and Navy, organized along centralized principles, could serve as an integrating element among non-Russians. Articles on the heroism of the Second World War and the friendship between Soviet forces and Baltic Pioneers and students proliferated. In February 1956, the Lithuanian party magazine *Komunistas* reproached writers for "trends toward pacifism and an abstract negation of war." Groups of "young cosmonauts" or "young border guards" were formed throughout the Soviet Union under the tutelage of officers to popularize the military among children.

There was a shift in emphasis on the roles of the native languages in the republics. This became particularly important, since national feelings among the Balts were largely based on linguistic distinctiveness. Officially, all languages of the USSR were equal, and during the Thaw this became more of a reality. A reaction accompanied the anti-nationalism campaign. One Soviet theorist depicted the goal of Soviet nationality policy as a melting-pot for "the creation of a single nation with a single language."[75]

The linguistic reaction appeared most strident in Latvia after the Berklāvs purge. LaCP Secretary Augusts Voss exuded love, respect and gratitude toward the "brotherly Russian nation" in an extensive editorial in *Cīņa* (10 June 1960). He admonished Latvians to learn Russian because it was "the language of socialist culture, of the most progressive literature and art, and of twentieth-century technology and progress." However, he observed that some comrades "lean toward national seclusion and do not support the progressive influence of the Russian language." All speeches at the joint session of the Latvian Supreme Soviet and CC held on 22 July 1960 were delivered in Russian. Streets in Riga began to be given Russian names. Literary evenings conducted in Russian proliferated, along with visits by prominent guests from Moscow at cultural gatherings.

The cry for vigilance against imperialists and bourgeois-nationalist agents and ideologies resounded through public pronouncements on cultural matters. Attempts to restore the old slogans of socialist realism — a projection of the current party line in the arts and a glorification of the mythical new Soviet man and Soviet patriotism — kept appearing in the mass media. Complaints were expressed about modernism and "a reversion to the old decadent formalistic schools and the outdated art of the bourgeoisie."[76] Frequently the absence of

75. A.A. Isupov, *Natsionalnyi sostav naseleniia SSSR* (Moscow, 1964), p. 9.
76. *Sirp ja Vasar*, 24 February 1961.

Soviet themes was lamented. Lithuania's graphic arts section at the 1960 Baltic Art Exposition in Moscow was faulted for an insufficient representation of proper historic, revolutionary and "international" themes. The Lithuanian State Publishing House was publicly reprimanded in 1961 for "uncritical" acceptance of a manuscript on lake research which gave too much prominence to the earlier work of émigré scientists, neglecting Soviet studies.

Expressions of local identification came under attack. In October 1962, *Komunistas* castigated the allegedly inaccurate and narrow-minded use of the term "our literature" in reference to Lithuanian literature; such an expression could supposedly only refer to the literature of the USSR as a whole. Lankauskas' short story, *A Bridge into the Sea*, was denounced for its numerous references to Lithuania as "the green country covered with the bones of forefathers who for centuries fought for their freedom." In early 1961, Voldemārs Sauleskalns and Voldemārs Melnis were dismissed from the Latvian Writers' Association. Three other writers (including, surprisingly, two Russians) received "strict party censure" for bourgeois nationalism.[77]

Attacks in the field of literature were paralleled in the other arts. The composer Vytautas Klova, who was preparing an opera on the theme of the Battle of Grünwald (Tannenberg) in 1410 which ended the threat of the Teutonic Knights to the medieval Lithuanian state, was faulted for seeking inspiration "behind the thick walls of the castle at Marienburg or the battlefields at Tannenberg," and his colleague Rimvydas Žigaitis was criticized for working on an opera based on Mickiewicz's long romantic poem *Konrad Wallenrod*.[78] The Kaunas State Opera was criticized for staging works by Lehar, Offenbach, Gounod and Strauss while ignoring current Soviet work.[79]

The writer Mykolas Sluckis was in effect subjected to a public self-criticism session at the 1963 Congress of the Lithuanian Writers' Union. The event — staged, perhaps significantly, in the Vilnius Russian Drama Theater — was attended by First Secretary Antanas Sniečkus. According to accounts current among Lithuanian intelligentsia circles, Sniečkus was late for his speech — having been, as he claimed, delayed by some agricultural business. He liked to present the image of a good farmer, and apologized in a rather Khrushchev-like

77. *Literatūra un māksla*, 8 April 1961.
78. *Literatūra ir menas*, 11 February 1961.
79. *Ibid.*, 4 April 1964.

manner: that morning, he is said to have claimed, the leadership had been concerned with manure, and now it would proceed to remove the dung from literature.

The exhibition of young artists at the Sixth Congress of the Union of Lithuanian Artists (December 1966) evoked another party blast directed against works permeated with "alien aesthetic conception," and even against "striving for world standards" if this did not help to shape the common national characteristics of Soviet art.[80]

Folk ensembles of song and dance were admonished to perform Soviet songs in place of archaic folksongs. In early 1960, the popular Latvian ethnographic ensemble *Saulgrieži* was disbanded as an undesirable propagator of nationalist ideology.

The poem "This Year's March" (1963) by Justinas Marcinkevičius unmistakably reflects the mood of uncertainty which had crept into the national cultural scene by the early 1960s:

> Maybe it is not spring, maybe only
> A new variety of winter?
> The earth appears through snow and frost
> As the shore of the sun.[81]

Consolidation of Cultural Autonomy.   The absence of Stalinist methods of control, however, weakened the attempts to re-impose orthodoxy in the realm of culture. The yearning of the younger cultural figures for a reunion with the mainstream of Western culture could hardly be dissipated by threats, admonitions or special seminars attended by party and Komsomol dignitaries designed to explain the party line on national characteristics in art or the role of the party leadership in creative work. Well publicized trips by young writers for inspiration in the Virgin Lands or Siberian construction projects yielded little results. The anti-nationalism campaign could not reverse the cultural revival which had begun with the Thaw.

Celebrations of particularly significant native cultural anniversaries came to be tolerated, provided that some ideological genuflections were made. The celebration in 1964 of the 250th birth anniversary of the Lithuanian poet Kristijonas Donelaitis tried to portray this eighteenth-century Lutheran pastor in East Prussia as a pioneer of socialist realism. A similar approach was taken to Jānis Rainis, the most eminent figure in Latvian poetry, whose birth centenary was

---

80. *Ibid.*, 24 December 1966.
81. Justinas Marcinkevičius, *Duoną raikančios rankos* (Vilnius, 1963), p. 77.

celebrated with commemorative evenings at the Opera and other theaters, and by the unveiling of a large monument in Riga. Rainis had been a member of Parliament and Minister of Education under the independent republic.

One reason for the failure of the cultural repression was an inability of the cultural authorities to agree consistently on what was permissible. The Estonian modernist composer Arvo Pärt took one of the seven first prizes awarded at the All-Union Final Competition for Young Composers held in November 1962 and involving some 1,200 works, although he had been criticized the previous March by Tikhon Khrennikov, perennial head of the all-Union Society of Composers, for his susceptibility to foreign influences. In popular culture, too, a similar lack of definition could be seen in 1964 when there was a controversy in Lithuania over the twist, a dance then popular in the West. A sign at a Vilnius youth center read: "Dancing the twist on our premises is strictly forbidden." The center's manager observed that "the twist is an unrealistic, unaesthetic, lewd dance of young Americans of a wealthy background. We have to uproot that dance by its roots," but a critic argued that the twist was no better and no worse than any other dance, and wondered whether proscription would stop it.[82]

The failure to reintroduce cultural orthodoxy also stemmed in large part from the mood of the indigenous populations. Cultural orthodoxy was identified with Russification. The Balts frequently refused to speak Russian in public, even when they were capable of doing so. Parents opposed intermarriage with Russians. Baltic tourists refused to pass for "Russians" in the East Bloc countries, and even managed to complain in the press of being introduced as such when abroad. Under these circumstances, any talk of a common Soviet style or school was immediately identified with attempts to impose Russian culture. Conversely, the striving for Western styles came to be viewed as cultural opposition to Russification.

Massive demonstrations of national cultural solidarity were manifested in the Latvian and Estonian song festivals. These important events in the national cultures, dating from the national renaissance in the nineteenth century, emerged as cultural expressions of non-Soviet moods. A large postwar Latvian festival, held at Daugavpils in July 1959, involved 5,000 singers, 2,500 musicians and dancers, and an audience of 70,000. The only principal conductor of the pre-war

---

82. *Meno saviveikla*, 1964/11, p. 23.

festivals still alive was asked to come to the podium to conduct a song and was rapturously received, as were several songs by émigré composers that were included in the program. The next Latvian festival, held in Riga the following summer, was billed as a festival of "friendship of nations," but the Red Army garrison chorus and orchestra drew little applause — unlike the Lithuanian and Estonian folk-dances which were greeted with great enthusiasm. The popular Latvian song "With a battle-cry on your lips," dating from the 1905 Revolution, was inexplicably dropped from the program. In 1965, the only encore was for the song "Jāņu vakars," about the summer solstice holiday which had been officially abolished after being allowed during the Thaw.[83]

Estonian festivals were even more massive, and followed a similar pattern. The 1965 festival involved 26,000 singers and drew an audience of 120,000 — one-eighth of the nation! The song "My homeland is my love," which had become the unofficial anthem of the Estonian people, was repeated at the insistence of a standing audience.[84] Although the tradition of massive song festivals was not so long-established in Lithuania as in Latvia or Estonia, the same intensity of national fervor was exhibited at such events. As in Estonia, a particular song, "Lithuania dear, you are my homeland," emerged as the *de facto* anthem of the Lithuanian people.

The creative intelligentsia soon learned to live with the new ebb and flow. The attacks, criticism, "opposition to one-sided depictions of the recent past in literary works and exaggeration of shortcomings in Soviet life," and warnings from party leaders and artistic hacks continued sporadically. In part, these might have served as ritual incantations to demonstrate alertness on the cultural front. The constant probing continued to test the regime's tolerance of efforts to preserve a national identity and culture. The tolerance of experimentation in the satellite People's Democracy countries provided some relief by making it possible to argue that modernism or a contemporary style were not necessarily anti-socialist. The anti-nationalism campaign in the Baltic republics abated after the fall of

83. ACEN, VII, pp. 79–80; IX, pp. 77–8, 109.

84. The number of singers was 25,800, according to *Nõukogude Eesti: entsüklopeediline teatmeteos* (Tallinn, 1975), p. 236. Including dance and gymnastics groups, the figure rises to 31,400, according to A. Mesikäpp *et al.*, *Laulusajand, 1869–1969* (Tallinn, 1969; no page numbers), which also confirms the standing-up event. The unbelievably large audience actually doubled to a quarter of a million at the next festival in 1969, according to Olt, p. 30 — almost a quarter of the nation.

Khrushchev. As a result, the late 1960s saw a great expansion of cultural possibilities.

The conditions for this development proved to be most auspicious in Lithuania. The local regime, the machine of Sniečkus — by now the doyen of republic First Secretaries — felt most secure against the political pitfalls of charges of cultural laxity. The quiet process of nativization of the party apparatus had continued unabated and possibly some of the new *apparatchiks* felt a certain sympathy for cultural modernization and "Westernism."

Greater cultural latitude prevailed in the Baltic republics than in Russia, due partly to lack of scrutiny by the world press. In Moscow, Western correspondents had become careful observers and commentators on any unusual or unexpected developments, a circumstance which increased the caution of the cultural bureaucracy for fear of political consequences. The lack of knowledge of the Baltic languages, both by the Moscow bureaucrats and the Western newsmen, and the infrequent visits by the latter to the Baltic republics insulated these cultures from scrutiny and thus lessened their politicization. While Camus was published in Estonia and subsequently in Lithuania without comment, this could hardly have happened in Moscow.

In sum, the decade after the Thaw was a time of clear re-emergence of national, Western-oriented and modernistic aspects of culture. While the organizational form saw little change toward autonomy, the content bore witness to an effective increase in cultural autonomy. Under Stalin only a few specified topics had generally been allowed, and everything not explicitly authorized was forbidden. By 1968 quite a number of topics remained on the forbidden list; but everything not explicitly forbidden was allowed, or was at least negotiable. For the national cultures, it meant the difference between suffocation and ability to develop within limits. These limits were set by a balance of forces and wills between, on one side, Moscow's desire to control the republics' cultural life and, on the other, each republic's desire and willingness to struggle for cultural autonomy. From the vantage-point of 1968 as compared to 1953, the struggle for cultural autonomy in the Baltic republics appeared quite successful.

Expansion of Contacts Abroad

An important psychological factor introduced by the Thaw was a reopening of foreign contacts. The Baltic populations had been all but cut off from the West since 1945, and vice versa. In the mid-1950s,

Soviet publications aimed at foreign audiences began to feature the Baltic republics. Selected foreign groups began to visit Riga and Tallinn. Riga was opened to foreign tourists in 1957, Vilnius and Tallinn in 1959, but apart from special exemptions, most of the territory of the three republics remained closed to foreign travel.

The appearance of foreign visitors was accompanied by the establishment in all three republics of Societies for Friendship and Cultural Ties with Foreign Countries, to arrange for exchanges of artists, tourists and publications. These societies were complemented by republic branches of the all-Union Societies for Friendship with specific countries, such as the USSR-France Society, which were responsible for enriching the cultural offerings in the three republics by inviting foreign performers. While most were from Eastern Europe, some Americans like the pianist Van Cliburn and the baritone Leonard Warren performed in Latvia. In June 1964, on its second visit to the USSR, the *Comédie française* gave a performance of Racine's *Andromaque* in Riga. Educational programs involving foreigners were also arranged. In 1962, a one-week seminar for teachers of French in all three republics was held in Riga, with instructors from France.

As a neighbor with a shared frontier and one with a friendly socialist government, Poland took on a special role in Lithuania's cultural life as a window to the outside. The shared Catholic milieu and, to a lesser extent, a common history enhanced Poland's position as a bridge to the West. Polish publications, despite the constraints of censorship, were much less fettered than the local output, and as a rule they were available. While Joyce, Kafka and Proust were still unmentionable locally, an intimation of their work could be gleaned by way of Poland. Two special Polish publications in 1957 on Lithuanian art and literature, issued in conjunction with an exchange of folk-art festivals between the two countries, praised the works of the pre-war period and almost disregarded more recent Lithuanian production. *Tiesa*, on 18 June 1957, carried a complaint by an "official" writer at such "unfair treatment of Soviet Lithuanian literature."

By the end of the 1960s, some Polish publications were no longer available in Lithuania. A general history of Lithuania published in Poland in 1967, for instance, contained too many items that were objectionable in Soviet eyes. Subscribers in Lithuania could not receive their copies, and these had to filter into the republic by way of Moscow or other parts of the USSR.

Although a good portion of Lithuania's Polish minority had been repatriated in the 1940s, enough remained for there to be a continuous flow of personal visits. The better-stocked Polish market for clothes and consumer goods thus began to supply a limited Lithuanian market, particularly for more contemporary Western-style clothing. Prayerbooks and Bibles, even though written in a foreign language, were also eagerly imported. By 1968, Polish TV, available to two-thirds of Lithuania, had become particularly popular because of its greater variety and freshness of programming.

Finland, though not an East Bloc country, assumed an analogous role for Estonia, especially after 1965 when the boat service between Helsinki and Tallinn, broken since 1940, was reestablished. However, the main beneficiaries were Finns coming to Tallinn on short visits for a drinking spree. The closeness of the Estonian and Finnish languages eased contact, but Finnish publications were less readily tolerated by Soviet authorities than those from Poland. Finnish TV could be picked up in northern Estonia. In 1964, Finland's President Kekkonen came on a visit to Tallinn — the first visit to the postwar Baltic republics by a Western head of state.[85]

The opening of the Baltic republics to foreign contacts also enabled some of their residents to catch a glimpse of the outside world. Initially, only carefully selected individuals were allowed to travel abroad, starting with the Soviet-appointed Archbishops Gustavs Tūrs of Latvia and Jaan Kiivit of Estonia, who visited Britain in 1955 and the United States in 1956. In 1958 the Latvian First Secretary, Kalnbērziņš, and the Chairman of the Latvian Council of Ministers, Vilis Lācis, visited the Brussels Expo. Baltic sports teams began to appear in international competitions. In 1958 the Latvian basketball team captured the European championship.

Even a trickle of legal emigration appeared. In 1956 ten elderly women from Latvia were allowed to join their children abroad. The stringent limits were dramatized by the Estonian sailor Viktor Jaanimets who, on 10 October 1959, defected from the Soviet ship *Baltika* when it was at anchor in New York harbor, on the occasion of Khrushchev's visit.

In spite of occasional defections, the numbers of Baltic performing groups allowed to tour foreign countries, and of individuals allowed to visit relatives abroad, continued to increase throughout the 1960s. In 1962, the Estonian Academic Male Choir was allowed for the first

85. *Teataja*, 7 March 1964.

time to perform in Helsinki, possibly in reaction to a similar performance by the refugee New York choir. Some of the performers began to be recognized internationally. The Lithuanian String Quartet was placed second in a Brussels competition in 1965.

The opening of the three Baltic capital cities to foreign travel affected the regime's policies on relations with the sizeable bodies of emigrants in the West, particularly those who had left in 1944–5. The emphasis changed from the postwar invitations to return to the fatherland to promotion and regulation of rather one-sided cultural contacts, with some intelligence activity included. The earlier committees for repatriation went through a mutation in the late 1950s into local "Groups of Initiators" within the USSR Committee for the Return to the Homeland and for Cultural Relations with Countrymen Abroad. Special newspapers were aimed at an émigré audience, such as the Lithuanian *Tèvynès balsas* (voice of the homeland). They were mailed free of charge from East Berlin, and were unavailable within the Baltic republics. They could afford to treat issues not mentioned by the local press, such as religion and some aspects of pre-war history. By 1964 the repatriation issue was dropped completely.

The new cultural contacts were accompanied by attacks on refugee political organizations and activities which had earlier been largely ignored. The Soviets appeared to be especially touchy regarding efforts by refugees which resulted in US Congressional resolutions on Baltic self-determination. In order to discredit refugee activists, several individuals prominent in pre-war society were harnessed to make anti-émigré statements in *Izvestiia* (e.g. Vilhelms Munters, the pre-war Latvian Minister of Foreign Affairs, 8 April 1962). While such declarations had little effect on refugee activity, they did reveal considerable information on refugee organizations to readers in the Baltic republics.

After the reopening of contact, many expatriates began to send parcels to relatives and friends in the home-countries, and the resale of such gifts, especially clothes, in the consumer-goods-starved Soviet milieu made some individuals quite wealthy by Soviet standards. The regime reacted by press attacks against those who had "lost the dignity of Soviet people and stretch a begging hand for some foreign rags,"[86] and by court actions against unearned income. In one instance, a hospital employee had built a small house for himself from the proceeds

86. *Tiesa*, 15 April 1960.

of only ten parcels sent by his sister in Canada. The local Executive Committee decided to confiscate it as having been built from funds not earned through "socially useful work," but a local judge reversed the decision, to the dismay of *Tiesa* (20 August 1965). While the attacks on speculation continued, the Soviet Treasury also profited directly from the parcels: duties, usually prepaid by the senders in hard currency, were set at extremely high levels.

Discussions of cultural interaction with the refugees were expanded during the late 1960s. In April 1966, a special conference of Soviet Lithuanian youth representatives met in Vilnius, and two years later the Committee on Foreign Affairs of the Lithuanian Supreme Soviet called a special conference on the matter. A Lithuanian Minister of Foreign Affairs was appointed after a vacancy of several years. The propaganda newspapers mailed from East Berlin to refugees in the West were replaced by weeklies published in the republics and available there as well. The works of several prominent émigré writers became available, at least in part, to residents of the home-countries. One Estonian and two Lithuanian anthologies published in 1967 included some émigrés, even though they had uttered quite a few pro-independence statements. The émigré theme was featured at the Vilnius Opera in 1967 with the première of the opera *Lost Birds*.

The level of personal interaction increased markedly. Wartime refugees and their children began to visit the home-countries. In 1967, about 500 such visitors went to Lithuania; six girls from Britain vacationed in a Pioneer Camp, and a Lithuanian-American basketball team played a series of games with local Lithuanian teams. Extended visits to relatives, while not numerous, had become fairly common.

Socio-Economic Trends

The major features of the Baltic socio-economic scene between 1953 and 1968 were industrialization and, in Latvia and Estonia, the accompanying immigration of Russians and other non-Baltic Soviet peoples. In agriculture, centrally enforced attempts to grow maize eventually gave way to a return to the dairy-centered approach of the independence period. Urbanization increased, the birthrate decreased, divorce rates soared and Protestant religious practices plummeted.

Industrialization and Regional Economic Councils.   After the intense and erratic reconstruction in the preceding decade, Soviet economic policy and practice in the Baltic republics stabilized in 1955–68. A set pattern of economic activity emerged by the mid-1960s and was to continue in the 1970s. Economic cost calculations agreed with imperial socio-political goals in the Baltic region, which was cheaper and easier to develop than the eastern part of the USSR, due to its relatively good rail and road networks and, above all, its skilled and well-trained labor force. Natural resources were limited to oil shale, fertilizers, construction materials and fairly good soil. Although some oil was discovered during the 1960s in western Latvia and Lithuania, the amounts were small. Ten tons a day spouted from two drill-holes in Lithuania in late 1968, but not much was heard subsequently about this oil.[87]

In industry, the emphasis was on labor-intensive products needing few raw materials. Skilled Baltic labor tended to be complemented by an influx of unskilled Russian labor. Only Lithuania maintained a considerable internal labor pool. The last cooperative enterprises were squeezed out of urban industrial production. In Estonia, their share declined from 12.6 per cent in 1950 to 5.5 per cent in 1960 and 4.9 per cent in 1965. The rest belonged directly to the state.

The product-mix largely continued and diversified the tradition of the independence period (radio-technical, food and footwear industries) or even of Tsarist times (electro-technical, machinery, transportation and textile goods). With only 2.8 per cent of the total Soviet population, the Baltic republics by the late 1960s produced 3.6 per cent of the Soviet gross national output.[88] This production included more than half of Soviet oil shale (Estonia), electric railway coaches (Latvia), telephones and automatic telephone stations (Latvia), electric welding equipment (Lithuania), various types of scientific and computing hardware, and motors for refrigerators and washing machines. The Baltic republics also produced 10 to 50 per cent of Soviet lightbulbs, radios, motorcycles (Latvia), refrigeration equipment and fish. For the sake of proper perspective, we should not forget that they produced little or no coal, iron, cars or cotton.

In money terms, Baltic visible exports tended to exceed visible imports by 10 per cent.[89] Such disparity might be interpreted as

---

87. Benedict V. Mačiuika, "The Role of the Baltic Republics in the Economy of the USSR," JBS, III/1 (Spring 1972), pp. 18–25. For more details on the economy in 1955–68, see King, pp. 207–95; Zundė 1965, pp. 141–69; Järvesoo 1978, pp. 131–90; Remeikis 1977, pp. 116–20.

88. Calculated from data in Remeikis 1977, p. 117. His figure of "almost 10 per cent" (p. 118) must be a misprint.

89. Mačiuika, "The Role," p. 21.

economic exploitation or an involuntary "foreign aid" to the less developed Soviet republics, but it may also have simply reflected an overpricing of industrial consumer goods by the Soviet non-market price system. Baltic wages and retail sales exceeded the USSR average, but so did their national incomes — so the question of possible exploitation by Russia cannot easily be settled at that level. The question of what the Baltic national income could have been in the absence of Soviet occupation remains open. Certainly the Baltic nations were paying for the upkeep of Soviet troops and police on their soil who, depending on one's point of view, were either protecting or oppressing the Baltic nations.

Within the USSR, the Baltic republics increasingly surpassed the other republics in *per capita* national income. In 1958, Latvia and Estonia were, respectively, 29 and 19 per cent above the Soviet average, while Lithuania trailed it by 8 per cent By 1968, Lithuania exceeded the average by 15 per cent, Latvia by 42 per cent and Estonia by 44 per cent. Compared, in particular, to the Russian republic, Latvia and Estonia were always higher, and Lithuania surpassed it in 1966. However, they all trailed the Moscow and Leningrad regions of Russia. Purchases by Russian tourists and soldiers also resulted in lower Baltic consumption. On the other hand, the strong Baltic "underground" economy had the opposite effect. While *per capita* income in the USSR increased by 67 per cent from 1958 to 1968, Estonia's and Latvia's went up by about 90 per cent, and Lithuania's by 108 per cent.[90]

The rise in living standards was more modest, since the increasing production largely went into industrial investment. Compared to the early postwar period, private consumption increased, but in many aspects it remained below the level reached during the independence period. It has been calculated that, compared to that period, the families of urban industrial families in Latvia consumed 30 to 50 per cent less meat, eggs and dairy products in 1961.[91] Regarding consumer durable goods, the pre-war level of consumption was reached again in the 1960s. Given the rapid advances in the West, this meant that the gap between Baltic and West European living standards had increased since the pre-war period — and by the 1960s, war destruction could no longer be taken as even a semi-plausible

90. H.-J. Wagener, "Regional Output Levels in the Soviet Union," *Radio Liberty Research Paper*, no. 41, 1970.

91. King, p. 266.

alibi. Introduction of the Soviet system had advanced the local time by one hour, but set back its growth in welfare by two decades.

It is not even clear whether income distribution had become more equal (as it did in Western Europe). Typical industrial wages in 1961 were around 90 new rubles per month. Many office clerks and female workers received the minimum wage of 45 rubles, but the director of a Latvian textile trust received 450 rubles, plus a hefty bonus and income in kind. Measures like socialized medicine worked to reduce such gaps in formal wages, but small income taxes and large indirect taxes had the effect of widening them. Nonetheless, median earnings increased by about 90 per cent from 1960 to 1974, while price inflation was less than 1 per cent.[92]

The quality of life improved considerably from what it had been in postwar times, yet it still left much to be desired. As in the rest of the USSR, the service sector had been particularly backward in the Stalin years. During the late 1950s, visible efforts were made to improve the situation, although the progress reported was at times pathetically limited. Between 1959 and 1961, some 500 new shops and restaurants were opened in Latvia.[93] Between 1959 and 1964, 10 laundries, 53 public baths, 5 dry-cleaning shops, 5 auto-service stations and 2 tailoring shops were reported to have been opened in Lithuania.[94] The positive effect of a greater number of better-stocked sales outlets in the Baltic republics was considerably offset by the influx of numerous shoppers from other parts of the USSR. A newly-opened radio repair shop in a small Lithuanian town began to attract a swarm of customers, some from as far away as the Kaliningrad *Oblast*, after its reputation for good service had circulated.[95] Service problems continued to persist. According to the First Secretary of the Lithuanian Komsomol, Vaclovas Morkūnas, in 1966 some 5,456 stores in Lithuania had an outdated "material technical structure," the service was frequently rude and prices were arbitrary. Meat stores were insufficient in number and poorly stocked. Stores in outlying areas had particularly meager offerings, and long lines were frequent when items in short supply appeared.[96]

92. King, p. 273; Järvesoo 1978, p. 144. The new ruble introduced in 1961 was worth 10 pre-1961 rubles.

93. *Cīņa*, 28 September 1961.

94. *Tiesa*, 26 February 1965.

95. *Valstiečių laikraštis*, 8 January 1965.

96. *Komjaunimo tiesa*, 29 November 1966; *Tiesa*, 5 November 1966.

Industry shared in the series of all-Union reforms and reorganizations and mirrored the all-Union errors and inefficiencies. The most significant reorganization was the establishment of the *sovnarkhozy* (regional economic councils) in mid-1957, already mentioned above. Each republic now became a unit of economic administration. The *sovnarkhozy* gave considerably more autonomy to the republic administrators, and reduced interference by central Soviet ministries. A number of industrial Union-republic ministries were transformed into branches of the republic *sovnarkhoz*, mostly headed by their former ministers. Estonia and Latvia now had ten such administrations and Lithuania eleven. About 420 Estonian enterprises — responsible for about 80 per cent of the republic's industrial production — were now subordinated to the republic *sovnarkhoz*. The Latvian *sovnarkhoz* was responsible for 486 enterprises, and that of Lithuania for 443 (approximately 83 per cent of all industry). This was in marked contrast to 1956, when central Moscow ministries had been in charge of 90 per cent of Latvia's industrial output.

In the long run, the *sovnarkhoz* system proved especially beneficial to Lithuania which, unlike its two northern neighbors, had not been subjected to rapid, centrally-directed industrialization during the postwar years. The later start of its industrialization allowed the Khrushchev era to have a greater impact on the manner in which it was carried out. The *sovnarkhoz* system gave local planners a far greater input than they had been allowed earlier. This led to dispersal of industrial projects within the republic in such a way as to maximize local natural and labor resources. The Khrushchev years also saw a modest shift in emphasis toward consumer-oriented production. Such an ability by local authorities to disperse new plants, as well as the increased possibility of opting for labor-intensive industries, made the industrial profile of Lithuania somewhat different from those of Latvia and Estonia. Important social consequences stemmed from there being little need in Lithuania for immigration of labor from other parts of the USSR, as had happened in Latvia and Estonia.

Formal recentralization began in 1962 throughout the Soviet Union. Baltic power generation, construction and fisheries were subordinated to supra-republic regional *sovnarkhozy*. The Northeast Power Industry System, for instance, included the three Baltic republics as well as the Leningrad and Kaliningrad *Oblasts* of the RSFSR. However, much was still left under local control. In 1964, the 160 republic *sovnarkhoz* enterprises in Estonia still represented 70 per cent of the republic's industrial output. This output doubled from 1958 to 1965. In spite of their apparent success in greatly increasing production, the *sovnarkhozy* of the Baltic republics were abolished in 1965 along with those in the rest of the USSR.

The reorganization that then followed has become known as the Kosygin Reform. Launched in September 1965, it aimed to introduce a criterion for appraisal of an enterprise according to results obtained through execution of production and profit plans. The USSR State Planning Committee was transformed from an all-Union to a Union-republic institution. The republics' planning committees were enjoined to prepare projects for all branches of the economy except defense, but in close coordination with the all-Union Committee. The majority of each republic's industry was placed under Union-republic jurisdiction. In Lithuania about 60 per cent of all industry fell into this category; 12 per cent was left under local supervision and 28 per cent was under purely central supervision from Moscow.

Friction between local units and a variety of central organs soon became apparent. The Lithuanian construction materials industry, for instance, came under the jurisdiction of at least eight all-Union ministries and agencies. As one critic observed, the all-Union agencies tried to regulate everything from above, to the last detail.[97] Such a situation made local planning efforts futile, especially when central agencies could and did frequently alter plans without full cognizance of or regard for local conditions. Complaints were also heard about attempts by all-Union agencies to impose supplementary production quotas at short notice, thus upsetting the internal work schedules of enterprises.

A lack of coordination between central and local agencies at times led to major problems. In 1965, Juozas Maniušis, LiCP Central Committee Secretary for Industry, complained to the all-Union Supreme Soviet that since 1961 the USSR State Planning Committee had been cutting down allotments of Lithuanian capital investment for the construction materials industry, despite the fact that construction projects within Lithuania were increasing. Hence an acute shortage of construction materials had developed. His request for an increased allotment, reiterated by the Deputy Chairman of the Lithuanian Council of Ministers, was not granted. In 1965 Lithuania's investment allocations in the construction materials industry remained at 1960 levels, although construction had doubled.

Construction of several massive enterprises was undertaken during

97. *Liaudies ūkis*, 1967/4–5, p. 127.

the *sovnarkhoz* period. The giant thermoelectric station at Elektrėnai, which began operations in 1962 and was completed in 1968, made Lithuania an exporter of electrical energy. Among other significant Lithuanian projects launched in this period were a chemical plant at Kėdainiai and a liquid-fertilizer plant at Jonava, using natural gas from the Ukraine as inputs.

The growth of Baltic industrial production slowed down somewhat during the 1960s (see Table 16), the main reason being increasing industrial maturity. However, obsolescent plants and lack of mechanization remained a problem. A furniture factory in Lithuania supposedly required four times the labor input of one in Finland, and took twice as long as a plant in East Germany to build a wooden wardrobe.[98] The high turnover in the workforce was another concern. In 1965–7 about a quarter of the Lithuanian workforce changed jobs every year. Idling, sluggishness and absenteeism aggravated inadequate or sporadic deliveries of raw materials. Frequently rushing to complete plant quotas toward the end of the month, workers paid little attention to quality. Around 1961, every fourth "Latvija" radio, every third telephone and every fifth automatic telephone exchange manufactured at the Riga Electronics (VEF) plant proved defective, and 38 per cent of the items manufactured at the Rigas Aditajs knitted goods factory were judged to be of inferior quality.[99]

Yet on the whole industry was developed in the Baltic republics more rapidly than in the rest of the USSR. In 1970 Lithuania's industrial production was 6.2 times higher than it had been in 1955. The comparable figure for the USSR as a whole was 3.7, while for Estonia it was 4.2 and for Latvia 4.7 (see Table 7). These were times when industrialization in any form throughout the world tended to be considered "progressive" by Western public opinion, regardless of the human or ecological cost; it began to lose its luster in the West only in the late 1960s. For a while longer, Soviet Baltic commentators continued admiring rather than abhorring the fact that the oil-shale ash heaps were higher than Estonia's highest natural hill.

Agriculture.   The relative improvement was most marked for farmers as state interference was reduced, the obligatory delivery system was abolished and prices paid were raised above confiscatory levels. Dismantling of the state MTS in 1958 was a major step.

98. *Komjaunimo tiesa*, 27 May 1966.
99. *Padomju Latvijas Komunists*, 1961/1.

Agriculture, which had languished in the "spook hostel" during the postwar period, presented a particularly sorry picture even in the late 1950s.[100] Total agricultural output had dropped to about 75 per cent of the pre-war level (see Table 8), and possible much lower. The Latvian party journal *Padomju Latvijas komunists* complained in its July 1958 issue that the total yield, while considerably increased lately, was still not sufficient to satisfy even the domestic needs of the collective farms completely. The area of land under cultivation had shrunk greatly since 1939. The 1960 figure for Latvia of 1.9 million ha. was about half that of 1939. Yields were down to half the pre-war level (see Table 8); thus grain production must have been much less than half. The general lack of fertilizer was partly responsible for lower yields: in Lithuania the single pre-war fertilizer plant had been shut down, and farmers were totally dependent on sporadic imports from other parts of the USSR.

The collective sector continued to be reduced in favor of the state sector. Inefficient and overefficient collective farms alike were frequently converted into state farms (*sovkhozes*), whereas the reverse process was not allowed. In Latvia the number of sovkhozes increased from 93 to 113 between March and October 1958 (in that year only 32 made a profit).[101] In Lithuania collective farms decreased between 1958 and 1961 from 2,185 to 1,867. The process continued through the 1960s, though at a much slower pace. The agriculturally useful area of Estonian kolkhozes decreased from 1,766,000 ha. in 1955 to 790,000 in 1970, while that of the sovkhozes increased from 118,000 to 576,000 ha.[102]

From the regime's point of view, sovkhozes represented a higher form of socialist ownership; from the point of view of the peasants, given the state-imposed restrictions on the kolkhozes, conversion to a sovkhoz assured small but regular remuneration, even though the farms might be operating at a loss, and some minimal social security for members. Pension plans for Soviet collective farmers were not introduced till 1965 (a non-mandatory plan based on deductions from income drew few applicants in Lithuania in 1961).

Initially, the wages of collective farmers under the new system generally remained low. In 1958, the average *annual* wage for a Lithuanian collective farmer stood at 68.4 new rubles and 452 kilos of cereal

100. Arnold Purre, *Soviet Farming Failure Hits Estonia* (Stockholm, 1964).
101. *Sovetskaia Latviia*, 11 April 1959.
102. Järvesoo 1978, p. 141.

grain. At 1963 prices, which were about the same as those of 1958, a kilo of sausages cost 2.8 rubles; a man's sweater 20.2 rubles; and a motorcycle 980 rubles. Many collective farmers earned less than half the pay of workers at state farms. Because of the enormous expenses for fodder and capital investments, a considerable number of Lithuanian collective farms could only afford to pay their members 10–15 per cent of their annual incomes.[103]

For this reason, a major portion of the livelihood of collective farmers depended on private plots. In 1959 the private sector in Lithuania, comprising 5.8 per cent of the cultivated land, produced 65.4 per cent of the most important livestock products, 72.4 per cent of the total potato crop and 80 per cent of the total fruit yield[104] (see also Latvian data in Table 15). High taxes and compulsory deliveries from private plots were abolished in 1958–9. At the same time, the cessation of payments of kolkhoz wages in grain had an adverse effect on the raising of livestock on private plots. However, this problem lasted only until new means of securing fodder could be found. The rumors, current in 1958, which attended these changes led to a drastic drop in the price of cows from 400–500 new rubles to 250–300. Many collective farmers managed to purchase cows at relatively low prices.

By 1965, a marked improvement in agriculture was noticeable. Capital and resource allocations to agriculture had increased, and yields reached and surpassed pre-war levels. In 1965 Estonian grain production reached the 1939 level, even though the area under cultivation was 45 per cent smaller. The high yields could be explained partly by the increased used of tractors and mineral fertilizers. Fertilizer use doubled in the 1950s, and again in the 1960s.

The earnings of collective farmers increased dramatically. In 1965, their average daily wage in Estonia stood at 3.7 rubles; the all-Union figure was 2.5 rubles. By 1964, all Estonian kolkhozes were on a system of guaranteed wages; this was envisaged for the whole USSR only for 1966. Various measures concerning the private sector increased incomes further in the mid-1960s. In late 1964, the special tax on private livestock was abolished and permission was granted to sell concentrated fodder to private individuals. Loans for the purchase of private livestock became available in Lithuania in 1965, and

103. *Komunistas*, 1962/3, pp. 36–41. All values are in the new 1961 rubles, worth 10 earlier rubles.
104. Zundė 1965, p. 155.

the number of privately-owned cattle increased by 9.5 per cent and pigs by 14.6 per cent, compared to 1964.[105] The average collective farmer's income in 1965 exceeded that of 1952 by 360 per cent. During the following two years, the average remuneration on Lithuanian collective farms increased by 90 per cent and on state farms by 30 per cent.[106] The comparable increases between 1960 and 1974 in Estonia were 278 per cent for kolkhozes and 177 per cent for sovkhozes. When sovkhoz "self-management" (with no government subsidies) was developed in the Soviet Union in 1967, all Estonian sovkhozes were immediately placed on the system. Latvia and Lithuania readily followed suit in 1970. Throughout the rest of the USSR, only 49 per cent of sovkhozes could get by without subsidies as late as 1973. By the late 1960s, average rural incomes in the Baltic republics, in marked contrast to other regions of the USSR, were approaching average urban incomes.

Urbanization and Immigration. Of the three Baltic republics, Estonia and Latvia tended to show quite similar social characteristics, while Lithuania usually followed the same path of development, though with some time-lag. This applies in particular to the urbanization figures shown in Table 10. The percentage of the workforce employed in agriculture was decreasing. In 1968 it stood at 22 per cent in Estonia and 24 per cent in Latvia and Lithuania, compared to 27 per cent throughout the USSR; here Lithuania *had* caught up with Latvia.

Urbanization went ahead at a fairly constant rate in 1955–68 (see Table 10). The absolute size of the rural population decreased steadily from 1940 on, a trend only briefly interrupted in the late 1950s and early 1960s when thousands of deported farmers returned. While the Baltic service sector also grew, agricultural labor shifted mainly to industry. In Latvia and Estonia, industrial surpassed agricultural employment around 1960. The three capital cities increased their shares of the republic populations (see Table 11). However, Tallinn's share in Estonia's industrial employment declined to 43 per cent in 1967 because of the growth of other cities. Changes were most dramatic in Lithuania. Its three major cities Vilnius, Kaunas and Klaipėda grew by 82 per cent between 1950 and 1965.

The flight to the cities had a significant effect on the countryside. In 1960–5, 100,000 Lithuanian farmers left to work in industry,

105. *Tiesa*, 29 January and 13 May 1966.
106. *Liaudies ūkis*, 1968/12, p. 35.

and some kolkhozes were so depleted of manpower that they were left with 35–45 ha. of arable land per collective farmer, in contrast to the average of 6 ha. Some farms were left with no males aged 16–30. At one kolkhoz in the district of Jurbarkas, 58 of the 165 households had no working-age men under 65 left.[107] Because of poor living conditions, over half of the newly-graduated agricultural specialists failed to stay on the farms for more than two years.[108] These bad conditions in the countryside resulted partly from the policy of discouraging private rural construction; collective farmers preferred to hold on to their old homesteads, many in a dilapidated condition, rather than engage in construction of new centralized settlements.

The rapid urban growth aggravated the housing shortage which had already appeared after the war (see Table 10). Moreover, an all-Union decree in 1962, motivated as much by cost as by ideology, forbad the building of individual dwellings in the republics' capital cities and allowed republic authorities to apply this prohibition to other cities as well. In June 1962, Estonia limited house-ownership to one dwelling per family. Bachelor-owned apartments in Vilnius were proscribed.[109] Despite shortages of building materials, a large construction campaign was undertaken. While living space had increased in Lithuania by 7.5 million square meters in 1946–64, it increased further by 5.2 million sq. m. in 1965–8 — about 3 sq. m. per urban inhabitant. Some Baltic urban projects, such as the Vilnius residential complexes of Žirmūnai and Lazdynai, stood out because of their attempts to vary the usual drab regularity of Soviet prefabricated housing.

Marriage patterns underwent a marked change as the countries became urbanized and modern technology penetrated the countryside: even while the marriage rate decreased, the divorce rate increased dramatically (see Table 12). Birthrates in Estonia and Latvia continued to be below the Soviet average, and reached their lowest levels in 1967 (14.2 and 13.5 per 1,000, respectively), after which there was a slight increase (see Table 13). In 1966–70, Lithuania's birthrate, though decreasing, temporarily exceeded the Soviet average, which had been decreasing even faster. This demographic difference, coupled with Soviet industrialization policy, produced a continuing heavy

107. *Tiesa*, 13 April 1966; *Komunistas*, 1967/1, pp. 6–7.
108. *Komunistas*, 1965/2, p. 59.
109. *Komjaunimo tiesa*, 28 March 1965.

immigration to Latvia and Estonia, but not to Lithuania (see Table 14).

Lithuania's rural labor pool was still large and could fill the labor needs of its relatively few cities; the influx of Russians was small compared to the natural increase of Lithuanians. In the absence of deportations, the percentage of Lithuanians in the country's population was even slightly increasing (see Table 1). The Russians could dominate Lithuania politically, but they were not in the process of swamping it. In contrast, the influx of Russians into Latvia and Estonia presented a threat to national survival.

Since Latvia and Estonia were already predominantly urbanized, the remaining rural labor reserve was comparatively small, and the low birthrates compounded the problem. Relentless Soviet industrialization plans ignored the shortage of indigenous manpower, or possibly even used this opportunity deliberately to bring in Russians. Latvia was quickly approaching the point where non-Latvian immigrants would exceed the Latvians. Estonia was following the same path, though more slowly.

The new immigration was different from that of the late 1940s, which had often been involuntary (functionaries assigned and forced labor dispatched to the Baltic area) and had been accompanied by forced emigration of natives. In 1954–9, immigration had remained low (except for Latvia in 1956) and included many returning Baltic deportees. In the early 1960s, the net immigration rate speeded up appreciably, amounting at times to almost 1 per cent of the existing population each year (see Table 14). Actually, although many more came, many also left every year. This flux made social, cultural and linguistic integration difficult, the more so since the Russian immigrants often expected the Balts to integrate with them. This was the situation that some of the Latvian Communist leaders had sought to alleviate in 1958, and the purge of these leaders made it even more difficult to control the influx. The immigration rate remained high throughout the decade. By 1970, Latvians were only 57 per cent of Latvia's population, and Estonians were down to 68 per cent of Estonia's (see Table 1).

The new immigration was voluntary, and consisted largely of individuals attracted by Baltic job vacancies and the more plentiful supply of consumer goods. However, jobs in the Baltic area sometimes seemed to be better advertised in Leningrad and Moscow than on the spot, raising the issue of possible purposeful Russification. In the 1960s many of the major labor-intensive industries were once again placed under the control of all-Union ministries and agencies which found it simpler to recruit in central Russia. By the late 1960s, immigration had become a major irritant to Latvian and Estonian national feelings, the more so since the immigrants often received the scarce housing for which local people had waited years. At times the Russian newcomers would simply invade newly-finished apartments, and no local functionary would dare to evict them and risk being accused of nationalism. "Friendship of peoples" meant accepting Russian colonization.

By 1965 the total number of Russians in the Baltic republics had topped a million. The Nazi *Generalplan Ost* had envisaged only 250,000 German settlers by that date![110]

Education.   The Khrushchev years saw considerable experimentation within the Soviet educational system. On the whole, developments in the Baltic republics followed the all-Union pattern of curtailing direct admission to higher education from secondary schools, and combining secondary education with on-the-job training. The USSR school reform laws promulgated in December 1958 were followed by republic counterparts early the following year. They envisaged a gradual transition between 1959 and 1963 to a new system in which pupils would attend classes for five days in every week and go to factories or kolkhozes to work on the sixth (usually Thursdays). Their school week was to consist of 31 hours in class, 6 hours in production and 2–4 hours in extracurricular activities. Furthermore, the new laws allowed parents to decide what languages their children would be taught. This meant that Russian became a "voluntary" subject in Baltic schools where it was not the language of instruction, and that the Baltic languages became voluntary in Russian-language schools. The realities of Soviet life, however, put pressure on the Balts to become bilingual, while no such pressure was out on Russian residents in the Baltic republics.

The adoption of the new system resulted in numerous criticisms. The Latvian CC Secretary, Pelše, as well as the Deputy Chairman of the Council of Ministers, Berklāvs, raised objections at the Supreme Soviet session at which the law was adopted. In March 1959 Latvia actually expanded compulsory Latvian studies in the Russian schools, and they were made voluntary only after the purge of autonomists.[111]

---

110. For the Nazi *Generalplan Ost*, see pp. 49ff. above.
111. *Pravda*, 24 December 1958; Widmer, pp. 542–5.

Problems of implementation appeared with the opening of the new school year. Shortages of adequate textbooks were universal, and resistance from parents and teachers had to be surmounted. The new system led to an immediate drop in the number of applicants to institutions of higher education, and in 1959, for the first time ever, there were fewer applicants than places at the Tallinn Polytechnic Institute.

After 1960, complaints appeared over the inability of young people who were sent to kolkhozes as laborers to continue their studies. By the 1961–2 school year, 30 per cent of all Lithuanian pupils in the ninth to eleventh grades combined classes with productive labor.[112] The quality of their production was poor, and many enterprises to which they had been assigned had difficulty in putting them to work. Many students did nothing, and 40 per cent of those assigned to kolkhozes were acquainted with tractors and machinery only through illustrations.[113]

In 1964, the optimal length of primary and secondary education became an issue, as it was becoming evident that the work-training programs had failed and would be abolished. The Lithuanian Minister of Education, Mečys Gedvilas, argued in *Izvestiia* on 22 March 1964 for an 11-year system in the national republics (instead of 10 years as in Russia), because of the need to learn a native language as well as Russian. Initially such arguments did not prevail, and the system was decreased to ten years in all three Baltic republics for the academic year 1964–5. In late 1965, however, after the fall of Khrushchev, the 11-year curriculum was approved for Baltic schools in which the language of instruction was not Russian. At the same time, the moribund work-study program was abolished.

The reinstitution of the 11-year system, as opposed to the 10-year system prevalent throughout the rest of the USSR, was viewed as a victory for those opposing forced Russification and concerned with the maintenance of the national languages as media for professional communication. However, in Latvia at least, nearly all of the extra time was allocated to the study of Russian.[114]

The anti-nationalism campaign was accompanied by a renewed stress on the teaching of Russian — with limited success. In 1962, nearly 5,000 students in Riga were made to repeat their whole school

112. *Tarybinis mokytojas*, 7 January 1962.
113. *Tarybinė mokykla*, 1963/10, p. 3.
114. Dreifelds 1976, p. 140.

year because of insufficient progress in Russian.[115] Numerous bilingual schools were introduced in Latvia; in 1967, 240 out of a total of 1,500 schools were bilingual.[116] Some were set up in areas where there was almost no Russian population, and therefore came to be seen as blatant instruments of Russification. Very few bilingual schools were established in Lithuania and Estonia.

A more orderly pace appeared in higher education. The postponement of obligatory military service for students in institutions of higher learning had been abolished in 1961, but was reinstated in 1966. Talk of a unified Baltic educational system — in which Estonia would train machine operators and electricians, Latvia nuclear physicists and technicians, and Lithuania specialists for the textile and leather industries — remained abortive. Difficulties in higher education caused by wartime loss of trained personnel and postwar Stalinist stagnation were largely surmounted by the late 1960s.

The widespread evaluations of the education-work curriculum in the early 1960s revealed numerous shortcomings which had existed since the war. While it had been claimed that by 1949 compulsory seven-year schooling was enacted in Lithuania, it appeared that in 1961 the drop-out rate in some rural areas reached 45 per cent. Many kolkhozes employed children, preventing their enrollment in school. Teacher shortages proved endemic, since the teaching profession was not considered an attractive career for males. In the 1966–7 academic year, 76.6 per cent of the teachers in Lithuania were women. In rural areas there was a chronic shortage of school buildings, and in the academic year 1961–2, more than 40,000 children in Lithuania had to attend school in two or even three shifts.[117] From the middle of the decade, some kolkhozes began to build their own schools, a common practice in the pre-war Soviet Union. Scarcities of textbooks, which had even extended to secondhand copies, were alleviated by 1967–8.

Religion.   The Thaw also affected religious life. Atheistic propaganda was toned down in 1954–6.[118] In Lithuania, two new bishops were consecrated in 1955. About 130 priests returned from deportation

115. *Skolotāju avīze*, January 1962.
116. Jānis Sapiets, p. 223; Augusts Voss, *Izvestiia*, 5 January 1967.
117. Vytautas Vaitiekūnas, "Sovietized Education in Occupied Lithuania," in Vardys (ed.), *Lithuania under the Soviets*, pp. 171–96.
118. Vardys 1978, pp. 80–8; Salo, pp. 191–222.

(amounting to one-third of those deported), along with two bishops — who, however, were not allowed to resume their positions. Some discussion of modern religion and its compatibility with socialism was even allowed in the press.

A new Union-wide campaign against religion was launched in 1957, and in the Baltic republics this soon merged with the drive against nationalism. There then followed a concerted effort to replace the religious customs and holidays which maintained wide currency among the population: a "Spring Holiday" was celebrated a week before Easter, and a "Winter Festival" on the Sunday preceding Ash Wednesday was billed as a Soviet *Mardi Gras*. A particular effort began in Latvia in 1960 to root out the traditional summer solstice feast of St John on 23–24 June, which had resumed during the Thaw. Its renewed prohibition apparently even led to a go-slow strike in 1960 at the Riga Electronics (VEF) and Railroad Car Plants.[119] The authorities finally yielded in 1968. Name-giving and Adulthood Day ceremonies appeared as efforts to replace baptism and confirmation. There was early realization that church ceremonies were more attractive and dignified, but efforts to spruce up civil ceremonies were slow. The most successful ceremony was the civil marriage, which was successfully invested with some solemnity and aesthetic aura. In Lithuania, the former Kaunas city hall, a graceful restored building in the old part of the city, became a particularly attractive wedding palace.

The campaign against religion was accompanied by the closure of churhes. In May 1959, Riga's towering Gothic cathedral was taken away from the Latvian Evangelical Church. The edifice, together with its massive organ, was restored and opened as a concert hall in June 1962. The eighteenth-century neoclassical cathedral of Vilnius had already been taken over in 1953, and converted into a picture gallery and concert hall. Other churches were also transformed into concert halls, including the church of St Simon (dating from 1283) in Valmiera, Latvia, in 1964, and in 1965 the seventeenth-century Reformed church in Riga was closed because its congregation could not raise the 55,000 rubles needed for repairs, and turned into a library. The Orthodox cathedral in Riga was closed in 1961 and emerged four years later as a new Museum of Science with a Planetarium. The church of St Casimir in Vilnius became a Museum

119. ACEN, IX, 76.

of the History of Religion and Atheism in 1962. One case of church closure stands out because of its peculiar circumstances: a permit to erect a Roman Catholic church in Klaipėda was issued during the Thaw, but the completed building was confiscated around 1960, and the parish priest was subsequently sentenced for alleged speculation. The Lutheran Aleksander church in Narva, destroyed during the war and restored by congregation members in 1958–60, was also confiscated and turned into a clubhouse.[120]

The campaign against religion included slander and police action against some clergy. Archbishop Julijonas Steponavičius of Vilnius was exiled to Žagarė (25 km. east of Akmenė) in January 1961, apparently because he expelled two policemen who had infiltrated the seminary in Kaunas and refused Soviet demands to issue orders contrary to canon law. Two other Lithuanian bishops, Teofilis Matulionis and his successor Vincentas Sladkevičius, had been banished from their diocese in 1958. In 1961–5, only one bishop remained who had not been exiled.[121]

A slackening in the anti-religious campaign set in during the mid-1960s, especially where it affected Roman Catholics, whose church is formally a part of a highly structured international organization. Delegations of Lithuanian priests (but no bishops) were allowed to visit Rome. In November 1964, Monsignor Julijans Vaivods, who had been allowed to attend the Second Vatican Council, was consecrated Bishop of Latvia. A year later, Bishop Juozapas Matulaitis-Labukas of Lithuania was also consecrated in Rome.

However, while the Kremlin was willing to go along with the Vatican's *Ostpolitik* at the official level, a crackdown on organized religious practices reappeared toward the end of the decade. State interference in the posting of clergy and the prohibition of religious activities such as the catechization of children had long been a cause of conflict between Archbishop Steponavičius and the regime. They were enacted into law in May 1966, when the Presidium of the Supreme Soviet of the Lithuanian SSR explained in detail the application of Article 143 of the republic's Penal Code, which concerned the separation of Church and state. It was probably an artificially low limit on seminarians accepted to study in the sole functioning Catholic

120. Klaipėda: Vardys 1978, p. 84; Narva: former congregation member A. Alliksaar's account in the bulletin of Estonian St Peter's church, Toronto, December 1967.
121. For the rather complex details, see Vardys 1978, pp. 83–6.

seminary. Various restraints on religious practice triggered reactions by the faithful during the late 1960s, which blossomed into dissent during the following decade (see section on dissent in Chapter 5).

Soviet policy on religion was characterized by two seemingly contradictory trends. On the one hand, there was the constant struggle against the "survival of superstition from the past." On the other, the churches and their dignitaries could be used as instruments of Soviet foreign policy in the context of the struggle for peace and coexistence. Jaan Kiivit, the Lutheran Archbishop of Soviet Estonia, and Archbishop Gustavs Tūrs of the Soviet Latvian Evangelical Church, were early travelers abroad, visiting Britain in 1955 and the United States in 1956. Two years later, Tūrs was a member of the delegation to a Stockholm peace conference which included, among others, the Secretary of the Latvian CC, Arvīds Pelše. Kiivit went on the air in 1958 to condemn the American intervention in Lebanon — the first time that a churchman was allowed to speak on Estonian radio since 1940. He traveled widely in the 1960s, attending Lutheran councils and lobbying with the World Council of Churches to unseat refugee Archbishop Johan Kõpp. In 1967 Kiivit resigned for health reasons, after close questioning in Moscow about his doings on the foreign visits.[122]

The effectiveness of the anti-religious campaign is difficult to judge. Statistical data concerning believers are not easily obtained and the concept itself is hard to define precisely. While some decline in religious practice could be expected anyway with modernization and industrialization, such losses could well have been offset, especially in Lithuania, by an identification of religious practice with national distinctiveness. In 1958, Archbishop Kiivit claimed that 80–85 per cent of Estonians were active members of the Lutheran Church, but his successor Alfred Tooming claimed only 300,000 by 1969.[123] An East German "progressive" Catholic journal estimated in 1969 that 75 per cent of the population of Lithuania confessed to the Catholic faith.[124] The Lithuanian and Polish populations of the republic, its two traditionally Catholic groups, made up 88 per cent of the total.

Whatever may have been people's internal convictions, it was clear that external religious practices declined sharply during the 1960s. In Estonia, christenings went down from 56 per cent of all children in

122. Uustalu 1970, p. 364, Salo, p. 204.
123. ACEN, V, p. 69, Salo, p. 204.
124. Vardys 1978, pp. 213ff.

1957 to 12 per cent in 1968. Church weddings dropped from 30 to 3 per cent of all weddings, and church funerals from 64 to 46 per cent. The secularization trend visible ever since 1920 may actually have been slowed down by the Stalinist onslaught, but was now catching up. Introduction of more dignified civil ceremonies also had an effect. Lutheran confirmations in Estonia reached a peak of 9,200 in 1957, the year when coming-of-age rituals were started at Komsomol camps. By 1959, both competitors netted about 6,200, with some young people possibly taking part in both rituals. By 1964, confirmations stabilized at around 500 and Komsomol camp rituals at around 6,000. The pattern may have been similar in Latvia. In Lithuania the percentage of children christened dropped from 80 per cent in 1958 to 46 per cent in 1972. The corresponding figures for marriages were 60 and 25 per cent and for church funerals 79 and 51 per cent.[125]

How the Baltic States looked in 1968

For the Baltic nations, the outlook was markedly different throughout 1968. The Soviet invasion of Czechoslovakia in August made the difference. It marked the end of the post-Stalin optimism, and of a hesitantly growing Baltic mood of cooperation with Soviet rule.

The late 1950s had turned out to be a period of major improvements in individual security and wellbeing as well as in national culture, despite setbacks such as the Latvian purge. By any standard other than the Stalinist past, the regime was still oppressive, but the changes that had already taken place encouraged a mood of optimism regarding those still to come. The early and middle 1960s saw a slowing down in the pace of reform, but a feeling persisted that headway was being made, despite Latvian and Estonian unease about the resurgent influx of Russians.

Readiness to cooperate within the Soviet framework increased, and confrontational tactics were avoided — for various reasons. The Soviet debit for having foisted Stalinism on the Baltic nations was gradually being canceled out by credit for overcoming it. As Russia itself evolved, so did the Baltic image of Russia. The renascent Baltic culture was increasingly appreciated by Russian cultural circles. This

125. Salo, pp. 202–4, Vardys 1978, p. 214.

recognition, combined with grudging Baltic respect for Soviet stability, added for the first time a fleeting element of goodwill to the complex mix of Baltic feelings toward the regime, a mix which had previously mostly ranged from (passive) total negation to abject, slavish eagerness to collaborate in some cases. It seemed that, in the end, problems could be talked through with Moscow rationally on the basis of respect for mutual interests. The general tenor may well have been aptly expressed by Rudolf Rimmel, an Estonian born in 1937 in Kazakhstan, in the opening verses of his poem "Looking Forward":

> mildew will wither forever wither
> and winds will carry away its musty stench
> eternal idols having become decrepit
> will scatter like seeds of daisies
> the air will be full as if with pollen
> unable to germinate unable to germinate
> shouts of joy will ring unable to germinate
>
> the hijacked ship will be cleared of pirates
> the rescued will discover a new New World
> sailors will not revolt against columbuses
> small fish will turn into dolphins
> so will the sharks so will the sharks because
>   it has to be so[126]

It was not a cry of triumph over the sharks but an expectation that they would evolve into dolphins; it was also a willingness to accept mutation without rancor. The term for "unable to germinate" (*idanemisvõimetu*) could also be understood as "unable to orient oneself." The poem was published in the August 1968 issue of the Soviet Estonian cultural monthly *Looming*. By the end of the month, the shark forecast was out of date.

Toward the end of 1968, there was widespread expectation of a general cultural purge. It never came, but the fleeting goodwill had been lost. Some, especially in Lithuania where the earlier process had been the most successful, began to wonder what benefit, if any, the nativization of the Communist Party had brought or could ever bring. Many reacted with a resigned, cynical attitude of pursuing material goods, which were still scarce though much less so than earlier.

---

126. Rudolf Rimmel, "Ettepoole," *Looming*, 1968/8, p. 1211.

Others became passive or active dissidents. Dissent, of which there had hardly been any evidence in the mid-1960s, was born. The confrontation was peaceful, but it was confrontation none the less. August 1968 can be said to have been a psychological watershed, marking the end of a cooperative evolution of Moscow's rule in the Baltic republics.

5

CENTRALIZATION AND
WESTERNIZATION, 1968–1980

The period from 1968 to 1980 might be termed years of contradiction for the Baltic countries. On the one hand, centralization of the economy and politics under Moscow's control continued and became more deeply entrenched, and immigration continued to strengthen the Russian hold on the Baltics. The Russification of education contradicted cultural autonomy. On the other hand, the development of a Western-oriented Baltic culture and lifestyle continued too. In particular, despite continuing strict controls, direct contacts with the West expanded. Dissent arose in the midst of increasing Soviet conformism.

Politics and Ideology

Immobilisme in Administration. In 1968, a variety of political developments seemed possible in the Soviet Baltic republics. On the one hand, a genuine political process could have evolved to complement the provincial administrations which, despite their trappings of autonomy, deferred all political decision-making to Moscow. On the other hand, the invasion of Czechoslovakia raised the possibility of a Stalinist crackdown on Baltic autonomy, limited as it already was. Neither of these potentialities materialized during the 1970s. We can hardly speak of government or politics in the republics, since these functions were reserved for Moscow; we can merely follow the rather uneventful changes of personnel within the Soviet Baltic bureaucracy. Other than their names, people tended to know little of Moscow's lieutenants in their countries, and politics was not a frequent topic of social conversation.[1]

1. For details of politics and ideology, see Pennar 1978, pp. 105–27; Taagepera 1978, pp. 75–103; Yaroslav Bilinsky, "The Background of Contemporary Politics in

Nativization of the ruling apparatus could have been expected in Estonia and Latvia in the 1970s. The Russianized cadres with native surnames, imported in the 1940s, had been subject to gradual re-nativization as well as mortality. At the same time, the indigenous pool of available talent was expanding in both numbers and seniority. Maintenance of an immigrant lieutenancy did not seem to be a basic element in Moscow's policy; in Lithuania, native cadres held most of the top posts after 1940. Nonetheless, there was no change in Latvia or Estonia, the chief cause perhaps being the increasing gerontocratic immobility in Moscow. This seemed particularly evident in 1978 when Estonia's First Secretary, Käbin, retired and was replaced by an utterly lackluster Yestonian technocrat, Karl Vaino, whose main qualification seemed to be an Estonian surname. Even after 30 years in the country, he had barely been able to learn his ancestral language.

The formal external relations of the Baltic republics seemed to expand somewhat around 1970. Like the other western republics of the USSR, they joined the East European International Radio and Television Organization, on a par with Poland and Finland. Some trade treaties were concluded on relatively minor matters with East Germany, Hungary, Czechoslovakia and Finland. However, this could not be considered even a formal extension of sovereignty, since the Leningrad *Oblast* also concluded comparable "border trade agreements" with Finland.

The death in office in 1974 of the Lithuanian First Secretary, Antanas Snieckus, was the first such occurrence among republic First Secretaries in the history of the USSR. Snieckus had been LiCP First Secretary since underground days in 1936, and by that time was second in seniority among national CP First Secretaries; only the tenure of Mao Zedong had been longer. The Lithuanian party had become its First Secretary's personal machine, probably to a greater extent than in any other Soviet republic. Snieckus had secured this relatively high degree of control through unhesitating allegiance to Moscow and his ability to foresee shifts in Kremlin policy. Although the Kremlin tended to have more trouble with Lithuania than with

the Baltic Republics and the Ukraine: Comparisons and Contrasts," in Ziedonis, Taagepera and Valgemäe (eds), *Problems of Mininations: Baltic Perspectives* (San Jose, Calif., 1973), pp. 89–122; Rein Taagepera, "Dissimilarities Between the North-western Soviet Republics," *ibid.*, pp. 69–88; Bruno Kalniņš, "How Latvia Is Ruled," JBS, VIII/I (Spring 1977), pp. 70–8; Remeikis 1970, pp. 121–56; also *EE/BE*.

the other two Baltic republics, somehow Snieĉkus seems to have metamorphozed the unruliness of his fief into proof of the toughness of his job rather than of his inability to handle it.

If one is to believe the interpretation of an alleged personal friend of Snieĉkus who sent an unofficial obituary to an émigré publication, the successful Lithuanization of the party over which he presided in the 1950s and '60s was partly due to a change in outlook on the part of the First Secretary. According to this thesis, Snieĉkus, who had been a fanatical Communist, ruthlessly executing orders from Moscow in Stalin's time, had later mellowed into an astutely pragmatic politician not blind to the intense nationalism of the people in his charge. Combining this pragmatic outlook with the inevitable expansion of prerogatives sought by the head of any bureaucracy and with his influential support in the Kremlin built up over his long tenure, he managed to secure some tangible benefits for his bailiwick, which might not normally have been forthcoming in the Soviet order of things.[2] Yet despite his seniority, it appears that Snieĉkus was posthumously snubbed. His funeral was a low-key affair, and no major Politburo figure attended. (The absence of Mikhail Suslov, a longtime personal friend, who had headed the CPSU Special Bureau for Lithuania in 1944–6, was perhaps particularly notable.)

His successor, Petras Griškevičius, had been a party member since 1945, and gradually risen through positions in press work (1950–5), the Vilnius Party Secretariat (1956–64) and the CC (1964–71) to become First Secretary of the Vilnius City Committee (1971–4). Indigenous staffing of the republic's top posts continued as before, and by 1970 native Lithuanians made up 67 per cent of the party (see Table 6). One of the few immigrant top functionaries was Juozas Maniušis, Chairman of the Council of Ministers from 1967 to 1981 (see Appendix A for other administrators).

The Latvian administration remained in the hands of Russian Latvians with a significant admixture of Russians and other non-Latvians. In 1971, only 3 of the 13-member Bureau of the LaCP CC had been born in Latvia. In 1975, 12 out of 42 members of the Council of Ministers had completely non-Latvian names.[3] The LaCP was headed by Augusts Voss, who had grown up in Siberia before being

---

2. T. Ženklys (pseudonym), "Su A. Snieĉkaus mirtimi pasibaigusi Lietuvos gyvenimo epocha," *Akiraĉiai* (Chicago), March 1974; republished as T. Zhenklis, "Proshchaias s Antanasom Snechkusom; chego my zhdem ot emigratsii, vstupitel'naia zametka A. Shtromasa," *Kontinent*, XIV (1977), pp. 229–50.

3. See lists in EE/BE, no. 27, p. 2 (1971), and no. 50/51, pp. 3–4 (1975).

sent to do party work in Latvia in 1945; he rose to the position of a CC Secretary in 1960, and succeeded Pelše as First Secretary when the latter was transferred to the all-Union CC Politburo. Pelše was the only person of Baltic origin to become a full member of the Soviet Politburo in the postwar years. He had left Latvia in his teens, joined the Bolsheviks in Petrograd in 1915, and returned to Latvia in 1940. After moving to Moscow, he ostentatiously downplayed any Latvian ties. While most non-Russian Politburo members had themselves voted into the Supreme Soviet from their respective republics, Pelše chose throughout most of the 1970s to represent Volgograd in Russia rather than Riga. The ceremonial chairmanship of the USSR Soviet of Nationalities was assumed in 1974 by Vitālijs Rubenis, who had previously been Soviet Latvia's titular head of state.

In 1970, Jurijs Rubenis, another Latvian from Russia, was appointed Chairman of the Council of Ministers. His official biography actually listed him as of Russian, not Latvian nationality.[4] Only in 1974 was an indigenous Latvian, Pēteris Strautmanis (a party member since 1944), given the ceremonial post of Chairman of the Presidium of the Supreme Soviet. By 1980 Latvians seemingly represented well below half of the LaCP membership. No direct Soviet data on this embarrassing issue seem to have been available (cf. Table 6).

Estonia continued to have fewer native top administrators than Lithuania, but many more than Latvia. In 1970 Estonians formed 52 per cent of the membership of the ECP, but an appreciable number of the Estonian members had grown up in Russia. However, after 30 years in Estonia, many of them were being re-Estonianized linguistically as well as culturally — a process which seems to have been less widespread in Latvia.

Top posts in Estonia still seemed to be awarded to those who remained the most Russianized. Johannes Käbin, First Secretary since 1950, was in 1978 kicked upstairs to become Chairman of the Presidium of the Supreme Soviet, the top ceremonial post which had previously been held by Aleksei Müürisepp and Artur Vader until their deaths. Käbin had spent the years 1910–41 in Russia, returning as Ivan Kebin. Having once been vocally anti-nationalist, he gradually re-Estonianized his name and relearned his mother-tongue. Conditions being what they were, Estonians came to consider him as a tolerable intermediary between themselves and Moscow.

4. *Deputaty Verkhovnogo Soveta Latviiskoi SSR Vosmoi Soziv* (Riga, 1972), p. 122.

Käbin's successor Karl Vaino, born at Tomsk in Siberia, came to Estonia first in 1947, apparently carrying the Russian name Kirill Voinov. He rose through a variety of party positions to become one of the CC Secretaries in 1960. His selection for the top post surprised many Estonians. His extremely limited ability and his reluctance to speak Estonian insulted national feelings. The deepening consumer goods shortage was blamed on his excessive zeal in shipping food products to Russia. In 1979, there was at least one attempt on his life: on his way to his country cottage, he was shot at by Imre Arakas, member of an underground armed group, who was given a 12-year sentence.[5]

Valter Klauson continued as Chairman of the Council of Ministers but by 1978 it was being rumored that he was in poor health. The two ranking home-grown administrators of the mid-1970s did not last: Edgar Tõnurist, First Vice-Chairman of the Council of Ministers, was demoted not long after Vaino's promotion in 1978, and Vaino Väljas, one of the CC Secretaries since 1971, was removed in March 1980, later to become Soviet Ambassador to Venezuela. After that date, the top administrators included only two home-grown Estonians, both with low party seniority: Arnold Rüütel, who replaced Tõnurist; and Rein Ristlaan, who replaced Väljas. Of all cabinet ministers, however, about 80 per cent were born in Estonia.

Civic Culture and Consumerism.   Administrative immobility and the absence of legally permitted political activity could not hold up change in civic culture. Generational change was causing memories of the Stalinist terror as well as of independence to fade. Consumerism arose to challenge both official ideology and dissent. Any study of it has to remain based on anecdotal accounts. Little social research has been carried out, and even less published.

By 1980, the Baltic population below the age of 40 had no experience of the independence period and little experience of Stalinism. This self-evident fact implies a series of consequences. A generation whose knowledge of the pre-Soviet period was hazy had grown to maturity. Soviet schools distorted facts, but corrective education at home was limited by people's fears of challenging a version of history backed by the police as well as by a prevalent modern tendency to leave education to the schools. For more and more Balts the independence period was receding into a past beyond that crucial personal watershed between

5. *USSR News Brief* (Munich), 31 May 1981, pp. 4–5.

the contemporary and the historical: one's own date of birth. As one of the present authors had occasion to observe personally, some could speak of the date when the Soviet Baltic republics were formed in 1940 as "the anniversary of the republic" with an indifferent matter-of-factness devoid of any pro-Soviet fervor, yet highly incongruous to anyone who applied the same term to the creation of the independent republics in 1918. In this sense, time was definitely on the Soviet side. However, the new generation also lacked the obedience which had been beaten into their elders by Stalinist terror. And even the older generation was opening up. People were less afraid than before to talk, to ask questions and, in some cases, to dissent openly. In this sense, time was working against Soviet efforts to maintain a tight police state.

Police-state methods certainly were not abandoned. Yet the penalties for real or imagined transgressions were obviously more lenient than the prison terms so easily meted out in Stalin's time. Foreign correspondence seemed to be registered and opened routinely (with contents sometimes replaced in the wrong envelopes), and phone calls abroad were sometimes interrupted at sensitive points, indicating continuous monitoring. Many people believed their houses to be bugged, and counteracted by playing the radio or television loudly or running the kitchen faucet when they were on the phone, speaking habitually in a low voice, or going to the park when talking about anything that might displease the authorities. Uncertainty over microphones and police reports, as well as over unexplained professional setbacks, became powerful weapons in the hands of a quasi-monolithic bureaucracy. Individuals found themselves put on the defensive and questioning themselves over which of their inevitable minor transgressions could have been the cause of a failure to be promoted or a friendly police chat. Even open dissent could be repressed by indirect means (such as firing from a job, house searches, interrogations, beatings of family members by "hooligans" whom the police would not catch, and general harassment) before open resort to imprisonment. The change in the totalitarian methodology was partly due to the rise of consumerism.

Consumerism developed with the rise in incomes — a Union-wide phenomenon — in which the Baltic republics were ahead of the Russian republic. After a period of general scarcity, the material good things of life now came within reach if one concentrated on getting them and did not rub the system the wrong way. A car, a summer cottage with a sauna bath, fancy food (often merely of US supermarket quality), elegant tableware and furniture, a trip abroad, and even an encyclopedia set made scarce through oversubscription by other, similar consumerists — these were attractive items for personal enjoyment and for vying with one's closest peers. The accompanying collaboration with the regime began to be rationalized in terms not only of yielding to the inevitable but of transcending the whole issue: Communist ideology was declared so despicably emptied of any content that it was beneath one's dignity even to bother taking an open stand against it. One voiced one's total opposition by going through all the required motions with an ironic meticulousness, thus presumably making the Communist liturgy even more void of content.

The regime's reaction to consumerism was mixed. Emphasis on material goods for private (or even group) consumption went against the official interpretation of Marxism. The regime lost idealistic supporters who succumbed to creature comforts, but it also lost idealistic opponents in even larger numbers. Consumerism faced political dissent with a weapon in some ways more powerful than terror or bureaucratic harassment: a mix of ridicule and boredom. While peaceful dissent looked criminal to the regime and morally imperative to the dissenters, to the consumerists it merely looked foolish. Consumerism was thus weakening the ideological underpinnings both of the regime and of dissent. It was not clear by 1980 which one would be more affected.

For those less cynical or egotistical, coping with repression led to a somewhat schizophrenic pattern of behavior, combining public collaboration with private dissent. The contrast became most marked among those writing in the course of their professions: managers, scholars, writers and educators. While praising the regime in their written output, such people frequently condemned it privately. The repression of loyal dissent blocked constructive criticism. Complete public support was obtained at the cost of cumulative private frustration and disaffection. As daily tasks continued to be performed, such split behavior served immediate Soviet objectives.

During the late 1970s, two new developments seemingly made it more difficult for the Baltic populations to maintain the stances of cynical consumerism or schizophrenic collaboration: an economic slowdown and Russification. The rise in the standard of living slowed down and probably even went into reverse. The availability of food declined; inflation could not be indefinitely masked by new and supposedly improved brands. Specific crises had their effect. The disruption of the flow of natural gas from Iran in 1979, coupled with

Soviet military moves during the Chinese border war with Vietnam, coincided with unexpected power-cuts in the Baltic republics.[6] For several decades, the Soviet regime had managed to deliver a rising standard of living to individuals willing to accept political restrictions as part of the bargain. By 1980 such times seemed to be about to end. Economic failure could give rise to questions about the regime's legitimacy. The Great Russian chauvinism, revived by the regime in its search for legitimacy at the Russian core of the state, affected all minority nationalities of the Union, the Balts among them.

The Russification Campaign of the late 1970s.   The slackening in the anti-nationalism campaign, which had followed the replacement of Khrushchev and the assumption of power by a collective leadership, showed signs of ending by the late 1960s. By the beginning of the 1970s a renewed pressure could be distinctly felt. The concept of a "Soviet people" continued to be a clear ideological tenet — in the present. This may have been perceived in the Baltic republics as a threat to the national cultures and thus have contributed a stimulus to their development as well as to dissent. The tightening of ideological controls and an intensification of "internationalist" propaganda were unmistakable. In Lithuania the brunt of the visible attack seems initially to have been borne by the popular ethnographic study groups and organizations which had emerged as points around which national cultural feelings tended to crystallize: these were directed to shift their attention to the "ethnography" of the Soviet period: revolutionary lore and the wartime experiences of the Soviet military.

The renewed effort to Russianize the non-Russian population of the USSR seems to have become more intense in the later 1970s. Ever since 1960, the Russian people had lost ground demographically within the USSR: although, according to the 1979 census, they still narrowly maintained an absolute majority, already by the mid-1960s more than 50 per cent of the Soviet newborn were non-Russian. In 1970 only 47 per cent of children under ten were Russian. The non-Russian population was growing most rapidly in Central Asia, but Moscow's response was Union-wide.[7]

6. Personal communications by Soviet citizens. Much in the section on consumerism is based on personal communications and on direct or indirect observation.

7. Rein Taagepera, "National Differences within Soviet Demographic Trends," *Soviet Studies*, XX/4 (April 1969), pp. 478–89; Lubomir Hajda, "Nationality and Age in Soviet Population Change," *Soviet Studies*, XXXII (1980), pp. 475–99; Michael

The brunt of the attack came in the realm of language. Union-wide conferences were called to consider methods of extending the use of Russian in public affairs and education. Secret instructions were sent to the republics decreeing implementation of what was still officially no more than under discussion.[8] Nursery schools were ordered to use Russian for half the day, and Russian was to be taught systematically, starting with the first grade. In the high schools at least two subjects were to be taught wholly in Russian. Such ordered use of Russian extended to parts of the university curriculum as well as to more informal activities such as amateur theatrical groups. Radio and television programs in Russian were expanded. Estonia's Pedagogical Institute expanded the training of Russian teachers for Estonian-language schools, but prepared no teachers of Estonian for the republic's Russian-language schools. The Estonian First Secretary, Karl Vaino, conceded that one should love one's own language and speak it every day, but he also maintained that Russian was the *lingua franca*, even within the Estonian republic, and the key to world culture. During the 1980 song festival, for the first time, all speeches at official receptions were in Russian only, although Estonian was used in some of the public speeches.[9]

The most blatant expression of this new Russification came from the Latvian Minister of Education, Mirdza Kārkliņš, who boasted of the moral superiority of Russian over other languages in *Sovetskaia Latviia* of 6 January 1979: "Russian safeguards the effectiveness of patriotic and internationalist education, promoting the development of high moral and ideological-political qualities among pupils." She

---

Rywkin, "The Political Implications of Demographic and Industrial Developments in Soviet Central Asia," *Nationality Papers*, VII/I (Spring 1979), pp. 25–52.

8. An unpublished decree of the USSR Council of Ministers, on 13 October 1978, was followed by a major conference in Tashkent on 22–24 May 1979. Its detailed and largely unpublished "recommendations" reached the West and were published in "The Tashkent Conference and its Draft Recommendations on the Teaching of Russian," *Radio Liberty Research Bulletin*, no. 232 (August 1979), pp. 4–24. The October 1978 decree was apparently delivered to republic educational officials by special couriers, to be read and memorized in a special room, without making written notes; the decree copy was then returned to the courier. (Private communication to one of the authors.) In their turn, the republic CP CC Bureaux issued detailed confidential decrees. That of the Estonian Bureau (Minutes no. 105, par. 1, dated 19 December 1978) was obtained and published in *Eesti Päevaleht* (Sweden), 15 November 1980.

9. Personal communications; *Perspektyvos* (a Lithuanian *samizdat* journal), no. 11, as reported in ELTA, October 1979, p. 11; *Nõukogude Kool*, no. 3 (March 1980), p. 14; *Rahva Hääl*, 14 June 1980; *Helsingin Sanomat*, 13 July 1980, p. 3.

confirmed in detail the planned expansion of instruction in Russian, and reproached Latvians for not "adequately appreciating the value of speaking Russian among themselves." Deepened and thorough mastery of the Russian language was only possible, she claimed, when informal conversation in the language was not restricted to discussions with Russian teachers. *All* teachers must speak Russian, "thus creating a Russian-speaking environment." The pressure of overt Russification seemed to be approaching that of the Tsarist government in the 1890s.

The well-developed Lithuanian underground press responded to the pressures with protests and calls to boycott classes taught in Russian. In Estonia the first reaction was shock and despair, combined with a determination not to yield a single cultural or educational position without argument or the use of delaying tactics. The 1979 census brought surprising results regarding the competence of Estonians in the Russian language. Through the 1970s, this self-declared knowledge of Russian as a second language increased in all Soviet republics except Estonia. Latvians claiming such fluency went from 45.2 to 56.7 per cent of the population and Lithuanians from 35.9 to 52.5 per cent, which was to be expected in view of the continued Soviet schooling and the mortality of the pre-Soviet older generation. However, only 29 per cent of Estonians admitted to being proficient in Russian in 1970, and by 1979 the figure had actually dropped to an unbelievable 24.2 per cent. The only possible explanation was that the Russification campaign had brought about a backlash.[10]

The open attack on national education may have elicited an active stand from many who had previously accepted the *status quo*. Pleas for support in the West were smuggled out by those who had never previously taken such risks. Consumerists, who had rationalized the slow Russification through immigration as harmless, could hardly pretend any longer that the national culture was not in danger. If the reaction to the Tsarist Russification drive of the 1890s could be taken as a guide, the means would be developed to resist denationalization. The end-result could be a heightened national consciousness and increased resentment of a regime which had turned more blatantly Russian-chauvinist.

10. Data from *Naselenie SSR: Po dannym vsesoiuznoi perepisi naseleniia 1979 goda* (Moscow, 1980). One of the present authors has direct information on specific cases where persons fluent in Russian denied such knowledge in a Soviet census report, and where census-takers casually suggested that extensive reporting of fluency in Russian might result in cuts in book publication in the language of the republic.

Demographic and Social Trends

The interaction between birthrates and immigration continued in 1968–80 to be of far-reaching importance for the social, political and cultural processes in the Baltic republics. Urbanization continued, but service industries replaced production as the main growth sector. Many new aspects common to all technologically overdeveloped countries emerged, but the basically established Soviet and Baltic patterns were maintained.

Demography. The gap between the labor demands set by imperialist economic goals and the labor-supply capacity of the Baltic population continued to be filled by immigration of Russians and Russianized members of other Soviet nations. Compared to the 1960s, the influx in the late 1970s decreased in Latvia and Estonia. In Lithuania it expanded, but was still less than in the other two countries. The differences could be explained in terms of the birthrates in the Baltic countries and in Russia.[11]

In Latvia and Estonia, the crude birthrate reached a low-point of 14 per 1,000 in the mid-1960s, and stayed in the 14–16 range thereafter (see Table 13). The rate seemed to be nearly the same for Estonians and Latvians (who had a high percentage of old people) and for immigrants (who were younger but included many footloose transients without children). Due to the ageing of the native population, the yearly deathrate climbed from 11 per 1,000 in 1970 to more than 12 in 1980, and was much higher for the local nationals (around 15) than for the immigrants (probably around 8). Because of this lower deathrate, the number of foreigners would have increased faster than the number of Latvians and Estonians, even if there had not been any further immigration in the 1970s. But immigration

11. For details on demography, see Taagepera, "Baltic Population Changes" and "The Population Crisis and the Baltics," JBS, XII/3 (Fall 1981), pp. 234–44; Gundar J. King and Juris Dreifelds, "Demographic Changes in Latvia," in Ziedonis *et al.* (eds), *Problems of Mininations*, pp. 131–6; Tõnu Parming, "Population Changes and Processes," in Parming and Järvesoo, pp. 21–74, and "Population Processes and the Nationality Issue in the Soviet Baltic," *Soviet Studies*, XXXII/2 (July 1980), pp. 398–414; EE/BE; *National Economy* yearbooks of the Baltic SSRs; Arnold Purre, "Ethnischer Bestand und Struktur der Bevölkerung Sowjetestlands im Jahr 1970," AB, XI (1971), pp. 41–60; Andrivs Namsons, "Nationale Zusammensetzung und Struktur der Bevölkerung Lettlands nach den Volkszählungen von 1935, 1959 und 1970," *ibid.*, pp. 61–86; Benedict Mačiuika, "Auswertung der Volkszählungsergebnisse von 1970 in Sowjetlitauen," *ibid.*, pp. 87–116.

compounded the threat of demographic denationalization of the two republics, reaching alarming proportions in 1970: about 11,000 immigrants entered Estonia in that year, compared to a natural increase of about 2,500 Estonians and 4,000 non-Estonians. In Latvia immigration peaked in 1973–4, with a net annual inflow of 15,000, compared to a natural increase of about 2,000 Latvians and 4,000 non-Latvians, but net immigration decreased appreciably thereafter (see Table 14). The decrease was clearly due to the drop in the Russian birthrate two decades earlier. The supply pool of immigrant labor was quickly being reduced.[12]

Even during its peak period, net immigration actually represented the combined effect of a massive influx largely cancelled out by an outflow almost as massive. In 1963 there were 72 departures for every 100 new arrivals in the Baltic cities; in 1968–9 Estonia received 35,300 immigrants but saw an outflow of 19,700 people.[13] By 1980 the ratio could stand at more than 90 departures for every 100 arrivals, with both flows consisting largely of footloose young Russians hunting for the "long ruble" (easy money) throughout the Soviet Union. The net emigration of Estonians seemed negligible, with a small outflow canceled by a similarly small return flow of previous Estonian settlers in Russia. Emigration of Latvians was also quite limited. The notably transient nature of the Russian-speaking colonies in Latvia and Estonia helped to reduce their vested interest and social power, but it also impeded cultural integration. They were guests who chose largely to ignore the republic's language and culture and expected their hosts to adjust themselves. Such behavior caused resentment well expressed in an Estonian ditty which was sung widely in private, and often openly in the streets during festivities such as New Year's Eve:

> *Välja, välja vabariigi seest,*
> *kes söövad eesti leiba ja ei räägi eesti keelt!*

(Out, get out from this republic's reach,
All eaters of Estonia's bread who do not use its speech)

Lithuania's birthrate was relatively high and, from 1965 to 1970, even surpassed the rapidly decreasing Soviet Russian birthrate by an appreciable margin (18 per 1,000 against 15); however, by 1980

12. Detailed data and calculation of estimates in this paragraph are given in Taagepera, "Baltic Population Changes."

13. V. I. Perevedentsev, in *Soviet Geography* (April 1969); Uno Mereste and Maimu Saarepera, *Rahvastiku enesetunnetus* (Tallinn, 1978), pp. 257–8.

it too had dropped to 15. Net immigration was actually rather larger in the 1970s (7,000 per year) than in the 1960s (an average of 4,300 per year). Even so, it remained small compared to Latvia's, and aroused little concern for national survival. The mechanization of agriculture, a higher birthrate and the successful decentralization of industrial development during the 1960s ensured that Lithuania's labor increase came predominantly from Lithuanian cradles.

In 1959 Estonia's population had been 75 per cent Estonian, but by 1970 the proportion had decreased alarmingly to 68 per cent. The third postwar census in 1979 showed a further decrease to 65 per cent (see Table 1) but it had noticeably slowed down. Similar trends brought the Latvians even closer to the prospect of being reduced to a minority in their own country; already down to 62 per cent in 1959, they represented 57 per cent in 1970 and 54 per cent in 1979. The psychologically important 50 per cent level was close, but there again the rate of attrition was slowing down. The Lithuanians continued to preserve a strong majority in their country. They actually increased their share in Lithuania's population from 79 per cent in 1959 to 80 per cent in 1970 and 1979, partly through a slow assimilation of the Polish minority.

Republic-wide trends in national composition were accentuated in the capitals (see Table 11). In Tallinn the Estonian share dropped from 60.2 per cent in 1959 to 55.7 per cent in 1970 and to 51.3 per cent in 1979. In Riga Latvians, down from 44.7 per cent in 1959 to 40.9 per cent in 1970, were outnumbered by Russians (42.7 per cent in 1970), and the remaining population tended to know Russian better than Latvian. In Vilnius, which had historically been a multinational city, the Lithuanian share (33.6 per cent in 1959) continued to rise, reaching 42.8 per cent in 1970 and 47.3 per cent in 1980.[14]

In the Baltic popular view of the immigrants, the poorly-educated and uncultured Russian construction worker seemed to loom large. However, statistics showed the Russians and Ukrainians in the Baltic republics as having had more schooling than the Balts. They dominated not only among bricklayers and miners but also in civil aviation, fishing fleets and railroad engineering. Reflecting the general lack of social interaction, intermarriage between Balts and immigrants remained quite low in the 1960s. It may have risen in the 1970s with most of the offspring apparently opting for Baltic nation-

14. *Itogi vsesoiuznoi perepisi naseleniia 1970 goda*, vol. IV (Moscow, 1973), pp. 275, 283 and 320; *Õhtuleht* (Tallinn), 27 February 1980; *Mokslas ir gyvenimas*, 1981/3, p. 27.

ality.[15] Around 1970 there was some propaganda for the immigrants to master the local language, and instances of those who had done so were described in the press. Results were limited. Especially in Latvia, even a single Russian within a *kollektiv* would often insist that official business be transacted in Russian.

Urbanization continued, but at a gradually decreasing rate (see Table 10). In Estonia, the most urbanized of all Union republics, the percentage of people living in cities and towns rose to 70 per cent in 1980, and Latvia's figure was almost as high. In Lithuania urbanization in 1970 was still below the Soviet average, but it almost caught up by 1980 (62 per cent, compared to 63 per cent for the USSR). The high degree of urbanization in Latvia and Estonia reflected the tendency of immigrants to settle in the cities. The urbanization of ethnic Latvians and Estonians was more limited. The Russian-penetrated cities continued to contrast with the overwhelmingly Baltic countryside, except in some eastern districts.

The share of agriculture in employment and national production continued its slow decline. However, industrial employment also peaked in Estonia (with 35.2 per cent of total employment in 1970 and 34.4 per cent in 1976), Latvia (down from 34.3 per cent to 33.1 per cent), and by 1980 probably in Lithuania as well.[16] As in all technologically mature countries, service became the major sector of growing employment.

Latvia's economy and culture continued to be dominated by a single large city — Riga (835,000 inhabitants in 1979). Lithuania maintained a two-center system, although Vilnius (481,000) was slowly gaining an edge over Kaunas (370,000). Estonia could be said to have a one-and-a-half-center system, with Tallinn (430,000) sharing some cultural leadership with Tartu (102,000 inhabitants in 1979).[17] An

15. Of a total of 15,552 Estonians who married in 1968, only 5 per cent (729) married Russians, according to *Nar. khoz. ESSR 1969*, p. 26. Of the children from Russian-Baltic mixed marriages who reached adulthood in 1960–8, 62 per cent opted for the republic nationality in Tallinn, 57 per cent in Riga, and 52 per cent in Vilnius, according to L. N. Terenteva, *Sovetskaia etnografiia*, no. 3 (May–June 1969), pp. 20–30, translated in *Bulletin of Baltic Studies*, no. 4 (December 1970), pp. 5–11. In Baltic mixed marriages with non-Russians, about 80 per cent opted for republic nationality. The percentages are likely to be higher in the countryside, but lower for those settled outside the republic.

16. *Nar. khoz. ESSR 1977*, p. 171, and *Nar. khoz. LaSSR 1977*, p. 212. In Lithuania, the combined share of industry and construction advanced very slowly from 37.6 per cent in 1971 to 38.0 per cent in 1975: *Ekonomika ir kultūra 1975*, p. 187.

17. Tönu Parming, "Roots of Nationality Differences," in Edward Allworth (ed.), *Nationality Group Survival in Multi-Ethnic States* (New York, 1977), pp. 24–57.

increasing proportion of the total population was living in the capital cities (see Table 11).

Western-Like Trends in Lifestyle. In many ways the Baltic lifestyle underwent changes similar to those in the West, with a time-lag that tended to become less as communications improved. Sometimes there was clear imitation of Western fads, while at other times similar technological changes may have brought similar results even independently of foreign examples. Analogous developments in Russia tended to lag behind the Baltic, but may at times have been affected by the Baltic examples.

Youth culture visibly imitated the West, and some establishment members were accepting it. "If a hippie plays a violin naked above the waist and with a cross around his neck . . . this does not mean that the music is bound to be bad," wrote the composer Uno Naissoo. "Let us remember that in fact we have always sanctioned (tacitly or even officially) everything that has acquired international circulation; only we have been up to ten years late."[18] Long hair was shocking to some Baltic parents and teachers throughout the early 1970s; they accused television of promoting "hairiness," which affected even the star team of the Estonian Student Corps (an apparently unique Estonian enterprise for summer work by high school students). Some schools had daily checking of pupils' dress, insisting on school uniforms and the removal of rings, and rejected long-haired boys and girls with tight pullovers. But at school dances leather jackets, Beatle outfits, weirdly-dressed bands and rock instead of polkas tended to prevail. In July 1971 a "Union-wide Congress of Hippies" reportedly brought 100 guests to a restaurant in Vilnius. Unable to expel the "Texas pants" (blue jeans) and unwilling to give up on having a school uniform, Estonian schools finally made the jeans compulsory.

Telemania expanded as in the West, despite a rather different program mix (except for Tallinn, where Finnish TV could be seen). TV broadcasting began in 1954, and started to reduce movie attendance by 1961. Color broadcasting was introduced in 1972. A Latvian study found people spending seven of their weekly total of 20 leisure hours watching TV, and the poet Lija Brīdaka felt the nation had become "comfortably ensconced on the couch in an intellectual stupor."[19]

18. *Sirp ja Vasar*, 29 October 1971; EE/BE, no. 29, p. 5 (1971).
19. *Literatūra un māksla*, 23 November 1974; EE/BE, nos. 48–9, p. 17 (1975).

Since most programs were in Russian (74 per cent in Estonia, 1975–6), if only for reasons of cost, the stupor also had a Russianizing component.

In the acquisition of private cars the Baltic republics were ahead of the rest of the Soviet Union. Although the "car explosion" was modest compared to American excesses, it began to overstrain the region's limited road, parking and servicing facilities. By 1970 Lithuania had 30,000 private cars and 160,000 motorcycles. Estonia's car sales leaped up by 400 per cent from 1971 to 1972. Rush-hours in Riga made planners start thinking about a subway. Waiting-lists for cars were still long, and some people in Latvia were ready to pay embezzlers 18,000 rubles cash for fake lottery tickets entitling the holder to get a 9,200-ruble "Volga" without waiting.[20] In Estonia's Kingissepa district (Saaremaa island), the right to buy a car without waiting was made a major prize in a socialist competition. Service remained so limited that the installation of a new eight-pump gas station in Tallinn (with no repair facilities) was front-page news, accompanied by a photo, in the republic's main daily.[21] An almost unbelievable degree of gasoline pilfering took place, with 30 per cent of all gasoline assigned to kolkhozes and state enterprises ending up in private hands through illegal speculation.[22]

Traffic accidents killed 667 people in Lithuania in 1970, 637 in Latvia in 1971 and 271 in Estonia in 1972. These seemed to be peak levels before the population adjusted to the car expansion. Of Lithuania's 4,678 car accidents in 1970, drunk driving caused 989. Truck drivers caused 57 per cent of Latvia's accidents, and tractor drivers 34 per cent. While 22,302 people received driving licenses in Estonia, 4,812 lost them for drunk driving in 1973. Fines were heavy. The ESSR Agriculture Minister, Harald Männik, was demoted to the post of sovkhoz director in 1970 because of a drunken U-turn in which he alone was injured. He was reinstated in 1975.[23]

As in the rest of the Soviet Union, highway construction failed to keep pace with the increase in vehicles, although the situation may have been marginally better in the Baltic republics. The four-lane

---

20. *Cīņa*, 1 July 1975.
21. *Rahva Hääl*, 29 September 1972.
22. *Ibid.*, 9 July 1969.
23. Traffic accident statistics compiled from Soviet press, in *EE/BE*, nos 33, p. 3, and 35, p. 4 (1972); nos 37, p. 4, 40, p. 3, and 41, p. 4 (1973); and nos 44, pp. 9 and 11, and 47, p. 12 (1974). For Männik: no. 24, p. 8 (1971), based on private communications; and *Rahva Hääl*, 25 December 1970.

highway linking Vilnius to Kaunas, a stretch of some 100 km. completed in 1970, was perhaps the longest such interurban expressway in the USSR.

The variety and quality of consumer goods improved, although continuing short supply was suggested by bulging savings accounts (one-third of yearly retail turnover around 1972, and close to half by 1977). Stereo hi-fis, vacuum cleaners, refrigerators and cassette tapes reached a sizeable fraction of the population. In 1970 "Estonia-Stereo" was the first Soviet stereophonic radio set. Meat began to be sold in vacuum-sealed plastic bags, and aluminum foil appeared. Even a Soviet invention of mailing-strength packing cartons was announced.[24] Washing-machine sales in Estonia and Latvia peaked in 1968, indicating saturation of the market, at least for the models available (and of the space in which to put them, inside cramped apartments). The partial switch from the traditional Soviet sellers' market to a buyers' market brought with it "socialist commercial advertising," in papers and on TV. Created in 1967 as a self-managing enterprise (see the section below on "Recentralization and Self-Management"), *Eesti Reklaamfilm* netted 3 out of 4 prizes at a 1971 Union-wide advertising film seminar, received in 1975 at least 120,000 rubles from regular customers, and was accused in the press of creating new artificial needs by persuading people that consumer goods can bring prestige and family happiness. In 1972, *Rahva Hääl* (23 February) for the first time ever ran an advertisement for credit buying: a 300-ruble TV set for 85 rubles down and the rest in monthly installments over two years. TV trade-in offers started in June 1972. In 1975 Latvia's *Padomju jaunatne* (6 June) was advertising a two-day moped, tent and outboard motor sale with no money down. It was a far cry from the Soviet Baltic market of the 1950s or even 1960s.

In 1972, the Soviet Union gingerly entered the bank-check age, and the following year personal checks were instituted for large purchases, with sums rounded off to the next 100 rubles. However, most Baltic customers still seemed to pay for their cars and apartments with thousands of rubles of cash nervously tucked into coat pockets.

The first comic book in Soviet Estonia (and possibly the Soviet Union) was published in 1973 — 128 pages of "Donald Duck, Mickey and others" — but no others followed. Two books on sex

24. *Rahva Hääl*, 12 May 1971.

and family life were published in massive quantities to take care of the backlog (1970: 50,000 copies; 1974: 80,000) for an Estonian-speaking population of one million, with about 8,000 marriages and 3,000 divorces each year. Estonia's first funeral home was established in 1975. Monthly TV press conferences by party and government leaders started in 1971, but did not seem to last long.

While officially there was no inflation, the only combined price index published (that for the kolkhoz markets in four Latvian cities) showed a yearly price increase of 1 per cent in 1965–70, 4 per cent in 1970–5 and 13 per cent in 1975–7. Price indices for individual goods on the Estonian kolkhoz markets tended on the average to increase by 2 per cent per year in 1965–70, and by 4 per cent in 1970–7.[25]

Other Social Trends.   In many other ways, life continued to follow established Baltic or Soviet patterns. Food — its cost and its availability — remained a major concern for the population. In 1968 Estonians were spending 62 per cent of their personal income on food and 21 per cent on clothing. The imbalance partly reflected the low cost of apartments (if one could obtain one), medical treatment and transportation. But food expenses also reflected recurring shortages of staple foods in state stores, and the high prices at the kolkhoz and the black market. Depending on domestic harvests and Soviet foreign-trade vagaries, there would be periods without meat, coffee, spices, onions and even potatoes. The Vietnam-China border war in 1979 and the United States' partial grain embargo in 1980 triggered panic buying which increased the daily sales of flour and grits in Tallinn sixfold.[26]

Official estimates of the Baltic diet indicated a higher protein content than in other Soviet regions and even in the satellite East European countries. Around 1970 consumption of eggs was rapidly increasing and that of meat was on a par with Hungary. Consumption of milk and dairy products (over 400 kilos per person) stood far above that in the East European countries. On the other hand, grain products were low in the Baltic diet, and only Poles were eating more potatoes. Potato consumption was decreasing rapidly (from 194 kilos per person in 1965 to 140 in 1975, in Estonia), but it was replaced by fats rather

25. Calculations based on data in *Nar. khoz. LaSSR 1977*, p. 292, and *Nar. khoz. ESSR 1977*, p. 233.
26. *Rahva Hääl*, 12 January 1980.

than vegetables. Rapid modernization resulted in people doing little physical work and yet eating the dream foods of their peasant grandparents. Rural Latvians were estimated on average to be 20 kilos overweight, in Estonia fats formed 69 per cent of calorie intake; and in Lithuania protein consumption decreased. The recurring meat shortages were aggravated by Russian tourists and holiday-makers raiding the stores in major cities and even in small resort towns, and sending food packages back to Moscow to the dismay of local residents.[27]

Servicing in the late 1960s compounded the shortages, since it too was often set up to suit the convenience of the store rather than the customer. To buy food one might have to stand in three or four separate waiting lines and then take the streetcar to separate bakery and vegetable stores, only to find some of them closed for lunch.[28] By 1980 the majority of shops seemed to have shifted to self-service, and overspecialization was attenuated.

After 1975, however, shortages of the goods themselves became increasingly frequent and acute, especially in Latvia. By 1979 people from Riga were to be found trying to purchase butter in Tallinn, and in Tallinn itself ham was all but absent from stores in the late 1970s. According to some local residents, by May 1980 little meat of any kind was available apart from pigs' trotters.

The shortage of housing remained a major social problem. By 1978, urban *per capita* living space in Estonia finally caught up with the pre-Soviet level of 1940, after 30 years of peace and worldwide technological progress. The pre-war level was not exceeded in Latvia or, probably, in Lithuania (see Table 10). Cramped quarters sharpened friction between married couples and between parents and their children. Living space was not redistributed just because of such purely personal reasons as divorce, and some remarried professional people avoided the resulting nightmare by sleeping in their offices. Distribution was unequal, and many people just above the legal minimum of 3 square meters were not even eligible for improved quarters around 1970. New building tended to be shoddy. Parents would move into a brand-new apartment before their children, to fill cracks, adjust doors and windows, and make sure the porch would not fall down. Architect

27. Food consumption data from EE/BE, nos 23, p. 4 (1970); 29, p. 8 (1971); 35, p. 3 (1972); and 44, pp. 7–8 and 47, p. 10 (1974). "Sausage tourists": nos 29, p. 2 (1971); and 32, p. 3 (1972).

28. *Eesti Kommunist*, May 1968, p. 36; EE/BE, no. 9, pp. 2–3 (1968).

Mart Port wondered whether city planners used apartment-dwellers as guinea-pigs in some socio-biological experiment:

Will they exist without stores and barber-shops? They will. How about trash-collection points a thousand feet away? They will carry it. Hoisting baby carriages up a narrow stairway to the fifth floor? They'll do it. No laundry facilities? They'll manage. But lower the room temperature by 10°C? They'll start complaining. So let us make a note: a boiler room is a must — that's the survival threshold.[29]

There were some notable improvements in the urban environment during the 1970s. The housing continued to grow, as new neighborhoods sprawled outward from the major cities, especially the capitals. The erection of new public buildings and restoration of old ones changed the older centers. Tallinn especially profited from its choice as the site of the yachting Olympics in 1980. In addition to a new yachting center on the outskirts of the city, linked to it by a 5-km. four-lane expressway, Tallinn also acquired a new 800-bedroom hotel and other amenities. Its picturesque center was given a facelift, and through the decade Riga and Vilnius also underwent considerable restoration. The 400th anniversary celebration of Vilnius University in 1979 occasioned a renewal of its centrally located old campus, and a new campus was opened in the suburbs. Earlier in the decade Vilnius built a new sports arena (1971) and opera house (1974), both considered outstanding by Soviet standards.

Because of a space shortage, nearly 18 per cent of Latvia's schools were operating two shifts in 1970. About 14 per cent of Lithuanian and 10 per cent of Latvian and Estonian students attended night shifts in 1975. This involved only about 1 per cent of all students in grades 1–8, but in grades 9–11 the night shift was attended by 48 per cent of all students in Lithuania and by 41 per cent in Latvia and Estonia. Hotels were crowded too. Tartu, with 100,000 inhabitants in 1977, had only two hotels, with a total of 319 beds and a remarkably high average occupancy rate: 1.31 persons per bed per night. Estonia's average was 0.97 persons per hotel bed, and Latvia's 0.95.[30]

Family structure showed some loss of masculine domination, but no let-up on the disproportionate share of housework done by women.

29. *Sirp ja Vasar*, 13 June 1969.
30. Schools: *Skolotāju avīze*, 25 March 1970; *Nar. khoz. LaSSR 1977*, p. 305, and *Nar. khoz. ESSR 1977*, pp. 261–3; *Ekonomika ir kultūra* [LiSSR] *1975*, p. 260. Hotels: calculated from *Nar. khoz. LaSSR 1977*, p. 297, and *Nar. khoz. ESSR 1977*, pp. 246–7.

Women also did most of the time-consuming everyday shopping, often in working hours. But life for single women was no easier in places like the Ogre textile firm in Latvia, which had dormitories for 4,000 young women without a single cafeteria, experienced a 20 per cent labor-turnover in half a year, and was used by mothers as a threat to their lazy school-age daughters. After a major increase in the 1960s, the divorce rate grew only slowly in the 1970s (see Table 12). Abortion continued to be the most prevalent birth-control method, reaching the proportions of an epidemic "in all social strata." Throughout the three Baltic republics, the incidence of abortions tended to equal or exceed live births. In 1973, Latvia registered 60,000 abortions and 34,000 births. When asked their reasons for avoiding having even a single child, most women stressed inadequate housing. Venereal disease became an acknowledged issue, encouraged by more relaxed sexual mores, continuing prostitution and clandestine brothels. As for rape, the Latvian Minister of Internal Affairs, Anrijs Kavalieris, cavalierly dismissed 60 per cent of the cases as provoked by the victim's "lustful behavior."[31]

Shoplifting tended to increase as more stores switched to self-service. Among those caught in Riga's "Children's World," the average hoard was worth under 7 rubles. On the more organized side, 34 people were indicted in 1972 for selling the examination papers of the Riga Trade Institute in advance for 200 rubles apiece. As in the West, the crime-rate was increasing (by 8.5 per cent annually in Lithuania from 1968 to 1970), the police complained of people's growing passivity in the face of criminal acts (partly to avoid tedious appearances in court), and juvenile delinquency seemed to spread to the middle class.[32] People depended heavily on "under-the-counter" dealings to make ends meet. "We are living on our *income*, not on our salaries," was a frequent explanation given to innocent visitors from the West.

Alcoholism became a source of worry both to Soviet managers concerned with labor efficiency and to Baltic patriots concerned with national survival. Around 1970, Estonia consumed 50 per cent more alcohol in terms of content *per capita* than did the RSFSR or the United States, and Lithuania and Latvia were close behind. This was

31. Ogre: *Padomju jaunatne*, 28 May 1975; abortion epidemic: *Nõukogude Õpetaja*, April 1972, and Dreifelds 1976, p. 147; venereal disease: *Veseliba*, no. 2, 1974; rape: *Literatūra un māksla*, 14 July 1973.

32. For crime reports, see EE/BE, nos 3, p. 3 (1968); 24, p. 2 (1971); 34, p. 4 (1972); 37, p. 2 (1973); 45, p. 9 (1974); and 48, p. 16 (1975).

on a par with beer-drinking West Germany, and well below wine-drinking France, but the Balts consumed mostly hard liquor and cheap wine substitutes. In Estonia, the yearly *per capita* consumption had risen from 3 liters of absolute alcohol in the 1930s to 6 liters in 1965. From 1965 to 1970 it increased by 52 per cent (while wages went up by 35 per cent, and *per capita* retail sales by 51 per cent), and was coming close to the previous historical record of 10 liters established around 1800 during the hopeless days of serfdom. Lithuania's hard liquor consumption doubled between 1959 and 1968 (from 4.5 to 8.9 liters of alcohol per person), in line with the general Soviet trend.

Drinking at work was widespread. Even during a 1972 Union-wide anti-alcoholism campaign, a major Tallinn plant ("Ilmarine") was proud to announce that it had broken up "group drinking," but admitted to having achieved only partial success with individual drinking. Penalties involved losing not only a bonus but also one's position in the waiting list for apartments. Truck and tractor drivers were the worst offenders, but they were also among the most indispensable workers. It was privately conjectured in Lithuania that if the laws on drinking and driving were strictly enforced, the republic's heavy vehicle fleet would become paralyzed. The leadership was accordingly not interested in full enforcement. More than 7 per cent of Estonia's tractor drivers lost their permits in 1968 for drunken driving, and the pattern was similar in 1972.[33]

A Latvian study showed that most collective farmers still felt that drinking in working hours was "not necessarily bad." Vodka had become standard payment for kolkhoz tractor drivers willing to plow up a farmer's private plot, and many other such services. Alcohol was involved in three-quarters of all drowning accidents and crimes, half of all car accidents and fire deaths, and many divorces. The death toll due to alcohol was estimated to be 1,500 in Latvia in 1972, and it accounted for one-third of male deaths in the 20–50 age bracket. Official responses ranged from producing more beer (to displace hard liquor) to increasing the penalty for selling moonshine to three years in prison in Latvia and five in Estonia.

Special services continued to be supplied to the upper class of the classless society. There were special stores for Communist Party leaders, and pharmacies reserved special items for these same privileged

33. "How Estonia Drinks," *ibid.*, no. 29, pp. 6–7 (1971), and various other reports; A. Garonas, "Gerti ar negerti?" *Švyturys*, 1964/9, pp. 25–6.

individuals, while others might have to wait almost a year for a prescription to be supplied. Republic CP CC buildings contained stores that were off-limits even to the party rank-and-file, and foreign lingerie used to be distributed at top-level party meetings even in the late 1970s. The development of a sense of hereditary élitism was illustrated by the angry establishment reaction to a short story in which a manager's son rejects middle-class values, drops out and becomes a truck driver. Although described in the story as a skilled and conscientious worker, he was termed a superficial anarchist in the anonymously authoritative critique which, interestingly, did not object to the description of workers living in hovels without hope of raising a family.[34]

Militarism in propaganda and education may have increased around 1970, at the same time as aggressive peace propaganda. After 1968 all factories and high schools were required to have permanent military workshops to get the boys "interested in warfare" and to develop "soldierly habits." The Estonian Lenin Prize-winning author Juhan Smuul proclaimed that "nowhere else is human character revealed so clearly, and nowhere do superficial virtues . . . crumble so quickly as in war." This mood was echoed in teachers' and children's magazines. Obligatory military training started in the ninth grade, including practice with combat weapons. High school competitions featured shooting and grenade-throwing from motorcycles, with gas masks on.[35] The great majority of Baltic youths spent their two or three years of obligatory Soviet army, navy, border guard or KGB service outside the Baltic area. In contrast to the Tsarist and early Bolshevik periods, the developed Baltic area supplied very few officers to the Soviet army; there seem to have been less than half a dozen native-born Balts above the rank of colonel. The distrust may have been mutual.

Large numbers of Soviet troops continued to be stationed in the Baltic republics. Soviet-inspired proposals for a denuclearized northern Europe did not include the eastern shore of the Baltic. An "earthquake" in northern Estonia (fall 1976) looked more like a nuclear accident at the Paldiski naval base 40 km. west of Tallinn. *The Guardian* (London) reported Soviet stationing of nuclear submarines

---

34. E. Tennov, "Margiti kadumine," *Looming* (October 1974), pp. 1592–1651; *Rahva Hääl*, 6 December 1974, pp. 2–3; EE/BE, no. 48, pp. 14–15 (1975).

35. Warfare interest: *Eesti Kommunist* (May 1970), p. 73; Smuul: *Rahva Hääl*, 10 October 1970; grenades: *Skolotāju avīze*, 18 November 1970.

in Liepāja (9 April 1978). Forced to serve as nuclear missile bases against Western Europe, the Baltic countries became potential nuclear targets themselves.

Economy and Ecology

The Baltic economic scene was characterized by a deepening labor shortage, and by two somewhat contradictory trends: a continuing shift of control from the republic to Moscow, and an increase in self-management on individual plants and farms. The labor shortage contributed to a reduction in the industrial growth-rate, and helped to boost the labor-saving aspects of self-management, which in turn consolidated the role of the Baltic republics (especially Estonia and Latvia) as a sort of socio-economic laboratory or testing ground for potential Union-wide reforms. Agriculture improved, but economic over-development started to create ecological problems. All these questions are discussed later.[36]

Recentralization and Self-Management. The *sovnarkhoz* economic councils of 1958–64 marked the peak of economic autonomy for the Soviet Baltic republics. The new leaders who replaced Khrushchev in 1964 clearly preferred administration on the basis of production branches rather than territorial units. Abolition of the *sovnarkhoz* was one of their very first steps. The need for territorial coordination was recognized in principle, but in practice the power of central ministries expanded greatly in the mid-1960s, and continued to expand later at a slower rate. Traditionally some Soviet ministries existed only in Moscow with no counterparts in the republics, while others were republic responsibilities with no central ministry in Moscow. A third category consisted of "Union-republic" ministries, where ministries of the same name existed both in Moscow and in the republics, interacting tightly. This last category was expanded at the expense of purely republic-level ministries. In this way, recentralization could take place without any republic ministry being

36. For details on economy, see EE/BE; Benedict Mačiuika, "The Role," pp. 18–25; George J. Viksnins, "Current Issues of Soviet Latvia's Economic Growth," JBS, VII/4 (Winter 1976), pp. 343–51; I. S. Koropeckyj, "National Income of the Baltic Republics in 1970," *ibid.*, VII/4 (Spring 1976), pp. 61–73; Järvesoo 1978; Endel Jakob Kolde, "Structural Integration of Baltic Economies into the Soviet System," JBS, IX/2 (Summer 1978), pp. 164–76; and the various annual editions of the *National Economy* of the Lithuanian, Latvian and Estonian SSRs.

conspicuously abolished. Yet the Union-republic format in practice shifted major decision-making from republic capitals to Moscow. The asymmetrical relationship was well illustrated by an Estonian delegate's complaint voiced at the 1969 Supreme Soviet session: if the combined operations resulted in a surplus the Union ministry got it, but if the year ended with a deficit this had to be absorbed by the republic ministry. The scope of the purely Union ministries (with no republic-level counterparts) also expanded. In Latvia only 3 per cent of industrial production had been under Union control in 1960. By 1971 the Union ministries controlled 34 per cent, and Union-republic ministries accounted for 56 per cent, leaving only 10 per cent (mostly food and light industry) under Latvian control.[37]

Baltic reactions to excessive centralization ranged from academic demonstrations of its inefficiency to complaints at Supreme Soviet sessions about central ministries' shortcomings, and attempts to widen the centrally mandated plant self-management program to include some republic ministries. The Estonian economist Vello Tarmisto argued that centralization might function well in less-developed areas, where the economic structure was simple, but hurt in well-developed industrial areas such as Latvia and Estonia. Before 1964, all of Estonia's industry was directed from six local centers, but by 1969 about 40 local and Union-wide command centers were involved. Union ministries often had a single plant in Estonia, with its day-to-day management carried out from Moscow some 1,000 km. away. Estonia's metallurgy and machine construction were subject to 15 different planning and command agencies, most of them outside Estonia. Industry was often expanded into cities where communal facilities were already overstrained, Tarmisto wrote, because the central planners were not obliged to consult with city agencies responsible for the wellbeing of the population. Others proposed that the efficiency measurements practised at single-plant level be expanded to ministerial level, to determine whether territorial or production-branch management would be more efficient in any given case. A similar argument was made out in 1978 by the Lithuanian economist Algirdas Maniušis, who underscored the importance of republic organs of administration in the establishment of genuinely efficient industrial units. He noted that management at the republic level was less fettered by rigid administrative boundaries, which could facilitate the creation of enterprises overlapping several existing industrial branches

37. *Nar. khoz. LaSSR 1971*, p. 79; EE/BE, no. 35, p. 3 (1972).

as well as drawing on the results of diverse research and planning institutes.[38]

At the Supreme Soviet session of 1970, Artur Vader (soon to become Chairman of the Presidium of the Supreme Soviet of the ESSR) castigated the Union Building Materials Ministry for its costly, shoddy and insufficient deliveries, and all Union ministries for giving premiums to plants located in Estonia but then failing to fulfill their plans for products that were needed locally. Such detailed complaints by Baltic Supreme Soviet delegates continued in the 1970s, but without raising the general issue of decentralization.

During the late 1960s, a "new planning and incentive system" of self-management was gradually introduced in Soviet enterprises. It involved relative administrative autonomy, financial self-dependence (and hence need for profitability), and the tying of workers' incomes to the enterprise's profits. This partial return to Western economic criteria was eagerly accepted and quickly implemented in the Baltic republics. In Estonia, plants using the new system represented 49 per cent of total industrial production in 1967 and 96 per cent by the end of 1970. In Lithuania the figure was 90 per cent by the end of 1969. Progress was slower in industries dominated by Union ministries, where the mentality that "production determines consumption" persisted and administrative methods were preferred to economic levers. The material stimulation of labor efficiency slowed down when payments into stimulation funds increased, but increased payments to the workers out of those funds were not allowed. Adjustments were gradual.

Stymied in their quest for decentralization from above, some Baltic technocrats tried to make use of the plant self-management approach for consolidation of republic authority from below. In 1973, the ESSR Food Industry Minister, Jaan Tepandi, argued that his ministry should be given self-management rights throughout the republic, reducing food industry decision-making by both local and all-Union enterprises. He thought this approach was suitable for many ministries in the smaller republics. The degree of implementation of such proposals was limited. The ESSR Transportation Ministry's Highway Agency

38. Vello Tarmisto, "Territorial Concentration and Decentralization of Industry in the Soviet Baltic Republics," *Eesti NSV Teaduste Akadeemia Toimetised — Ühiskonnateadused*, XVIII/3 (1969), pp. 208–11; M. Kuniavskii, "Territorialnye problemy upravleniia," *Kommunist (Litvy)*, no. 11 (1979), p. 86; review of A. Maniushis [Maniušis], *Sovershenstvovanie upravleniia narodnym khoziaistvom soiuznoi respubliki* (Vilnius, 1978).

apparently could not shift to self-management under that name, but was able to do so once it was reorganized as a "Highway Construction and Maintenance Trust" in 1970. Even minor production and personnel decisions continued to be made in Moscow. Knowledgeable Balts combined frequent business trips with personally making sure that their files in Moscow were "in the right pile."

Agricultural Efficiency.   The agricultural efficiency of the Baltic republics continued to surpass the Soviet average by wide margins (86 per cent in Estonia, 1968), and farmers' living standards continued to improve.[39] State farm employees profited from enterprise self-management, and the relaxation of various restrictions turned some kolkhozes into genuine collective farms which at times became relatively wealthy. By 1972 collective farmers' average income (including income from private plots) had exceeded that of urban workers in Estonia and Latvia, and the traditional labor flow from the countryside to the cities started to be cancelled out by an opposite flow. Kolkhoz chairmen continued to be effectively appointed by the party-state apparatus, but in some cases the kolkhoz council came to be genuinely elected.

The number of farms continued to be slowly reduced through mergers. Both very poor and very rich kolkhozes ran the risk of being turned into sovkhozes after an irreversible *pro forma* vote by the collective farmers. The poor ones would receive improved management, while the state could extract a fatter slice of profits from wealthy farms under the sovkhoz format, even though total profits might suffer. Kolkhoz-sovkhoz mergers almost always resulted in sovkhozes, but there was at least one conversion in the opposite direction.

Auxiliary industry on collective farms was a major factor in their new wealth. Although an all-Union edict of 1938 had prohibited any kolkhoz industry, many kolkhozes started to process their products in the mid-1960s. By the time farm industry was declared legal in 1967, it already produced 54 per cent of all Estonia's starch and 27 per cent of its sawn timber. By 1970 many Baltic collective farms derived most of their profits from mills, canneries, wine factories and mineral-

39. For details on agriculture, see (in addition to sources in note 36) Elmar Järvesoo, "Progress Despite Collectivization," in Ziedonis *et al.* (eds), *Problems of Mininations*, pp. 137–49, and "Private Enterprise in Soviet Estonian Agriculture," JBS, V/3 (Fall 1974), pp. 169–87; Jonas Glemža, "Die Landwirtschaft Sowjetlitauens, 1960–1973," AB, XV (1975), pp. 211–79.

water bottling. They made furniture, bakery products, barbed wire, special nails and various wooden and metal consumer goods. Inter-farm industry developed, such as a large cannery built by 24 kolkhozes in Latvia's Liepāja district. Some kolkhozes (and sovkhozes) built their own stores in the cities. The kolkhozes were supposed to use only their own labor and agricultural raw materials, but in practice success-ful farms often bought raw materials from other farms and brought in city labor. The 1972 plan for Latvia envisaged 64,000 minks, but farms produced 36,000 more for the private market. State pleas for "party-mindedness" only partly convinced kolkhozes to deliver cheap milk and grain rather than make more profitable maltose and starch. A firm line was drawn by state control when four Estonian kolkhozes started to act as marketing agents for individual producers of wooden buttons throughout several districts. Farm industry made headway in many parts of the Soviet Union, but the Baltic farms seemed to be among the most active. In 1972 auxiliary industry formed 14 per cent of Estonia's total agricultural production.[40]

The Kirov fishing kolkhoz near Tallinn seems to have been unique. It gradually acquired nearly 100 trawlers, boats and processing ships, but most of its income came from fur animals, trout, canning, furni-ture, garden products and souvenirs. Mergers made it stretch 120 km. along the coastline. Already by 1971, the monthly income was 650 rubles per member (compared to the ESSR average of 240 and USSR average of 140 rubles). Membership stood at 3,400, with a long waiting list. This piece of the Adriatic on the Baltic coast seemed to be accepted by the authorities because it was a convenient showcase of collective-farm wellbeing. Visiting VIPs from Romania's President Ceauşescu to the Shah of Iran as well as tourist groups from abroad could be taken to admire Kirov's health and consumer services build-ing, its restaurant, clubhouse and sports stadium.

Despite occasional collective wealth, a large part of collective farm income continued to come from the tiny private plots — 44 per cent in Latvia in 1970 and 43 per cent in Lithuania five years later. In 1975, the private sector still produced 39 per cent of Lithuania's total agricultural output and 17 per cent of Estonia's *marketed* agricultural produce, on a basis of 5 to 7 per cent of total arable land and an

---

40. For documentation on farm auxiliary industry, see "Can Farmers Can?" EE/BE, no. 20, pp. 3–4 (1970); and also nos 14, p. 8 (1969); 19, p. 2, and 23, p. 5 (1970); 24, p. 6, and 29, p. 8 (1971); 33, p. 4 (1972); 37, p. 2 (1973); and 42, p. 3 (1974).

obviously much larger share of labor input.[41] However, the state and collective sectors were expanding; the Latvian figures in Table 15 are typical.

Soviet feelings toward private agriculture were negative in principle, and there were frequent attempts to make it inconvenient. Some of these clearly backfired. As livestock feed came to be priced higher than bread, many privately owned pigs, not surprisingly, started to be fed bread and even macaroni. At a practical level, however, the Soviets realized the importance of private farming in feeding the cities. As thousands of farmers were being relocated from the traditional scattered farmhouses into newly-created kolkhoz villages, it was determined by a Latvian survey that many had given up their cows and most planned to stop all private farming as being inconvenient. While official social commentators were pleased with the apparent diminution of the instinct for private ownership, they also noted that a collective farmer who gives up his cow "not only stops producing milk but will also demand milk from the local store."[42] When Baltic efficiency seemed to bring a completely deprivatized agriculture possibly within their reach, the Soviets hesitated. Official support for the vanishing privately owned cow reappeared. The Tartu Experimental Automotive Plant even built a special bus for collecting milk from private owners of cows.

Although rural incomes, including the significant proceeds from private plots, tended to exceed those of urban industrial workers, the rural environment continued to offer a less attractive lifestyle than the cities. In 1973, about half of Lithuania's rural population lived in some 200,000 scattered individual homesteads (down from 265,000 in 1967). Some 100,000 of these dated from the nineteenth century and were of log construction and badly in need of repair. Their rate of diminution was low, about 10,000 annually, but apart from a few showplace settlements, their replacements were also not uniformly attractive. Of the 130,000 residential units in Lithuania's 3,870 rural settlements (38 per cent of the total rural housing), only 17 per cent had running water and 6 per cent a working sewage-disposal system. Only one-fifth of the settlement streets were paved, and most had no trees or greenery.

41. *Ibid.*, no. 47, p. 13 (1974); *Ekonomika ir kultūra* [LiSSR] *1975*, pp. 104 and 113; *Nar. khoz. ESSR 1977*, pp. 90 and 97.

42. *Literatūra un māksla*, 27 January 1973.

The ageing of the rural population also continued. By 1970, two-thirds of Lithuania's pensioners lived in the countryside, numbering 357,000 or 23 per cent of the rural population. This placed a great strain on the underdeveloped social-care and social-welfare systems. The average rural pensioner found it difficult to live on a pension which in 1972 averaged 23 rubles. In 1968, it had been calculated that a monthly expenditure of 45 rubles was necessary to maintain a minimum standard of living. This led many to work for their collective farms after retirement, to continue backbreaking labor on their private plots for some supplementary income, or to join their children in already overcrowded urban housing. Such solutions did not lighten hardship and could alert younger people to the difficulties of remaining in the countryside. The prevalent attitude of looking down on rural workers remained widespread.

While Baltic agricultural efficiency continued to be much higher than the Soviet average, it also remained much below that of Scandinavia. The average 1970 milk production per cow was 2,110 kilos throughout the USSR, 2,950 in Latvia, but 3,950 in Denmark. Disparities led to an interesting cooperation between Estonia and the neighboring underdeveloped Russian Pskov *Oblast*, which delivered Estonia's flax quota while Estonia took care of the Pskov potato deliveries to the state and helped in land drainage. Baltic experimentation with an extensive type of farming offered a possible development model for the less advanced regions of the USSR.[43]

Laboratory Role and Labor Shortage.   According to the French Communist journal *Démocratie nouvelle*, in 1965 Estonia, because of its high level of material, social and cultural development, was explicitly assigned a role as a socio-economic laboratory for the Soviet Union, which made it in the journal's opinion a representative miniature, a "reduced model" of the future economy of the Soviet Union.[44] This laboratory role, which was shared by Latvia, was receding by the late 1970s, but around 1970 its importance in determining the direction of Soviet planning seems to have been appreciable. It was not so much a question of having the largest milk tank in the Soviet Union or

43. M. L. Bronshtein, "Estonskii eksperiment," *Pravda*, 18 June 1972. For preceding description of rural life, see Benedict Mačiuika, "Contemporary Social Problems in the Collectivized Lithuanian Countryside," *Lituanus*, XXII/3 (1976), pp. 9, 14, 16.

44. *Démocratie nouvelle*, March 1965, p. 91.

building the world's most powerful crane (although these achievements were announced by the Soviet Estonian press), or even realizing by 1970 that trucks are more economical than railroads for small freight — Estonia's main role was in the adoption of computerized methods in economic management.

Estonian scientists were assigned "a leading role" in developing republic-wide automated management systems.[45] They were to write the standards regarding the structure, data banks and transmission. The Cybernetics Institute in Tallinn, founded in 1960, had been the first Soviet institute devoted entirely to cybernetics. In 1969 an econometric model of Estonia's economy was constructed, scheduling of trucks began to be computerized, and two years later republic-wide automated planning and managing of construction were introduced — all Soviet "firsts." Increasingly, all-Union ministries were turning to Estonia and the other Baltic republics for the first implementation of systems later to be applied Union-wide. Computerization of agricultural management was another focus of Baltic pioneering. The limited supply of advanced computers was compensated for by ingenuity.

The Baltic industrial product-mix remained basically the same as before. Overall, the structure of Baltic industry differed from the average of the USSR in the preponderance of food processing and light industries. In 1970, 32.7 per cent of Lithuania's industrial workforce was engaged in machine construction, 24.8 per cent in light industry and 13.0 per cent in food processing. *Per capita*, Lithuania in 1970 was fifth in the USSR in the production of electrical energy, third in mineral fertilizer, second in wool fabrics, first in meat and third in fish. In 1977, Estonia stood first in the USSR in *per capita* production of electrical energy, mineral fertilizer, paper, cotton fabrics, fish and butter. Latvia continued to produce about 30 per cent of all Soviet electric railroad cars, 50 per cent of all motorcycles and mopeds, and 20 per cent of radio sets.

The share of consumer goods varied. In Estonia consumer goods industries expanded, and surpassed heavy industry in 1973. In Latvia, on the contrary, the share of heavy industry expanded from 50 per cent of the total in 1965 to 57 per cent in 1977. In Lithuania it expanded from 58 per cent in 1970 to 60 per cent in 1975.[46]

---

45. *Rahva Hääl*, 15 February 1973.

46. Järvesoo 1978, p. 143; *Nar. khoz. LaSSR 1977*, p. 68; *Ekonomika ir kultūra* [LiSSR] *1975*, p. 57.

Quality still remained a problem. A check-up made in 1973 in Latvia found that 106 out of 185 production units produced substandard goods. The merging of small production units met resistance, and bureaucratic squabbles sometimes became grotesque. For more than a year, no door hinges could be bought in Estonia, the Deputy Minister of Trade Aleksander-Voldemar Rebane complained in 1970, because the Price Committee refused to assign a price for hinges without screws, and no suitable screws could be found.[47]

Despite such impediments, industrial production in the late 1960s continued to rise steeply (see Table 16). The growth was slightly above the Soviet average in Estonia and Latvia, and much higher in Lithuania. As Baltic industry matured, growth slowed down in the 1970s, falling below the Soviet average (which itself was decreasing) in Latvia and Estonia, and barely maintaining this average in Lithuania.

The increase in produced national income followed a similar pattern (see Table 16). In 1965–70, it was very close to the Soviet average for Latvia and Estonia, and higher for Lithuania. In 1970–5, it was very close to the Soviet average in all three Baltic republics.

Around 1970, Soviet sources were claiming that Baltic *per capita* national incomes were among the highest in Europe, with Estonia slightly ahead of Denmark, Latvia and West Germany. However, Baltic visitors to the West felt that their people had markedly lower purchasing power and living standards, in spite of their *per capita* national incomes certainly being some 50 per cent above the Soviet average, and higher than those of any other Union republic.

Integration of the Baltic economies into the all-Soviet framework was extensive, but nonetheless a quite surprising degree of self-sufficiency was maintained. In 1971 Estonia exported 31 per cent of its "material production" (88 per cent of it into other parts of the USSR), which is low compared to other countries throughout the world of comparably small population size.[48] The import pattern was similar, with imports and exports in approximate equilibrium. It seemed that restrictions on trade with non-Soviet countries were partly compensated for by Soviet trade, but partly too by producing

47. *Rahva Hääl*, 23 September 1970.
48. Laine Tulp, "Meie vabariik Nõukogude Liidu majandussüsteemis," *Eesti Kommunist*, XXVIII/2 (February 1972), pp. 11–18, and "The Estonian SSR and Socialist Integration," in *Estonia: Geographical Studies* (Tallinn, 1972), pp. 151–9; Rein Taagepera and J. P. Hayes, "How Trade/GNP Ratio Decreases with Country Size," *Social Science Research*, VI/1 (March 1977), pp. 108–32.

locally what could have been found more cheaply on the world market. Soviet trade through the Baltic ports expanded, with Klaipéda and Ventspils exporting coal and oil. Riga shipped iron, timber and industrial products, with regular connections to Le Havre in France. Tallinn's maritime connections with West Africa specialized in sugar imports. Throughout the 1970s, rumors circulated that Moscow was planning to make Tallinn the main Soviet Baltic maritime center, doubling its population to nearly a million. Local planning in all three republics stressed the need to develop smaller towns around which rural labor reserves still existed.

Labor shortage was becoming a major problem for the Soviet Union in the 1970s, and in the Baltic republics it was becoming a visible brake on plans for industrial expansion. By 1969, Lithuanian economists began to speak of the labor shortage (already prevalent in Latvia and Estonia), and suggested a slowdown, since Lithuania's industrial production was on the point of reaching the Soviet average. In Latvia the number of industrial workers did not increase in 1970–2, and in Estonia the increase was much less than 1 per cent per year. At the highest level in Moscow the labor shortage was acknowledged, and emphasis was placed on raising labor efficiency. Baltic republic agencies, keenly aware of the shortage in their own republics, generally tried to achieve the planned production growth through increases in efficiency only. However, the basically territorial issue of labor economy was hard to solve through the mechanisms inherent in centralized management. Thus Latvia's Deputy Director of Planning, Elerts Āboliņš, protested against the five-year plans for industries under Union-wide control which, instead of freeing labor for other needs, expected "an increase in the number of workers by an unrealistic 13,000."[49]

Baltic labor efficiency was markedly above the Soviet average, but below Western standards. The "Kalev" candy factory in Tallinn exported some of its production and used the resulting foreign currency bonus to buy an assembly line from Italy around 1969. Designed for 11 Italian workers, the line was set up to operate with 18 Estonians. A series of 24-hour analyses of all machine and instrument construction factories in Latvia between 1967 and 1971 found 25–32 per cent of basic production equipment idle, mainly for lack of workers. Auxiliary tasks consumed an increasing share of labor — 42 per cent in 1971.[50]

49. *Padomju Latvijas komunists*, May 1973, p. 12.
50. *Cīņa*, 23 July 1972.

The very shortage of manpower which demanded higher efficiency made its achievement more difficult, since workers fired for continual tardiness, absence and drinking on the job could easily find jobs elsewhere. The yearly turnover in apparently typical plants and farms was around 15–20 per cent, saddling the economy with additional time losses and retraining costs, on top of a heavy bureaucratic overload. In the words of senior engineer, Heino Tominga: "Building organizations unfortunately have so much empty senseless paperwork that it is hard to take it seriously. We make fun of these documents, but we must nonetheless send them in by the deadline." He also said that labor shortage forced the management "to treat the construction workers with more tender loving care than they merited."[51] In Tartu the competition between construction enterprises led to wage increases, but such regulation through market mechanisms was stopped in 1972; strict wage ceilings were imposed, and scarce labor was distributed by administrative means.

The labor shortage ranged from police to milkmaids. The seasonal nature of agricultural work emerged as another labor drain, with 70,000 farm workers underemployed in Latvia alone. Farm ancillary industries gave only limited help, since their peak period tended to coincide with that of agricultural work. Commuting to winter work in nearby cities was under discussion both in Latvia and Estonia, but the non-market wage structure imposed by bureaucratic fiat seemed to offer no incentives. A popular way of avoiding wage ceilings was to work on two full-time jobs simultaneously, and 40,000 people in Latvia were officially acknowledged to be thus engaged in 1973.[52]

In 1969, pension rules for retired persons were relaxed in Estonia, where 17 per cent of the population were over 60, compared to the Soviet average of 11 per cent. In some fields, pensioners could now receive full retirement benefits on top of a salary of up to 300 rubles a month, if they continued to work (which 55 per cent did). An official "people's industry enterprise" named *Kodu* ("Home") was also created to distribute materials and collect products from a sort of cottage industry where pensioners, disabled people, housewives and seasonal workers produced various consumer items. In addition to such efforts to collectivize private production, restrictions on non-cooperative work were relaxed. Private tailoring and photographic

51. *Sirp ja Vasar*, 15 September 1972.
52. EE/BE, nos 25, p. 4 (1971); 32, p. 3 (1972); 37, p. 3 (1973); and 42, p. 2 (1974).

work were already legal under the 1949 rules. Permitted private enterprise was now extended to hairdressing, watch and TV repairs, and toy and furniture manufacture. Printing, brewing and transportation remained expressly forbidden. All private enterprises had to be registered. In Latvia, construction and carpentry income up to 730 rubles was tax-free in 1973.[53]

As the spontaneous labor inflow from Russia leveled off in the late 1960s, enterprises took to active recruitment through advertisements in the Baltic Russian-language press, and directly in Russian cities. The accompanying promises of housing especially irked the Balts, who were themselves short of living space. In Estonia a special Labor Reserves Committee was created in 1968. Its centralized employment bureau ran advertisements in the Estonian and Russian-language press for unskilled and construction laborers, typists, electricians, salespeople, nurses and farm tractor-drivers. There was visible inconsistency between the Baltic economic goals set by Moscow and official statements that manpower recruitment from outside the republic was "not in agreement with our Party's policy."[54] While 22,000 job vacancies in Estonia were allegedly caused by the decreased labor influx from outside, an increasing population growth-rate around 1970 could be explained only by increased immigration. The labor demands of the economic plan had been excessive from the viewpoint of Baltic national interests ever since 1945, but now they also exceeded the availability of the Russian labor supply. In the late 1970s the planned overexpansion was reduced, and a better balance with the still decreasing labor supply seemed to result.

Energy and Ecology.   The policy of overdevelopment brought increasing ecological problems, especially in connection with boosted energy needs.[55] Baltic energy supply remained limited. Oil was discovered in Lithuania's Klaipėda district in 1968, but in insufficient quantities for exploitation. Instead, a large oil refinery was built in Mažeikiai to

53. *Ibid.*, nos 10, p. 4 (1968); 14, p. 4 (1969); 18, p. 1, and 23, p. 5 (1970); 25, p. 2 (1971); and 43, p. 9 (1974).

54. Arno Köörna, in *Eesti Kommunist*, June 1971, pp. 3–10.

55. For details on energy and ecology, see Henry Ratnieks, "Baltic Oil Prospects and Problems," JBS, VII/4 (Winter 1976), pp. 312–19, "Baltic Oil Shale," *ibid.*, IX/2 (Summer 1978), pp. 155–63, and "Energy Crisis and the Baltics," *ibid.*, XII/3 (Fall 1981), pp. 245–59; Mare Taagepera, "Pollution of the Environment and the Baltics," *ibid.*, pp. 260–74; Augustine Idzelis, "Response of Soviet Lithuania to Environmental Problems in the Coastal Zone," *ibid.*, X/4 (Winter 1979), pp. 299–308.

refine crude oil piped in from Bashkiria and the Ob region. It was begun in 1972 and completed in the early 1980s. The refinery had originally been planned for Jurbarkas, but a protest by 21 members of the intelligentsia over its danger to the Nemunas River delta led to the inland site at Mažeikiai, near the Latvian border, being chosen instead. In Latvia, a large hydroelectric power station was built at Pļaviņas, on the Daugava River, 120 km. from Riga. More industrialized than the other two Baltic republics, Latvia received 42 per cent of its 1970 energy from Lithuania and Estonia.

Estonia's oil-shale mining far exceeded its internal energy needs, but with energy exports its own needs were barely covered. The degree of electrification of Estonia's industry in 1970 was only 64 per cent of the Soviet average. It produced 10 billion kilowatt-hours, but consumed only 3.5 billion. The pattern of oil-shale use changed over time. Gas made from oil-shale had been supplied to Leningrad in the 1950s, but in 1968 the flow direction was reversed as Tallinn started to receive cheaper natural gas from the Urals. Oil-shale gasification thus remained static, but shale-based electricity continued to expand. The "Baltic Thermoelectric Station" was completed in 1965, and the "Estonian Thermoelectric Station" reached its full capacity of 1.6 million kilowatts in 1973. While growth worshippers waxed enthusiastic about Estonia's having the world's two largest shale-based power plants, scientists increasingly questioned the wisdom of digging up 30 million tons of oil shale each year and then burning most of it. Shale oil was seen as a valuable chemical raw material. An ammonia fertilizer plant was opened in 1969, but few other chemical applications followed. For most chemical uses it was cheaper to import oil than to extract it from shale. At the least, Estonian oil-shale activity brought to Tallinn a nine-day UNESCO-sponsored International Oil Shale Symposium in 1968, a valuable boost to the self-confidence of the long-secluded Estonian technologists and engineering students.

By 1975 all major Baltic cities were connected to natural gas pipelines. In the face of this cheap and convenient means of energy supply, oil-shale mining seemed to level off, but by 1980 the energy outlook had changed. With its oil and gas projections reduced, Moscow seemed to want to increase oil-shale mining to levels that could deplete the Estonian reserves in much less than the previously envisaged 200 years. From the empire's viewpoint it was a quick energy fix, but from Estonia's viewpoint it was colonial over-exploitation of the country's only energy and industrial raw material reserves.

Considerable reliance on nuclear energy was apparently foreseen in the future. In the late 1970s, construction began by Lake Drūkšiai in northeastern Lithuania on the first quarter of a planned massive generation complex. A new city named after the late First Party Secretary Sniečkus was also begun nearby to house construction workers and, eventually, workers at the plant.

Baltic concern about ecology first emerged in the mid-1950s with a Latvian debate about clean rivers.[56] In Estonia there was a debate in *Eesti Loodus* (March 1965) about pesticides, and in 1968 Rachel Carson's *Silent Spring* was translated. Both Latvia (around 1966) and Estonia claimed to be the only republic in the USSR (and possibly the world) completely to ban the use of DDT, hexachlorane and other long-lasting and highly toxic organic chlorine and phosphorus preparations. River pollution was the next concern. In 1969 the effluents of a chemical factory in Panevėžys killed all the fish in the Nevėžis River, and the Venta, the Šešupė, the Minija and other Lithuanian rivers were also reported to be suffering from pollution. The freshwater fish catch in Estonia had been reduced to one-eighth of what it had been ten years earlier, and several popular beaches were becoming unhealthy.

> This is the last song about this river.
> No new ones will be made
> and the old ones will soon be forgotten.
>
> Nothing but a dead, dirty flow
> circling around mounds of ashes.
> This river no longer has a soul.
>
> The factory, this bright-eyed titan,
> has buried the sun and the moon
> with hot flakes of soot,
> while it pours its excrement
> into the river.[57]

These Estonian verses by Kersti Merilaas were a far cry from the Soviet First of May slogans which in 1970 still made no mention of the need to abate pollution — just "Improve product quality in every way, and reduce production costs!" (Slogan 24). Sewage-disposal problems arose even in minor cities such as Viljandi, and water-supply

---

56. Juris Dreifelds, "Implementation of Pollution Control Policy in Latvia: A Case Study of the Sloka Pulp and Paper Mill," *Co-Existence* (Glasgow), XVII (October 1980), pp. 178–92.

57. Kersti Merilaas, *Kuukressid* (Tallinn, 1969), pp. 141–2.

problems were ever-present. By 1980 Tallinn was receiving water from all over Estonia, from Lake Peipsi in the east and the Pärnu River in the southwest. In 1972 an ESSR Water Code was promulgated to regulate water use and forbid construction of new plants without pollution-control devices. The paper industry was a main polluter, but talks with the visiting USSR Minister for the industry seemed to make no progress. The republic's code was not binding on the Union-wide ministry. Soviet industry in Estonia recirculated only 22 per cent of its water, compared to 81 per cent in Lithuania and a Soviet average of 53 per cent.

Protection of the environment gradually became accepted by Moscow as necessary in principle. However, continued emphasis on Union-wide management by each branch of production made it very difficult to preserve the inevitably territorial ecological balance. In Lithuania's fragile coastal zone pollution increased despite republic-level efforts. The Klaipėda Cellulose and Paper Combine continued to discharge 35,000 tons of waste annually into shallow waters. Waste treatment facilities began to be built only in 1974, and were not yet finished four years later. Despite moderate fines, 63 ships discharged waste oil into the Klaipėda harbor in 1974. Protests at the USSR Supreme Soviet (e.g. by the Vilnius CP Secretary, Vytautas Sakalauskas, in 1977) brought only partial response from Union-wide ministries, and the LiSSR Deputy Prime Minister, Aleksandras Drobnys, started to advocate "the adoption of territorial principles in the planning of surface-water protection measures."[58] However, the Lithuanian Party and government appeared to be powerless *vis-à-vis* the all-Union ministries. A number of international conferences and projects on pollution took place in the Baltic republics, mostly with Soviet and Finnish but also some American participation (December 1974, in Jūrmala).[59]

Culture and the Expansion of Western Contacts

One of the most striking socio-cultural developments in the Baltic republics after 1968 was the expansion of contacts with the West. The submerged Western traditions had resurfaced during the rebirth of national cultures under the Thaw, and direct contacts began to develop during that period. Their expansion after 1968 was so gradual

58. *Liaudies ūkis*, no. 5, 1979; see Idzelis 1979, pp. 304–8.
59. *Veseliba*, no. 2, 1975.

that only comparing them with the reports and comments of the mid-1960s reveals the extent of cumulative change by 1980.[60]

The Expansion of Travel.   By the 1970s, the small amount of travel which began in the late 1950s had become an appreciable flow, though hardly a torrent. In 1967, 2,500 individuals from Estonia took vacations outside the USSR, most of them probably in Eastern Europe. In 1970 about 1,700 Estonians visited Finland alone. While still very limited in comparison with West European countries, these figures had probably risen much higher by 1980.

Increasing numbers visited relatives abroad, sometimes for several months. More scholars spent up to a year abroad, sometimes accompanied by their spouses, though with children usually left behind. Soviet Baltic attendance at international scholarly conferences increased. In 1979, for the first time ever, several Soviet Baltic scholars attended the biennial Conference on Baltic Studies in Scandinavia. Artistic performances abroad by Soviet Baltic individuals and ensembles became ever more frequent.

Nevertheless, impediments to foreign travel continued. Many people repeatedly applied for permission to travel abroad but without success, even though relatives abroad were willing to cover all expenses. Scholars and scientists with papers accepted for presentation at international conferences were sometimes denied exit visas at the last minute, with no explanation. Permission and denial of foreign travel had become one of the means for social control by the authorities.

Permanent emigration was also somewhat expanded. During the 1970s most emigrants from the Baltic republics were either Jews or Volga Germans who had settled there during the Thaw.

The flow of Western visitors continued, at probably ten times the rate of Balts going to the West. During the early 1970s, several Scandinavian lines supplemented the Helsinki-Tallinn boat line which had been started in 1965, attracting vodka weekenders from Finland. Several hundred Finnish construction workers came to Tallinn between 1969 and 1972 to build the modern high-rise Viru Hotel, and a number of them married Estonians. However, such projects did not continue after that time.

60. For details of travel and interactions, see EE/BE; V. Stanley Vardys, "The Role of the Baltic Republics in Soviet Society," in Roman Szporluk (ed.), *The Influence of East Europe and the Soviet West of the USSR* (New York, 1977), pp. 147–79.

Émigrés continued to make up a large percentage of Western visitors. In 1968 at least 600 Estonian émigrés revisited their homeland, and over 900 Latvians did so in 1972. By 1980 the number for all three countries together was very likely several thousand. Some of these visitors stayed for several months. A few students from abroad began to attend courses at Vilnius University and in Tallinn. An annual Lithuanian summer program at Vilnius University specially designed for the children of émigrés was started in the early 1970s, to be followed by similar programs in Latvia and Estonia.

Cultural Interactions.   Increasing numbers of Baltic performing artists were allowed to make themselves known abroad. The most eminent was probably the Estonian conductor Neeme Järvi, who performed extensively in the West and had a favorable reception at the Metropolitan Opera in New York in 1978. The following year he and his Jewish wife emigrated permanently, and at once became unmentionable in the Soviet Estonian press. The Lithuanian tenor Virgilijus Noreika gave some performances abroad.

Many attempts by Baltic performers to participate in Western musical life met obstruction from the authorities. The Estonian composer Arvo Pärt, whose music had become known outside the USSR since the mid-1960s, had several premières of his works in Finland and in Britain. However, his own travel abroad was severely restricted, which led him to ask for a permanent emigration permit. It was granted in 1979; Soviet bureaucracy seemed to prefer a total loss of talent to sharing it with the West. The Lithuanian bass Vaclovas Daunoras, who won a Gold Medal at the Toulouse competition in 1971, apparently also experienced difficulties in performing outside the USSR until 1979.

In spite of such pettiness, Soviet Baltic artists and their art continued to reach the West far more widely than earlier, and began to create a modernist Baltic image distinct from the general Soviet one. Writers also travelled more widely than ever before, and ties with émigré communities were expanded.

Western impact on the Baltic cultures, occurring through reciprocal visits, radio and Finnish (and, somewhat less, Polish) TV, translation of Western books, production of Western plays and musicals, and screening of Western films expanded steadily throughout the 1970s. The effect was striking, not only in comparison with the previous decade, but also in comparison with the rest of the USSR.

Serious Western drama seems to have been more in evidence on Baltic stages than in those of other Soviet republics. Eugene Ionesco's *Rhinoceros*, which had already been published in Estonia in 1967, and Samuel Beckett's *Krapp's Last Tape* were given notable stage performances in Tallinn. Riga saw a production of Tennessee Williams's *Night of the Iguana* in 1973. Arthur Miller's *Death of a Salesman* opened in Panevėžys in the late 1960s, and his *The Price* appeared in Vilnius somewhat later. Friedrich Dürrenmatt's *The Visit* and *The Physicists* and Tennessee Williams' *Orpheus Descending*, *The Glass Menagerie* and *A Streetcar Named Desire* were all performed in Lithuania in the 1970s.

The 1968 Vilnius production of Sławomir Mrożek's *Tango* was removed from the repertoire shortly after the invasion of Czechoslovakia. Its author, resident in France, had protested publicly against Poland's participation in the affair, and as a result became unmentionable in his home-country. The story was widespread in Vilnius that the Cultural Attaché of the Polish Embassy in Moscow had lodged a protest over this sole remaining production of a Mrożek play in the bloc. The Lithuanian production of *The Price* also disappeared because of Arthur Miller's public expression of opinions unwelcome to the Soviet authorities.

Popular Western theatrical entertainment also made inroads. The Estonian production of *West Side Story* in 1965 seems to have been the first in the USSR of an American musical. By 1968 the "Estonia" Theater had also staged *Kiss Me Kate* and *My Fair Lady*. In 1974, a sexually explicit Estonian musical based on *Love Story* was performed. In 1969, a Latvian musical based on Mark Twain's *The Prince and the Pauper* was produced in Liepāja, and *Oklahama!* appeared on the same stage four years later. *My Fair Lady* was also given a Lithuanian production in Kaunas, and *Man of La Mancha* was staged in Vilnius. While such Baltic productions can hardly be considered unique, their number appears to have been greater than anywhere else in the USSR, especially in view of the size of the potential audience.

Interaction with émigrés sometimes proved fruitful in explaining Western phenomena to Soviet Balts — who in turn were able to "translate" them into concepts understandable to Soviet Russians. Émigrés continued to supply contacts with Western scholars and artists, and channeled Western consumer goods and fashions to the Baltic countries. In the absence of Stalinist methods of persuasion, Russian culture was clearly losing out to what the West had to offer.

Of course, interaction with Eastern Europe and the Soviet Union continued, but it became more balanced in several ways. In addition to Western works, the Balts translated Mrożek from Polish and Havel from Czech. They also discovered the Soviet East beyond Russia, from medieval Central Asian classics to contemporary Georgian and Armenian ways of coping with Russian hegemony. The Balts may have had some Westernizing influence on Russia itself in the 1960s through the ties to the West which they had established earlier.

The Baltic impact on the smaller nationalities within the Russian republic has been little noticed, but it may prove to have been of more than local importance, especially in the case of Estonia. The developed Estonian culture within the Soviet Union was an obvious role-model for other Soviet nations of around one million people, and Estonians were well aware of it. In 1968 the Vanemuine Theater in Tartu organized a seminar for theater producers of the autonomous republics and *oblasts* within the RSFSR. Estonia became the natural leader in Finno-Ugrian language studies in the USSR, and attracted graduate students from all the five Finnic autonomous republics. In 1970, a week-long Mari Cultural Festival was held in Estonia to introduce Estonians to this emerging fellow-Finnic culture in the Volga Bend and vice versa.

The Development of National Cultures.   The powerful cultural rebound of the early 1960s was followed in 1968–80 by a period of more mature and less spectacular development. Conditions continued to be the most difficult in Latvia, where the battle for cultural autonomy was still undecided.[61] In June 1968 Czechoslovakia's National Assembly Chairman, Josef Smrkovsky, visited Latvia and spoke on the "need to democratize socialism." In August students in Riga grilled and shouted down the regime spokesmen who tried to justify the Soviet invasion of Czechoslovakia. In December, LaCP Secretary Jurijs Rubenis launched a counterattack. Seven leading literary figures — Priede, Bels, Belševica, Čaklais, Vācietis, Auziņš and Purs — were accused of writing "from unacceptable positions." In the summer of 1969, the editors of the cultural weekly *Literatūra un māksla* were replaced, but the new team was also soon criticized for publishing ideologically erroneous works. (Estonia's cultural weekly *Sirp ja Vasar* also lost its editors in early 1969 after they were accused of "ugly

61. For details of cultural developments, see Ekmanis 1978; Kurman 1978, pp. 247–80; Valgemäe, pp. 281–317.

attacks" against Stalinist attackers of modernism.) However, later criticism (e.g. at the January 1976 LaCP Congress) tended to become more impersonal.

Attacks went beyond words. A play by Laimonis Purs, *To Behold the Sea*, became a box-office hit and was praised in the newspapers, until it was suddenly removed from the repertory in September 1968 because of "politically equivocal dialogues." The censors banned Gunārs Priede's *Mushrooms are Fragrant* even before it opened. Vizma Belševica became the most denounced writer of the period because of her two-tiered symbolism "liable to create utter ideological chaos among politically inexperienced readers" (*Cīņa*, 7 June 1969). Starting with her fourth poetry collection (*Annual Rings*, 1969), the witch-hunt continued for years. Many were bound to be displeased with verses like

> O servile nation! In sweet joy you tremble
> Because the master whips your brothers
> Instead of you. Waiting, you bare your teeth
> To fall upon a brother's bloodied nape,
> For in the master's hand a medal glitters
> To be bestowed on you . . .[62]

The setting of the poem was medieval, with one marked anachronism. For three years (1971–4), not a single poem by Belševica was published, but she was later gradually allowed to return. Another member of the Writers' Union, the French translator Maiji Silmale, was arrested in 1971 and made to testify in a political dissidence case. Although never tried herself, she was nonetheless confined to the prison psychiatric ward in Riga until shortly before her death.

Despite such harassment, Latvian culture made headway. In literature, new young talent appeared. Established poets sometimes switched to prose (Imants Ziedonis, *My Kurzeme*, 1970–4, and *Epiphanies*, 1971 and 1974; Belševica, *Misfortune at Home*, 1979). Poems were published that would have sounded bold even by the reputedly more relaxed standards in Lithuania and Estonia:

> Like pestilence, the regiments of Sheremetev
> Brought you double bondage
> Because His Excellency Peter the First
> Felt like hewing a wider window to Europe.

62. Vizma Belševica, "The Notations of Henricus de Lettis in the Margin of the Livonian Chronicle"; translation by Baiba Kaugara, *Lituanus*, XVI/1 (Spring 1970) pp. 15–21, followed by comments by Gunārs Saliņš, pp. 22–32.

This observation, made in 1968, was expressed in more general terms in 1970 by another poet:

> No one shall transform our land
> neither with Bibles
> nor various theories, courts, idols, hells.
> Alas, many have come to remake us,
> to give us their faith, their gods,
> to take our harbors — ice-free!
> to occupy our shores — amber shores![63]

Latvian prose was finally allowed to catch up, in terms of stylistic experimentation, with that of its neighbours. Poignancies of everyday life, alienation (*The Pedestrian*, 1974, by Jānis Mauliņš), war and postwar events (*Joker and a Puppet*, 1971, by Visvaldis Lāms), and sex (*Nakedness*, 1970, by Zigmunds Skujiņš) became acceptable topics. Drama remained a weak point, partly because of harassment.[64]

In Estonia prose writing and drama caught up with the earlier expansion of poetry. Here too a number of established poets shifted into a new genre. Historical novels by Jaan Kross set out to "reconquer the national past" by demonstrating the Estonian ties of reputedly Baltic-German cultural figures such as the sixteenth-century chronicler Balthasar Russow and the fifteenth-century painter Michel Sittow. Mats Traat described more recent tribulations in novels like *Dance around the Steam Engine* (1971), where every potential central figure dies, mostly in war, as soon as the author tries to focus on him. Aimée Beekman portrayed contemporary life with vivid realism, Arvo Valton wrote abstract short stories and a major novel on Mongol-Chinese intellectual interactions, Vaino Vahing emerged as a writer of psychological short stories, and Aino Pervik shocked many with her merciless description of sterile consumerism, sleeping around and pseudo-intellectualism.

In poetry the major new debut was that of the actor and TV performer Juhan Viiding (his early collections were written under the pseudonym Jüri Üdi), whose playful and ironic tone at times concealed deep despair. Writing in a somewhat similar tragi-comic vein,

---

63. Imants Auziņš, *Skumjais Optimisms* (Riga, 1968), p. 35; Māris Čaklais, *Karogs* (May 1970), p. 59; both as translated in Ekmanis 1978, pp. 344 and 347. Only one European power has been chronically short of ice-free ports.

64. *The Blue One*, a play representative of Gunārs Priede's production in the 1970s, is available in English translation by Andre Šedriks, in Alfreds Strautmanis (ed.), *Confrontations with Tyranny* (Prospect Heights, Ill., 1979), pp. 225–62.

Hando Runnel was repeatedly attacked in the official press for "impro-prieties" and "statements tending to nationalism," such as the follow-ing description of the postwar guerrillas:

> Many men were found, deported
> Many men to arms resorted.
> Bunkers in the woods were built.
> Many mouths were filled with silt.[65]

Absurdist theater reached a peak with Mati Unt's *Phaethon* (1968) and Paul-Eerik Rummo's *Cinderella Game* (1969; performed at La Mama in New York, 1971), and continued with a series of plays by Enn Vetemaa.[66] Political pressures in Estonia were similar to those in Latvia, but in general they remained milder.

Lithuania had already reached a state of stability following the Thaw by 1968, in almost all branches of writing, and further change was less eventful. The highly complex and intellectually sophisticated poetry of Tomas Venclova (*A Sign of Speech*, 1972) clearly proclaimed the incompatibility of art and politics. In "Tell Fortinbras" the allusion to Lithuania is unmistakable:

> So may they rest. White islands,
> Rock salt replenish their blood,
> Snowstorms rise from the shores of Connaught,
> The forests wrapped in steam, the shaggy orchards,
> And Denmark, Denmark is no more.[67]

Kazys Saja emerged as Lithuania's most prominent exponent of the didactic function of drama, focusing on such diverse questions as public morality, alcoholism and the conservation of natural resources. His *A Hunt for Mammoths* (1968) employs grotesque hyperbole and psycho-logical paradox to lampoon a variety of bureaucratic and social short-comings. *The Holy Lake* (1970) treats the damage caused by the excessive draining of swamps. Perhaps his most successful effort, which was translated into other Soviet and East European languages and had several productions within the bloc, was *Nine-Calamity Village*

65. Hando Runnel, *Lauluraamat ehk mõõganeelaja ehk kurbade kaitseks* (Tallinn, 1972); for full translation of the poem quoted, see Taagepera, "A Portrait," p. 85. For documentation on official attacks, see EE/BE, no. 37, p. 4 (1973).

66. *The Cinderella Game* has been translated into English by Andres Männik and Mardi Valgemäe, in Strautmanis 1979, pp. 273–322.

67. Tomas Venclova, *Kalbos ženklas* (Vilnius, 1972), p. 29; English translation by Algirdas Landsbergis in *Lituanus*, XXIII/4 (Winter 1977) p. 27.

(1976), an American-style musical based on folk themes.[68] *The House of Terror* (1968) by Juozas Glinskis is a philosophic investigation of the life of the early nineteenth-century folk bard Antanas Strazdas. Elements of the grotesque, along with stylistic and linguistic contrast and juxtaposition, are used to good effect in reflecting upon social, ethical and, in a veiled form, political issues. The production enjoyed unprecedented success. *Barbora Radvilaitė* by Juozas Grušas (1972), an extremely poetic treatment of the tragic fate of a beautiful sixteenth-century queen, Barbara Radziwiłłowna, continued to figure in the active repertoire long after its director, Jonas Jurašas, was forced to leave the country because of his open opposition (see p. 257).

However, a significant chill crept into the Lithuanian cultural scene in 1972, a follow-up at the local level of slightly earlier all-Union developments. In Vilnius the new atmosphere was heralded by a review article in *Tiesa* entitled "The Poetization of Chaos" on the latest poetry by Sigitas Geda, *26 Chants of Autumn and Summer* (1972). While the attack on Geda for his "subjective super-individualistic manner of depiction" was somewhat restrained, its weighty message of official dissatisfaction resounded clearly through cultural circles. The party organ did not usually concern itself with reviews of poetry, but in that year the editors of the official cultural weekly *Literatūra ir menas* and of the trendy youth magazine *Nemunas* were removed and the tone of both magazines noticeably changed. The year can also be said to have marked the end, for a time at least, of the theater's ability to discuss contemporary issues by allusion through historical drama. The innovative director of the Kaunas State Theater, Jonas Jurašas, was removed from his post and became a stone-cutter after he had protested publicly against political tampering with his productions (see next section, on dissent).

Baltic cultures received inspiration not only from the contemporary West but from their folkloric past, and often the two influences were blended. Remarkable ethnographic films on the Finno-Ugrian peoples were made by Lennart Meri. The oral folksong tradition, with motifs and styles going back centuries or as much as a millennium, still survived through the mouths of ageing bards in the middle of the twentieth century. However, people in general were more familiar with written texts and "Europeanized" tunes than with the original musical style. The spread of tape-recorders and the worldwide interest in

68. Translated under the title of *Village of Nine Woes* by Eglė Juodvalkis, in Alfreds Straumanis (ed.), *The Golden Steed* (Prospect Heights, Ill., 1979), pp. 277–325.

folksong coincided with the advent of a self-assured Baltic generation no longer ashamed of the simplicity of the old folktunes. The archaic singing style became quite popular with some groups in Estonia, while some others produced jazzed-up versions. A modernistic folksong-based oratorio by Veljo Tormis, *The Cursing of Iron* (1975), was officially criticized as pacifist. Folklore influenced many Baltic writers, from Latvian poets like Imants Auziņš and Jānis Peters to Lithuanian playwrights like Saja.

Dissent

It could be said that dissent — disagreement with or opposition to the system — was, almost by definition, endemic within the Baltic republics.[69] The realization that persistent dreams of independence, or at least of genuine autonomy, required fundamental change in political conditions throughout the USSR fostered a continuous series of attempts to secure or maintain whatever piecemeal benefits to national self-identification were obtainable under existing conditions. A whole spectrum of individuals, encompassing a major portion of the Baltic populations, could be characterized as falling within this group, and their general goal was shared by, among others, passive nationalists seeking to preserve and maximize the national forms of the Soviet system, members of the intelligentsia striving to enrich the national cultures and thus make them more attractive and immune to denationalization, and even some national Communists. All seemed to be striving for an improvement within the system. Broadly, Soviet reality turned any non-Russian Soviet citizen fully aware of his identity into a dissident because the survival of his ethnic group was likely to be seen by the regime as incompatible with its aims.[70]

69. For English-language reports on dissent and its repression, see various Amnesty International publications on the Soviet Union; *UBA Information Service* (United Baltic Appeal, New York), news release series; ELTA Information Service monthly newsletter (Supreme Committee for the Liberation of Lithuania, New York, from 1956 on); *Latvian Information Bulletin* (Latvian Legation, Washington, D.C.); EE/BE; Lituanus. Overviews and translations of underground publications: Vardys 1978; *Documents from Estonia on the Violations of Human Rights* (Stockholm, 1977); full texts (in German) of *The Chronicle of the Lithuanian Catholic Church*, from no. 7 on, in *Acta Baltica* (from 1975 on); Peter Reddaway (ed.), *Uncensored Russia: The Human Rights Movement in the Soviet Union* (London, 1972); Andres Küng, *A Dream of Freedom* (Cardiff, 1980).

70. Alexander Shtromas, *Political Change and Social Development: The Case of the Soviet Union* (Frankfurt, 1981), p. 80.

However, dissent was normally used to describe a more narrow type of overt activity. It included dramatic action like mass demonstrations or rioting, though these were infrequent and sporadic. Usually, the term connoted more restrained activity by those who felt a need to protest publicly or to counteract any of the basically negative influences permeating Soviet society. Dissidents generally sought to make their protests within Soviet law, but this nonetheless brought down upon them the full repression of the system, thus highlighting its pervasive hypocrisy.

At times dissent which could be labeled "apolitical" achieved its purpose. The appeal in 1966 by 21 members of the Lithuanian intelligentsia over the planned building of a refinery at Jurbarkas led to its relocation at Mažeikiai. Within a Soviet context, however, only a very limited range of issues could appear not to be politically inspired.

At the other end of the spectrum, some survivors of the postwar guerrillas still maintained an armed existence in the Baltic woods. On 5 October 1978 August Sabe, aged 70, drowned rather than surrender, like the swagman in "Waltzing Matilda."[71] He had been a forest brother in southern Estonia since 1944. Other similar cases have been reported, but after 1954 opposition to Soviet rule tended not to resort to arms.

Spontaneous Manifestations of Dissent. Numerous minor indications of the latent opposition smoldering beneath the surface constantly reappeared on the Baltic scene in the late 1960s and '70s. The simplest forms were usually the most numerous, consisting of ostentatious refusals to speak Russian in everyday situations when addressed in that language. Another form consisted of small symbolic gestures such as placing flowers at places whose significance the regime was seeking to minimize. An Estonian hero of the 1919 War of Independence, Julius Kuperjanov, had no living relatives, yet flowers regularly appeared by his grave. The pre-war Latvian independence monument in downtown Riga, which had not been destroyed by the authorities, was a similar magnet. Also the colors of the pre-war national flags were very unobtrusively introduced into souvenir items. More dramatic were the occasions when these flags were surreptitiously flown in prominent public places. It was reported that the slogan "Sakharov our conscience" was painted on trains as well as in the Riga Railroad Station in the spring of 1976 (see Plate III).

---

71. *Sõnumid* (Stockholm), no. 71 (March 1979), pp. 3–5.

Then there were the times when non-Soviet competitors were cheered by the spectators at sporting events, especially when they had acquired resistance symbolism. Czech teams were particular favorites in the period after 1968. Sporting events also triggered more massive demonstrations. These did not even have to be witnessed "live", as on 20 April 1972 when several hundred students from the Tallinn Polytechnic Institute celebrated a televised Czech hockey victory over the Soviets by shouting "We won" on the streets. In Vilnius a soccer match against a Russian team from Smolensk on 10 October 1977 provided the occasion for a demonstration against the new Soviet Constitution. A crowd of sports fans took to the streets shouting "Down with the Constitution of the occupying power!" Four months later, the Soviet press confirmed the event by castigating the émigré press for having exaggerated it, and "interviewed" some of the "rowdy" participants somehow to prove that simple hooliganism had triggered the outburst.[72]

Pop concerts sometimes had similar results. In the Estonian university town of Tartu on 3 December 1976, local officials decided to ban one of these because of its supposed political nuances. A crowd of students, estimated at about 1,000, streamed through the town shouting anti-Soviet slogans through the evening till about 2.30 the next morning. A similar incident followed a concert in the Latvian port city of Liepāja on 11 August 1977. Around 11 p.m., when an Estonian rock group was banned from performing at an open-air theater, the audience of young people proceeded to wreck the place to vent their anger at the authorities. About 1,000 of them later roamed through the streets shouting "Freedom!"[73]

There were full-scale riots in Lithuania at least three times after the war. The first was in 1956, and coincided with the dramatic events in Hungary and Poland. In July 1960 disturbances broke out in Kaunas after a boxing match between Lithuanian and Uzbek teams. Moscow's chief ideologue Mikhail Suslov was reputedly in the town that day, the anniversary eve of Lithuania's incorporation into the USSR. Few details are available.

The most massive manifestation in Lithuania was on 14 May 1972, when a 19-year-old student, Romas Kalanta, poured gasoline

72. Rein Taagepera, "Estonia: Uppity Satellite," *The Nation*, 7 May 1973; *Literatūra ir menas*, 11 February 1978, p. 12.

73. "Student Demonstrations in Tartu, Estonia," *Radio Liberty Research Paper*, no. 107 (May 1977); "Reports of Youth Demonstration after Pop Concert in Latvia," *ibid.*, no. 243 (October 1977).

over himself at noon in a park at Kaunas, struck a match, and subsequently died in hospital. Rioting began on the day of his funeral, when several thousand youths roamed the streets shouting "Freedom for Lithuania!" and fought with the authorities, who had to be reinforced by paratroopers and KGB units. Some 500 were arrested. Within a few days, three other self-immolations took place in other places in Lithuania. Some claims have been made that the Kalanta suicide had been planned as a joint Baltic protest, but that the Latvian and Estonian participants were somehow prevented from carrying them out.[74]

The meat shortage in Latvia reportedly led to an economically motivated workers' strike on an officially imposed "fish day" in May 1976 and the sentencing of four Riga dock workers to terms of two to three years in labor camps.[75]

October 1980 saw unprecedentedly large student demonstrations in Estonia, and up to 200 workers went on strike, possibly for the first time since the strike of the "Red Krull" workers in December 1940. A youth protest started on 22 September when a pop concert following a soccer game was abruptly interrupted by officials. Several thousand young people marched toward Tallinn's city center, and 200 were briefly arrested and expelled from school. Repression triggered new and better organized marches on 1 and 3 October, with 2,000 high school students converging on the government buildings from four separate assembly points. Some were severely beaten by the police, and several hundred were briefly arrested. Demonstrations spread to the Tallinn Polytechnic Institute, the Pärnu Merchant Navy School and Tartu University, and recurred in Tallinn on 10 October. Their calls ranged from demands for better cafeteria food to "Russians, get out!" A particular target was Elsa Gretškina, Soviet Estonia's newly appointed semi-Russian Minister of Education. *Rahva Hääl* on 14 October 1980 announced court proceedings against the "initiators and propagators" of "recent gross breaches of public order by groups of youths." Meanwhile, workers went on strike on 1 October at the Tartu Experimental Repair Factory, demanding reduced work norms and the payment of long-withheld bonuses. They were perhaps encouraged by the success of Polish workers. The next day a

74. The events in Lithuania received widespread press coverage. Among others, see *New York Times*, 22, 26 and 28 May and 8 June 1972; *The Economist*, 27 May 1972; and *Le Monde*, 23 May 1972. The reference to an abortive joint Baltic demonstration appears in the Lithuanian *samizdat* publication *Aušra*, no. 1 (1975).

75. *The Times* (London) and *New York Times*, both 1 November 1976.

special commission rushed in from Moscow and acceded to strikers' demands.[76]

Dissent was persistently manifested in *samizdat*. The varied documents, magazines, memoirs, appeals, open letters and news reports, though generally produced by the intelligentsia, together represented the tip of an iceberg of gradually mounting internal pressure for change affecting all levels of society. On the all-Union scene, the trial in early 1966 of the writers Siniavskii and Daniel is usually considered the beginning of the *samizdat* age. Most of those who, as a result of the Khrushchev years, had hoped for things to get better within the system and that their society would finally throw off its Stalinist shackles, now realized how futile their expectations had been. As official channels for serious criticsm remained closed for the foreseeable future, the most eager advocates for change began to act unofficially.

Lithuania. As has been noted, the Khrushchev Thaw lasted somewhat longer in Lithuania than in Moscow. The CP First Secretary Sniečkus managed to avert the unseemly problems posed by national Communism in Latvia. Although carefully controlled, there was a greater cultural latitude and diversity, enriched by the pre-war heritage which had still not entirely faded. This produced achievements of unquestioned value and nourished the hope that a distinct Lithuanian culture would be preserved. The feeling of futility took longer to sink in than in Moscow. But from 1968 on, Lithuanian *samizdat*, first a mere trickle, began to reflect mounting dissident activity. The trickle later became a massive flood. Around 1980, Lithuania was probably producing more *samizdat* compared to the size of the population than any other region of the USSR.

Whereas in Moscow dissent was a phenomenon among the secular intelligentsia, the first manisfestations of *samizdat* activity in Lithuania showed a clear religious orientation and encompassed a broader spectrum of society. Roman Catholicism provided a core for the national opposition, and the issue of religious discrimination attracted widespread attention. As in neighboring Poland, religious strength had come to be equated in Lithuania with national identity. However,

76. Alex Milits, in *Välis-Eesti* (Sweden), 10 November 1980, p. 2; *New York Times*, 5 and 18 October 1980; *Daily Telegraph*, 6 October 1980; *The Economist*, 11 October 1980, p. 57; *Los Angeles Times*, 23 October 1980, p. 1–2; *Time*, 3 November 1980, p. 57. Exaggerated figures have been reported. Dissidents who later emigrated put the number of strikers at "200 workers at most" (personal communication).

the Soviet reality curiously metamorphosed the generally conservative political traditions of Roman Catholicism into the championing of traditionally secular political ideals. Although religiously oriented *samizdat* may not reflect the whole spectrum of opposition, they accounted for by far the greatest number of publications.

The first phase of overt Lithuanian religious dissent, dating from 1968, consisted of petitions to the authorities as well as to the Church hierarchy — some two dozen such documents have become known — and when the regime counter-attacked by prosecuting several priests for teaching religion to children, this only served to inflame the issue. In December 1971 a mass petition was organized, asking the Soviet government

to grant us freedom of conscience that is guaranteed by the Constitution, but which has so far not been secured in practice. We do not want beautiful words in the press or over the radio; we ask for serious governmental efforts to make us, Catholics, feel that we have equal rights as Soviet citizens.[77]

Despite efforts by the KGB to obstruct the gathering of signatures, 17,054 were appended to sheets of paper each carrying the full text of the petition. The collection was addressed to Brezhnev and sent to him through the UN Secretary-General Kurt Waldheim. Two other mass petitions followed in 1973. One, with 14,604 signatures, went to the Ministry of Education of the Lithuanian SSR; the other, with 16,800, to the republic's Commissioner for Religious Affairs. The government merely intensified propaganda alleging freedom of religious practice, and coerced the Church hierarchy to condemn such "divisive" practices by religious activists. Mass appeals of this nature seemed to cease after 1973. In 1979, however, a new one appeared regarding the church in Klaipėda, containing some 150,000 signatures (4 per cent of the republic's population).

The chief *samizdat* publication of religiously oriented dissent in Lithuania was *The Chronicle of the Lithuanian Catholic Church*. Its first issue was dated 19 March 1972, and the journal appeared continuously until circumstances changed in the late 1980s and the need for it ceased. Evidently modeled on the Moscow *Chronicle of Current Events*, it sought at first to register events connected with the repression of religious practice in Lithuania. Each issue, consisting of some 40–70 single-spaced typewritten folded-sheet

77. Full text in Vardys 1978, pp. 261–2.

pages, provided a glimpse, at times in minute detail, of various aspects of everyday life in the republic. The first six numbers were largely documentary, but later issues also included opinion. The initial exclusive focus on specific violations of religious rights expanded into treatment of other matters of general national interest, especially the effect of ideological demands on Lithuanian culture. This expansion also introduced a change in tone. The earlier issues had sought a level factual approach. Inventories of the social ills introduced by the system — physical destruction of the population, denationalization and moral decay (including alcoholism, juvenile delinquency, venereal disease and increased divorce) — inexorably led to expressions of judgment on the whole system, which at first was avoided. In 1976, however, the diversification of Lithuanian *samizdat* led the *Chronicle* to revert to its initial exclusive focus on religious questions.

In late 1973, a major KGB offensive labeled "Case 395" was launched against the *Chronicle* as well as other religious activism in Lithuania, and within a year several prominent activists had been arrested. Five were tried in December 1974 on charges of producing and distributing "libelous fabrications directed against the Soviet system." The youngest of the group, 27-year-old Virgilijus Jaugelis, was also its most outspoken member:

Here we stand before the Supreme Court. It is here that the most law-abiding and just people should be in charge. But what do we see? Corruptions, lies and brute force . . .[78]

The trial, as reported in a subsequent issue of the unvanquished *Chronicle*, bore out this evaluation: the judges disregarded evidence in favor of the defendants, two of whom publicly repented, acted as prosecution witnesses and were rewarded with suspended sentences. Jaugelis received two years. The *Chronicle*-related trial of Nijole Sadūnaitė followed in June 1975. Although the proceedings were held *in camera*, the *Chronicle* managed to print the speech she made in her defense, in which she compared the publication to a mirror

. . . which reflects all the criminal acts of atheists against those who believe. No evil act likes to look at its own horrible image, it hates its own reflection. That is why you hate everyone who tears off the veil of falsehood and hypocrisy behind which you are hiding. But the mirror does not lose its worth for all that.[79]

78. *Lietuvos Katalikų Bažnyčios kronika 13* (Chicago, 1975), II, p. 304.
79. *Ibid.*, 17, III, p. 64.

She was sentenced to three years in a labor camp, to be followed by three years in exile inside the USSR but outside Lithuania.

"Case 395" also involved two prominent Moscow dissidents. In December 1974 Andrei Tverdokhlebov was interrogated and Sergei Kovalev, a biologist and founding member of the Moscow chapter of Amnesty International, was arrested. At his trial, nearly a year later in Vilnius, Kovalev was given seven years in a labor camp and three in exile from his home region.

In 1976–9, several additional religiously oriented *samizdat* journals and the non-religious *samizdat* discussed below joined the *Chronicle*. These varied from a nationalistic and somewhat intolerant *Dievas ir tėvynė* (God and Fatherland) to one with a primarily pastoral function, *Rūpintojelis* (Sorrowing Christ). The issue "Bažnyčia ir *LKB Kronika*: mintys, svarstymai ir pageidavimai" (The Church and *The Chronicle of the Lithuanian Catholic Church*: Thoughts, Reflections and Desiderata) in 1977 was an attempt to present an alternative loyal Roman Catholic position, and general consensus holds that this was inspired by the KGB. Aside from its content, this *samizdat* publication was alone in being typed in double-spacing, at least in those copies earmarked for foreign consumption.

Around 1980 religiously oriented dissent in Lithuania seemed to move towards more open confrontation with the regime — possibly a reflection of the boost to morale which the election of Pope John Paul II in 1978 gave to religious activism. In the fall of that year, a five-member Committee for the Defense of the Rights of Catholics was announced at a Moscow news conference. Together with the attention devoted at that time in some issues of the *Chronicle* to the rights of Roman Catholics in Moldavia, this indicated an expansion of concern on the part of Lithuanian Roman Catholic dissenters beyond purely Lithuanian questions.

Religious dissent was the longest-standing and most widespread manifestation of organized opposition in Lithuania. The country's strong religious heritage, interrelated as it was with nationalism, made such dissent potentially the most powerful. However, it did not appear alone on the scene.

Several prominent figures on the Lithuanian cultural scene became dissidents individually with public protests against some negative facets of Soviet reality. In August 1972, as mentioned above, Jonas Jurašas, Senior Director of the Kaunas State Theater, addressed a letter to several cultural agencies in the republic denouncing the compromises forced on him as an artist by the arbitrary limitations placed on his activity by cultural officials. He was removed from his post and later allowed to emigrate.

In May 1975 the poet Tomas Venclova, son of a pre-war leftist writer who became the People's Commissar for Education in 1940, declared in a letter to the CC of the LiCP:

The Communist ideology is alien to me and, in my opinion, is largely false. Its absolute reign has brought much misfortune to our land. . . . I take a serious view of Communist ideology, and therefore I refuse to repeat its formulas in a mechanical or hypocritical manner.[80]

He was subsequently allowed to accept an invitation to take up a visiting professorship at the University of California, and while there he was stripped of his Soviet citizenship.

The case of Mindaugas Tomonis should also be included in the catalogue of actions by individuals. In November 1975 he was found dead alongside a railway track, supposedly having committed suicide though many felt he had been driven to it, if not actually killed beforehand by the KGB. As head of the laboratory in the Institute for Monument Restoration, Tomonis refused to inspect a crumbling monument to the Red Army at Kryžkalnis (40 km. north of Jurbarkas) and gave his frank opinion of the significance of the memorial in writing. He was placed under psychiatric care, but continued public manifestations of dissent by writing his opinions in the visitiors' book at the Vilnius Museum of the History of Religion and Atheism, and sending the Lithuanian Soviet administration memoranda on the Helsinki Agreement. Tomonis had been known as an unofficial poet who had published abroad, and after his death his poetry circulated in *samizdat*.

Several standing groups emerged, formed for specific non-religious purposes, though some of their members were also religious activists. The most significant of these was the committee established by five individuals in November 1976 to monitor Soviet compliance with the Helsinki Accords; it is usually referred to as the "Helsinki Committee." In effect it fulfilled the function of a citizens' initiative civil rights committee. Its name and concerns were similar to those of committees in several other parts of the USSR with which it maintained ties. Its method of operation was through *samizdat* publication of statements on alleged human rights violations brought to its attention. Because human rights were of more than purely national

---

80. *Lituanus*, XXIII/3 (Fall 1977), p. 76.

concern, the documents of the Lithuanian committee were not limited to Lithuanian questions. Document no. 7 (26 May 1977), for instance, dealt with the case of Erik Udam, an Estonian electrical engineer and former wrestling champion who had been approached by the KGB to form a Soviet-controlled "dissident" committee with ties to American diplomats in Moscow. The Lithuanian Helsinki Committee's ties with its Moscow counterpart made its memoranda more accessible to the outside world.

Of the five founders of the Lithuanian Helsinki Committee, the Rev. Karolis Garuckas died from natural causes in April 1979. Tomas Venclova, as already mentioned, went to reside in the United States. Viktoras Petkus was arrested in the summer of 1977 and in 1978 received the especially harsh sentence of ten years' imprisonment, to be followed by five years of internal exile. The two others, Ona Lukauškaitė-Poškienė and Eitan Finkelstein, were interrogated by the KGB; Finkelstein was accused of "collecting and transmitting to foreign intelligence centers and anti-Soviet propaganda organs slanderous fabrications and information defaming the Soviet social and state system."[81] After the departure of these, new members kept the Committee going.

Samizdat intimated the existence of several other Lithuanian groups. A National People's Front — consisting, among others, of a Lithuanian Free Democratic Youth Alliance and a Lithuanian Catholic Alliance — claimed in 1975 to have been in existence since 1955 and to have organized an illegal countrywide conference in June 1974. The program of struggle supposedly discussed at that time, and submitted to the entire freedom movement, was predicated on a rather gloomy world-view and appeared rather general and unrealistic. A strongly-worded declaration in May 1976 makes its authenticity seem doubtful; at best, the authors may have been a small unrepresentative group. This was probably the case also with a "Lithuanian Communist Movement for Secession from the USSR," for which there are two *samizdat* references.

A second Lithuanian *samizdat* periodical began to appear in 1975. By its name, *Aušra* (Dawn), and its numeration it sought to establish a symbolic continuity with the first Lithuanian newspaper, published

81. As reported in *Draugas* (Chicago), 9 September 1977. See also Yaroslav Bilinsky and Tõnu Parming, "Helsinki Watch Committees in the Soviet Republics: Implications for Soviet Nationality Policy," *Nationality Papers*, IX/1 (Spring 1981), pp. 1–26.

in East Prussia in 1883–6 and smuggled into the Russian Empire. *Aušra* was not a chronicle of specific events or issues but a magazine with an avowed emphasis on spiritual values and cultural progress as indispensable elements for the preservation of a Lithuanian national character. Implicit in its advocacy of nonviolent resistance was the idea that the Lithuanian nation would survive if it managed to maintain a cultural superiority over its oppressors. *Aušra* focused attention on a series of questions involving human rights as well as social, economic and cultural issues. It devoted attention to various facets of Russification as well as to the distortion or insufficient coverage of the nation's history.

At least six other Lithuanian *samizdat* periodicals appeared after 1975. Some indicated the circulation of source materials unavailable to Soviet citizens under normal conditions; others referred to ties and cooperation with dissident elements outside Lithuania. *Alma Mater* made its appearance in 1979, Vilnius University's 400th anniversary. It was a thick quarterly of some 300 typed pages with a distinctive cover. In the late 1970s, several books also appeared in Lithuanian *samizdat*. One volume consisted only of the memoirs of Petras Klimas, a pre-war statesman and diplomat; another, those of the second President of the interwar republic, Aleksandras Stulginskis. *Tarybų Sąjungos Komunistų Partijos Programa ir Gyvenimas* (The CPSU Program and Life), by Gintautas Tautvytis (a pseudonym), analyzed political and socio-economic realities in the republic. *Sofijokratija ir geodoroviniai jos principai* (Sophiocracy and its Geomoral Principles) (1977) was a theological-philosophical work by a dissident activist, Algirdas Statkevičius, who was subsequently persecuted. A 300-page manuscript entitled "Spiritual Genocide in Lithuania" was confiscated in November 1979 during a search of the apartment of another prominent dissident, Vytautas Skuodis.[82]

Latvia.   The first intimations of Latvian opposition date from 1960, when three individuals were tried for allegedly plotting an armed uprising. One of them, Vilnis Krūkliņš, received a ten-year sentence, being released in 1970. In 1961, the poet Knuts Skujenieks was sentenced to seven years' forced labor for activities connected with Latvian patriotism. In 1962 eight Latvians were given sentences of between eight and fifteen years for planning to form an organiza-

---

82. Richard J. Krickus, "The Case of Vytautas Skuodis, U.S. Citizen," *Commonweal*, CVIII/17 (25 September 1981), p. 525.

tion, to be named the Baltic Federation, to oppose Russification and economic exploitation of the Baltic republics. Viktors Kalniņš, who served a ten-year sentence, continued with dissident activities after his release and in 1971 was allowed to emigrate.[83]

In early 1968, Jānis Jahimovičs, chairman of a collective farm near Daugavpils, sent a letter to Mikhail Suslov and the CPSU CC protesting at the persecution of Iurii Galanskov, Aleksandr Ginzburg and others:

Only one remedy can liquidate *samizdat* — the development of democratic rights, not their violation; observance of the Constitution, not its violation; the realization in practice of the Declaration of Human Rights.[84]

Jahimovičs was expelled from the party and subsequently removed from his post, but he continued to sign protests against human rights violations. He considered himself a national Communist, a stance clearly reflected in a moving letter he wrote in March 1969, just before his arrest. While the people are sovereign, he claimed, "they are made up of living persons, of real lives. When human rights are violated, especially in the name of socialism and Marxism, there cannot be two positions."[85] Jahimovičs was declared to be mentally ill and forced to receive treatment which continued till 1971.

The year 1969 proved to be dramatic for individual Latvian dissent. On 13 April a young Jewish student, Ilia Rips, set himself on fire by the Riga Independence Memorial, in a protest against the Soviet occupation of Czechoslovakia. He survived and was allowed to emigrate to Israel in 1972. In 1970–1, at least a dozen Latvian Jewish activists were sentenced. A journalist, Ivars Žukovskis, received a five-year sentence for criticizing the intervention in Czechoslovakia; after finishing his sentence, he was rearrested and imprisoned for six months for carrying a petition addressed to the UN Commission on Human Rights, and was later again arrested and given a two-year sentence on an apparently fabricated charge of shoplifting. In November 1969 three young men, Gunārs Bērziņš, Laimonis Markants and Valerijs Luks, distributed 8,000 leaflets commenting on various aspects of Soviet foreign policy. They were sentenced to up to three

83. Interviews with Viktors Kalniņš have been published in several Canadian newspapers, including *St. Catharines* (Ont.) *Standard*, 8 May 1978, and *The Daily Mercury* (Guelph, Ont.), 14 May 1979.

84. Text in *Sunday Telegraph*, 3 March 1968, and *New York Times*, 8 March 1968. For dissent in Latvia, see Ekmanis 1978, pp. 305–8.

85. *New York Times*, 13 April 1969.

years for anti-Soviet propaganda and alleged illegal possession of weapons. One of the signatories of the 1918 Latvian Declaration of Independence, the Social Democrat Fricis Menders, was tried in November for "anti-Soviet agitation and propaganda": he had supposedly given some notes and memoirs to a visiting émigré couple. He was banished from Riga, but allowed to return a year later and soon died, aged 86.[86] In December 1970, Lidija Doronina-Lasmanis and several others received shorter sentences, and in 1971, as we have seen, it was the turn of the translator Maija Silmale.

The most notable document of Latvian dissent, dated July-August 1971, was the long "Letter of the Seventeen Communists" addressed to party leaders in Romania, Yugoslavia, France, Austria and Spain.[87] Although its origin in Latvia and authorship by Communists in particular later came to be questioned, the "Letter" received much attention in the West. Its anonymous authors claimed to be veterans of 25 to 35 years' service who had joined the party when it was operating underground in the pre-war republic. They detailed numerous violations of Marxist-Leninist nationality policy and called on the fraternal parties to help correct "certain actions and events that cause great harm to the Communist movement, to Marxism-Leninism, and to our own as well as other small nations." They said that Latvians (including Russian Latvians) formed only 42 per cent of the LaCP CC staff, 47 per cent of District Secretaries and 17 per cent of the basic Party Group Secretaries; in Riga Latvians accounted for only 18 per cent of the LaCP members and there were none among the City Committee section leaders. They listed by name and function 25 native Communists purged in 1959. The authors said they had all fought on the Soviet side in the war, and had actively participated in building socialism in Latvia. They had long thought that Russification was an unintentional temporary phenomenon, but had reluctantly come to believe that the Soviet Communist Party had "deliberately adopted a policy of Great Russian chauvinism."[88]

86. See Bruno Kalniņš, "The Social Democratic Movement in Latvia," in *Revolution and Politics in Russia: Essays in Memory of B.I. Nicolaevsky* (Bloomington, Ind., 1972), pp. 134–56.

87. English text in George Saunders (ed.), *Samizdat: Voices of the Soviet Opposition* (New York, 1974), pp. 427–40, and in *Congressional Record*, 21 February 1972, pp. E1426–30; German text in AB, XI (1971), pp. 117–30.

88. Factual information in the "Letter" was not contradicted in Soviet Latvian press comment ("Atbilde apmelotājiem," *Cīņa*, 24 February 1972) after the "Letter" was published in the West. Western press reports included *The Economist*, 26 February 1972; *New York Times*, 27 February 1972; and *Le monde*, 8 March 1972.

The Baptist Khristianin Publishing House near Cēsis was the most prominent exponent of religious dissent in Latvia. However, its publications appeared only in Russian, and individuals connected with the effort seem to have come together from all over the USSR. Another facet of religious dissent in Latvia was the tortuous process of emigration by Baptist Pastor Jānis Šmits and his relatives, the Bruvers family, which stretched over three years (1973–6), and involved hunger strikes, harassment and even the sentencing of one member of the family to a six-month term in a labor camp.[89] A petition signed by 5,043 Roman Catholic faithful in Daugavpils in 1975 over the threatened demolition of their church can also be classed as Latvian religious dissent.

The activities of three political dissent groups in Latvia also became known. A letter dated 27 July 1975 addressed to Latvian émigrés first indicated the existence of the Latvian Independence Movement. It contrasted the positive developments of the independence period with the overwhelming problems of the present — among them oppression, Russification, moral degradation, family instability and alcoholism — which threatened the survival of the nation. Émigrés were asked to remind the world of this reality. The second group, Latvia's Democratic Youth Committee, likewise sent a letter to Latvians abroad, on 5 October 1975, surveying the steps which had to be taken to reestablish independent Baltic states. It carried the signature of the group's chairman, Jānis Briedis, and the seal of the organization. Later that year, the clandestine Pali Publishing House in Riga printed a New Year's greeting card from the Committee. The third group, Latvia's Christian Democratic Organization, became known from a letter to émigré leaders, also written about this time after a clandestine observance of Latvian Independence Day, 18 November. As well as voicing political concerns, it said that Latvians needed to lead Christian lives as a prime condition for regaining independence, and expressed particular concern for the plight of the Baptists in Latvia.

The three groups coordinated their efforts in 1976. The first two produced a handbill in March, and in June they sent a letter to the government of the Latvian SSR signed by their chairmen. Written on the anniversary of the entry of the Red Army in 1940, the document protested at the subsequent Sovietization and Russification. All

89. See, e.g., "Latvian Minister Tells of Plight of Clergy in the Soviet Union," *Christian Science Monitor,* 17 August 1976.

three organizations sent a joint letter to the Australian Prime Minister Malcolm Fraser thanking him for his new government's decision to abrogate the earlier Australian recognition of the incorporation of the Baltic states into the USSR. Each of the three groups sent greetings to the United States on its bicentennial.[90]

A fourth Latvian group of this type, the Organization for Latvia's Independence, became known from a small pamphlet (in spring 1977) calling for a referendum on the republic's secession from the USSR. The four-page pamphlet was said to be the third statement of the organization, abridged from a larger work, and to have been printed in an edition of 25,000. The group claimed to consist of 210 representatives, each from a particular constituency. The tract provided some practical suggestions for showing discontent: these included whistling whenever ideological statements were being expressed, boycotting elections and using the tritest phrases of official jargon as often as possible. Whenever anyone was arrested, the population could show solidarity by turning on all lights and appliances for ten minutes during the peak period of usage; the resulting blackouts would be noticed by the authorities. A list of positive goals for a liberal independent state was appended.[91]

Latvian *samizdat*, less copious than Lithuania's, showed a pessimistic concern for the future of the nation. As in the other two republics, the implementation of human rights was emphasized. Latvian dissidents managed to smuggle to the West a unique three-minute film of a Soviet labor camp near Riga: columns of prisoners, armed guards, watchdogs, trucks with barred cages and watchtowers. The documentary was seen on television in 1975–6 in Britain, the United States, Canada, West Germany and France.

The case of Žanis Skudra is particularly notable. In 1979 he was tried and given a 12-year sentence for allegedly transmitting photographed information about military objectives to the West. This was done with the help of Jānis Niedre, a Swedish citizen of Latvian birth, who was arrested on a visit to Latvia and sentenced to ten years but released after six months and returned to Sweden. The material, published in two volumes by the Latvian National Fund in Stockholm, consisted among other things of photographs of churches,

90. Aina Zariņš, "Dissent in the Baltic Republics: A Survey of Grievances and Hopes," *Radio Liberty Research Paper*, no. 496 (December 1976), pp. 18–20.

91. The untitled four-page pamphlet was republished in 1978 in Bonn by the emigré publisher Gaismas Akcija.

farms, rural scenes and architectural monuments, accompanied by a diary. Together they presented a panorama of the changes in the Latvian countryside under Soviet rule and formed an indictment, in the shaped of an illustrated travelogue, of the neglect and destruction suffered by Latvia's national heritage.[92]

The existence of an underground branch of the Latvian Social Democrat Party (complementing its exile branch in Sweden) became known when its leader, electrical engineer Juris Bumeisters, was arrested in 1980 and sentenced in June 1981 to 15 years' imprisonment.

Estonia.   Organized Estonian dissent became known mainly through a series of *samizdat* essays and memoranda which began to reach the West in the late 1960s. Nearly all of them reflected concern over the survival of the Estonian nation, and embodied appeals for moral regeneration and the fostering of spiritual values.

The earliest notable piece was an essay of July 1968 entitled "To Hope or to Act," written by "Numerous Members of Estonia's Technical Intelligentsia" in reply to Andrei Sakharov's *Thoughts on Progress, Peaceful Coexistence and Intellectual Freedom.*[93] Its anonymous authors took issue with Sakharov's implicit belief in the basic goodness and common sense of humanity, as well as with his faith in the ability of science and technology to solve contemporary problems. They felt that Sakharov ignored the spiritual side of human nature, and argued the need for new moral values. Materialist ideology, they claimed, had destroyed Christian values without providing any adequate alternative. On a more practical plane, they called for a specific program of action, which they felt Sakharov failed to enunciate: renunciation of the aggressive foreign policy of the Soviet Union, establishment of a democratic form of government, and the right of nations to exercise self-determination.

About a year later, a group of officers of the Soviet Baltic fleet were tried in Tallinn on charges of having founded a society called the "Union for Struggle for Political Rights," whose membership involved some Estonians but extended beyond Tallinn to Leningrad and Kaliningrad. Searches connected with the affair reportedly uncovered a printing press. On 11 December 1969, four Estonians

92. J. Dzintars, *Okupētas Latvijas dienas grāmata, 1944–1972* (Stockholm, 1976 and 1980; 2 vols); see also Jānis Sapiets, "Out of Latvia," *Index on Censorship*, X/2 (1981), p. 58.

93. *Münchener Merkur*, no. 306 (1968); *Frankfurter Allegemeine Zeitung*, 18 December 1968.

were arrested in Tartu for being members of a secret organization as well as possessing weapons.

In 1972 evidence reached the West of the existence of two Estonian resistance groups: the Estonian National Front (ENF) and the Estonian Democratic Movement (EDM). The former supposedly published a political program in the fifth issue of the *samizdat* periodical *Eesti demokraat*, published since 1971, but the publication did not reach the West. As summarized in the Moscow *Chronicle of Current Events* (no. 25), the program sought to work out principles for the political and social systems of an independent Estonia and to strive for a referendum on self-determination. In October 1972, both groups addressed a joint memorandum to the UN General Assembly and a letter to the Secretary-General, Kurt Waldheim,[94] outlining the *raison d'être* for both groups and detailing the course of Russification in Estonia. The memorandum demanded the restoration of an independent Estonia, its admission to the UN and the formation of a democratic government through free elections administered by the world body. The Soviets responded to the publication of these documents by house searches and arrests in December 1974, as reported in a new appeal to Waldheim by the two groups (23 December 1974):

In spite of these gloomy events, we consider that our primary goal has been achieved. . . . The monopoly of the Soviet Estonian puppet regime to represent the Estonian people has ended. No one can state any more that the Estonian nation as a whole agrees with the 35 years of occupation and perspective of assimilation.[95]

The same themes appeared in a letter written on 25 December 1974 by a group of "Estonian Patriots" to several principal instruments of the Western mass media such as the BBC and the *New York Times*. In June 1975 "Representatives of Estonian and Latvian Democrats" addressed all governments participating in the Helsinki Conference on Security and Cooperation in Europe. In September, the ENF and the EDM joined four other Baltic organizations in an appeal to Baltic émigrés as well as to leaders of freedom-loving nations and organizations throughout the world. These activities may have been interrelated.

94. The road to the West was long. Texts were first published in *Baltic Events*, no. 46 (October 1974), and later in *Documents from Estonia*, pp. 19–26.

95 The 1974–5 texts in EE/BE, nos 48, pp. 2–6, and 52, pp. 2–10 (1975), and *Documents from Estonia*, pp. 10–18 and 27–31; the June 1975 text also in *Lituanus*, XXI/3 (Fall 1975), pp. 63–73.

Five members of the EDM were tried in Tallinn in October 1975 (these proceedings established a connection between the group and the human rights movement in other parts of the USSR), and of the defendants one pleaded guilty and received a suspended sentence in return for testifying against the other four, all of whom were engineers. The defendant Kalju Mätik argued that the EDM had not sought to overthrow the Soviet regime: "The constitution guarantees the right of the constituent republics to secede from the Soviet Union. We demanded a referendum. This is not the same as overthrowing the regime." His colleague Mati Kiirend found it difficult to believe that anyone could be tried for activities which were sanctioned by the Soviet Constitution. Sergei Soldatov, whose dissident activity had already surfaced during the trial of the Baltic fleet officers, characterized the EDM as motivated by moral and ethical principles in its struggle for human rights. Artjom Juskevitš protested against being imprisoned in a dirty and dark cellar, a treatment which made him believe Solzhenitsyn's *Gulag Archipelago*. The four unrepentant defendants received sentences of 5–6 years in strict-regime labor camps, but they were not silenced. In February 1976, they joined 15 other political prisoners in the Potma camp in Mordovia in an appeal to all who cherished "the principles of democracy, freedom and human rights," asking them to demand that the USSR adhere to the provisions of the Helsinki Agreement which it had signed.[96] Kiirend and Juskevitš were released in 1979, and Soldatov and Mätik in 1980. Soldatov, given the choice between living permanently in a rural area and emigrating, chose Western Europe in 1981.

A long statement dated April 1976 was addressed by an "Association of Concerned Estonians" to ESTO '76, an American-Estonian festival of culture. It expressed concern over the moral erosion which had accompanied 32 years of Soviet rule. Christian ideals and faith in the future had been replaced in Estonia by widespread skepticism, materialism, pragmatism and egoism. A moral renaissance of the Estonian people was seen as a *sine qua non* for the re-achievement of independence. In October 1976 "Representatives of Estonian Democrats" sent another plea to Amnesty International and to UN and United States human rights bodies.

---

96. Texts of court proceedings and of Potma appeal in *Newsletter from behind the Iron Curtain*, nos 490/1 (April-September 1976) and no. 492 (December 1976), and also in *Documents from Estonia*, pp. 32–61.

In May 1977, 18 naturalists addressed an anonymous letter to colleagues in Northwestern Europe, protesting against ecological damage by Soviet oil-shale and phosphorite mining in Estonia, which was described as a short-sighted colonialist practice of turning large stretches of land into a lunar landscape.

One later manifestation of organized dissent in Estonia showed some unusual features for such activity in the USSR, though it too shared the reflective concern over the future of the nation which seemed to be the main theme of Estonian *samizdat*. In late 1978 a "White Key Brotherhood" and a cultural organization calling itself Maarjamaa circulated six issues of a mimeographed periodical called *Poolpäevaleht* (which could mean either "the Saturday Paper" or "the Semi-Daily") in Tartu. The first issue outlined its goal, which was principally the uncensored publication of literary and cultural writings of the membership. One editorial in the journal viewed Christianity as the "carrier of the idea of Germanism" and, as such, poison. The Estonian people were in need of spiritual independence from Europeanization. In May 1979 several members and contributors were expelled from the University of Tartu.

In addition to identified individuals connected with some of the groups, several other names were significant in Estonian dissent. Mart Niklus was first arrested in 1958 for sending abroad photos of shoddy construction and of a radio-jamming station, and a year later was sentenced to ten years in a labor camp for "agitation and the spread of anti-Soviet propaganda." He was again taken into custody for two months in 1976 when he went to the prosecutor's office to demand the return of tape-recordings and texts seized during a search of his apartment. In 1970, four young workers were sentenced to 2–5 years for political organizing and alleged possession of firearms. In 1971 Vladimir Eichvald was committed to a psychiatric ward for, among other things, protesting at the expulsion of Aleksander Solzhenitsyn from the USSR Writers' Union. Olev Meremaa, a mathematician with the Tallinn Construction Institution, kept applying unsuccessfully for permission to attend international conferences which had accepted his papers. On 1 May 1974, he publicly carried a placard in Tallinn with the inscriptions "Put human rights into practice" and "Sakharov-Solzhenitsyn." He was physically attacked by four party activists, arrested and held for nearly four days before being released, and he lost his position. In January 1975, a theater employee, Sven Kreek, was arrested for distributing poems and a socialist reform manifesto. Soon after being forced to undergo mental treatment, he died — the Soviet authorities claimed it was suicide, but they buried him secretly in an unknown place.

A new major phase in Baltic dissent was introduced on 28 October 1980, when 40 Soviet Estonian writers, artists and scholars signed an open letter to *Pravda* (which did not publish it). Among the signatories — 13 of whom were listed in the *Estonian Soviet Encyclopedia* — were the writers Lehte Hainsalu, Jaan Kaplinski, Heino Kiik, Paul-Eerik Rummo, Mati Unt, Arvo Valton and Juhan Viiding, and the sociologist Marju Lauristin, daughter of the first (1940–1) Chairman of the ESSR Council of People's Commissars. Their unprecedented step was triggered by the "violence associated with the events in Tallinn" during the high school student demonstrations already mentioned, which they termed "an unexaggerated reflection of the dissatisfaction of numerous older Estonians." They mentioned food shortages, but more specifically called for a candid discussion of Russian-Estonian relations, mentioning specifically the following aspects:

— the rapid relative decline of the Estonian segment of the population;
— restrictions on the use of the Estonian language in business, everyday matters and science;
— the growing scarcity of Estonian-language journals and books;
— the exaggerated and inept propaganda campaign pushing the teaching of Russian;
— immoderate and overtaxing development of industry;
— unilateral demand for bilingualism among Estonians, without a similar effort being made among aliens;
— the appointment of persons with inadequate knowledge of Estonian culture.[97]

While half a dozen less well-connected dissidents were arrested in late 1980, the regime's response to the memo of the 40 intellectuals seems to have been limited to a search of Jaan Kaplinski's apartment on 6 November. Their writings continued to be published.

Cooperation among Baltic Dissidents.   In the late 1970s, some hints of cooperation among dissidents appeared in the three republics. There

97. Full text in *Radio Liberty Research Paper*, no. 477 (15 December 1980). Interviewed by Sweden's State Radio on 4 May 1981, the ESSR Minister Gustav Tõnspoeg acknowledged the letter's existence, but declined to discuss its details (*Vaba Eestlane*, 30 June 1981). See also Rein Taagepera, "Peril of Uprising Keeps Moscow Cautious," *Los Angeles Times*, 20 May 1981, pp. 11–15.

was no indication that the 1962 Baltic Federation extended beyond Latvia. The EDM defendants in 1975 were accused of contacts with Moscow, Latvia and especially Lithuania. There was the June 1975 Estonian-Latvian appeal. A Baltic dissident gathering in August 1976 was mentioned in the Lithuanian *samdizat* periodical *Perspektyvos* (no. 9, 1979). A decision was made to appeal to the West with a memorandum outlining the reality of conditions in the Baltic republics and pointing out Western indifference to the situation. The Estonian human rights activist Mart Niklus was arrested during the drafting of the memorandum. Some of the participants in the Riga gathering also sought to establish an Estonian-Latvian-Lithuanian National Movement Committee and to appeal to the democratic states of the world in its name. According to the account in *Perspektyvos*, one of its organizers, Viktoras Petkus, was arrested before the final stage of establishment of the Committee, and its activity ceased. A Committee decision of 20 August 1977 was reported in the Lithuanian *samdizat* publication *Aušra* (no. 8). Three days later, on 23 August, Petkus was arrested.

On 23 August 1979 a statement protesting at the Molotov-Ribbentrop Pact of 1939 and demanding that the USSR publish its full text including the secret protocols on the division of Eastern Europe, appeared in Moscow.[98] Although most had Lithuanian names, four Latvians and four Estonians were among the 45 who signed it. The Estonian signatories Mart Niklus and Erik Udam had been mentioned in Lithuanian *samizdat* since 1977. The statement requested that the Pact be specifically declared null and void by the USSR as well as by the two German states, which were further requested "to assist the Soviet Government to nullify the consequences of that Pact: namely, to withdraw foreign troops from the Baltic states." Unconfirmed reports claimed that 35,000 signatures were gathered in Lithuania in support of this statement, which is remarkable for its skillful avoidance of terms that could be interpreted as "anti-Soviet" and by its specific request for nullification placed at West Germany's door.

Police harassment of the signatories began immediately. Among others, Antanas Terleckas was arrested in October 1979, and Mart Niklus in March 1980. Also arrested was a chemistry lecturer at Tartu University, Jüri Kukk, after he had condemned the Soviet invasion

---

98. *New York Times*, 25 August 1979, p. 5. Full text in *UBA Information Service*, news release nos 330/1 (11 November 1979), supplement.

of Afghanistan in a statement with 21 signatures from all three Baltic countries.[99] On 8 January 1981 Kukk was sentenced to two years in prison, and died in suspicious circumstances on 27 March. Niklus received a harsh sentence of ten years in prison plus five of internal exile.[100] Terleckas was sentenced to three years in prison plus five of internal exile.

These varied manifestations of dissent indicated gradually mounting pressures in the Baltic republics for a more pluralistic society which would grant legitimacy to indigenous nationalism, including Lithuania's religious heritage. The continued existence and circulation of Baltic *samizdat* seemed to evoke an increasing defensiveness on the part of the regime, whose power, long eroded by institutionalized hypocrisy, was accompanied by an astounding moral weakness.

99. David K. Willis, "Fresh Burst of Baltic Nationalism Hits Kremlin," *Christian Science Monitor*, 29 January 1980; further articles on 16 January and 6 February 1980.
100. *Rahva Hääl*, 13 January 1981; Murray Seeger, "In Estonia, an Uncelebrated Martyr," *Los Angeles Times*, 20 May 1981, p. 11–15; Rein Taagepera, *Softening without Liberalization in the Soviet Union: The Case of Jüri Kukk*, Lanham, MD, 1984; Jānis Sapiets, "New Waves of Dissent," *Index on Censorship*, X/3 (June 1981), pp. 51–3.

6

THE APOGEE OF STAGNATION,
1980–1986

After the years of deepening despair from the mid-1940s to the mid-1950s and the years of rising hopes from the mid-1950s to the late 1960s, the 1970s were years of contradictions for the Baltic nations. Internal autonomy did not increase, but neither was there marked erosion of the modest gains of the early 1960s. Centralization of economic decision-making was counterbalanced by more plant-level autonomy. Economic development continued, new products whetted consumers' appetites, but food shortages reappeared. Russian immigration reached alarming new peaks, but then started to subside rapidly. Western influences penetrated the Baltic lifestyle more than at any time since 1940, but a new campaign for Russification of culture started in the late 1970s. Travel contacts with the West became commonplace, but heavy and petty restrictions remained. The structure of Moscow's rule in the Baltic did not change appreciably, but the very lack of reforms represented a change. In terms of passive submissiveness, the Soviet rule gained further acceptance by simply lasting for another dozen years and sinking deeper into the collective memory. Yet dissent became vocal. It was repressed harshly, but less brutally than before.

In 1940, the Soviet Union annexed three nations with ancient roots but with very young national identities in the modern sense; their modern national framework was recent and fragile. It was possible to wonder whether they would survive under new conditions, or whether political annexation would soon be followed by socio-cultural absorption, but the fact that their linguistic and cultural roots were quite different from the dominant Russian veneer in Soviet society argued against this happening easily. However, sustained national-language literature, press and theater were less than a century old. Higher education in the national languages had come

with the emergence of the nation-states in 1918, as had administration above the level of the commune. Nearly every adult in the
three national groups was a child or grandchild of peasants. The
possibility existed that the sense of national identity could be shaken,
that gifted individuals could be lured to Moscow or elsewhere in the
empire, and that the collective sense of identity would shift from
the local to the empire level. In many ways, Lithuanian, Latvian and
Estonian identities may have appeared to rest on shallower ground
than those of the Basques, the Welsh or the Bretons — who, in spite
of their linguistic distinctiveness, also looked like vanishing peoples in
1940.

Predictions of imminent demise were still there 40 years later;
and so were the Baltic nations. It has been said that, according to
the laws of aerodynamics, the bumble-bee should not be able to fly,
but it does so nonetheless, since it is too ignorant to know any
better. Perhaps according to the social laws of modernization, devised
mostly by members of large national groups, such entities as the
Baltic or the Ibero-Celtic mini-nations should have been collapsing,
but they did not know it, and kept going. Culturally more suppressed
than the Balts during the period 1940–75, the Basques seemed to
achieve, in 1979, a meaningful political autonomy which was still
beyond the reach of the Balts. Autonomy for Wales was an issue more
alive in the late 1970s than 40 years earlier, and there were new stirrings in Brittany.

Cultural assimilation in the Soviet Union may have been overestimated by many earlier observers. Correctly noting the utterly
limited political and economic autonomy of its national republics,
such observers underestimated the boost to national identity supplied
by the mere existence of those republics, not to mention the very real
cultural autonomy that existed in many of them. The Baltic nations
made full use of their restricted opportunities, and by so doing they
appreciably extended their historical depth as modern nations, compared to the situation as it was in 1940.

By 1980, the Baltic nations could look back to six rather than
two decades of native-language universities and republic-level administration. In the 40-year perspective, the use of Russian in those
fields had advanced; but in the perspective of 80 years, the overall
picture was still one of a massive shift from Russian to the national
languages. The very territorial units called Estonia, Latvia and Lithuania, as applied to the ethnolinguistic areas, were only two decades old
in 1940. They too had now tripled in age: the two decades of real

sovereignty had been augmented by four of shadow sovereignty in the form of secession rights in the Soviet Constitution, and of non-recognition of Soviet annexation by the United States and other Western powers.

The increase in socio-cultural depth may be the most important consideration. Large numbers of young Balts in 1980 saw college-educated grandparents as nothing unusual. Instead of vehement doubt-tinged declarations that one's co-nationals were as capable as members of any large Western nation, the Balts of 1980 took such parity as self-evident. The centennial celebrations of national press and theater came and went; factually and mentally the Baltic nations were now in their second century of modern cultural nationhood. They could expect to be there for their bicentennial. The bumble-bee was still flying.

Politics and Ideology

Administration.   As before, Baltic history during the 1980s continued to depend on the interplay of local aspirations with decisions made in Moscow. The administrative *immobilisme* that had set in during the late 1960s and became the hallmark of the Baltic political scene in the 1970s continued into the 1980s with little evidence of sub-stantial change. After the death of the CPSU General Secretary, Leonid Brezhnev, however, some indications of change began to appear.

It was still too early to assess the impact of Gorbachev's much heralded campaign to increase the economic efficiency of adminis-tration in the Baltic republics. Some of the all-Union attempts to streamline economic administration were already making themselves manifest in the three Baltic republics by late 1985. State agroindustrial committees merging several ministries were formed, parallel to an all-Union body formed in November that year. There were intima-tions of an intent to streamline the process of economic planning throughout the USSR, increasingly downgrading the bureaucracies of the republics and allowing plant managers to deal directly with planners in Moscow. However, any practical implementation was still at an early planning stage and vulnerable to opposition from entrenched bureaucratic interests throughout the USSR. Some of the reorganization up to 1986 had already brought about changes in personnel.

The Hill of Crosses near Šiauliai, Lithuania, became a symbolic center of
living Lithuanian Catholicism. Despite persistent efforts by the Soviet
authorities to weed out the crosses, new ones kept appearing on the site,
up to a total of some 3,000. The upper photograph is a view from prewar
times, and the middle one was taken in the summer of 1977. The lower
photo shows Father Algirdas Mocius, a postwar deportee who was not
allowed by the authorities to serve as a parish priest, beginning a
70-kilometer walk carrying a cross to the Hill of Crosses in June 1979.

"In Russia there lives a bear whose appetite is hard to bear." This poster at the "Song of Estonia" (Tallinn, 11 September 1988, 300,000 people) went somewhat further than the organizers of the meeting, the Popular Front of Estonia, wished. It put responsibility for stealing the Baltic states firmly on Russia rather than on the USSR, and thus irritated the local Russian colonists, who were disinclined to forget it, and attributed sinister meanings to its message.

One day after the reactionary CPE First Secretary, Karl Vaino, was replaced by a reformist, Vaino Väljas, more than 100,000 people came out to celebrate in Tallinn (17 June 1988). It was among the highlights of the "Singing Revolution."

Baltic opposition to the Soviet *status quo* received significant support from the minority populations in the republics. These demonstrators in Latvia hold a sign reading: "We Russians support the demands of the Latvian people."

Russian monks from a monastery near Pskov attended a meeting in Vilnius wearing *Sajūdis* support buttons. Their identification labels read "Pskovo — Pecherokü Monastery in the Pubaltika." The monastery is in a region of pre-war Estonia annexed by the Russian Federation in 1945. Estonia still claimes the area.

On 23 August 1989, the fiftieth anniversary of the Molotov-Ribbentrop Pact which sealed the fate of the independent prewar Baltic republics, some 500,000 demonstrators formed a human chain, the Baltic Way, stretching from Tallinn to Vilnius. In the above picture, the Soviet military are engaged in transporting tanks past demonstrators in Latvia.

A detachment of Latvian police guard the entrance to the parliament building in Riga on 15 May 1990 from possible anti-independence demonstrators. A transitional period to independence was declared on 7 May 1990.

In mid-January 1991, reactionaries in the Kremlin staged the last massive attempt to reimpose their control in Lithuania and Latvia by trying to unseat the elected pro-independence governments. In a series of bloody incidents several key buildings, most notably the television tower, were occupied in Vilnius by Soviet special forces. Lithuanians streamed *en masse* to defend the parliament building, as the last bastion of independence. The Kremlin lost heart and the stalemate continued for another seven months.

Mass demonstrations were frequent in all three Baltic capitals during the last three years of the *ancien régime*. Above is the state funeral in Vilnius of the six border guards killed at their post in Medininkai on the Belarus border on 31 July 1991 by Soviet special forces.

Lenin statues were toppled throughout the former USSR in the aftermath of the failed coup in Moscow in mid-August 1991. The statue in Vilnius resisted to the end.

Instead of reconstructing the damaged city of Königsberg, the Soviets chose to demolish most of what remained at the end of the war and to replace it with a modern newly-designed Kalinigrad of their own design. Several decades later, most of the block housing has begun to crumble. The massive City Hall (above), of questionable aesthetic value, was never finished. Insecure foundations caused cracks in the concrete structure which cannot be repaired.

Changes in Latvia.   Up till 1986, the process was most dramatic in Latvia, with the elevation in April 1984 of the republic's KGB chief Boriss Pugo to the post of First Secretary of the LaCP. The previous incumbent, Augusts Voss, was promoted to Chairman of the Council of Nationalities of the Supreme Soviet of the USSR, an honorific position occupied from 1954 onwards, with one brief exception, by figures from Latvia and Lithuania before their retirement. Pugo, born (probably in Moscow) in 1937, the son of a Latvian Communist exile, represented the younger generation of the non-native administrators so prevalent in the Baltic political apparatus. There can be no doubt that personal connections played a significant role in his rapid rise through the Latvian Komsomol and Latvian party apparatus. Reputedly the stepson of the late Arvīds Pelše, First Secretary of the LaCP from 1959 to 1966 and thereafter Chairman of the CPSU Party Control Committee and a full member of the CPSU Politburo, Pugo emerged in 1968 as head of the organizational department of the Riga City Party Committee. One year later, he was elected First Secretary of the Latvian Komsomol CC and shortly thereafter went to Moscow as Secretary of the all-Union Komsomol. In 1973 he was Inspector in the CPSU CC Department of Organizational Party Work. The following year he returned to Latvia as head of the LaCP CC Department of Organizational Party Work. He was elected First Secretary of the Riga Party Committee in 1975 and became a candidate member of the LaCP Bureau. Pugo went back to Moscow in late 1976, apparently in preparation for appointment as head of the Latvian KGB. He returned in 1977 as First Deputy to the then Chairman of the Committee for State Security in Latvia, General Longins Avdjukevičs, whom he succeeded in 1980. At that point Pugo again became a candidate member of the Bureau of the LaCP and was still not a full member of that body when he emerged as First Secretary, an apparently unprecedented occurrence. Although Pugo began his political career during the Thaw, his activity did not seem to reflect much of the "liberalism" of that time. As head of the Latvian KGB, he gained a reputation for being unscrupulous and lacking in any moral restraint in the pursuit of his objectives. He achieved particular notoriety in the 1983 crackdown on dissident activity.[1]

While Pugo lost no time in proclaiming his intention of improving economic performance and combatting corruption at the LaCP CC

---

1. For a discussion of the emergence of Pugo see Sergei Zamascikov, "The Ascent of Boriss Pugo or Voss's Long Road to Moscow," *Baltic Forum,* I/1 (Fall 1984).

Plenum of June 1984, the first since his accession, little of note apparently happened in Latvia during the remainder of Konstantin Chernenko's brief tenure as all-Union First Secretary. With the accession of Gorbachev, however, personnel changes in the Latvian *apparat* were announced. While the incumbent Chairman of the Council of Ministers, Jurijs Rubenis, continued in office, certain changes took place at the top levels of government and the Bureau of the CC, reflecting Pugo's efforts to introduce younger functionaries, presumably of his own stripe, into the leadership of the republic's *apparat*. March 1985 saw the early retirement (at the age of 62) of Imants Andersons from the post of Bureau Secretary for Ideology and his replacement by Anatolijs Gorbunovs. In June 1985 the Chairman of the Presidium of the Supreme Soviet, Pēteris Strautmanis, retired and was succeeded by the indigenous party activist Jānis Vagris, who at that point in his career was First Secretary of the Riga Party Committee. In late 1985 and early 1986, other personnel changes in the government and party leadership were announced. Two Deputy Chairmen of the Council of Ministers and four ministers, five chairmen of state committees, the Chairman of the Supreme Court, two LaCP CC Secretaries and four heads of departments were all replaced in 1985. The most noteworthy in this group was the retirement in November 1985 of Viktors Krūmiņš, who had been Deputy Chairman of the Council of Ministers for a quarter of a century since the purges of 1959–60 and Minister of Foreign Affairs since 1967. Vladimirs Kaupuzs, Minister of Culture since 1962, was retired in January 1986, apparently under a cloud, and replaced by Jāzeps Bārkans, deputy chief of the CC Department for Culture, an agency headed by an outspoken ideological hardliner, Aivars Goris.[2] The most interesting change in the Council of Ministers was the replacement, announced in *Cīņa* on 31 August 1985, of Mikhail Drozd by Vladimir Egorov as Minister of the Interior. Egorov, who had previously been Deputy Minister of the Interior in the Belorussian Republic, had up to that time not worked a single day in Latvia. While Drozd, like Egorov, was a Belorussian, he had resided in Latvia for a long time. The retirement of Drozd aged 52 suggested removal, and the appointment of Egorov appeared to be connected with Gorbachev's drive against ingrained corruption at the local level. It also provided an example of Gorbachev's proclaimed intention to assign cadres according to merit,

2. Dzintra Bungs, "New Minister of Culture," RL Research, Baltic Area SR/1 (27 January 1986).

without any regard for republican national boundaries. This practice had hitherto been limited mainly to the Central Asian republics. Egorov did not last long in his position, however. On 12 November 1986, *Cīṇa* reported that he had been "transferred to other work." His successor was a native Latvian, militia Major-General Bruno Šteinbriks, who had headed the main administration for criminal investigation of the USSR Ministry of Internal Affairs.

Throughout 1985 there was widespread replacement of district party leaders throughout Latvia which also seemed to reflect Pugo's intention to restructure the party as his own political machine. The passing or retirement of many of the prominent beneficiaries of the purges of 1959–60 may have made possible a muted rehabilitation of some of the victims of those purges. In September 1984, the monthly magazine *Liesma* carried an interview with Vilis Krūmiņš, who had been Second Secretary of the LaCP in 1953–6. The purged Minister of Culture of that era, Voldemārs Kalpiņš, also appeared in the press that fall. He wrote about other former comrades who had disappeared from public view since those days. In August 1985 *Cīṇa* published a decree awarding the Order of Friendship between the Peoples to Kārlis Ozoliņš, erstwhile Chairman (1952–9) of the Presidium of the LaSSR Supreme Soviet; Kalpiņš provided the accompanying biographical article.[3]

Changes in Lithuania.   Analogous processes were taking place in the other two republics as well, although apparently on a much smaller scale. In Lithuania most of the publicized changes were retirements of aged officials. In 1984 74-year-old Ksaveras Kairys, First Deputy Chairman of the Council of Ministers, resigned. His position was assumed by another full Bureau member, Vytautas Sakalauskas, First Secretary of the Vilnius City Party Organization. The following year, the three oldest members of the Council of Ministers were retired and replaced by considerably younger individuals. The most important of the former was Deputy Chairman of the Council of Ministers and Chairman of the Lithuanian State Planning Committee Aleksandras Drobnys, who had served in a ministerial capacity since 1944. None of these three changes, however, appeared to be more than overdue retirements.

There appears to have been a widespread feeling that First Secretary Griškevičius, an eminent product of the Brezhnev era, would soon

3. "Berklāvs Group Rehabilitated?" *Baltic Forum*, 11/2 (Fall 1985), pp. 102–5.

be replaced. Such speculation was fanned by the release in August 1984 of Vytautas Sakalauskas from his newly-acquired position as Deputy Chairman of the Council of Ministers and from the Bureau of the CC of the LiCP, in connection with a transfer to an undisclosed position. It was rumored that he had been posted to the CPSU CC in Moscow as an instructor, a move which seemed to suggest he was being groomed as a replacement for Griškevičius. In September 1985 a resolution of the USSR Supreme Soviet addressed to the Presidium of the Supreme Soviet of the LiSSR contained unspecified criticism of Lithuania's economic performance, which by Soviet standards had not been that poor. This seemed to presage imminent personnel changes which in all likelihood had already been decided in Moscow. Sakalauskas did indeed return to Vilnius. However, in November 1985 he resumed his position in the CC Bureau and replaced the incumbent Chairman of the Council of Ministers, Ringaudas Songaila, who in turn replaced the retiring Antanas Barkauskas as Chairman of the Presidium of the Supreme Soviet.

In addition to the party and government changes, the replacement of Genrikas Zimanas as editor of the party journal *Komunistas* was worthy of note. His removal, though clearly justifiable on grounds of age, came without a public announcement, and seems to have been engineered rather suddenly. Zimanas, who was of Jewish background, had been a Soviet partisan in Lithuania during the German occupation and a member of the CC of the LiCP from 1949 to 1964. He had been editor of the party paper *Tiesa* from 1945 until his appointment to *Komunistas* in 1971.

The March 1985 Plenum of the LiCP CC was noteworthy for its attention to personnel questions. Griškevičius, the First Secretary, criticized various facets of the selection, training and appointment process for responsible positions. He particularly decried the lack of qualified personnel. Under normal circumstances, he reasoned, a replacement reserve of qualified individuals should have existed, but this had not happened. Factory directors dismissed for failure to fulfill quotas had been replaced by poorly trained people who achieved even worse results. Griškevičius mentioned that several local officials had been dismissed for wrongdoing. The Chairmen of the executive committees of the districts of Trakai and Širvintai and a Secretary of the Utena district Party Committee had been dismissed for illegally constructing cottages on collective orchard land.[4] However, there

4. *Tiesa*, 17 March 1985.

seemed to be no intimation of large-scale replacements of local officials such as had happened in Latvia.

Changes in Estonia. Estonian CP First Secretary Karl Vaino was a typical example of the late Brezhnev appointments: stable, unimaginative and unproductive. As such, he looked like a prime candidate for replacement under the presumably more dynamic Gorbachev, and the ECP Congress in February 1986 was an opportune moment for such a move. Nonetheless, Vaino survived.

Meanwhile, the struggle between the home-grown Estonians and the Russian-bred "Yestonians" focused on the position of Chairman of the Council of Ministers. As the ageing Yestonian incumbent, Valter Klauson, approached retirement, jockeying for the post of First Vice-Chairman intensified. Since 1979 this position had been held by a home-grown agriculture specialist, Arnold Rüütel, who had joined the CP at the age of 36 (in 1964). In April 1983 Vaino apparently wanted to replace him with his Yestonian crony Vladimir Käo, the ECP Secretary, who was notorious not only for his corruption but also for his foulmouthed and abrasive treatment of underlings. Rüütel was promoted to ceremonial head of state (Chairman of the Presidium of the Supreme Soviet of the ESSR), bouncing the Yestonian incumbent, the former ECP First Secretary Ivan Kebin, into full retirement. However, opposition to Käo resulted in a compromise: not one but two First Deputy Premiers were appointed: Käo and the home-grown Heino Veldi.

Incidentally, the appointment of two First Vice-Premiers required a change in the Constitution of the ESSR. Such a fundamental step, which in democratic countries requires a lengthy legal process, was carried out in Soviet Estonia with a speed worthy of an entry in the *Guinness Book of Records.* In the middle of a speech by Vaino the constitutional issue was pointed out and, without the least discussion, hands were raised in approval of the change.

When Klauson actually retired in January 1984, the picture had changed appreciably. Käo had apparently lost a patron in Moscow (and his corruption later brought about his unceremonious dismissal in March 1985, accompanied by barely veiled personal criticism in the press). Veldi did not advance any further either. Instead Bruno Saul, an Estonian-born communications engineer, one of the third-ranking ECP Secretaries since 1983, became the new Premier. Saul had established his credentials by marrying a Russian in his student days in Leningrad, but he put his son into an Estonian-language school while he gradually advanced from Vice-Minister to Minister of Communications, and subsequently became one of the Deputy Premiers. The advancement of Rüütel and Saul meant the shift to home-grown Estonians in two major posts — formal head of state and Premier — which had been held by Yestonians ever since the 1950s.

The long tenure of Konstantin Lebedev as ECP Second Secretary and hence as Moscow's chief watchdog ended in May 1982. He was replaced by Aleksandr Kudriavtsev and then, in December 1985, by Georgi Aleshin, both Russians with no previous Estonian connection. These changes seemed to have no local cause or effect. The replacement of the Estonian KGB chief Ado Pork by a Russianized Karelian, Karl Kortelainen, received attention abroad primarily because of the recent Soviet promotions from the KGB to higher office (as with Andropov and Pugo). In Estonia, however, such a course was very unlikely in view of Kortelainen's lack of any trace of local ancestry.

After Käo's promotion to First Vice-Premier in April 1983, all three third-ranking ECP Secretaries were home-grown Estonians: the incumbents Rein Ristlaan and Artur-Bernard Upsi, plus the newcomer Saul. The last-named was replaced in April 1984 by a Russian, Nikolai Ganiushov. Another Yestonian crony of Vaino, Nikolai Johanson, was pensioned off in October 1986, his post as Chairman of the Council of Trade Unions going to Mati Pedak, former First CP Secretary for Tallinn, who was replaced by Enn-Arno Sillari; both were home-grown Estonians.

Party Membership. These personnel changes apparently did not basically alter the composition of the parties in the three republics. The Latvian party, membership of which was estimated at 172,500 full or candidate members at the time of the LaCP's Twenty-fourth Congress in January 1986, seemed to have a more or less constant turnover during the 1980s despite the anticorruption drive of the new leadership.[5] No figures were available on the nationality composition of the Latvian party.

The Lithuanian CP continued to grow faster than the CPSU. On 1 January 1986 it had 197,283 members,[6] and its growth rate of 60.5

---

5. Dzintra Bungs, "The 24th Latvian Communist Party Congress," RL Research, Baltic Area SR/2 (4 March 1986).

6. Pranas Vaitkūnas, "Lietuvos Komunistų Partija," *Švyturys*, 1986/2. Inexplicably he gives the same figure on p. 5 for 1986 and on p. 6 for 1985.

per cent between 1970 and 1984 was the second highest among the constituent republics of the USSR. Nevertheless, in 1984 the percentage of party members in the total population (5.25 per cent) was still lower than the corresponding average for the USSR (6.74 per cent). The percentage of Lithuanians in the party continued to increase slowly: in 1970 it stood at 67.1 per cent, in 1980 at 69.4 per cent and in 1986 at 70.4 per cent. That figure was still well below the Lithuanian percentage of the population of the republic, which in 1979 was 80 per cent.

In the Estonian CP, the Estonians (including the relatively few ageing Yestonians) probably lost their slim majority around 1985. Slowly recovering from Stalin's purges, the Estonian share had passed the 50 per cent mark in 1963; it peaked in 1969 with 52.5 per cent of the ECP membership, again well below the Estonian share of the general population. By 1975 a steady decline had begun, and in 1981 Estonians were reduced to 50.8 per cent of the ECP membership.[7] This phenomenon could not be completely explained by the continuing flow of immigrants, given that the Estonians still represented more than 60 per cent of the country's population.

Society

Demography.   Immigration continued to be a long-range threat to the survival of the Baltic nations, and for the first time Lithuania seemed to be as seriously affected as the other two countries. The pattern for the 20 years from 1965 to 1985 was as follows (in thousands of immigrants over five-year periods):

	Estonia	Latvia	Lithuania	Total[8]
1965–9	45	71	29	145
1970–4	40	64	40	144
1975–9	24	46	31	101
1980–4	31	45	59	135

The trend of the late 1970s toward less immigration was reversed, except in Latvia. In Lithuania the marked decrease in birthrates in

7. *Estonskaia Kommunisticheskaia Partiia v tsifrakh, 1920–1980* (Tallinn, 1983), pp. 109, 181, 182.

8. For 1965–1979, data condensed from Table 1 of Rein Taagepera, "Baltic Population Changes, 1950–1980," *JBS*, XII/1 (Spring 1981), pp. 35–57. For 1980–4, based on population and natural increase figures in *Eesti NSV rahvamajandus 1984, a.*, pp. 8, 10, 12; *Latvijas PSR tautas saimnieciba 1984. gada*, pp. 20–1, and *Narodnoe khoziaistvo Litovskoi SSR v 1984 godu*, pp. 7–8.

the early 1960s was bound to weaken the local labor supply in the 1980s, but since the same situation existed in the RSFSR, only a purposefully imperialist Russification policy could explain the new immigration. The same applies to Estonia, where the increase in immigration was largely caused by the construction of a mammoth new harbor near Tallinn (discussed in the section on the economy) — a prime example of a colonial outpost. Plans for huge new phosphorite mines also seemed to be pushed harder in labor-poor Estonia than in the adjacent Leningrad *Oblast*, which apparently had equally rich deposits.

As a result, the percentage of Latvians and Estonians in their respective republics continued to decrease, and the same phenomenon began to appear in Lithuania for the first time since the deportations of the early 1950s. After the census of 1979, the following changes took place:[9]

		Estonia	Latvia	Lithuania
Total population	1/79	1,466	2,521	3,399
(thousands)	1/85	1,530	2,604	3,570

		Estonia	Latvia	Lithuania
Republic nation's	1/79	64.7	53.7	80.0
per cent share	1/85 *est.*	62.6	52.6	79.8

It would seem that about 16,000 Latvian-speaking Latvians emigrated to the RSFSR in 1970–9, in a reversal of previous trends,[10] although there was little Lithuanian or Estonian emigration.

Mixed Baltic-Russian marriages seemed to be on the increase, and the offspring of more than half of such marriages seemed to opt for

9. For total population, see previous note for sources. Percentage breakdown is extrapolated from the 1979 and 1989 census figures.

10. Thorough tables on the ethnic aspects of the 1979 census are presented in Egil Levits, "Die demographische Situation in der UdSSR und in den baltischen Staaten unter besonderer Berücksichtigung von nationalen und sprachsoziologischen Aspekten," *Acta Baltica*, XXI (1981), pp. 18–142. The number of Latvians and Estonians residing outside their respective republics but speaking their ancestral language was almost the same in 1959 (54,074 vs. 54,304) and 1970 (45,262 vs. 43,963), but a gap of 18,500 developed in 1979 (52,484 Latvians vs. 33,954 Estonians). If attrition through denationalization between 1970 and 1979 was the same, 17,200 new Latvian-language immigrants would be needed to balance the count. Within the RSFSR alone, 15,600 new Latvian-speaking immigrants would balance the count. Levits estimates the emigration at 10,000, which can be taken as the minimum estimate. See also Juris Dreifelds, "Demographic Trends in Latvia," *Nationalities Papers XXII* (1984), pp. 49–84.

the Baltic nationality when the family remained in the Baltic republics. Thus such marriages tended to work rather in favor of the Baltic peoples. In general, however, the immigrants' knowledge of the republican language remained low; the fraction of Russians who deemed themselves fluent in the language of the republic in 1979 was 37.4 per cent in Lithuania, 20.1 per cent in Latvia and 13.0 per cent in Estonia. The regime's educational policies actively contributed to this lack of integration. While in the republican-language schools the beginning of Russian study was shifted from third to first grade and efforts were made to introduce it in kindergarten, no teachers were specifically trained to teach Estonian in the Russian-language schools of the republic until 1982, when a yearly quota of ten teachers were established and a textbook of Estonian for Russians was issued.

Although the Soviet authorities published little of the 1979 census material (as compared to previous occasions), some of their confidential information regarding the nationality composition of individual towns and rural districts in Latvia and Estonia was leaked to the West. In both countries the population was divided almost equally between the capital city, other urban centers and rural areas. In both cases, too, the capital was heavily Russian, the provincial urban population had a narrow native majority, and the countryside was solidly Latvian or Estonian in 1979. In Lithuania, where the ethnic ratio of the population was a less sensitive issue, comparable data were published. Both rural and provincial urban populations were solidly Lithuanian, and the capital city had a large Lithuanian plurality:

Percentage of	*Capital*	*Other Urban*	*Rural*	*Total*
Latvians in LaSSR	38.3	51.5	71.9	53.7
Estonians in ESSR	51.9	56.9	87.6	64.7
Lithuanians in LiSSR	47.3	84.6	86.0	80.0

If one combines major cities with their surrounding districts, the following geographical pattern emerges for 1979. Latvians were a minority in two zones: in the Riga district with its massive population concentration (over 1 million out of the republic's total population of 2.5 million), and in three southeastern districts (Daugavpils, Krāslava, Rēzekne). The Latvian majority was precarious (under 60 per cent) in three other districts with major cities (Liepāja, Jelgava, Ventspils). In the remaining, predominantly rural 19 districts, the Latvian proportion ranged from 60 per cent in eastern Ludza to 88 per cent in northwestern Talsi. Estonians were a small minority

(23 per cent) in the Kohtla-Järve oil-shale district (including Narva) in the northeast and a precarious majority in Harju/Tallinn. In the remaining 13 districts the Estonian share ranged from 77 per cent for Tartu to 95 per cent on the island of Hiiumaa. The Lithuanian majority was solid (over 90 per cent) in 32 of that republic's 44 rural districts, while two districts had Polish majorities (the Vilnius rural district was 68 per cent Polish). The Russian element reached 20 per cent to 30 per cent in Klaipėda and Vilnius, and in the districts of Ignalina and Zarasai in the neighborhood of the nuclear power plant.[11]

Birthrates in the early 1980s were stable — around 15 per 1,000 — in all three republics. The deathrate in Latvia and Estonia reached a plateau at just below 13 per 1,000, while in Lithuania it was slightly above 10 per 1,000 and rising, mainly because of the changing shape of the age-pyramid. In Lithuania the number of female children per woman decreased to 0.97, i.e. slightly below the population reproduction level. This situation had been reached much earlier in Latvia and Estonia, but the low reproduction rate among the unstable immigrant population was the main cause. Latvians and Estonians actually seemed to have maintained a reproduction ratio of slightly more than 1, and the same can be presumed for the Lithuanians as well.[12]

Marriage and divorce rates changed little. Further urbanization slowed in Latvia and Estonia as the rural share of the population fell below 30 per cent. In Lithuania it fell from 38.4 per cent in 1980 to 34.3 per cent in 1985. The share of the capital cities in the overall population of the republics continued to edge upwards, mainly because of Russian immigration. Estonians lost their majority in Tallinn around 1982 and were down to 48 per cent by 1985, while

11. Data reworked from leaked parts of restricted-circulation reports: *Chislennost, sostav i razmeshchenie naseleniia Latviiskoi SSR po gorodam i raionam po dannym perepisi naseleniia 1979 goda*, Riga, Tsentralnoe statisticheskoe upravlenie Latviiskoi SSR, 1980, as reproduced in "Nationality Composition of the Population in Latvia," World Federation of Free Latvians, press release 24 September 1984 and commented upon in *Baltic Forum* II/1 (Spring 1985), pp. 145–9; and *Itogi perepisi naseleniia po Estonskoi SSR 1979*, Tallinn, ESSR Central Statistics Office, no date known, as reproduced and analyzed in Rein Taagepera, "Size and Ethnicity of Estonian Towns and Rural Districts, 1922–1979," *JBS*, XIII/2 (Summer 1982), pp. 105–27. For Lithuania: Petras Gaučas, "Dabartiniai ethniniai procesai Lietuvoje," *Mokslas ir gyvenimas*, 1981/3, pp. 27–8.

12. *Komunistas* 2/1985: 63; Rein Taagepera, "Baltic Population Changes, 1950–1980," *JBS*, XII/1 (Spring 1981), pp. 35–57, especially p. 49.

the Latvians in Riga were reduced to approximately 36 per cent. The increasing Lithuanian share in the population of Vilnius reached 47.3 per cent in 1979.

Lifestyle. The food shortages of the late 1970s were alleviated in the early 1980s. The prices of some consumer items were at times raised sharply, without any previous warning. The resulting overall rate of inflation is difficult to estimate. The introduction of Western-style features into the retail sectors, such as buying on credit and the sale of comic books, which had been characteristic of the early 1970s, seemed to stagnate, with a few exceptions. Rock bands proliferated and obtained recognition to the extent that recordings of their music were officially produced and sold. For more expensive purchases such as automobiles (around 8,000 rubles) a savings bank check instead of the traditional cash became mandatory in June 1986. The amount of savings was even more overwhelming in the Baltic republics than in Russia. Estonia had close to a million savings accounts for a population of 1.5 million, and *per capita* savings amounted to 1,000 rubles.[13]

The continuing housing scarcity throughout the USSR was highlighted by Gorbachev's promise to supply every family with its own apartment by the end of the millennium. The shortage was reflected in the local Baltic press (which could not be mailed abroad). For example, a reader's letter in the Tartu *Edasi* (12 May 1986) described the family of a war veteran who had waited seven years to get a two-room apartment. Before moving in, the family spent a further 24 days and 100 rubles to find a private entrepreneur to smooth and paint the floor. Two weeks after the actual move they still had no electricity, water or gas.

Some consumer goods, such as color TV sets and cars, became more readily available. Video-cassettes, though rare, presented special control problems for the Soviet authorities. *Izvestiia* (15 October 1985) reported that 415 underground Western cassettes had been confiscated in Riga alone, while the total Soviet cassette production as of October 1985 amounted to only 200 different programs, issued on average in editions of 125 copies. In October 1984 four Lithuanians were sentenced to up to two years in prison for showing videotaped Western pornographic films for profit.[14]

13. *Rahva Hääl*, 13 June 1986.
14. Ojārs Kalniņš, "Underground Videos — Another Problem for Soviet Leaders", *New York City Tribune*, 31 March 1986; *Komjaunimo tiesa*, 9 October 1984, as reported in *Baltic Forum* II/1 (Spring 1985), pp. 163–5.

The need for greater computer skills was recognized in Moscow, but "personal computer" tended to mean a "microcomputer" housed in schools and workplaces only. In Estonia a special computer was devised for school instruction. The élite's lack of familiarity with office duplicators was highlighted by a top establishment writer's high-tech dream: using a computer to print out several copies of the same draft of a novel.[15]

The continuing Soviet aggression in Afghanistan aroused fears for the young Balts drafted into the Soviet army, and indeed a number returned home in sealed caskets.[16] In June 1986 over 10,000 Ukrainian and Belorussian refugees from the Chernobyl disaster area were settled in the Baltic republics. Over 10,000 Baltic youths were sent to the site to do nuclear decontamination work, sometimes being summoned in the middle of the night with only an hour's notice. Stories about radiation deaths of these workers abounded (sometimes with names supplied), as did rumors of contaminated food being sent to the Baltic republics. The official press reported that 300 Estonians had staged a work stoppage when their stay was prolonged from two to six months, and underground sources added that 12 men had been shot.[17]

The general mood in the Baltic republics at the beginning of the 1980s was somber, given the stagnating consumer economy and increasing pressure of Russification. However, Andropov's and then Gorbachev's accession aroused hopes for some kind of change. Its direction was unclear, but even a change for the worse would have been more stimulating than dull stagnation, and the brain was kept more active by hope than by despair. Nonetheless, the first year of Gorbachev's rule offered little that was new. Promises, exhortations to work harder and a crackdown on private entrepreneurship had all been seen before. The only unprecedented move was the crackdown on alcohol.

15. Vladimir Beekman, *Looming* 4/86.

16. A blunt interview with an ex-soldier was published in the Estonian underground publication *Isekiri* no. 2 (1984); full translation in Peter Philips, "A Soviet Estonian Soldier in Afghanistan," *Central Asian Survey* V/1 (1986), pp. 100–15. See also *Baltic Forum* II/1 (Spring 1985), pp. 178–82.

17. See, e.g., Tönis Avikson, series of articles in *Noorte Hääl*, 12 to 19 August 1986, Ants Kippar, "Tshernobol ja Eesti" (Chernobyl and Estonia), *Vaba Eestlane*, 18 November 1986, the elements of which are confirmed by many other reports. Around 4,000 men were dispatched from Estonia to Chernobyl; Latvian and Lithuanian contingents, if proportional, could have been 6,000 and 9,000 respectively. Over 3,000 refugees had been settled in Tallinn alone, displacing locals who were on apartment waiting-lists.

Restrictions on alcohol came in June 1985, and their impact in the Baltic republics was so marked that the move came to be known in Estonia as "the second changeover of June," the Soviet occupation in June 1940 having been the first. Alcohol consumption in the Baltic republics was among the highest in the USSR,[18] and was a national threat second only to Russian immigration. However, being self-inflicted, it was by far the more popular of the two threats. The prohibition of alcohol from office birthday parties came to many as a most unwelcome change. Nonetheless, it was clearly in the Baltic national interest that the anti-alcohol campaign should succeed at least as well in the Baltic republics as in Russia. Throughout the Soviet Union, however, the long-term effects of the campaign remained uncertain. While less drinking on the job was bound to increase productivity and possibly workers' incomes, little was offered on which to spend the time and money previously spent on vodka. It was all stick and no carrot, and the consumption of illegally distilled alcohol seemed likely to increase.

In 1986 there was expanded coverage of economic and social problems in the Soviet Baltic press, which thus became much more interesting to read than it had been in the previous decade. Much more information now became available about social conditions and problems, the existence of which had previously been merely hinted at.[19] The problems of youth in Latvia were graphically presented in a film by Juris Podnieks, *Is It Easy To Be Young?*, which received wide

---

18. In 1970 expenditure on alcohol per adult (aged 15 and over) was highest in Estonia (189 rubles), the RSFSR (186), Latvia (179), Kazakhstan (164) and Lithuania (142) — see Vladimir G. Treml, *Alcohol in the USSR: A Statistical Study* (Durham, NC: Duke University Press, 1982), p. 77. By 1979 total Soviet consumption was up by 36 per cent, and the regional distribution had not changed appreciably.

19. In the Estonian daily *Rahva Hääl*, the official statistics were shown to be misleading and insufficient (Siim Kallas, 8 August 1986). A republic committee for mineral resources was proposed (Kalju Kask, 27 August 1986), and alleviation of individual producers' fears in the face of official inconsistencies was urged (Imre Raig, 3 October 1986). The tremendous bureaucratic roadblocks were illustrated in the issue of 28 September 1986: a director faced fines and possibly prison because his plant used diesel oil for cleaning purposes, and this time-honored practice was suddenly declared illegal by a control committee who interpreted a rule in the narrowest sense possible, happily oblivious of the lack of any substitutes. The Estonian cultural weekly *Sirp ja Vasar* published suggestions that the coverage of foreign countries in the Soviet press was distorted (26 September 1986) and that the city of Kuressaare, renamed after Bolshevik leader Kingissepp "in a leftist excess" of the early 1950s, should have its historic name restored. The name of the weekly itself (meaning "Hammer and Sickle") also came under criticism as incompatible with its Latvian and Lithuanian counterparts, entitled "Literature and Arts."

acclaim in the USSR and attention in the international press. In the mid-1980s several pieces of Hare Krishna *samizdat* from Lithuania reached the West, and in 1987 one Hare Krishna group in Lithuania attempted to register itself as a religious congregation. In 1986, a man-slaughter trial in Vilnius involving an Uzbek guru and his disciples was given prominent coverage in the Soviet Lithuanian press under headlines such as "In the Whirlpools of Extrasensory Perception." And the problem of prostitution, especially in the port cities of Riga and Klaipėda, was discussed in the press of Latvia and Lithuania.[20]

Whether the new relative openness would be translated into changes in actual bureaucratic practice remained to be seen. A Baltic joke of 1986 claimed that the population had been deprived of its two remaining consolations: vodka was prohibited and cursing the administration had been made compulsory.

Economy and Ecology

Economy. The growthrates of national income and industrial production in the Baltic republics were lower in 1980–5 than during previous 5-year periods. The average yearly percentage growth figures reported by the Soviet authorities were as follows:[21]

ANNUAL GROWTH (%)

	National Income			Industrial Production			Population[f]		
	E.	La.	Li.	E.	La.	Li.	E.	La.	Li.
1970–5	5.5	5.8	5.7	7.1	6.4	5.1	1.0	0.8	1.0
1975–80	4.2	3.6[b]	2.9[d]	4.4	3.7[b]	4.9[d]	0.7	0.5	0.8
1980–5	3.0[a]	3.2[c]	3.0[e]	2.5[a]	3.2[c]	4.4[e]	0.7	0.6	0.9

20. *Trud*, 12 April 1987; *Daily Telegraph*, 18 April 1987; *Washington Post*, 2 May 1987; *Baltic Forum*, 1987/1, pp. 101–7; *Sovetskaia Latviia*, 16 May 1987; *Tiesa*, 6 June 1987; *Komjaunimo tiesa*, 7 May 1987.

21. Data from Appendix, Table 16, unless otherwise indicated. The Soviet sources shown below at times use different definitions so that the figures may not be directly comparable.

(a) *Rahva Hääl*, 26 January 1982, 26 January 1983, 31 January 1984, 29 January 1985, 29 January 1986.

(b) *Latvijas PSR tautas saimniecība 1982. gadā* (Riga, 1983), p. 28.

(c) J. Porietis, "Intensifikācijas stratēgija," *Skolotāju Avīze*, 14 May 1986.

(d) *Narodnoe khoziaistvo Litovskoi SSR v 1978 godu* (Vilnius, 1979), pp. 29 and 54; *Tiesa*, 27 January 1980; *Liaudies ūkis*, 1981/3, p. 26.

(e) *Tiesa*, 26 January 1982, 26 January 1983, 29 January 1984, 29 January 1985, 22 January 1986.

(f) See note 8 above.

The slowing growth in production reflected industrial maturity, but it came while living standards were still far below those of Western Europe. Hidden inflation played its part, mainly in the form of manipulation of the consumer price index by the central authorities and manipulation of the producer goods price and quantity by enterprises. The United Nations estimates put real growth at about 2 percentage points lower than the official Soviet figures. Close to 1 per cent growth was needed merely to stay abreast of the population increase. Thus, an officially reported 3 per cent growth in the table above represented stagnation in real *per capita* national income or industrial production, and a reported growth rate of 2 per cent definitely represented negative growth.[22]

Slow growth also reduced the economic incentive for further immigration. Estonian oil-shale-based production of electrical power was a case in point. The workforce in this industry consisted mainly of immigrants. Oil-shale production reached a peak of 31.3 million tons in 1980, slid to 26.4 in 1985, and was planned to drop still further to 24.9 million tons by 1990. The production of electricity peaked a year earlier (1979) at 19.4 billion kilowatt-hours, and fell to 17.7 in 1985, with the plan calling for 18.1 in 1990. Oil-shale stockpiles were accumulating, but their lower quality resulted in more frequent shutdowns of the ageing power plants for ash removal. The anticipated depletion date of this national resource was thus pushed further into the twenty-first century, and the reduced manpower needs were a welcome harbinger of more balanced development.[23]

In Lithuania the energy picture was dominated by the construction of what was billed as the world's largest nuclear power station (6,000 megawatt, compared to 4,000 for the largest Soviet operating plant, near Leningrad). Located at Lake Drūkšiai in the Ignalina *raion*, the plant was close to the Latvian and Belorussian borders and thus able to supply all three republics with power — and with fallout, if there

---

22. The UN figures in *Economic Bulletin for Europe* XXXI/2 (1980) are reproduced by Jan Winiecki, who considers them minimum estimates of hidden inflation ("Are Soviet-type Economies entering an era of long-term decline?", *Soviet Studies*, XXXVIII/3 (July 1986), pp. 325–48). The 1970–80 changes in GNP *per capita* are estimated to be +8 per cent in Lithuania, −1 per cent in Latvia and +2 per cent in Estonia by George J. Viksnins, "The Latvian Economy: Change under Gorbachev?" *JBS*, XVII/3 (Fall 1986), pp. 238–55.

23. Data mainly from *Rahva Hääl*, 27 January 1980, 26 January 1982, 29 January 1986 and 17 June 1986. The latter carried the report of Chairman of the Council of Ministers Bruno Saul on the 1986–90 socio-economic plan for the ESSR.

were an accident. The four uranium-graphite channel-type reactors were similar to those at Chernobyl, and violations of work discipline and shoddy workmanship were reported in the Soviet Lithuanian press. No public debate preceded the decision to build, which was made at the all-Union level without any input from the republican authorities. Some Lithuanian scientists protested against the construction, especially since the plant lacked cooling towers to contain contaminated water in case of malfunction. Even normal functioning was expected to bring the average temperature of Lake Drūkšiai to 30°C., thus destroying the existing ecosystem. The first reactor began operating in January 1984, and a second one was scheduled to go on line in 1985. Russians occupied the posts of power station director and executive committee chairman for the newly-built city of Sniečkus in the Ignalina *raion*. As a result of the influx of the new workforce, the Lithuanian share in the population of the *raion* decreased from 79.0 per cent to 64.3 per cent in 1979.[24] In Latvia, too, a nuclear power plant was planned (at Pāvilosta, on the Baltic coast between Liepāja and Ventspils). Like Ignalina, it increased the energy capacity for industrial growth in a labor-poor area, as if designed on purpose to induce further immigration.

Port facilities were expanded in Klaipėda, Liepāja and Ventspils, but the main push came at Muuga, 12 km. east of Tallinn, where building began in 1982 and was scheduled to be completed by 1990.[25] The Tallinn "New Harbor" was to become the largest and the deepest port on the Soviet Baltic coast, serving first of all as a site for the import of grain and the export of fertilizers. Most of the labor force involved in the construction came from Russia, and this immigration seems to have provided the main rationale for this dinosaur of a harbor. Economic considerations alone would have dictated a more southerly location, shortening transport time and avoiding ice in the winter. Estonian economists were not consulted at all, and public discussion of the project's ecological, demographic, and cultural impact was glaringly absent; the project was not even mentioned in the general press until 1982, when the official opening presented the Estonian public with a *fait accompli*. Much later, the official press poked fun at the rumors about the project that had been circulating since 1976,

24. Augustine Idzelis, "The Socioeconomic and Environmental Impact of the Ignalina Nuclear Power Station," *JBS*, XIV/3 (Fall 1983), pp. 247–54; see also Erik Lettlander, "Baltic states oppose Soviet nuclear reactor, siting of SS-20s," *Christian Science Monitor*, 26 January 1984, p. 13.

25. See Henry Ratnieks, "Soviet Hydrocarbon Exports and the Baltics," *JBS*, XV/4 (Winter 1984), pp. 282–92.

but it did not bother to explain why the population had been denied better information for six years, and it quoted ridiculously low figures for the immigration resulting from the project: an alleged total of 100 persons, including family members. This was no way to build credibility.[26]

The record of Baltic agricultural production during the period was uneven. Estonia apparently took a pioneering role in the late 1970s in organizing agricultural complexes that coordinated the collective and state farms of an entire district. The partial US grain embargo of 1981 reduced the fodder supply so severely that instructions on how to feed tree branches and fir needles to cattle were issued.[27]

Workplace Autonomy: The Acceptance of "Contractual" and "Collective Task". Parts of state or collective farms began to be assigned to self-organized groups on a long-term basis around 1980, but the practice was rarely mentioned in the press. It seemed to represent a marked shift in Soviet farm policy. Only on 3 October 1984 did the Estonian main daily *Rahva Hääl* dare to use the term "family farm." More often the euphemism "collective task acceptance" was used.

The traditional brigades had been formed by farm managers and shifted from one field to the next. In contrast, the new teams that chose to work together consisted of family members or close friends. They effectively obtained a long-term rental contract for certain fields or stables and had a personal economic interest in doing a good job during the entire yearly production cycle. Success stories in the Soviet Baltic press stressed not only productivity and personal profits but also the more flexible work schedules. The situation became somewhat similar to that of the mid-nineteenth century, when passive agricultural workers on large estates coexisted with rental farms offering more autonomy, responsibility and opportunity for profit. However, the next step taken in the late nineteenth century — family-owned farms — was not yet in sight. The motivation of farmers to increase profits was limited to their own consumption needs; they still could not invest their profits in a productive way. As in the early nineteenth century, it was pointless and even imprudent to improve the land to a point where the owner would be tempted to evict the tenant. Considerable internal capital to finance reindustrialization could be raised by selling farms to individual farmers, but like the

26. *Rahva Hääl*, 5 March 1982 and 26 August 1986.
27. Ülo Oll, *Rahva Hääl*, 11 February 1982; see Rein Taagepera, "Why Are We Feeding the Ravenous Russians?", *Los Angeles Times*, 7 November 1982.

Baltic barons before the 1850s, the Soviets did not entertain such an idea. Even the survival of rental farms was not certain. The regime had a reputation for killing the goose that laid the golden eggs as soon it began laying.[28]

In services, especially repairs, an analogous development was taking place, known as "contractual task acceptance," but it involved individuals rather than groups. A service worker would apparently take orders directly from clients, carry out the work required and receive payment. He or she would pay a fixed sum to the enterprise to cover rental and the cost of materials. This setup seemed equivalent to private artisans working in the same building and using the same source of raw materials. In Estonia 1,200 service workers were on such contracts in April 1986, and their average yearly "production" amounted to 6,000 rubles, compared to 4,400 for traditional service workers. They probably netted some 100 rubles more in average monthly income, even though the profit of the enterprises was also higher. Some service enterprises which had regularly operated at a loss of 30–40 per cent were now turning in a profit.[29] The appearance of officially sanctioned private taxis in all three Baltic capitals was another facet of the same development.[30]

In part, the new measure merely legalized the existing moon-lighting practices of repairmen and drivers, but enabled the state to take its cut of the profits. Allowing the craftsmen to do this work during official working hours could increase productivity and the convenience of the customer, provided there was sufficient price flexibility. In the summer of 1986, however, the Baltic public did not seem to notice any difference. The measure still fell short of the Hungarian and Chinese experiments in that the artisans were still unable to set their own prices or to invest in expanding or improving their means of production.

Ecology.   New measures to preserve the environment and fight pollution were taken in the old problem areas, only to be stymied by the rise of new problem areas and by the need of managers to fulfill production plans. Water pollution was the severest problem in all three republics. In addition to industrial waste and domestic sewage, the

28. See *Baltic Forum*, II/1 (Spring 1985), pp. 132–4.
29. Andres Root, in *Rahva Hääl*, 25 June 1986, p. 2; see also David Buchanan, "Estonia Demonstrates how it's Done," *Financial Times*, 19 March 1986.
30. *Izvestiia*, 23 January 1987; *Komjaunimo tiesa*, 1 April 1987.

run-off of agricultural fertilizer was a major contributing factor. Acid rain, largely of Central European origin, also began to have a harmful effect on local forests. Air pollution was becoming a problem near certain industrial sites, such as the Mažeikiai oil refinery in Lithuania, and in larger cities throughout all the three republics, where private cars were becoming more numerous.

In Latvia, severe pollution of the shallow Gulf of Riga by the effluents of the Sloka Pulp and Paper Mill was largely stopped by 1977 as a result of pressure from environmentalists, but in the city of Riga only 4.5 per cent of waste water was receiving proper treatment as late as 1983. Dams slowed the movement of water on the lower Daugava from 50 km. a day in 1950 to 50 km. a month, reducing the potential for self-purification.[31] An oil spill from a tanker near Klaipėda in 1980 spread pollution over a wide area.

Because of Soviet emphasis on the "branch principle," most of the polluting industry was under the control of central ministries in Moscow, while pollution damage was most evident to territorial agencies. This discrepancy forced the republic governments to assert their limited powers. In particular, the former Chairman of the LiSSR Council of Ministers, Juozas Maniušis, called for reform in branch-territorial relations:

In order to create more favorable conditions for the integrated development of a union republic, the USSR State Planning Committee should plan the allocation of funds and material resources for the nonproductive sector and the entire infrastructure not through all-Union ministries and administrations but through the republic Council of Ministers.[32]

The Lithuanian Nature Protection Association grew from 20,000 members in 1971 to 320,000 (close to one-tenth of the republic's population) in 1983, reflecting public awareness and heightening it still further. Concern with preserving the natural setting of the republic often looked to the Soviet authorities like nationalism. The sentencing of the environmental activist Vytautas Skuodis to 7 years in prison plus 5 years' internal exile for dissident activities in 1980 seemed to be a warning to the environmental movement. More sinister was a report in *Literatūra ir menas* (19 March 1983) that two environmental protection inspectors had been murdered by unidentified persons and that two others had narrowly escaped the same

31. Juris Dreifelds, "Participation in Pollution Control in Latvia, 1955–1977," *JBS*, XIV/4 (Winter 1983), pp. 273–95.

32. J. Maniušis, *Komunistas*, 1/1983, p. 53.

fate, apparently in two separate incidents. The intimidation seemed intentional, since the Soviet press usually did not report crimes, complete with names of victims, except when announcing that the culprits had been caught, sentenced and executed.[33]

Estonian environmentalists prepared a republic-wide plan for the protection and rational use of natural resources and succeeded in publishing a synopsis of it in the popular *Eesti Loodus* (Estonian Nature) in June 1983. The areas of greatest concern were on the northern coast: the oil-shale area, the Kunda cement works and Tallinn with the nearby Maardu phosphorite mines and new harbor construction. However, the huge phosphorite mines planned at Toolse near Kunda threatened to contaminate water supplies as far as Lake Peipsi, dwarfing all previous environmental problems by comparison.[34] There was similar republic-wide expression of environmental concern in Lithuania in 1986. In June of that year the Chairman of the LiSSR Council of Ministers, Vytautas Sakalauskas, revealed at a session of the USSR Supreme Soviet that a search for oil had been going on in Lithuania's waters south of Klaipėda. The question evoked public opposition from many prominent figures in the Lithuanian scientific and cultural establishments, and in December it was announced that the drilling projects had been suspended.[35]

A Soviet decree on "increasing the role of local soviets" ordered the formation of republic committees for protection of the environment and made any polluters (including those subordinate to central ministries) subject to fines from the republic. The decree further ordered territorial planning experiments in Latvia, Estonia and a few Russian *oblasts*.[36] In general it seemed to widen republican prerogatives by a modest amount.

Culture: Continued Modernization and Russification

The stalemate between increasing modernization and Westernization of style on the one hand and exhortations to ideological vigilance on the other, which characterized the cultural scene of the three republics

33. Augustine Idzelis, "Institutional Response to Environmental Problems in Lithuania," *JBS*, XIV/4 (Winter 1983), pp. 296–306.

34. Mare Taagepera, "Ecological Problems in Estonia," *JBS*, XIV/4 (Winter 1983), pp. 307–14.

35. *Literatūra ir menas*, 15 November 1986; *Pergalė*, 1987/3.

36. *Rahva Hääl*, 1 August 1986.

during the 1970s, continued largely unchanged during the early 1980s. As before, new literary and dramatic production continued to explore the limits of the possible, and occasional transgressions of orthodoxy were met with official reprimands. Still, as in the 1970s, there was no wholesale cultural reaction, and each successful minor overstepping of the bounds seemed to establish a precedent, expanding the boundaries of the permissible for subsequent efforts. Ideological exhortations came and went, almost in ritual fashion, and cultural life at times appeared almost oblivious to them. Very gradually, the ideological element appeared to be pushed out of serious literary creation. An apparently more serious problem was the failure of supply to meet demand. Literary works of quality were frequently published in small editions, unlike political literature, and tended to become black market items as soon as they appeared.

Historical subject matter, which had provided a medium for the discussion of sensitive contemporary political questions in the 1960s, continued to serve that function. For example, *Vilniaus kalneliai* (The Hills of Vilnius, 1986) by Alfonsas Bieliauskas sought to examine the options that had been available to Lithuania during the fateful two months, September and October 1939, when its fate hung in the balance between Germany and the USSR. Bieliauskas' not altogether negative portrayal of some prominent interwar figures caused a minor sensation. Likewise, *Paskutinis atgailos amžius* (The Last Age of Repentance, 1986) by Vytautas Petkevičius, used settings in various historical periods from the Middle Ages to the twentieth century to enable the present-day fate of the Lithuanian nation to be discussed. Such historical approaches were joined by surprisingly frank literary investigations of contemporary urban life. The novels of the Lithuanian Lenin Prize-winner Jonas Avyžius, *Chameleono spalvos* (The Colors of a Chameleon, 1979) and *Degimai* (Burnings, 1982), were praised by some for their daring and castigated by others as little better than imitations of Western soap operas striving for sensationalism. However, they provided an intriguing glimpse into the lifestyles and social problems of the new Soviet Lithuanian society.

The first novel of the Estonian poet Viivi Luik, *Seitsmes rahukevad* (The Seventh Peacetime Spring, 1985), was acclaimed for its child's eye rendering of rural life around 1950, including some previously unmentionable aspects of the guerrilla war and deportations. A rather unlikely theatrical success was Valter Udam, a district party secretary. His play *Vastutus* (Responsibility, 1985), while lacking literary quality, was a hit with both Estonian and Russian audiences because of its remarkably blunt description of Soviet bureaucratic tangles.

In the later 1970s, several talented poets appeared on the Latvian literary scene, notably Uldis Bērziņš, Leons Briedis, Māra Misiņa, Velga Krile, Māra Zālīte and Klāvs Elsbergs. Jānis Rokpelnis emerged as a master of paradox sustained by a truly polyphonic texture of dissonant voices, incongruous pairings of words, mocking rhymes and other sound effects. In the 1980s a number of young prose writers, chiefly women born in the 1960s, came to the fore, among them Eva Rubene, Aija Vālodze, Gundega Repše and Andra Neiburga. Particularly noteworthy is Rudīte Kalpiņa, who at the age of 22 became the voice of a generation no longer willing to swallow "the unappetizing porridge" that had been fed to it for so long, a generation with the courage to ask questions. Her short story "Let's Say Goodbye to Zinc Overcoats" (the reference is to the metal caskets used to bring home the bodies of dead soldiers) was perhaps the first piece of fiction published in the USSR to criticize the war in Afghanistan, although that country was never mentioned by name.[37]

A renewed Russification campaign began in the late 1970s and continued at least till 1986. Its most obvious manifestation was increased Russian-language instruction in the school system (including kindergartens) and an increased Russian-language presence in the media of the three republics.

In Estonia, the question of Russification emerged prominently in an open debate in the press. On 26 February 1985 the Russian-language daily *Sovetskaia Estoniia* published an article by the Scientific Secretary of the Council of Nationalities in the USSR Academy of Sciences, M. Guboglo, arguing that in many places (mainly in Estonia) a disproportionately large amount of material was being published in the indigenous language. He proposed increased local publication in Russian in the interests of increasing effective bilingualism. The article was widely interpreted by the republic's cultural élite as an expression of imminent intent on the part of the authorities and came to be seen as a threat to Estonian culture. The wide discussion it provoked, *inter alia* at a meeting of the Writers' Union, received little coverage in the press. However, an article published by Savvati Smirnov in the cultural monthly *Looming* of December 1985 took issue with some of Guboglo's contentions. In a particularly

37. *Literatūra um māksla*, 24 October 1986.

graphic passage, Smirnov ridiculed Guboglo's attempt to compare the 80 per cent rise in the total number of books printed in Estonian in the 1960s and '70s and the 4.8 per cent decrease in the number of Estonians fluent in Russian over the same period: "According to this logic the relationship between the rise in the yearly grain harvest and the decrease in the number of wolves should be of equal interest."[38]

Another facet of the Russification campaign was the stress on Soviet political themes in public events not intrinsically connected with politics. Such politicizing was particularly noted during the song festivals held in all three republics in the summer of 1985. The anniversary of the Soviet victory in the Second World War figured prominently as a theme at those events. In Latvia, non-Latvian Red Army choruses participated in the program — to a disproportionate degree, according to some observers.

In the early 1980s a new propaganda approach to Roman Catholicism manifested itself in Lithuania. The earlier line that religion was a remnant of the past which was dying out had virtually become untenable in the face of increasing evidence of popular identification of Roman Catholicism with Lithuanian nationalism. While the process was far from being as developed as in neighboring Poland, it apparently caused concern to the ideological establishment. Increasingly, works appeared which stressed a historical accidental association between Lithuanian nationalism and Roman Catholicism. This line of argument became most pronounced during the celebration in 1984 of the 500th anniversary of the death of St. Casimir, a sixteenth-century prince revered as the country's patron saint. Although the anniversary was celebrated in Lithuania, the Vatican and among émigrés, the regime managed to prevent a joint celebration from taking place. Pope John Paul II revealed publicly that the Soviets had not allowed him to attend the commemoration in Lithuania, and three years later he was again denied permission to visit Lithuania on the 600th anniversary of its Christianization. However, a delegation of Lithuanian clergy did participate in the solemn ceremonies in the Vatican, which drew several thousand Lithuanian émigrés from all over the world. A year earlier, an analogous celebration had been held there to mark the 800th anniversary of the introduction of Christianity in Latvia.

The expansion of foreign contacts, which had been developing since the 1960s, continued. As earlier, the stream of émigré visitors

---

38. *Looming*, 1985/12, p. 1665; for an overview of the discussion, see *Baltic Forum*, 1985/2 and 1986/1.

to the homeland brought with it not only material benefits but also living examples of the lifestyles of non-Soviet societies. The earlier prohibition of foreign visits outside the three capital cities seemed to be relaxed somewhat, and day-trips in rented cars with a chauffeur and a guide, all paid for in foreign currency, became common.

Longer stays for study purposes also continued, at least in Lithuania. Individuals managed to arrange sojourns at the universities and other places of higher learning, although most of the student visitors were participants in the summer programs for younger émigrés which became an almost annual event, albeit with several interruptions. The Latvian program was discontinued, apparently due to lack of émigré interest; of the three it had been most transparently a Soviet intelligence operation.[39] The Estonian program took the form of one week every two years, while Lithuania had a yearly three-week program.

Prominent performing artists and cultural figures were able to visit the West in response to individual invitations, most of them from the émigré community. In 1985, for instance, four prominent figures from the Lithuanian literary world were specifically sent, for the first time, as participants in an annual émigré cultural gathering in the United States, and in the spring of 1986 several members of the Lithuanian opera and ballet went on an American recital tour. Although their visit was arranged by individuals in the émigré community, they also performed in non-émigré settings where they were joined by émigré performers. Others went for professional reasons unconnected with the émigré community. The Estonian conductor Eri Klas was named conductor of the Royal Swedish Opera, a post which he assumed in 1985. In the previous spring the Tallinn Opera, under his direction, had visited Stockholm and given eight performances at the Royal Opera House. The Latvian poet Imants Ziedonis visited Lugano, Switzerland, as a guest of the local government to celebrate the anniversary of the sojourn there, in the first part of the twentieth century, of the poets Jānis Rainis and Aspāzija. Soviet Baltic scholars also appeared in several West European countries and the United States as participants in ongoing educational exchange programs, and in contrast to earlier practice, not all of them were specialists in the natural sciences. Historians, for example, were visiting scholars at the Universities of Stockholm and Wisconsin in the

39. Imants Lešinskis, "Cultural Relations or Ethnic Espionage?", *Baltic Forum*, 1985/1, pp. 26–7.

1985–6 academic year. That same year, a Soviet Lithuanian lawyer visited Columbia University Law School in the United States.

The regime also continued to use Baltic settings for international gatherings, presumably as a means of asserting the legitimacy of its control of the region. The first important occasion of this kind was in 1980, when the yachting events of the Moscow Olympic Games were held in Tallinn. In November 1985 Vilnius was selected as the meeting-place for a Soviet-US writers' colloquium, and in September 1986, Jūrmala outside Riga provided the setting for a Soviet-US Town Meeting on the Chautauqua model involving official delegations of citizens from both countries. The US delegation to the latter event included some members of the American Latvian Association.

In 1982 the Soviet Union introduced severe restrictions on the mailing of printed matter to foreign countries, a measure strongly criticized by the Estonian establishment writer Vladimir Beekman at the Moscow Writers' Congress in June 1986.[40] Indeed, the meetings of all three republics' writers' associations that year were marked by protests against various aspects of censorship.

Dissent

Cooperation among Baltic dissidents reached a new stage of sophistication in October 1981, with an open letter "Concerning the Establishment of a Nuclear-Free Zone in Northern Europe." Latvians were most numerous among the thirty-eight signatories, who asked that their three republics be included in the zone.[41] The heavy sentence given to the Estonian chemist Jüri Kukk at the beginning of the year and his subsequent death in prison seemed to boost rather than dampen the protest. The potentially most serious challenge came when an underground movement called for a "silent half-hour" on 1 December 1981 — a brief work stoppage to be repeated once a month until a number of non-nationalist demands were met. Inspired by the Polish Solidarity (crushed that same month), the center of the movement seemed to be in Tallinn, but leaflets were distributed as far away as Vilnius and Moscow, and the authorities later admitted to being frightened by it. The strike activities in Tallinn were fairly limited in

40. *Sirp ja Vasar*, 27 June 1986.
41. Rein Taagepera, "Inclusion of the Baltic Republics in the Nordic Nuclear-Free Zone," *JBS*, XVI/1 (Spring 1985), pp. 33–51; Rein Taagepera, "Citizens' Peace Movement in the Soviet Baltic Republics," *Journal of Peace Research*, XXIII/2 (1986), pp. 183–92.

scope, but they nonetheless supplied a blueprint for potential future action.[42]

In 1983 there was a visible crackdown by the regime on dissident activity — which may have been connected with the elevation of KGB head, Iurii Andropov, to the leadership of the Soviet state.

In Lithuania, clergy were subjected to arrest and trial for the first time since 1971. Singled out were Alfonsas Svarinskas and Sigitas Tamkevičius, two of the most outspoken leaders of the Lithuanian Roman Catholic movement; they had been members of the Catholic Committee for the Defense of the Rights of Believers, which had ceased to function publicly as a result of severe harassment by the authorities. Subsequently, two other members of the group were physically assaulted: in August 1985 Vaclovas Stakėnas was thrown into a pond by unidentified attackers, and in February 1986 Juozas Zdebskis was killed in a motor accident that, according to several sources, bore the marks of having been arranged by the KGB. Evidence from the *Chronicle* suggests that the regime also made a concerted effort to eliminate the underground seminary which was seeking to train the additional priests that the limited official seminary could not provide. The Commissioner for Religious Affairs in Lithuania, Petras Anilionis, was reported to have threatened a reduction in the number of students in the official seminary for each unofficial graduate to appear.

The repression succeeded in reducing the volume of Lithuanian *samizdat*. The only such publications to reach the West in 1984 were the *Chronicle of the Lithuanian Catholic Church* and *Aušra*, the oldest and probably the best organized among them. The two are known to have continued publication through 1985, although copies had greater difficulty in reaching the West. Indeed, the LiSSR Minister of Foreign Affairs accused the US Embassy in Moscow of abetting their export from the USSR. In 1985, one issue of a new publication, *Juventus Academica*, which claimed to be the organ of a Lithuanian Youth Association, also reached the West.

In the early 1980s the dissident and human rights movements in Latvia and Estonia appeared to have been crushed. The texts of the appeals by the Latvian human rights activists Lidija Doronina-Lasmane and Jānis Barkāns to the Presidium of the Supreme Soviet

42. For a more detailed description of Estonian dissent in 1979–83, see Rein Taagepera, *Softening without Liberalization in the Soviet Union: The Case of Jüri Kukk* (Lanham, MD, 1984).

of the USSR provide evidence of the crackdown in Latvia. Doronina-Lasmane was arrested in January 1983 and sentenced to five years' imprisonment and an additional three years' exile; Barkāns was arrested on 26 April and later sentenced to four years in a hard labor camp. It was not his first taste of the Gulag; he had spent 1971–81 in a camp near Riga. Later in 1983, Gunārs Astra was sentenced to seven years in a strict-regime labor camp, to be followed by five in exile, for dissemination of a *samizdat* novel, *Piecas dienas* (Five Days), a fictional account of a tourist visit to present-day Latvia. He was also accused of possession of émigré Latvian literature and a copy of George Orwell's *1984*. His final statement to the court that sentenced him, smuggled out to the West in *samizdat* form, eloquently depicted the effect of the lack of freedom of information in Latvia. The same charge — possession and dissemination of anti-Soviet literature — was leveled at two young Baptists, Jānis Rožkalns and Jānis Vēveris. Ints Cālitis, who had signed the appeal for a nuclear-free zone in the Baltic and had earlier signed the protest on the fortieth anniversary of the Molotov-Ribbentrop Pact, was also jailed.

The Estonian activists Lagle Parek, Heikki Ahonen and Arvo Pesti were tried and sentenced in late 1983. In 1984 the last prominent dissident active in Estonia, Enn Tarto, was sentenced to 10 years in a strict-regime labor camp for signing appeals labeled "anti-Soviet agitation and propaganda," among them a letter on nuclear disarmament. The sentence was harsh even by Soviet standards.

Nonetheless, dissent reemerged in Estonia and Latvia in 1984 when eight people signed another open letter on world disarmament and the abolition of censorship. In March 1986 an anonymous group of Estonian scientists issued a protest against the port construction and phosphate mining — which, they argued, would lead to Russification.[43] The Estonian underground journal *Lisandusi* . . ., published since 1978, put out its twenty-third issue in 1986.

In May 1985 there were unconfirmed reports of a riot in Riga: teenage students of polytechnic and other specialized educational institutions who had gathered there for an official convention staged a *de facto* demonstration, walking from the railroad station to the independence monument carrying posters reading "Down with the Party — Down with the Russians." They were attacked by Russian youths, and the authorities intervened in force. Three hundred were

---

43. See e.g., Bohdan Faryma, "Estonian Scientists Warn of Damage from Planned Soviet Mine Harbor," *New York City Tribune*, 18 July and 24 July 1986.

detained, and three Russians who had been thrown into the Daugava River apparently drowned. In Tartu, hundreds of Estonian and Russian youths clashed during preparations for Soviet Constitution Day in the fall of 1985.

Among an increasing number of defecting Soviet Baltic functionaries, an Estonian couple received considerable media attention because the Soviets refused to allow them to be reunited with their one-year-old daughter. After more than two years of adverse international publicity about "the world's youngest political prisoner," the Soviet authorities let her go in November 1986.

A number of Baltic political prisoners, some of them only recently sentenced, were released in early 1987 as part of a general policy decision in the Kremlin. Among them were the Estonians Parek, Ahonen and Pesti; the Latvians Rožkalns, Doronina-Lasmane and Barkāns; and the Lithuanians Vladas Lapienis and Antanas Terleckas. However, the most prominent repressed Baltic dissidents — the Estonian Mart Niklus and the Lithuanians Balys Gajauskas, Viktoras Petkus, Alfonsas Svarinskas and Sigitas Tamkevičius — remained in detention. Niklus and Tamkevičius were briefly returned to Tallinn and Vilnius, but would not sign confessions and recantations and so were returned to labor camps.[44]

The extent of quiet dissent among the Baltic population was reflected in Vaino's speech to an ECP Central Committee plenary meeting. After commenting on the "multi-national" nature of the republic, the ECP First Secretary continued:

It is especially important to achieve the understanding among the indigenous population that the historical fate of the Estonian people is inseparably tied to the Soviet state — the Union of Soviet Socialist Republics — and to the development and strengthening of the great Russian people.[45]

After 40 years of uninterrupted rule from Moscow, understanding of subservience to the Russians still remained something to be "achieved" rather than "maintained."

44. Niklus in a letter to his mother, late March 1983; Tamkevičius, Lithuanian Information Center News Release, 10 February 1987.

45. *Rahva Hääl*, 25 August 1985.

7

THE NATIONAL RENAISSANCES,
1987–1990

1987 — The Latvian Phase: Ecological Protest and Beyond

The year 1987 can, in hindsight, be said to have been a watershed in the history of the Baltic lands. The period of stagnation, to use Soviet parlance, largely prevailed in the three Baltic republics through 1986. By early 1987 *glasnost* and *perestroika*, vociferously resounding in certain Moscow circles, had only fleetingly surfaced elsewhere in the Soviet Union. Some modest expressions of opposition to centralizing trends and cultural Russification had cropped up. But their scope and tone of expression still did not radically differ from analogous instances of dissent throughout the preceding three decades.[1]

By the end of the year, several noteworthy events pointed unequivocally to a drastically changed situation in which the regime had clearly found itself on the defensive. Unofficial demonstrations in all three republics heralded a massive open opposition to the *status quo*. The success in stopping an ecologically unsound hydroelectric project in Latvia underscored the possibility of successfully confronting the designs of the central bureaucracy in Moscow and its toadies in

---

1. For details and documentation of the period 1987–90, see Walter C. Clemens, Jr., *Baltic Independence and Russian Empire* (New York, 1991); Alfred Erich Senn, *Lithuania Awakening* (Berkeley, CA, 1990); V. Stanley Vardys, "Lithuanian National Politics," *Problems of Communism*, XXXVIII/3 (July–August, 1989), pp. 53–76; Juris Dreifelds, "Latvian National Rebirth," *Problems of Communism*, XXXVIII/3 (July–August 1989), pp. 77–94; Rein Taagepera, "Estonia's Road to Independence," *Problems of Communism*, XXXVIII/6 (November–December 1989), pp. 11–26; Rein Taagepera, "Estonia in September 1988: Stalinists, Centrists, and Restorationists," *JBS*, XX/2 (Summer 1989), pp. 175–90; "Glasnost in the Street," *Baltic Forum*, V/1 (Spring 1988), pp. 64–80; "The National Renaissance of 1988," *ibid.*, V/2 (Fall 1988), pp. 1–21; "On the Road to Sovereignty," *ibid.*, VI/2 (Spring 1989), pp. 38–51.

the local *apparat*. Such confidence in turn succored opposition to analogous dictates in a wide array of other facets of national life.

Ecological Protest.   Not surprisingly, the first sustained expressions of dissatisfaction with the *status quo* arose in the area of ecology and environmental protection, which was relatively neutral in political terms. Up to 1987, most dissatisfaction with the regime's steward- ship of national life had been channeled into cultural matters. To a large extent, such critiques, although doubtless enjoying wide- spread popular support, remained primarily the concerns of the national cultural élites. The policy of *glasnost* allowed considerable expansion of their public expression. But more significantly, *glasnost* also invited public re-evaluation of all other facets of everyday condi- tions. The focus of concern soon shifted to ecology and environmental protection. The catastrophe at Chernobyl underscored the irrespon- sibility of official economic development in planning as well as execu- tion. It also graphically demonstrated the incompetence of the regime in handling the fallout, physical as well as ideological. National dis- content began to crystallize around concern over the environment. Such questions possessed the added advantage of being intrinsically apolitical.

Environmental issues surfaced to prominence first in Latvia. The principal ecological question there centered around the planned hydro- electric complex at Pļaviņas. A project for a hydroelectric station at the site was first announced in 1958 and had elicited protest even then.[2] In October 1986, a young journalist Dainis Īvāns and his col- league, a computer specialist Artūrs Snips, published an article ques- tioning the value of the massive long-planned project: "We cannot allow technicians to determine singlehandedly the future of our common home, our river of destiny."[3] Their broadside in the after- math of Chernobyl and the successful opposition in Russia to the Siberian river diversion scheme soon initiated a swell of popular opposition. The issue began to predominate in the Latvian press, especially in publications focusing on national culture. In the fall of 1986, a letter-writing campaign developed. Between 17 October and 26 November the cultural weekly *Literatūra un māksla* received approximately 700 letters with about 30,000 signatures. Within eight

---

2. Juris Dreifelds, "Two Latvian Dams: Two Confrontations," *Baltic Forum*, VI/1 (Spring 1989), pp. 11–24.

3. *Literatūra un māksla*, 17 October 1986.

weeks, the LaSSR Council of Ministers adopted a recently concluded ecological study characterizing the project as unsound.[4] By mid-summer, the USSR Academy of Sciences in Moscow had likewise become convinced. On 7 November 1987, about a year after the initial article, the USSR Council of Ministers bowed to pressure and cancelled the project.

The import of the Pļaviņas victory extended beyond ecology. The mass mobilization effort fueled confidence in the possibility of successfully opposing the designs of the bureaucratic regime. That in turn heartened the national demonstrations which began in 1987.

Somewhat later, the role of environmental issues as a catalyst in crystallizing opposition to the *status quo* proved even more dramatic in Estonia. As in Latvia, opposition to a massive ill-conceived project by central planners in Moscow ministries gave rise to a national movement of considerable proportion. The immediate cause was the planned excavation in north-central Estonia of Europe's largest phosphorite lode.

The excavation, processing and enrichment of the phosphorite would, the opposition claimed, affect not only Estonia but ultimately the entire littoral of the Baltic Sea. Mining operations around Rakvere in the Pandivere Highlands, site of the lode, would render the region, a particularly rich agricultural area, infertile. Moreover, the region is the source of approximately two-thirds of Estonian rivers and provides about 40 per cent of the water supply of the republic. Excavation would lower the water-table approximately 20 meters up to a radius of 50 kilometers from the mining site and would introduce a constant flow of radioactive elements into Estonian groundwater and eventually into the Baltic Sea. Such problems of seepage of radioactive waste had already chronically complicated phosphorite mining operations at Maardu near Tallinn.[5] But Maardu was not located near a principal water-supply source. Seepage in the Pandivere Highlands could result in the contamination of the underground waterbed of a large part of Estonia. In addition, the project called for local processing of the phosphorite into various forms of fertilizer. Similar operations had already nearly devastated the Kola Peninsula, and there was no reason to believe that the processing in Estonia would be done

4. Nīls Muižnieks, "The Daugavpils Hydro Station and *Glasnost* in Latvia," *JBS*, XVIII/1 (Spring 1987), pp. 66–8.

5. Mare Taagepera, "The Ecological and Political Problems of Phosphorite Mining in Estonia," *JBS*, XX/2 (Summer 1989), pp. 168–70.

more cleanly. Prevailing winds would, moreover, carry much of the pollution into neighboring Finland.

In addition to the purely environmental dangers, the mining plans exacerbated Estonian perceptions of the demographic threat. The country was already short of labor, due largely to various other massive development schemes carried out by Moscow. Estimates in the Estonian press held that in the initial stages the project would require an immigration of 30,000–40,000 people. That included only the miners and their families. Additional service personnel would also be required. Inevitably, the percentage of the indigenous Estonian population would suffer a significant decline.

The policy of *glasnost* allowed a relatively open discussion of the question. The Estonian intelligentsia was able to propagate opposition in a quite unhindered fashion and opposition snowballed. In early 1987, at the time of Gorbachev's visit to Estonia, the head of the Writers' Union, Vladimir Beekman, raised the issue openly. In the spring of that year, the University of Tartu issued a warning, to which the Rector added his name as signatory, on the real risks involved in the project. The Estonian Lawyers' Association issued a declaration that, according to the Constitution of the USSR, the use of the ground, forest and water as well as environmental protection was under the competence of the republic's own authorities and not under that of an all-Union office like the Ministry of Mineral Fertilizers in Moscow. The declaration urged that the project be discontinued until the requisite technology for proper environmental control could be developed. The university town of Tartu was full of wall paintings on the phosphorite danger, and on 1 May 1987 the students substituted green ecological banners for the standard red ones during the traditional parade.[6]

Surprisingly, even some among the local Estonian party satraps joined those working against the Ministry of Mineral Fertilizers in Moscow. The Chairman of the Council of Ministers of the ESSR, Bruno Saul, promised to stop the undertaking if scientific analysis could prove that irrevocable ecological damage would result, and his deputy, Indrek Toome, affimed that the ESSR authorities would not sanction continued planning until all ecological concerns had been met.[7]

---

6. "Phosphorite and Politics," *Baltic Forum*, IV/2 (Fall 1987), p. 90.
7. *Sirp ja Vasar*, 1 May 1987.

Past experience indicated that local authorities had little if any decisive say in environmental matters affecting their republic. This instance, however, appeared different, especially because the proponents of the project in Moscow saw a need to justify their plans. Iurii Iampol, head of the mining agency *Soiuzgorkhimprom* in Moscow, noted the importance of the Rakvere find to the all-Union economy and urged proceeding in the shortest amount of time possible.[8]

In October 1987, the USSR Council of Ministers decided to stop projects for new phosphorite mines in Estonia, to which the Estonian leadership readily concurred. The decision may have been conceived as a temporary retreat, but further political developments subsequently made resumption of the project even more difficult.

Glasnost in the Streets.   The inability of the regime to cope with the ecological protests no doubt contributed to a spill-over effect into other areas of national life. Opposition to the *status quo* received increasingly open expression. Significantly, it began to be tolerated by the regime. The earliest and most dramatic manifestations of this new situation occurred in Latvia. Mass demonstrations in June, August and November 1987 commemorated significant anniversaries in the modern history of the nation. A new ebullience in the public atmosphere in Riga conducive to such activity had begun to be noticeable already in the spring of 1987. On 19 April, several hundred Latvian youths — described as "punks" because of their age and appearance — had danced in a snake line through the center of the city and around the Freedom Monument. This event coincided with reported incidents of violence between Latvian and Russian youths in the city.[9]

The first demonstration in June saw some 5,000 participants file past the Freedom Monument in Riga on the anniversary of the massive deportations in June 1941 which preceded by one week the German attack on the USSR. The date also coincided with the occupation of the Baltic states by the Red Army in mid-June 1940. The event was organized by the working-class human rights group "Helsinki '86" which had been founded the preceding year. Planning had begun in March by the founders of Helsinki '86, Linards Grantiņš and Rolands

8. *Noorte Hääl*, 28 February 1987.
9. Viz. Jānis Peters, Chairman of the Writers' Union of the LaSSR in *Literatūra un māksla*, 1 May 1987.

Silaraups. A few days before the event, Grantiņš was arrested and sentenced to six months' imprisonment — allegedly for refusal of military service, although he was 37 and held a medical exemption. The authorities unsuccesfully pressured Silaraups to move the planned demonstration outside the city center.

The June commemoration in Riga served as a rehearsal for more imposingly massive events later that summer in all three Baltic capitals. On 23 August, the anniversary of the Molotov-Ribbentrop Pact of 1939 which sealed the fate of the independent pre-war Baltic states, demonstrations took place in all three Baltic capitals and several other cities as well. The one in Riga, which even by conservative estimates drew over 10,000, was probably the largest unofficial demonstration up to that time in the recent history of the Soviet Union. Some violence occurred as Helsinki '86 activists were filing past the Freedom Monument to lay flowers. Police attempted to move back the crowd, which broke through police lines and occupied the base of the monument. It was surrounded by police who in turn were surrounded by a larger crowd on the outside. Several clashes resulted. Official reports claim that 86 were arrested, although unofficial witnesses cite a higher figure. Just before the march, in an obvious attempt to disrupt its organization, KGB and plainclothes police detained several of the leaders of Helsinki '86. Their efforts were in vain.

On the same day, analogous demonstrations were also organized in Tallinn and Vilnius. Judging by photographs subsequently brought to Sweden, a crowd numbering at least 5,000 marched from the town hall square to Harju Hill in Hirvepark to lay flowers at the statue of Linda, the mother of Kalevipoeg, the hero of the national epic. The crowd was led by persons carrying placards with the words "*Eesti, Latvija, Lietuva*", the names of the Baltic states in their native languages, and the flags of the independent states which were at the time still proscribed. The demonstrators also carried placards prominently demanding freedom for Enn Tarto, a dissident then serving a 10-year sentence for anti-Soviet activity. He had signed a joint Baltic appeal for a nuclear-free zone.

The event in Lithuania, the only one of the three attended by foreign correspondents, drew a crowd of over 1,000. Flowers were laid at a recently unveiled statue of Adam Mickiewicz, the great Polish poet of Lithuanian origin (1798–1855). According to Western analysts, one of the reasons for the relatively low turnout in Lithuania may have been the favorable status of national relations there;

it was the least Russified of the three republics, and many could have felt that demonstrating would only harm the interests of the largely native Lithuanian party and state apparatus. The paucity of Lithuanian workers in Vilnius could also have been a factor. Although the city's population was approximately half Lithuanian, most of these were members of the intelligentsia, bureaucrats, and white-collar workers — elements less likely to risk an anti-regime stance in public.

From the outset, it was clear that the local regimes were at a loss how to cope with these events. There was no experience in dealing with massive unofficial demonstrations, especially in an atmosphere of self-proclaimed *glasnost*. And initially, at least, the demonstrations did not concern matters other than those which the regime itself had halfheartedly acknowledged as past mistakes which had been swept under the rug and required open airing. Official reactions nevertheless betrayed considerable unease. Vituperative denunciations accompanied attempts to belittle the size and significance of the demonstrations. TASS understandably focused on the one in Lithuania, the smallest of the three, pronouncing its turnout a flop. No mention was made of crowds in Riga and Tallinn. The Latvian media furthermore made a concerted effort to depict the leaders of Helsinki '86 as atypical and in some cases reprehensible individuals. TASS quoted a claim by the hardline Mayor of Riga, Alfreds Rubiks, that some of the participants wielded knives and that others, by implication, were just "hoodlums" who had been "seduced" into coming to the Freedom Monument "with the promise of an interesting show."[10] The old timeworn theme of blaming foreign incitement was also resurrected. As part of the effort, Kim Philby, the Soviet spy in Britain and prominent defector to the USSR of another era, was brought out of mothballs. In an interview with KGB General Janis Lukasevics (*alias* Iakov Konstantinovich Bukashev, First Secretary at the USSR Embassy in London, 1972–80) broadcast on Latvian television on 18 November, Philby discussed the sending of agents to Latvia by the British Secret Service in the postwar years and implied that the current upsurge in national feeling was of foreign inspiration: "They're doing just the same now as in my day."[11] On more than one occasion, the role and responsibility of foreign radio broadcasts in fuelling such activity was underscored in press accounts, and a number of official demonstrations of protest at US interference were organized.

10. TASS, 25 August 1987.
11. Tom Bower, *The Red Web* (London, 1989), p. 191.

Delegations from the Supreme Soviets of the Baltic republics were even sent to the US Embassy in Moscow. Television coverage, however, proved surprisingly extensive and was virtually live in all three capitals.

In Latvia and Estonia, though not in Lithuania, several of the leaders were subsequently pressured into emigration. Silaraups arrived in Vienna in late July on a Jewish emigration visa, although he has absolutely no Jewish connections. Madisson and several others left in the aftermath of the August demonstration.[12]

The relative indecision on the part of the regime which appears to have preceded the June and August demonstrations disappeared in Latvia during the fall of 1987, before preceding the upcoming anniversary of the national proclamation of independence on 18 November 1918. As the date approached, hints and warnings began to proliferate in the media. Then LaCP Bureau Secretary for Ideology Anatolijs Gorbunovs went on record to warn Latvians against demonstrations on 18 November:

Let it be known to those who go, either intentionally or out of naiveté or curiosity, to the Freedom Monument on 18 November . . . that the majority of society considers it to be their moral duty to oppose such irresponsible people.[13]

On the same day, the LaCP First Secretary Boriss Pugo issued a warning on television that strong measures would be taken against all demonstrators. Efforts were made to keep down the size of the possible crowds. A correspondent of *Le monde* who spent 18 November in Riga reported that she had been told by a local resident that "special Latvian history lessons" had been given to schoolchildren and that they had been warned that "things would turn out badly for them" if they went to the monument on 18 November. A school located close to the monument was closed for the day and the pupils were sent off on an excursion. Students at the university and at technical institutes were allegedly warned of the possibility of expulsion if they demonstrated. Employees at various enterprises suddenly found themselves on special duty, something which had not happened for years. Prominent dissidents also found themselves under house arrest.[14]

12. For surveys of the summer events and interviews with Tiit Madisson and Rolands Silaraups, see "*Glasnost* in the Baltic: Summer Demonstrations," *Baltic Forum*, IV/2 (Fall 1987), pp. 1–29.

13. TASS, in Russian, 17 November 1987.

14. *Le monde*, 20 November 1987; *Daily Telegraph*, 19 November 1987.

In spite of the spate of precautions, 18 November 1987 was an eventful day in Latvia. On the morning, individuals were allowed to place flowers by the Freedom Monument as well as by gravestones in the Cemetery of Brothers and the Forest Cemetery, both places of commemorative significance. During the afternoon, security forces made a concerted effort to close off all areas where people might gather because of their symbolic importance. Some youths tried to penetrate the police cordons, but without success. Vigils were held by the National Theater, where the original declaration of independence had been signed. Witnesses of the June and August demonstrations estimated that about 10,000 people participated. However, due to the efforts of the authorities they were prevented from demonstrating as a group. The following day, Radio Stockholm reported that 6,000–7,000 had been involved in commemorative activities of various kinds in Riga and that there had been 40 arrests. Such reports were officially denied by the LaSSR authorities. Ironically, the extreme security measures imposed in the center of Riga on 18 November also impeded access to an officially sponsored demonstration at the monument to the Red Riflemen which had been planned as a counterweight to the expected nationalist demonstrations. Western correspondents reported seeing some 2,000 people there rather than the constantly repeated 15,000 claimed by the official media; most of them appear to have been Russians who could not even understand the Latvian placards which they were carrying.[15]

1988 – The Estonian Phase: Striving for Autonomy

The momentum begun in 1987 gathered force in 1988 and developed into significant mass political movements in all three republics. Baltic efforts increasingly focused on broader demands for autonomy, especially in economic matters. This year saw political change of great consequence in all three republics. Broad popular fronts appeared; these occupied the middle ground between the incumbent CP leaderships and dissidents. The old party leaderships were changed, and their successors sought to acquire popularity by espousing national causes. Old national symbols such as the flags of the pre-war states, strictly proscribed throughout the period of Soviet occupation, reappeared. In that year too, the indigenous language was declared the state language in Estonia and Lithuania; in Latvia, this happened early in 1989.

15. *"Glasnost* in the Streets," *Baltic Forum,* V/1 (Spring 1988), pp. 70–4.

Demands for independence remained in the realm of former dissidents; however, repression of their demonstrations gradually ceased. Part of the Russian immigrant population also organized themselves to counter perceived threats to their privileges, especially in matters of language.

The process appeared first and in the most pronounced form in Estonia, which by the end of 1988 became the first republic in the USSR to proclaim its sovereignty and the primacy of republic law over all-Union legislation. One of the leaders of the Estonian movement, Marju Lauristin, compared Baltic developments to a bicycle race in which different members of a team take over the lead at different times. In 1987, Latvia had been in the forefront of developments; by 1988, Estonia was clearly the pathfinder. This Estonian phase can be said to have lasted 17 months, from September 1987 to February 1989. From a comparison of 11 significant developments which occurred in all three countries on fairly clearcut dates it appears that during this period Lithuania trailed Estonia by an average of 3.5 months and that Latvia trailed Lithuania by about 1.5 months.[16]

The Hirvepark demonstration in Tallinn on 23 August 1987 trailed Latvia in terms of numbers of participants, but it may have accelerated developments of proposals for far-reaching economic autonomy in Estonia. Closet reformists in the establishment who had been testing the waters came to realize that they faced a loss of initiative to popular forces whose activity could provoke the backlash that they were trying to avoid by going slowly. The "Four Man Proposal" for economic autonomy published on 26 September 1987 provides a good example. Throughout late 1987 the proposal came under official criticism. In their attempt to prove the impossibility of economic autonomy, the opponents fell into the trap of documenting the extent to which Estonia's economy was directed from Moscow, even in petty detail. One of the four signatories, the future Prime Minister Edgar Savisaar, then just a former minor planning committee official, turned their argument around to demonstrate that overcentralization had reached absurd proportions.[17]

Public discussion of the crimes of Stalin in Estonia had already begun

16. Rein Taagepera, 1989, p. 24.
17. Toivo Miljan, "The Proposal to Establish Economic Autonomy in Estonia," *JBS*, XX/2 (Summer 1989), pp. 149–64.

in late 1987, and in that year Christmas was rehabilitated. In January 1988, the hardline ECP CC Secretary for Ideology, Rein Ristlaan, was replaced by Indrek Toome, who established a dialogue with the autonomists.

From the beginning of the year, the dawning of a new era on the Baltic political scene was most evident in Estonia. The possibility of a backlash was still clearly present. On 2 February, a demonstration in Tartu to commemorate the Estonia-Soviet peace treaty of 1920 was brutally attacked by the police, but this proved to be the last such incident in the country. There were analogous repressions in Lithuania in the fall of that year and in Latvia as late as March 1989.

The different reactions later that month in Estonia and in Lithuania to the independence anniversaries of the pre-war states provide a more revealing illustration of the changing atmosphere in Estonia. In Lithuania, it was still business as usual. As in Latvia the preceding November, equally blatant efforts were made to prevent, manipulate and misrepresent events on the occasion of the anniversary, on 16 February 1988, of Lithuania's declaration of independence in 1918. These included a specially arranged Potemkin-like village tour for a group of selected foreign correspondents. After witnessing an evidently staged pro-Soviet demonstration, they left Vilnius on the afternoon of 16 February. This naturally minimized the number of foreign witnesses of the spontaneous national demonstrations which developed in Vilnius, Kaunas and elsewhere in the evening. Official pronouncements also attempted to lessen any impact. TASS admitted that "following divine service in the churches of Vilnius and Kaunas, individual extremist and nationalistically minded elements tried unsuccessfully to incite believers into committing anti-Soviet action." TASS furthermore quoted the Minister of Interior of the LiSSR, Major-General Stasys Lisauskas, as claiming that there had been ". . . no anti-Soviet national actions in Lithuania. Only thirty-two people were detained in the Republic for antisocial and hooligan actions yesterday. After an investigation, all of them were released."[18] However, the uneasiness of the regime was clear. The official press continued a campaign of denigration of nationalist elements lasting at least a month thereafter.

18. "*Glasnost* in the Streets," *Baltic Forum*, V/1 (Spring 1988), pp. 73–5.

Such clumsy attempts at manipulation which characterized the independence anniversaries in Riga on 18 November 1987 and in Vilnius on 16 February 1988 seem on the whole to have been avoided in Estonia. Its independence day, 24 February, passed somewhat differently. Although, as in Latvia and in Lithuania, a pro-Soviet demonstration was staged, it proved a transparently halfhearted effort; the largely non-Estonian audience had difficulty in understanding the speeches and in applauding at the correct places in the script.

The unofficial demonstration clearly overshadowed the official one. Ater 5 p.m., sizeable crowds began to gather in a downtown Tallinn park, laying flowers by the monument honoring the novelist Anton H. Tammsaare. The title of his principal work, *Truth and Justice*, was inscribed on the monument, and this had served as a symbolic rallying-point for protest in Estonia. By 6 p.m., the militia seemed to have lost control of the gathering. According to the official press, the area was packed with people. By 7 p.m. prominent cultural figures began to exhort the crowd to go to several specially designated halls which the authorities had prepared for discussions. By all accounts both the Estonia Opera House and the hall of the Building of Political Education were filled to overflowing, and a momentous meeting was held in the latter hall, which included a frank discussion of several hitherto taboo topics such as the necessity for opposition, the return of national symbolism and an admission by one of the official speakers that the pro-Soviet demonstration had been staged in order to demonstrate "order" to the rest of the USSR and to the outside world.

In Estonia, the spring of 1988 is remembered as the spring of blue-black-white, the national flag of the pre-war independent state. In April the Estonian Heritage Society (EHS), an organization formed legally in December 1987, began openly and with impunity to display the as yet prohibited colors during demonstrations throughout the land. Somewhat later, the Lithuanian and Latvian colors also reappeared. Eventually, these came to be legalized in all three republics as "national" emblems.

Subsequent developments in Estonia proved even more significant. A mood of defiance prevailed at a meeting on 1–2 April of the leaders of the Estonian creative unions. The press reported a public mention by a member of the establishment, Rein Veidemann, editor of the monthly *Vikerkaar*, of the possibility of Estonia leaving the USSR. The meeting adopted radical proposals for the upcoming Nineteenth Conference of the CPSU along with a vote of no-confidence addressed to the leadership of the republic.

On 13 April, Edgar Savisaar proposed the creation of a "Popular Front for the Support of Restructuring in the USSR". It soon became the Popular Front of Estonia (PFE), a still informal group, though including significant members of the republic's more nationally minded Communists and prominent members from among the national intelligentsia. It called for "economic sovereignty" in the form of republic self-management, legalization of private enterprise, control of immigration and concern for the environment.

Increasingly out of touch with the mood of reform, ECP First Secretary Karl Vaino decided to follow long-standing practice and in effect appoint the Estonian delegation to the upcoming conference of the CPSU in Moscow by not holding multi-candidate elections. When the PFE called for a mass meeting on 17 June to meet these delegates, Vaino is believed to have requested Moscow for military action. However, the new ECP CC Secretary for Ideology, Indrek Toome, split ranks with Vaino. The Kremlin agreed to Vaino's dismissal on 16 June 1988. The following day, a celebratory demonstration drew 150,000 people.

Vaino's replacement as First Secretary, the native Estonian Vaino Väljas who had lost out in the power struggle of 1978 and who had subsequently been removed from the scene as Soviet Ambassador to Venezuela and Nicaragua (see Chapter 5, p. 208), soon openly made common cause with the PFE. At the Moscow conference Väljas openly advocated the PFE platform on extensive autonomy, in contrast to his incumbent counterparts from Latvia and Lithuania. By September, the ECP leadership had come fully to share this goal. In November, the entire Estonian leadership passed into the hands of the reformists. The Chairman of the Council of Ministers, Bruno Saul, resigned and was replaced by Indrek Toome. The Chairman of the Presidium of the Supreme Soviet, Arnold Rüütel, had made common cause with the reformists earlier. By then, however, the PFE had moved further, calling for "the transformation of the Soviet Union from a federal state into a confederation of states," with juridical guarantees and a political mechanism for secession if this were needed.[19] The ECP leadership was again lagging behind rapidly moving developments.

Analogous popular mass movements appeared in Lithuania and Latvia as well. On 3 June 1988, after a visit by several Estonian economists, the "Lithuanian Reconstruction Movement",

19. *Sirp ja Vasar*, 5 August 1988.

subsequently known as "*Sąjūdis*" (Movement) was formed. Then, on 21 June, an analogous Popular Front of Latvia (PFL) was initiated. Both movements shared the Estonian goals of political and economic reorganization. All three leaderships consisted of an even mix of rank-and-file CP members and non-members. They sought to avoid open conflict with the CP establishments; however, unlike in Estonia, which did experience a change in leadership, relations between the front and the existing CP leaderships remained cool.

The national renaissances demonstrated their growing strength at several mass meetings during the summer at which politics and national feelings were mixed with song and expressions of ecological concern. These represented a remarkable outpouring of emotion, apparently with no drunkenness or rowdyism.

Sąjūdis held its first mass rally on 24 June. More than 50,000 people gathered on Cathedral Square in Vilnius to meet the delegates to the CPSU conference, that is those delegates who agreed to attend. The turnout was particularly impressive in view of the lack of any announcement by the media and the bad weather. A subsequent *Sąjūdis* "meeting" with congress delegates in Vingis Park in Vilnius on 9 July drew a crowd of more than 100,000.[20]

On 14 June between 50,000 and 100,000 people gathered in Riga to commemorate the deportations of 1941. There were smaller gatherings in other cities. On 16 July, some 30,000 joined in a rally in Riga to demand that the pre-war maroon-white-maroon flag be restored as the official flag of the republic. The anniversary of the Molotov-Ribbentrop Pact on 23 August occasioned demonstrations in all three republics. The one in Riga drew at least 60,000, that in Vilnius 250,000.

The PFE demonstrated its strength by calling a song-and-speech meeting on 11 September at which 250,000, one-quarter of the ethnic Estonian population, participated.

Political change came more slowly to Lithuania and Latvia. The incumbent CP chiefs held on in both republics until October. Their removal proved less dramatic than that of Vaino had been early in the year. Like Vaino, Boriss Pugo in Latvia and Ringaudas Songaila in Lithuania had effectively appointed their republics' delegations to the CPSU conference in Moscow in June. However, they were unable to contain the surging growth of the popular fronts. Indeed, some of the members of the old ruling élite, no doubt sensing the way

20. For details see, Senn, 1990, pp. 74–95.

the wind was blowing, began to make common cause with the fronts. In Lithuania, two LiCP CC Secretaries, Algirdas Brazauskas for the economy and Lionginas Sepetys for ideology, addressed the massive *Sąjūdis* gathering in July.

A visit to Riga and Vilnius by Gorbachev's troubleshooter, CPSU CC Secretary Aleksandr Iakovlev, in early August sent a clear message to the reformers that the Kremlin would sanction the toppling of the existing leaderships. Since the death of Griškevičius in December 1987, Songaila had hardly had time to establish himself in office. He reputedly had been backed by a majority of local LiCP bosses because of a do-nothing reputation which indicated that he was not likely to interfere in affairs at the local level. He was replaced on 20 October by Algirdas Brazauskas in the aftermath of the popular reaction against the suppression of a demonstration in Cathedral Square in Vilnius. Brazauskas was evidently chosen as the most acceptable among the existing leadership to the *Sąjūdis* organisation. As in Estonia, the LiCP espoused the goal of autonomy.

In Latvia, the change in leadership was occasioned by the transfer to Moscow in September of the First Secretary, Boriss Pugo. The choice of Jānis Vagris as his successor on 4 October was a compromise and was made in the face of opposition demonstrations. The leading reformist in the LaCP leadership, Anatolijs Gorbunovs, clearly the favorite of the LPF, was made Chairman of the Presidium of the Supreme Soviet of the LaSSR. Vagris, a lackluster bureaucrat, was at least a native Latvian, the first since 1959 to hold the position of First Secretary of the LaCP. The Chairman of the Council of Ministers, Vilnis Bresis, was also a passive politician.

All three fronts, still unregistered informal organizations, held founding congresses in October. The congress of the Popular Front of Estonia came first (1–2 October 1988), and was attended by ECP First Secretary Väljas. Among 3,267 delegates, 22 per cent were members of the CP. Only 5 per cent were non-Estonian; however, their role in the organization was somewhat greater than their numbers would indicate. They delivered 10 per cent of the speeches, and made up 13 per cent of the standing assembly of 105 which was formed. None of them, however, was elected to the seven-person leadership of the EPF. This unintentional result, produced by ill-advised electoral rules, was to have consequences in Estonian politics later. According to the statute, the chairmanship was formally a rotating one, but in practice Savisaar clearly ran the show, both during the congress and subsequently. The charter adopted a goal of sovereignty for the ESSR, "while recognizing the Estonians' right to self-determination." The monopoly on power by any organization, without an explicit electoral mandate, was declared undemocratic.

On 8–10 October, the Popular Front of Latvia held its founding congress in Riga. Over 1,000 deputies were present, and they elected Dainis Īvāns President of the Front. The charter adopted called for a variety of social measures to increase democracy, social justice, economic sovereignty and environmental protection. It also addressed in some detail several specific matters such as the need to take Riga off Moscow time. A potentially explosive call made for full publication of the minutes of the July 1959 LaCP plenum and a clarification of the role of its organizers Arvīds Pelše and Augusts Voss. That plenum had been followed by a wide-ranging purge of native elements in the LaCP (see Chapter 4, pp. 140–6).

The founding congress of Sąjūdis took place on 22–3 October; 1,027 delegates elected a 220-member assembly and 35-member council, 17 members of the latter belonging to the LiCP. The resolution adopted called for relations with other Soviet republics based on Leninist principles of federalism, national equality and self-determination. A mood of euphoria permeated the congress. Just two days before its gathering, the conservative head of the LiCP, Ringaudas Songaila, was replaced by the popular Algirdas Brazauskas. On the eve of the opening, it was announced that the cathedral of Vilnius would be returned to the Roman Catholic Church. An open-air mass held in Cathedral Square on Sunday morning (23 October) was attended by 5,000 people and broadcast live on television.

By the fall of 1988, the popular fronts had clearly emerged as the leading political forces in their republics. The PFE claimed some 100,000 supporters, but the figure is hazy since no dues-paying membership was introduced. The situation was similar with Sąjūdis. Vytautas Landsbergis, who emerged as its head, put the membership at between 100,000 and 500,000. The Popular Front of Latvia was the only one of the three to introduce formal dues. In October 1988, its membership stood at 110,000, of whom one-third were also members of the LaCP.[21] During the spring and summer, the fronts had received tacit support from Moscow. However, when it became increasingly clear that their notion of *perestroika* did not coincide with what Gorbachev had in mind, such support ceased.

21. Dreifelds, 1989, p. 85.

The CPs, still in charge of the administrations, had clearly been placed on the defensive. Their relationships with the fronts remained schizophrenic. While officially the CP leaderships not only tolerated the movements but also participated prominently in their opening congresses, it was clear that they were not fully at ease with the new situation; it was also clear that they did not know how to cope with it. The situation was even more strained at intermediate and lower levels where old-style conservatives still held sway in the *apparats*. Although this state of affairs was somewhat more apparent in Latvia than in the other two republics, it was unmistakably present in Estonia and Lithuania as well.

Various measures were utilized by the CP *apparats* in their attempts to neutralize or limit the impact of the fronts. The Russian settler populations became pawns in a political balancing act in resisting the push for more rapid change, especially in Estonia and Latvia. The process of registration of the fronts as legal entities, which would have meant formal acquiescence in their continued existence and activity, also met with resistance. The process became long-drawn-out. In Estonia, registration was completed only in February 1989 and in Lithuania the following month. In Latvia the issue remained unresolved for even longer.

As the largest organized opposition, the popular fronts were in the forefront of changing the political spectrum in the three republics. Other groupings also soon made an appearance, reflecting finer political differentiation. Some were outgrowths of specifically oriented movements. The Estonian National Independence Party (ENIP) was formed on 20 August 1988, and was a continuation of a group established to propagate the publication of the secret protocols of the German-Soviet arrangements in August and September 1939 as a first step towards a clearcut public labeling of the events of 1940 as a Soviet occupation. The group was successful. The publication of the documents in the ECP daily *Rahva Hääl* (11 and 12 August 1988) was the first such instance in the USSR. The Lithuanian cultural weekly *Literatūra ir menas* (20 August) and the Latvian Komsomol daily *Padomju jaunatne* followed suit. However, the group's success removed its *raison d'être* and it metamorphosed itself into the ENIP. Relations between this party and the PFE were at times strained; for the ENIP, any members of the ECP were suspect, and the PFE all too often tended to label the ENIP as "extremist".

In Lithuania and Latvia, such political differentiation did not as yet produce an analogous cleavage. The Latvian equivalent to the ENIP, the Latvian National Independence Movement (LNIM), first appeared in public on 10 July 1988 and worked under the Latvian Popular Front umbrella. Its most prominent leader was Eduards Berklāvs, an old Communist who as Deputy Chairman of the Council of Ministers had been the most prominent individual purged in 1959. The pro-independence Lithuanian Liberation League (LLL), which counted several prominent dissidents and former repressees among its leadership, emerged from the underground in 1987. After some initial criticism, it achieved a *modus vivendi* with *Sąjūdis*. The LLL was offered and accepted seven seats (out of a total of 1,121) at the founding congress of *Sąjūdis*.

The political organization of the indigenous nationalities also catalyzed the Russian-speaking populations to form their own political groupings. The indigenous groups can be faulted in part for making insufficient efforts to attract Russians and members of other minorities to their movements. At the founding of *Sąjūdis*, 96 per cent of the delegates were Lithuanian, and — as already noted — the Russians were similarly underrepresented at the PFE congress. Only in Latvia did the organizers of the popular front succeed in attracting a fair number from among the minority population, thus preparing the ground for more cooperation in years to come. It should be noted that a significant proportion of Latvia's Russian population does not consist of postwar Soviet immigrants.

After the local CP apparatus had come under the sway of nationally-minded party members, the more active and imperialist-minded among the recent settler populations began to organize against the indigenous fronts. The Internationalist Front of Estonia, which emerged in July 1988, later called itself the Intermovement while its Latvian counterpart, dating from October 1988, kept its original name, Interfront. In Lithuania, where the settler population was considerably smaller and where native elements had predominated in the party leadership since 1940, the analogous *Edinstvo* organization, dating from November 1988, was considerably smaller and less significant in the political spectrum. Its attempts to include the native Polish-speaking population around Vilnius met with only limited success.

A political balance of power between the nationalists and the Kremlin can be said to have prevailed until the late fall. It was broken not through a Baltic initiative but rather as a reaction to a move by Moscow. In November 1988, Gorbachev sought to force through changes in the Constitution of the USSR. Either on purpose, or through insensitive wording, these changes were read as a nullification of Article 72 which guaranteed the right of USSR republics to leave the union. Appeals by the popular fronts to postpone the amendments received millions of signatures within one week: 1.8 million in Lithuania and 0.9 million each in Latvia and Estonia.[22] Evidently the general mood in the Baltic favored retention of Article 72 in the USSR Constitution in an unambiguous form. The outcome was the adoption by Moscow of a somewhat watered-down version of the constitutional amendment, which introduced an even greater measure of ambiguity.

On 16 November, ECP First Secretary Väljas guided the ESSR Supreme Soviet through a tense meeting which adopted a "Declaration about Sovereignty" ("about" not "of").[23] It stopped short of declaring Estonia's secession from the USSR, yet it formally legislated an interpretation of the existing USSR Constitution most favorable to Estonia's sovereignty. For a while, the ECP gained in popularity.

Doubtless affected by stern warnings from Moscow, LiCP First Secretary Brazauskas prevailed on the Supreme Soviet of the LiSSR at its 18–19 November session not to follow the Estonian example. As a sop, Lithuanian was declared the state language, the interwar anthem was made the official anthem of the republic, and the national tricolor flag was made the state flag, a step which Estonia and Latvia took only in May 1990. For a while, Lithuania became the only republic in the USSR to have eliminated the hammer and sickle from its official pennant. However, the victory for Brazauskas was Pyrrhic. While he won the battle in the Supreme Soviet, in spite of massive demonstrations to follow the Estonian example, the LiCP lost support on two flanks. The language law and the adoption of the old state flag displeased *Edinstvo*; *Sąjūdis* activists talked of betrayal of Estonia. The honeymoon between *Sąjūdis* and the LiCP was over. Faced with the Lithuanian example, Latvia's Supreme Soviet desisted from any action.

The Estonian leadership, in particular Rüütel, withstood coarse verbal assaults in the Kremlin. The Presidium of the Supreme Soviet of the USSR declared the Estonian legislation on sovereignty unconstitutional, but the ESSR Supreme Soviet stood firm. Its position was that the USSR Constitution was itself contradictory, especially after

---

22. "The National Renaissance of 1988," *Baltic Forum*, V/2 (Fall 1988), p. 17.
23. English text in *Baltic Forum*, V/2 (Fall 1988), pp. 74–9.

the most recent changes. A stalemate resulted, and a prolonged stalemate between a queen and a pawn works in favor of the latter. When, half a year later, Lithuania (18 May) and Latvia (28 July) made analogous declarations, it hardly raised a ripple in Moscow. Subsequently sovereignty declarations were passed by supreme soviets in virtually every republic of the USSR.

Official registration of the Popular Front of Estonia in February 1989 proved to be the last Estonian "first." Estonia's initiative came to be increasingly weighed down by its Russian immigrant population.[24] These provided half of the CP membership of the Estonian Party and predominated demographically in the northeast corner of the republic. The very speed of the changes had left the immigrant population behind. In Latvia, however, the slow pace provided time for adjustment. In Lithuania the non-indigenous numbers were low. By the spring of 1989, the initiative had clearly shifted to Lithuania and the emphasis was no longer autonomy but independence.

1989 — The Lithuanian Phase; Push for Independence

In 1989 the push for restructuring political and social life gathered momentum. Indeed, by the end of the year, the thrust of political activity had shifted perceptibly from attempts at reform of the old structures to unequivocal striving for political independence. At the beginning of the year, the key term in the operative political lexicon of the opposition was "sovereignty" — loosely defined and not necessarily clashing with official ideology. The initially cautious steps in the spring and summer of 1988 had ostensibly sought merely to reform the ossified one-party regime. Relatively rapid success in dislodging the old republican party leaderships provided an impetus toward radicalization. The clear victories by the fronts in the elections in the spring of 1989 to the new USSR Congress of People's Deputies fuelled the trend. Even the old republic supreme soviets, "elected" under the old system, began to assert the primacy of their republics. By the end of the year, national political independence had emerged as the predominant political goal in all three republics.

In early 1989, the CP establishments had not yet reconciled themselves fully to the emergence of the popular fronts as the principal forces in the republics. Last-minute attempts by the old regime to

---

24. The atmosphere in January 1989 is described by David K. Shipler, "A Reporter at Large: Symbols of Sovereignty," *The New Yorker*, 18 September 1989, pp. 52–9.

eliminate the growing threat were made, but they proved unsuccessful. An ideological counterattack was launched in Lithuania during a LiCP plenum in February. Supreme Soviet Presidium Secretary Jonas Gureckas called for the closing of most of the independent publications. It was feared that a pre-election crackdown on *Sąjūdis* was imminent. In Latvia, the attempts at obstruction by functionaries of the old regime dragged out the registration of the Latvian National Front and the opening of its bank account. In Estonia, the increasingly tense relations between the PFE and the CP were somewhat alleviated by a call from the Interfront for the ECP leaders to resign, a move which had the effect of making the ECP appear more centrist.

The overwhelming victories by front-supported candidates in the elections to the USSR Congress of People's Deputies in the spring of 1989 underscored the demise of the old political system. In Lithuania, front-supported candidates were elected in 36 of the 39 (out of a total of 41) districts in which they fielded candidates. In Latvia, about three-quarters of the elected deputies were associated with the front. In Estonia, 27 of the 36 seats went to candidates supported by the front; these included several leaders of the ECP.

The demise of the old system set the stage for raising the fundamental political question in the lives of the three nations: independence. It was first openly propounded by the smaller uncompromising groupings such as the Estonian National Independence Party, the Latvian National Independence Movement and the Lithuanian Liberation League, all of which held founding congresses in late 1988 and early 1989. Such radicalism on the supposed fringe provided an aura of moderation to the majority popular fronts which, at the beginning of 1989, officially still sought "sovereignty" within a Soviet framework. The ultimate goal of all the indigenous groupings, however, was identical — political independence from the USSR. The differences concerned only tactics. In Lithuania, the Popular Front espoused eventual independence in a resolution passed on the eve of the 16 February 1989 independence day celebration. Its Latvian and Estonian counterparts were somewhat more cautious. However, by the end of the year, the nebulous term "sovereignty" had been all but replaced by "independence" as the avowed goal of almost all indigenous groupings.

The shift towards independence proved most dramatic within the ruling CPs. Their electoral fiascos in the spring of 1989 necessitated radical changes. The process was most marked in Lithuania. The first post-election plenum in June saw the replacement of 15 full members and ten candidate members of the CC Bureau. A subsequent plenum on 10 July discussed the draft of a new program calling for an independent state, the rule of law, humanism, freedom, democracy, social legality and the welfare of working people. The traditional ritual invocation of the leading role of the party was dropped. And the draft envisaged a separation of the functions of the party from those of the government, which were to be based on a democratically elected Supreme Soviet.

In the fall, more dramatic developments occurred. A plenum on 12–13 October voted overwhelmingly (97 out of 111) for the convocation of an extraordinary party congress on 19 December to discuss the separation of the LiCP from the CPSU. The move was an open and direct rebuff to Gorbachev, who had telephoned First Secretary Brazauskas urging that the party congress be delayed until the following year in line with all the other republic congresses. On 16 November, the Lithuanian Bureau was called to Moscow for consultations with the CPSU CC Politburo. The CPSU CC subsequently issued a resolution criticizing Lithuanian hesitations and deviations in implementing CPSU resolutions and calling on the LiCP to implement the policy of preserving the unity of the party without delay. On 29 November–1 December Politburo member Vadim Medvedev travelled to Vilnius with a similar plea. He played a recorded message from Gorbachev to the LiCP plenum asking Lithuanian Communists not to vote for separation from the CPSU.

The attempts were in vain. The Twentieth LiCP Congress, held 19–23 December 1989, voted overwhelmingly for independence. The vote on 20 December was 855 against 160 with 12 abstentions. Subsequently, those in opposition established their own party as a territorial unit of the CPSU. Its membership consisted largely of individuals from the minority populations and immigrants.

Party developments in Latvia and Estonia, while somewhat less dramatic than those in Lithuania, also resulted in splits between proponents of independence and those favoring continued affiliation with the CPSU. However, unlike in Lithuania, such splits occurred in the following year.

The new political currents became evident, too, in the government apparatus. Up till 1989, the supreme soviets of the three republics had been largely *pro forma* institutions meeting a few days each year to ratify decisions made in the party bureaux. That year, considerable change was noted. Even though these legislatures had been "elected" under the old system, they began to take their government functions more seriously. All three began to pass legislation called for in the programs of the fronts.

The question of declaring the indigenous languages the state languages of the republics had already appeared in 1988, and a constitutional change to that effect was adopted in Lithuania on 19 November 1988, with specific legislation being passed the following January. The same month, the Supreme Soviet of the ESSR passed similar legislation and Latvia followed suit in May 1989. All three laws were in effect compromises. With some variation between the three, they mandated a specified period for all government officials and sales personnel to become sufficiently proficient in the state language as well as Russian. Previously, Russian had been the sole requirement while the indigenous language had been optional.[25]

The measures fueled opposition among the non-indigenous populations and exacerbated the political situation. Extremists among the immigrants considered such measures "discriminatory" while natives felt that it countered the *de facto* predominance of Russian which the system had imposed for decades. It was a difference of perception. The indigenous Balts considered their lands to be distinct countries while the colonialist premise was that these republics were merely provinces of a Greater Russia. Needless to say, arguments based on such divergent premises were hard to settle. The platforms of the interfronts railed against the "nationalism" of the indigenous populations. Ironically, most of the Russian immigrants who labelled themselves "internationalists" were monolingual while the "nationalist" natives were mostly bilingual.[26]

On 18 May, the Supreme Soviet of Lithuania reversed its stand of the previous November. A declaration of state sovereignty was adopted, and a constitutional amendment giving primacy to Lithuanian law over that of the USSR was enacted. During the summer, a series of particularly significant pieces of legislation in this vein followed. Laws declaring economic sovereignty, to go into effect on 1 January 1990, followed legislation in the USSR Supreme Soviet setting up such arrangements.

25. For details on the language legislation in the three republics, see Riina Kionka, "Are Baltic Laws Discriminatory?" *Report on the USSR*, 12 April 1991, pp. 21–2.

26. For an overview on the language question, see Romuald J. Misiunas, "Baltic Nationalism and Soviet Language Policy: From Russification to Constitutional Amendment," in Henry R. Huttenbach (ed.), *Soviet Nationality Policies: Ruling Ethnic Groups in the USSR* (London, 1990), pp. 206–20.

Attempted measures by all three republics aimed at moving toward economic self-management were largely ineffective. The practical integration of their economies into the by then rapidly deteriorating all-Union system precluded any significant practical effect resulting from the various pieces of legislation adopted at various times in all three republics. The absence of their own currency and the ability to conduct direct foreign trade presented nearly insurmountable obstacles. Even the much heralded all-Union legislation in July 1989 on economic self-management by the republics proved stillborn in practice for the same reasons. The only moves which did have some practical effect were the restrictions on exports of scarce consumer goods from the republics imposed by each of the three legislatures. By 1989, almost all consumer goods could be classified as scarce.

In July 1989, the Supreme Soviet of the LiSSR coopted several prominent Sąjūdis figures into the government. The economist Kazimiera Prunskienė was appointed Deputy Chairman of the Council of Ministers. In August, a commission appointed by the Supreme Soviet to investigate the German-Soviet treaties of 1939 published a conclusion to the effect that the secret protocols of the Molotov-Ribbentrop Pact "contravened universally recognized principles of international law and were absolutely invalid from the moment of their conclusion." In effect, the republic Supreme Soviet questioned its own legitimacy. In the fall, laws on citizenship, on referendums and on the rights of religious congregations were passed. Lithuania's law on citizenship, passed on 3 November 1989, was, at the time of writing, the only such law adopted in the Baltic lands. It limited citizenship to those who had been citizens of the pre-war states on 15 June 1940 and to their descendants residing permanently in the republic. All other residents were given a two-year period to decide whether or not to opt for citizenship. The status of such permanent residents who would not opt for citizenship remained unclear. New immigrants were required to possess ten years' residence, and a knowledge of both the language and Constitution of the state.[27] Likewise, in the face of massive public opposition, the republic's contribution to funding the completion of the third reactor at the Ignalina nuclear facility was blocked.

Latvian and Estonian legislation, while not as dramatic as that of Lithuania, followed in the same vein. On 28 July, the Supreme Soviet

27. Saulius Girnius, "Lithuania," *Report on the USSR*, 29 December 1989.

of Latvia adopted a declaration of republican sovereignty analogous to that of Estonia of November 1988 and Lithuania of May 1989. On 10 November, the pre-war independence day was made an official holiday. The most notable Estonian legislation consisted of an election law, passed on 8 August, setting a two-year residence requirement. The law elicited considerable opposition, including strikes among the non-native immigrant population, and was declared unconstitutional by the USSR Minister of Justice. In October, the Estonian Supreme Soviet decided not to make an issue of the question and suspended the law; provisions mandating ten-year residence in Estonia by candidates, however, were retained.

National Demonstrations. One of the most noteworthy aspects of the Baltic scene in 1989 was the ebullience which accompanied the national renaissance. By the end of the year, almost all the hitherto proscribed national symbols had been rehabilitated. The old tricolor flags were to be seen everywhere; the Lithuanian variant had already been the official state emblem since the fall of 1988. The old coats of arms were still only tolerated as national symbols, but only a few months later these too replaced the Soviet hammer and sickle variants.

In 1989, the pre-war days of independence were celebrated as official holidays in all three republics. In Latvia, 18 November 1988 had already been celebrated as such, with half a million people participating in a demonstration stretching 2 miles along the Daugava River. Lithuania's independence day, 16 February 1989, was particularly notable in that it provided the occasion for unveiling a reconstruction of the old pre-war independence monument in Kaunas which had been razed in the early 1950s. Almost all notables in the republic from the First Secretary of the LiCP to the Cardinal Archbishop of Kaunas, the head of the Roman Catholic Church of Lithuania, took part in the ceremony.

In early August, a long human chain was organized along the Baltic coast to dramatize the ecological problems of the seashore. The most dramatic demonstration of 1989, however, was on 23 August, the fiftieth anniversary of the Molotov-Ribbentrop Pact. A human chain of close to a million individuals holding hands stretched from Tallinn to Vilnius. The manifestation elicited a harsh response from hardliners in the CPSU Central Committee. On 26 August the CPSU CC issued a statement vaguely threatening the existence of the Baltic nations:

Matters have gone far. There is a serious threat to the fate of the Baltic peoples. People should know the abyss into which they are being pushed by their nationalist leaders. Should they achieve their goals, the possible consequences could be catastrophic to these nations. A question could arise as to their very existence.[28]

While attempting to remain conciliatory, the increasingly beleaguered Baltic CP leaderships stood firm. According to Jānis Jurkans, a leader of the Latvian front, the Secretary for Ideology of the Bureau of the CC of the LaCP, Ivars Kezbers, called the Kremlin statement irresponsible and "intended to provoke the people of Latvia." A telegram to Gorbachev and the CPSU CC was sent by Latvian delegates to the USSR Congress of People's Deputies, "who were enraged by this declaration," demanding an explanation of who had drafted the statement and how and when it came about.[29] The party leaderships in Estonia and Lithuania likewise refused to accept condemnation by the CPSU.

Baltic Cooperation.   The dramatic events of 1989 saw a formalization of the *de facto* cooperation between the three Baltic national movements. On 12 May, members of the three popular fronts gathered in Tallinn for a two-day conference. The meeting, attended by several hundred participants from all three republics as well as some notable foreign guests, aired a whole series of topics affecting the Baltic situation: the meaning of independence for the Baltic countries, the role of CP members in the national movements, calls for the removal of Soviet armed forces from Baltic territory, and the effect of cultural and ecological conditions throughout the USSR on the Baltic scene.[30]

Throughout the summer, Baltic delegates to the USSR Congress of People's Deputies put great effort into lobbying to place the question of the secret protocols attached to the German pacts with the USSR in 1939 on the agenda of that legislative body. Their efforts were successful. In the past, the Soviet government had refused to acknowledge the existence of secret protocols attached to the pacts which had divided Eastern Europe into Soviet and German spheres of influence; an admission of their existence would have undercut the legitimacy of Soviet rule in the Baltic area by virtually negating the official version that the three states had joined the USSR of their own volition in

28. *Komunistas*, 1989/10, p. 5.
29. *New York Times*, 29 August 1989.
30. For details see *Baltic Forum*, VI/2 (Fall 1989), pp. 59–62.

the summer of 1940. Baltic efforts secured the naming of a special commission chaired by Politburo member Aleksandr Iakovlev and comprising 25 other deputies, of whom 11 were from the Baltic republics and five from Belorussia, Ukraine and Moldavia, areas also affected by the territorial arrangements of 1939. The publication of the commission's report demonstrated the difficulty which the question alone engendered. By midsummer, the commission seems to have unequivocally confirmed the existence of the secret protocols. On 18 August, Iakovlev admitted in an interview in *Pravda* that, without any doubt, the Soviet Union and Germany had secretly and illegally divided up Eastern Europe into spheres of influence. However, he continued to insist that it was farfetched to seek a connection between the present status of the three Baltic republics and that treaty. Apparently, the Baltic chain demonstration of 23 August made the issue too sensitive for adoption. On 29 September, members of the commission claimed that their findings had been ignored, delayed and distorted. At that point only four members of the commission had not signed the report. These included the three members of the CPSU Central Committee, Iakovlev, Falin and Georgi Arbatov; the fourth, Vladimir Kravets, Foreign Minister of the Ukrainian SSR, was a member of that republic's Central Committee. It appears that they had been enjoined by party discipline to take the position that they did.[31] Eventually, in December 1989, the Congress of People's Deputies did adopt the report. On paper, at least, the USSR appears to have admitted its wrongdoing in 1939 and by extension undercut the legitimacy of its rule in the Baltic republics.

1990 — The First Stage towards Independence

By the beginning of 1990, the restoration of Baltic independence had become an entrenched goal. Lithuania continued to lead the process. The USSR had surrendered its suzerainty over East Central Europe with amazing ease, and the Balts were encouraged to speed up their timetable so as "not to miss the Central European train." Although formally the "economic autonomy" declared with much fanfare in the summer of 1989 had gone into effect on 1 January 1990, in practice the instinctive precautionary reaction in Moscow ministries effectively restricted rather than expanded autonomy. For instance, savings accounts were centralized, as were transactions with foreign banks.

31. "Goal: Independence," *Baltic Forum*, VI/2 (Fall 1989).

Such worthless "economic autonomy" contributed to persuading the Balts that independence was the only solution.

The first step toward independence had already been taken with the secession of the LiCP from the CPSU in December 1989. In January Gorbachev visited Vilnius, perhaps hoping that somehow his presence there would rally those opposed to independence. His encounters there with Lithuanians, both on the street and in a formal meeting with the republic's intelligentsia, made it clear how illusory were notions that independence was just an unrealistic dream of an élite cultural intellingentsia and that the masses supported the Soviet system. Even Gorbachev himself implied that independence was negotiable when stating that in case of "secession" Lithuania would have to pay reparations to the USSR. The idea of independence for ransom was outrageous and even hardened the Lithuanian resolve.

Under such circumstances, the elections to the supreme soviets in all three republics were in effect turned into referenda on the question of independence. Despite the electoral participation of Soviet military garrisons and non-native officials, pro-independence forces won overwhelmingly in all three republics.

Elections were held first in Lithuania. Ninety of the 141 seats were decided in the first round. *Sąjūdis*-supported candidates won 72 of these. In subsequent run-off elections on 4, 7, 8 and 10 March, *Sąjūdis*-supported candidates picked up another 26 seats. A significant proportion of the non-*Sąjūdis*-supported winners were members of the independent LiCP which was equally on record in favor of independence. Two of those elected overwhelmingly in the first round, Romualdas Ozolas and Bronislovas Genzelis, were members of both the LiCP Bureau and the Council of *Sąjūdis*; several other members of the LiCP Bureau also received *Sąjūdis* support.[32]

The elections in Lithuania were the first multi-party elections held in the USSR. The Supreme Soviet of the Lithuanian SSR had abolished the constitutional monopoly on power of the CPSU in December. The pre-election phase passed quite smoothly, and few irregularities in the process of nomination of candidates were reported. And the pre-election mood was described by one foreign reporter as calm and nonchalant.[33] Among the republic's major problems the economic situation was unlikely to be improved, irrespective of the

32. For detailed results, see *The Lithuanian Review*, 2 March 1990, pp. 4–5.
33. *New York Times*, 23 February 1990.

electoral results. And the basic decision, independence, had in effect already been taken. It was enshrined in the platforms of both major political groupings in the republic, *Sąjūdis* and the LiCP, and only remained to be ratified. The LiCP, attempting to salvage its position, had become the first republic party in the USSR formally to split off from the CPSU. One question briefly disturbed the calm. In December 1989, a petition with 300,000 signatures asked for a referendum on the participation of Soviet military personnel in Lithuanian elections. However, in view of the population composition of the republic, the problem was more symbolic than real, and it was difficult to believe that such personnel could affect the results significantly. The most frequent question put to candidates by the electorate involved Communist Party membership. Those who had or still belonged frequently had to justify their status.

On 18 March, elections were held in Latvia and Estonia. In Latvia, 120 of the 170 candidates winning in the first round had endorsed the PFL platform and independence. In run-off elections held on 25 March, 1 April and 29 April, the proportion of supporters of independence elected exceeded the necessary two-thirds (134) for control of the Latvian Supreme Soviet.[34]

In Estonia, the anti-independence forces won 25 of the 105 seats, including four reserved for the Soviet occupation forces, thus falling four seats short of the one-third necessary for exerting a minority veto through blockage of legislation. However, the formula of proportional representation used in Estonia (the Irish-style "single transferable vote") prevented an overrepresentation of the largest group (as was the case with the single-seat district system in use in Latvia and Lithuania). As a result, supporters of the EPF made up only 43 per cent of the assembly — by far the largest group but necessitating political deals with the reform Communists and the relatively few radical nationalists. In a principled but politically self-defeating maneuver, most ardent nationalists had refused to run for the Supreme Soviet because of its illegitimate origin.

The pro-independence results were somewhat lower in Estonia and Latvia with their large immigrant populations. But even there, large numbers of non-Balts must have voted for pro-independence candidates or stayed at home. The one-seat electoral districts used in Latvia

---

34. Dzintra Bungs, "Supreme Soviet Elections in Latvia: Preliminary Results Indicate Victory for People's Front," *Report on the USSR*, 30 March 1990; American-Latvian Association (Rockville, Md.), news, *Election Report #7*, 3 April 1990.

and Lithuania worked to the advantage of independence forces. The outcome, however, cannot be explained without marked support among non-Balts.[35] The results in all three also showed the limited popularity of the Communist Party. In general even members of the independent CPs did not fare well unless they enjoyed support from the fronts.

The question of independence became the first order of business for the newly-elected legislatures. The new situation presented a legal quandary. The case for independence of the Baltic countries had been premised on the notion of the illegality of the Soviet occupation and annexation in 1940. That in effect had also been conceded by the USSR Congress of People's Deputies in December 1989 through the recognition of the secret protocols of the Molotov-Ribbentrop Pact. In theory, then, the existing state structures, including the newly-elected republic supreme soviets, were therefore also illegal. While the recent elections were by all considerations the first free elections in those lands since 1940, they also presented some intrinsic problems. One stems from the participation of Soviet military personnel and labor immigrants who were technically illegal aliens and certainly not citizens.

However, it was difficult in practice to avoid the use of the existing government structures in the pursuit of independence. To complicate matters, the extant Soviet-imposed borders of the republics differed from those of June 1940. After the Soviet occupation, Lithuania had gained some territory southeast of Vilnius and in 1945 the Klaipėda area (which it had been forced to cede to Germany in 1939). Latvia and Estonia had lost territory to the RSFSR in the immediate postwar period.

The necessity of balancing between legal continuity and extant reality was least pressing in Lithuania. The Russian immigrant population was too small to block any action in the Supreme Soviet. There was little interest in Lithuania for a return to the pre-occupation borders and even less so to those of 1939 when the region of Vilnius had been under Polish rule. In effect, the extant structures could be utilized to underscore the fact of a half-century of occupation. Participation in the Soviet system had occurred under duress. If the first freely elected representative body of the Lithuanian people did not declare independence, it would in effect be participating in the system

---

35. For the intricacies of the electoral rules and politicking, see Rein Taagepera, "The Baltic States," *Electoral Studies*, IX/4 (December 1990), pp. 303–11.

of its own free choice. Perhaps that figured in Gorbachev's calculations in allowing admission of the secret agreements of the Molotov-Ribbentrop Pact which had resulted in the occupation of the Baltic states.

On 11 March, the newly-elected Supreme Soviet of the LiSSR met. Its first meeting presented an unambiguous legal denial of Soviet legitimacy. A restoration of the Republic of Lithuania with its pre-war coat of arms and flag was voted with no opposition and six abstentions. A new provisional Constitution, a hybrid of that of 1940 and the extant Constitution of the LiSSR, was proclaimed. The old formal designation, "Republic of Lithuania," was restored.[36] The head of *Sąjūdis*, Vytautas Landsbergis, became Chairman of the Supreme Council and as such head of state. In an attempt at a broadly based government, Kazimiera Prunskienė, a prominent *Sąjūdis* leader but also a former member of the Buro of the CC of the LiCP, was named Prime Minister. Algirdas Brazauskas, the head of the independent LiCP, became one of the deputy prime ministers. The Lithuanian move preceded by one day the adoption of a new "secession law" by the USSR Supreme Soviet, which in effect was intended to hinder secession.[37] From that point on, the history of modern Lithuania becomes one of a struggle for implementation of its declaration of restored independence.

The legal quandary of legitimizing occupation through free participation in the Soviet system posed much more serious practical political problems in Estonia and Latvia. In both, sizeable groups among the native populations considered any participation in the Soviet system as tantamount to treason, and they organized elections to alternative parliaments. Thus in both, there appeared non-Soviet national congresses, elected through a franchise giving the vote only to citizens of those two countries in 1940 and their descendants. Non-citizen residents could only elect advisory members.

In such circumstances, the need to choose between a pragmatic approach based on the existing situation and a strict adherence to

36. Strictly speaking the designation of the supreme soviets was not changed back to pre-war forms, apart from the deletion of "SSR" from the name of the country. In the Baltic languages, the term "soviet" is rendered by the native word for "council." That was retained, and the legislatures became "supreme councils". We have used the Russian form "Supreme Soviet" for references until the meetings of 1990 to accentuate the foreign provenance of the institutions and changed references to "Supreme Council" after the declarations of independence.

37. For an overview of its absurdities, see *The Wall Street Journal*, 3 July 1990 and *Los Angeles Times*, 12 April 1990.

legal continuity fell most heavily on the popular fronts. In Estonia, the Popular Front decided at the last moment to participate in the congress elections of 24 February. However, it gathered less than a quarter of the seats while a total of 38 per cent went to the EHS and the ENIP, which together dominated the congress. Initially, the congress counterposed only a lame-duck non-elected Supreme Soviet. That changed after the elections of 18 March to the Estonian Supreme Soviet when independence forces, including reform Communists, won about 75 per cent of the votes and seats. Enjoying a plurality of 43 per cent, EPF leader Edgar Savisaar formed a fairly broad-based center cabinet including only two Communists (but many recent ex-Communists). The incumbent Chairman of the Supreme Soviet, Arnold Rüütel, was reelected as head of state. On 30 March 1990, perhaps in view of the harsh Kremlin reaction to Lithuania, the Estonian legislature declared Estonia to be "in a transition phase toward independence." By early May, the Supreme Soviet of the ESSR had metamorphosed itself into the Supreme Council of the Republic of Estonia.

The Supreme Council initially paid lip-service to the Estonian congress as "restorer of Estonia's independence", and the latter, in turn, declared that some power was delegated to the Supreme Council. This arrangement left the congress without any political leverage except a claim to greater legitimacy. Once it had reestablished the symbolism of the Republic of Estonia, the Supreme Council largely managed to surmount such a gap in legtimacy, and its leaders thereafter felt little need to pay attention to the congress. The leadership of the congress felt cheated, and often appeared like bad losers in a game in which they had misplayed their hand.

Although the situation in Latvia resembled that in Estonia, its practical effect was less marked. The non-Latvian population of 48 per cent included a high proportion of old settlers who had been citizens of the pre-war independent state. Unlike the situation in Estonia, relations between the Latvian Popular Front and the Latvian National Independence Movement were cooperative. Moreover, the Latvian Popular Front made a concerted effort, with considerable success, to coopt the non-Latvian population. With its allies it won two-thirds of the seats in the Supreme Soviet of the LaSSR. That outcome was already evident in April, when a Latvian national congress analogous to that in Estonia was elected. The resulting participation was low, and the Latvian congress never succeeded in becoming a political force of much significance.

On 8 May 1990, the Supreme Soviet of the LaSSR passed a declaration on renewing the independence of the Republic of Latvia. As in Estonia, a transitional period leading up to *de facto* independence of the republic was declared. The role of national Communists in the government remained stronger than in either Estonia or Lithuania. The incumbent Chairman of the Presidium of the Supreme Soviet of the LaSSR, Anatolijs Gorbunovs, was retained as Chairman of the Supreme Council, i.e. head of state. A leader of the popular front, Ivars Godmanis, became Prime Minister.

In early 1990, all three Baltic states had formally declared the restoration of their independence. The implementation of such declarations remained an unachieved goal. However, circumstances had changed drastically from those prevailing throughout most of the period of Soviet occupation. In 1980, any Baltic political initiative had looked severely limited, but a socio-cultural initiative had been possible. A decade later, political initiatives were being pursued to the full, while cultural concerns had fallen into the background.

The Baltic peoples had successfully managed to draw on the strength of their cultures in their striving for independence. Irrespective of future political developments, the staying power of these cultures precludes any easy eradication of their national identities.

In the words of Vizma Belševica:

> Winds rage. Winds howl. Riga is silent.
> The nude stone women are silent.
> The heraldic beasts are silent.
> The steeples are silent. Rooster
> Weathervanes are silent.

> Winds rave. Winds roar. Riga is silent.
> Like a key that is silent
> When the pulse beat of the sweaty hand
> That took it throbs around the iron.
> Struck down, the conqueror shall always fall,
> And on the cobblestones his blood
> Will guard its silence.

> Winds whip. Winds beat. Riga is silent.
> Indifference? Obtuseness? Cowardice?
> Ask not. You won't be answered.
> The transitory must shout.
> Must plead. Must prove.
> The eternal can dwell in silence.[38]

38. Vizma Belševica, *Gadu gredzeni* (Riga, 1969), p. 55.

Postscript

THE KALININGRAD *OBLAST*:
A NEW BALTIC LAND?

Throughout most of the postwar period, the Kaliningrad *Oblast* of the RSFSR remained an almost forgotten corner of the USSR. Its formally unsettled status, heavy militarization and slow rate of postwar reconstruction may have induced the Soviets to avoid any focus of attention on the area. Likewise, the inevitable interaction of its very existence with Lithuanian national sensitivities doubtlessly contributed to the low profile of the region in the mass media of Lithuania. Although foreigners were occasionally taken for visits, the *oblast* remained essentially out of bounds for non-Soviet citizens. In the late 1980s, the changed atmosphere in the USSR as a whole as well as in Lithuania affected the *oblast*. By 1990 its enforced seclusion from the outside world had been breached, and the question of the future role of the region in a reconstructed USSR had become current. That, in turn, gave impetus to a rise in a distinctive self-identity among its inhabitants.

Three Decades of Oblivion.   Russian possession of the region is a consequence of the outcome of the Second World War. The question of its annexation appeared quite early after the German invasion of the USSR in 1941. Culturally and historically, it had had close ties with Lithuania, and its pre-war population of some 1.5 million included a significant proportion of Germanized Lithuanians. As late as 1931, 61,000 still spoke Lithuanian.[1] Before 1945, the expressed Soviet intention was to incorporate the northern third of East Prussia into the Lithuanian SSR; this was suggested by the Soviets to Britain and reiterated in wartime Soviet broadcasts to Lithuania.[2] The

1. Bronius Kviklys, *Mūsų Lietuva* (Boston, Mass., 1968), IV, p. 623.
2. Tony Sharp, "The Russian Annexation of the Königsberg Area, 1941–1945," *Survey* (Autumn 1977–8), p. 156. V. Žemaitis, *Sūduvos praeitis* (Chicago, 1964),

preparation in 1944 by two Soviet propagandists of publications on the ethnic Lithuanian past of the region might well have been indicative that discussion of the question would appear during a postwar peace conference.[3]

However, historic and ethnic considerations do not seem to have figured in the discussions at Potsdam. Stalin's expressed claim at the time was based on a pragmatic Soviet need for a icefree port. He also stressed the symbolic compensation which the territory would give to the USSR for its heavy wartime losses. It is also not unlikely that he was seeking the benefits which a Russian enclave in the area could bring to any future settlement of the status of the Baltic states.

Western reactions were mixed. On the one hand, George Kennan pointed out that after the annexation of the Baltic states in 1940 the USSR had gained three icefree ports: Paldiski, Ventspils and Liepāja. Moreover, Königsberg lay 49 km. inland at the end of a canal which froze for several months of the year. However, there were those in the British Foreign Office who saw some merit in Stalin's arguments, pointing out that the three other icefree ports were inferior to Königsberg in every way and that in particular they were not as well connected with their hinterlands.[4]

The conference reached an agreement in principle for a division of East Prussia. The northern third, comprising 15,100 sq. km. including the capital city Königsberg, was placed under the administration of the USSR. The final border with the rest of the region, which came under Polish control, was to be determined by experts. For the time being, a provisional straight line of demarcation was cut across East Prussia without any regard to local geography. Although formally the Soviet portion of East Prussia was only included in the Soviet occupation zone of Germany, and as such fell under the jurisdiction of the Allied Control Commission, the United States and Britain declared their intention to support a permanent cession of the region to the USSR at the forthcoming peace conference. This provided a diplomatic way of getting around the problem of the Western allies' non-

---

p. 108. According to the Lithuanian *samizdat* publication *Varpas* (no. 6 [1977], p. 11), a Lithuanian-American pro-Communist convention held on 18–19 December 1943 adopted a resolution to that effect.

3. Iu. Zhiugzhda (J. Žiugžda), "Zapadnie litovtsy," *Arkhiv Instituta Etnografii AN SSSR*, 1944; P. Pakarklis, "Litovskoe naselenie v Prussii," *Arkhiv Instituta Etnografii AN SSSR*, n.d.

4. Sharp, p. 162.

recognition of the incorporation of the Baltic states into the USSR — although a formal transfer of the enclave to the USSR could hardly have avoided such a question. No such problem seems to have attended the unilateral return by the USSR, on 7 April 1945, of the extreme northern tip of East Prussia, the territory around Klaipėda (Memel), to Lithuania. That region, part of the pre-war Lithuanian state, had been ceded to Germany under duress in March 1939. A statement of the British position at Potsdam clearly defined the borders of "Germany" as those in existence on 31 December 1937.[5]

After Potsdam, the USSR took two formal steps affecting East Prussia without the concurrence of the Western allies. On 17 October 1945, the Soviet portion of East Prussia was incorporated into the RSFSR, and in the following year, on 4 July, Königsberg was renamed Kaliningrad. A Soviet-Polish treaty of 16 August 1945 and a Demarcation Protocol of 7 May 1947 designated the provisional line drawn at Potsdam as the boundary between the two states.

The effort to eradicate traces of the area's past and replace them with a Russian veneer began in 1947 with a total overhaul of geographic designations. Mostly, these had consisted of the original Baltic names rendered in Germanized variants. The Lithuanian equivalents of many were recognizably close. The city of Tilsit (Tilžė in Lithuanian), which had entered the annals of European history with the meeting there in 1808 of Tsar Alexander I and Napoleon, now became Sovetsk. At times, attempts were made to find historic ties with Russia for the new designations. The city of Preussisch-Eylau, for instance, became Bagrationovsk after the Russian general of Georgian origin who had fought a battle there with the French in 1807. But since the historic Russian presence in the area was limited to a few campaigns, most of the new place-names were simple *ad hoc* concoctions like Polessk, Primorsk or Zhekeznodorozhnyi. Linguists' observations on the staying power of hydronyms, however, seem to have been borne out. Many rivers retained recognizable forms of the original names; the principal river, the Pregel, became the Pregolia.

In addition to the incorporation of the enclave into the RSFSR and its outward Russianization, an ethnic argument for Soviet possession was also formulated. An expectation during the early 1950s that East

5. "Conference Proceedings, July 23, 1945," *Foreign Relations of the United States: Diplomatic Papers, The Conference of Berlin, 1945* (Washington, DC, 1960), II, p. 305; "Memorandum by the British Delegation, 'The Eastern Frontier of Germany as it Affects the Principles Governing the Treatment of Germany and the Authority of the Control Council'," *ibid.*, II, p. 1137.

Prussia might become a subject of negotiation during a peace conference to end the Second World War generated a series of studies, mostly by the Institute of Ethnography of the Academy of Sciences of the USSR, designed to bolster a Soviet claim for possession based on demonstration of the Baltic and Lithuanian past of the region.[6] The second edition of the *Great Soviet Encyclopedia* went even further by referring to East Prussia as the ancient land of the Baltic Slavs (Pribaltiiskie Slaviane),[7] a group that had never hitherto been heard of. On a more popular level, that group became simply Russian. In 1953, the Kaliningrad writer Fedor Vedin observed: "By all laws these lands belong to us . . . we are traversing Russian land. We settled accounts with the fascists and retook our land."[8] The expected peace conference never took place, and the studies, relegated to oblivion, have become bibliographic rarities. The spurious Baltic Slavs likewise quickly became extinct in Soviet sources.

By the late 1960s, a quarter-century of Russian possession had created a new Soviet claim for possession. This made a distinct appearance in a spate of articles reacting to various West German discussions preceding the inauguration of Willy Brandt's *Ostpolitik*. The great postwar Soviet investment now appeared in the forefront of justifications for continued ownership. As the then First Secretary of the Kaliningrad CPSU Obkom, Nikolai Konovalov, stated in typically bombastic Soviet bureaucratese: ". . . we had to build anew, and not only to build but to create in a different quality." The process of physical reconstruction had somehow fused a group of people with a new identity tied to that land:

Over two decades passed together in unceasing work by workers, *kolkhozniks*, members of the intelligentsia which drew together, befriended and merged into a wonderful fusion yesterday's Muscovites and Leningraders, emigrants from many *oblasts* of Russia, united through a word native and dear to the hearts of all — Kaliningraders. We also have a special relationship which cannot be called by a different name from a blood relationship. Every meter of land is touched here by the best sons and daughters of our motherland: Russians, Ukrainians, Belorussians, Lithuanians and Latvians.[9]

---

6. The most notable is P.I. Kushner (Knyshev), *Etnicheskie territorii i etnicheskie granitsy* (Moscow, 1951).

7. *Bolshaia Sovetskaia Entsiklopediia*, 2nd edn (Moscow, 1953), XIX, p. 426.

8. Fedor Vedin, *Gorod budet* (Riga, 1953), as cited in *Literatūra ir menas* (1 January 1989).

9. *Sovetskaia Rossiia*, 31 December 1968.

In general, however, the sense of self-identity among the Kaliningrad population, a significant part of whom continued to be transient, remained weak. At times, efforts to emphasize the region's "Russian-ness" reached extremes. The exchange of "days of culture" between the *oblast* and Lithuania in the fall of 1979 provides a graphic example. A feeling of unreality accompanied the *kokoshniki*-crowned girls in traditional native Russian national costume representing the *oblast*. The Lithuanian Minister of Culture's incantation to "old internationalist ties of brotherhood which connect Lithuania with its good neighbor, the Kaliningrad *Oblast*,"[10] at best merely stretched the meaning of the word "old." The paean to Kaliningrad as a unifying bond between Russians and Lithuanians, however, must have sounded ominous to nationally conscious Lithuanians:

White-winged seagulls seem to carry a song about the Baltic and its amber shores, which have eternally united the Lithuanian and the Russian nations.[11]

The artificiality of the region's Russian cultural heritage was perhaps unwittingly underscored by the painter Aleksandr Balabaev, a member of the *oblast*'s 30-strong artists' union, who as its representative declared:

. . . I especially like Suzdal and Vladimir [ancient cities near Moscow] — I find inspiration in the old architecture of those places. There I deeply feel the Russian spirit.[12]

The general tenor of articles then published about the area indicate extreme Soviet sensitivity to some German writings arguing that the Kaliningrad *Oblast* remained largely devastated after the war. All sorts of descriptive enumerations were trotted out to show how the region had flourished under the beneficent Soviet power, and often these were accompanied by typical Soviet comparisons with pre-war economic statistics. One commentator went as far as to claim that pre-war East Prussia as a whole had been an undersettled and underdeveloped part of Germany from which 2,559,300 people had emigrated throughout the 86 years preceding 1930.[13]

10. *Tiesa*, 5 April 1979.
11. *Tiesa*, 19 October 1979.
12. *Literatūra ir menas*, 31 March 1979.
13. A.V. Salikhov, "Kritika faltsifikatsii deiatelsnosti KPSS po sozdaniiu i razvitiiu ekonomiki Kaliningradskoi Oblasti," *Vestnik Leningradskogo Universiteta*, I/2 (1975), p. 19.

According to almost all contemporary sources, the reconstruction of the region has been inadequate. The destruction during the spring of 1945 was severe. The *Wehrmacht* put up particularly stiff resistance in and around Königsberg, the center of which had already been largely leveled in August 1944 by British air bombardment. One Soviet source claims that by the end of hostilities in 1945, 90 per cent of the buildings in the area had been destroyed.[14]

Kaliningrad itself appears essentially a new city with wide, straight boulevards linked by broad squares and flanked by pretentious imitation-classical buildings and nondescript housing units which are the hallmarks of all Soviet urban development. One Soviet commentator proudly contrasts this supposedly light airy and modern city with its pre-war predecessor:

We know from photographs and books how dreary this city appeared before the war. Heavy forts were interspersed among the grey financial buildings, the luxury of banking and commercial offices in the center and sentimentally elegant villas in the suburbs. And everywhere there were barracks and squares as indispensable appurtenances of the urban landscape. All this came in two colors: either dark grey or brick red.[15]

According to almost all witnesses, the bulk of construction carried out in Kaliningrad dates from the 1970s or later, when West German *Ostpolitik* and the Helsinki Treaty added a touch of reassurance to the permanence of Soviet possession. However, the reconstruction remains far from complete. In the late 1970s, an eyewitness noted how much remained of the wartime destruction, and how pervasive was the "crumbling stone or red brick with clear imprints of bullets and shells," painful testimony to the horrors of war.[16] More recent impressions are almost uniformly of disorder. One visitor noted that the city once known as "the pearl of the Baltic" now resembled a "cluttered construction site in which people are trying to live."[17] It is possible, on the basis of pictures, to agree with the same commentator and others that the Soviet building of gargantuan proportions being erected on the site of the old castle would have been a prime candidate for the distinction of being the ugliest building in the world.

14. TsSU RSFSR, "Statisticheskoe Upravlenie Kalinigradskoi Oblasti," *Kalinigradskaia Oblast v Vosmoi Piatiletke* (Kaliningrad, 1972), p. 3.

15. *Sovetskaia Rossiia*, 6 May 1969.

16. *Literatūra ir menas*, 27 October 1979.

17. *Süddeutsche Zeitung*, 16 April 1991.

The need for reconstruction appears to be even more acute outside Kaliningrad. One traveller noted in June 1991 how extensive were the ruin and desolation all the way from the Lithuanian border to the sea. The city of Cherniakhovsk (formerly Insterburg) remained largely in ruins; visible construction projects were mainly barracks and garages, many of which were in repaired pre-war buildings, including historic churches. Although the main street of Sovetsk (formerly Tilsit) just across the river from Lithuania had been rebuilt, there were still 4,500 families in the city waiting for apartments even though the total population of the city was only about two-thirds of what it had been before the war.[18]

Because of the postwar political division of East Prussia along a purely arbitrary line, it is difficult to make exact population comparisons with pre-war times. In 1925 the whole of East Prussia contained 2,256,349 people.[19] Even though the present Russian portion only covers about one-third of that area, it includes the major urban concentration in the region. This portion may therefore have accounted for at least half the total population before the war. During the war, many people were evacuated or fled before the Red Army; according to one estimate, only 500,000 people remained in the whole of East Prussia by February 1945. Of these, 100,000 civilians and 15,000 foreign workers were concentrated in Königsberg, and many died during the severe fighting. Others succumbed to the hunger and disease which followed, or managed to filter into Lithuania which was much less devastated, or were deported to other parts of the USSR. In 1948 most of the 25,000 Germans remaining in Kaliningrad left for Germany.[20]

Immigration from other parts of the USSR began to fill the vacuum. By 1959, the population of the *oblast* had reached 610,000; in 1970, 731,900; in 1978, 804,900; and in 1988, 849,000. By any estimate, the current population remains much smaller than it was before the war. Most of the immigrants are East Slavs; in 1970 Russians made up 77.1 per cent of the population, Belorussians 9.4 per cent and Ukrainians 6.9 per cent.[21]

The *oblast* is heavily urbanized, being 77 per cent so in 1978. In 1988, about half its population lived in the city of Kaliningrad alone.

18. *Lietuvos rytas*, 2 June 1990; *Respublika* (Vilnius), 3 June 1991.
19. *Encyclopaedia Britannica* (1962), VII, p. 873.
20. *Frankfurter Allgemeine Zeitung*, 19 April 1990.
21. TsSU RSFSR, p. 3; *Tiesa*, 28 March 1978; *Kaliningradskaia Oblast: Ocherki stanovleniia i razvitiia* (Kaliningrad, 1988), p. 24.

No figures are available for population mobility; however, in view of the preponderance of military and naval presence in the *oblast*, a significant portion of the total population, especially in the city of Kaliningrad itself, consists of families and dependents of servicemen on station, and apparently the military population increased during the military pull-out from Poland and Germany. Under the circumstances, the population turnover is in all likelihood quite high. Such a state of affairs is also underscored by the evident rural underpopulation which is noted in the press from time to time.[22]

The predominant industry in the *oblast* is fishing, and in 1988 it accounted for about 40 per cent of industrial production in the *oblast* and 10 per cent of total Soviet seafood production.[23] In 1972, more than 52,000 Kaliningraders, about one-sixth of the city's total population at the time, were directly or indirectly connected with the fishing industry,[24] though one cannot judge whether this figure included the shipbuilding activity in the port.

Two other important industries appear to be based on reconstructed pre-war facilities. Kaliningrad figures as one of the main Soviet centers for the production of railway cars, and the *oblast* contains a significant portion of Soviet paper and cellulose production. In 1963 it accounted for 50 per cent of all Soviet production of paper used for offset printing, a proportion which had risen to 70 per cent by 1988.[25] Additionally, the area produces some fur and oil. Amber mining is a notable minor industry; 94 per cent of the world's known resources are located there.[26]

Stirrings of Change. In the era of *glasnost* and *perestroika* Kaliningrad began to emerge from the virtual oblivion which had enwrapped it previously. The policy of enforced isolation from foreign contact became difficult to maintain, and the artificial attempt to eliminate the pre-Russian past of the area from public consciousness eroded rapidly. Nevertheless, the undue concentration of conservative military influence in the area continued to serve as a brake on such developments.

The relationship of the region with Germany and Germans as well as with Lithuania became increasingly important, with the significant

22. Viz. *Sovetskaia Rossiia*, 28 January 1979.
23. *Kaliningradskaia Oblast*, p. 104.
24. *Izvestiia*, 6 July 1972.
25. *Tiesa*, 21 February 1963; *Kaliningradskaia Oblast*, p. 112.
26. *Tiesa*, 28 March 1979.

number of former East Prussians in Germany providing a natural source of interest in the region. The Baltic push for independence opened up the question of its future position as an enclave of the RSFSR territorially separated from it. The Lithuanian national renaissance inevitably raises the historic cultural interaction of the region with Lithuania. General détente and demilitarization in Europe undercut its *raison d'être* as the westernmost outpost of the Soviet military machine. In addition, despite the conservative influence of the heavy military presence, the region could not escape the pressures for change which manifested themselves throughout the USSR.

In March 1988, the German banker F. Wilhelm Christians, a leading expert on Eastern Europe and the USSR in the Deutsche Bank, proposed a general plan to make the *oblast* into a special economic zone for interaction with Western Europe. Christians, who as a young man had served in the German army defending the city in 1945, envisaged the area as a natural entity for North European interaction. Such status would grant a new *raison d'être* to the region, whose economy was disproportionately tied to the Soviet military-industrial complex, with 93 of the 100 largest enterprises being managed by either USSR or RSFSR ministries in Moscow.[27]

The plan received ardent support from the Mayor of Kaliningrad, Nikolai Khromenko. In July 1990, the Supreme Soviet of the RSFSR passed a resolution to that effect. However, the mere question of opening up the city to foreign visitors aroused considerable opposition in the establishment. The issue was forced by the Kaliningrad city soviet by unilaterally sanctioning visits by foreigners. The *oblast* committee of the CPSU denounced the action as a violation of Soviet law,[28] but it was powerless to stop foreign arrivals.

Another unexpected new development was the proposal to promote settlement of the largely underpopulated area by Soviet Germans who had been deported *en masse* from their Volga republic to Central Asia during the war. Like the other deported peoples, Germans have sought to undo wartime wrongs and return to their lands along the Volga. The precariousness of European rural settlement in Central Asia became evident in the aftermath of the riots in the Fergana valley in 1990, and the idea of their resettlement in the Kaliningrad *Oblast* appeared even more attractive if it could be coupled with financial aid from Germany. Some movement in that direction has begun. By

27. *Die Zeit*, 10 August 1990.
28. *Report on the USSR*, 3 August 1990.

early 1991, about 800 Germans had established themselves in Kaliningrad itself and about 5,000 more had settled in its environs. A German cultural society was already functioning. One of its organizers, Vladimir Jahnke, referred to the region as "the land of our historical forefathers." He had little faith in the possibility of resurrecting the Volga Republic. Another activist, Keller, was interested in moving an entire village of some 1,000 individuals from Kirghizia to Sovetsk (Tilsit). However, not all the new arrivals were satisfied with the possibilities in the area and some looked on it as a staging post for emigration to Germany itself.

The immigration of Germans at the time of writing is still extremely circumscribed and its future remains uncertain. Nevertheless it has been sufficient to arouse alarm among some Kaliningrad Russians who are afraid of suddenly finding themselves surrounded by Germans in a "Western environment". Viktor Harbach from Tadzhikistan, along with 20 others, opened a pig-raising farm outside Kaliningrad. The group rented a sovkhoz, fired about half its workers and raised wages by 40 per cent, and within six months the number of pigs had doubled. The lease called for an annual delivery of 120,000 tons of pork, but the remaining 130,000 could be sold on the free market at a considerable profit. The local government appeared hostile to the new kulaks. No apartments were assigned to them and permission to renovate ruined dwellings was denied. An application by a German from Alma-Ata to move 800 Germans into the area floundered in the face of local opposition.[29] Aleksandr Savkin, deputy CPSU leader in Kaliningrad, expressed his apprehension to a Western correspondent that the Russian population of the region would in time become the object of a German-Russian deal.[30]

Another visible element of change is the attempt by some to restore to the area an awareness and acknowledgment of its pre-1945 past. Such tendencies appear most pronounced among the younger generation of Russians who do not appear to share the anti-German attitudes of their parents; some among these are also active in seeking closer ties with their Baltic neighbors. A young representative of the Kaliningrad Reconstruction Front appeared in Tallinn in May 1989 at the Baltic Assembly, the joint gathering of the three Baltic popular fronts, seeking at least a symbolic union with the Baltic efforts through the unfurling of the organization's distinctive

29. *Der Spiegel*, 7 January 1991, p. 126.
30. *Süddeutsche Zeitung*, 16 April 1991.

flag.[31] In view of the expectation of closer interaction with Germany in the future, the German language has been introduced in primary schools of the *oblast*. The Kaliningrad Institute of Economics has already sent two groups of management students for training in Munich.[32]

The head of the Kaliningrad Culture Fund, Iurii Ivanov, was writing as early as 1988 about the need for the region to restore its history,[33] and in the summer of 1990 the first exhibition on the true history of the region was organized. The following March, the Culture Fund, jointly with the newly established "Prus" society, organized a conference in the former Queen Louisa church, converted into a puppet theatre, on "The Old Past of Our Land."[34] In 1987, in connection with the millennium of the Christianization of Rus, the first working church since 1945 was opened in the city.[35] Restoration of the massive cathedral — which, apart from the restored tomb of Immanuel Kant, remains a ruin — is planned through a joint effort between the Russian Orthodox Church and Lutherans from Germany. On Easter Sunday, 1991, the last pastor of the cathedral, Reinhold George, now resident in Berlin, visited Kaliningrad as a guest of the *oblast* Culture Fund and conducted a service in the ruins.[36] It is possible that the movement to restore original names, which is sweeping the former USSR, will also touch the region. Kalinin is no more noteworthy than Molotov, Voroshilov or Kirov, all of whom have been expunged from the Soviet geographic lexicon. In addition to its original German name Königsberg, the Slavonic form Krolevets has been proposed on the grounds that the knights which founded the city in the thirteenth century were largely from Bohemia. Likewise, Kantgrad, in honor of the city's most illustrious former resident, has been suggested.

Connections with Lithuania. The historic and modern relationship of the region to Lithuania remains a particularly sensitive question. Throughout the postwar years, the question of the very existence of the Kaliningrad *Oblast* received scant attention in the official

31. *Baltic Forum*, VI/2 (Fall 1989), p. 60.
32. *Süddeutsche Zeitung*, 16 April 1991.
33. *Literatūra ir menas*, 2 July 1988.
34. *Lietuvos aidas*, 30 March 1991.
35. *Berliner Morgenpost*, 8 November 1987.
36. *Literatūra ir menas*, 6 April 1991.

Lithuanian media. In the 1960s and '70s, rumor circulated in Lithuania to the effect that in 1945 Stalin had offered the region to Lithuania but that the then First Secretary, Antanas Snieckus, had adroitly managed to refuse. Lithuania possessed neither the manpower nor the resources to absorb and reconstruct the territory, and if it had been incorporated into the LiSSR the latter's population, thus enlarged, would have been less than 60 per cent Lithuanian rather than around 80 per cent, which it has remained since the early 1960s. Cynics have interpreted such rumors as a clever move to defuse a potentially troublesome question while simultaneously raising the stature of the long-serving First Secretary in the eyes of nationally-inclined Lithuanians. Whether there is any factual basis for such conjectures cannot be ascertained, but their currency underscores the significance of the question in Lithuania.

During Khrushchev's reorganizations and consolidations of the late 1950s and early '60s, it appeared probable that the *oblast* would be attached to Lithuania. In the spring of 1957 a suggestion appeared that the Couronian Bay should be entirely incorporated into Lithuania, and in 1963 the management of its industry was turned over to Lithuania; its railroads and inland waterways had been under Lithuanian administration for many years.[37] Agriculture, however, was not at that time attached to the Lithuanian sovnarkhoz, and it remains unclear whether any of these arrangements with Lithuania would have survived the abolition of the sovnarkhozy in 1965 and if so in what form. A description of commercial relations in 1979 singled out the cooperation of ten industrial enterprises in the *oblast* with Lithuania, but did not elaborate on the nature of such collaboration.[38]

Discussion of the role of the Kaliningrad area in the cultural past of Lithuania remained even more muted than references to economic interaction. The most important exception was the restoration and opening of the Donelaitis Museum at his restored home in Chistye Prudy (Tolminkiemis) not far from the Lithuanian border. Kristijonas Donelaitis (1714–80) was a Lutheran pastor whose neoclassical poem *Metai* (The Seasons) is considered one of the principal works of Lithuanian literature. During the restoration work in the 1970s, organized and carried out by Lithuanians rather than the Kaliningrad

37. V. Stanley Vardys, "How the Baltic Republics Fare in the Soviet Union," *Foreign Affairs*, IVL/3 (1966), p. 513; *Tiesa*, 19 April 1957; *Tiesa*, 21 February 1963.
38. *Tiesa*, 30 March 1979.

cultural authorities, his grave — hitherto believed to be lost — was discovered.[39]

The Lithuanian population of the region also received scant attention until very recently. Officially, according to the 1979 census, there were 19,677 Lithuanians resident in the *oblast*: 3,475 in Kaliningrad (1 per cent of the population), 2,132 in Sovetsk (5.3 per cent), 2,099 in Neman (9.3 per cent) and 1,348 (2.7 per cent) in Cherniakhovsk. Many, including Iurii Ivanov, head of the Kaliningrad Culture Fund, thought that this figure was too low and that their real number was at least 40,000.[40] In 1989 there was not a single school, kindergarten or newspaper in the *oblast* for its Lithuanian residents. However, the nature of the Lithuanian population explains its reticence over drawing attention to its presence. Of the total number of these Lithuanians it has been estimated that about 30 per cent are former deportees or refugees from one type of repression or another. Many of them were released from the Gulag or exile in the late 1950s but without permission to reside in Lithuania. Another 20 per cent were postwar Soviet activists who were running away from their home areas in Lithuania out of fear for their personal safety. And among the rest were many seekers after easy wealth (in rubles) who were naturally disinclined to embrace causes or national concerns.[41]

The changed conditions in the late 1980s occasioned a renaissance of Lithuanian interest in the area. In December 1989, the Presidium of the Supreme Soviet of the LiSSR established a Lithuania Minor Council to preserve the monuments of Lithuanian history in the *oblast* and care for the cultural needs of the *oblast*'s Lithuanian population. Through its efforts the first Lithuanian kindergarten was founded in Sovetsk, and Lithuanian sections were established in the Kaliningrad and Sovetsk libraries.[42] Initially the Council faced an uproar in Kaliningrad, but after a short time it seemed to be accepted, and succeeded in establishing good relations with the Kaliningrad Culture Fund.

German interest in the area and the spill-over effects of the economic blockade of Lithuania in 1990 served to assist the rise of Kaliningrad's

---

39. Tomas Venclova, "Dabartinė padėtis Mažojoj Lietuvoj," *Aidai*, 1978/4, p. 172.

40. *Literatūra ir menas*, 1 January 1989.

41. *Gimtasis kraštas*, 2 August 1990.

42. *Lietuvos aidas*, 30 March 1991.

sense of its own identity. It is clear that if its status of a free economic zone, proclaimed in 1990, is to acquire any substance, the region will in the future be drawn into interaction with its neighbors far more than has been the case hitherto. Some steps have been taken, like turning the clocks back by one hour from standard Moscow time in 1991 to standardize the zone with that in effect in the Baltic states, but they remain so far primarily symbolic. If the trend continues, the *oblast* will inevitably become in time a very unusual part of the RSFSR whose ties are emphatically not with the center. Perhaps then the separate multi-national republic dreamed of by those like Iurii Ivanov will not seen so very farfetched.

MAJOR BALTIC GOVERNMENT LEADERS AND ADMINISTRATORS, 1938–1990

	ESTONIA	LATVIA	LITHUANIA
		1938 — early June 1940	
President	Konstantin Päts 1938–21 July 1940	Kārlis Ulmanis 1936–21 July 1940	Antanas Smetona 1926–15 June 1940
Prime Minister	Kaarel Eenpalu 1938–October 1939	Kārlis Ulmanis 1934–19 June 1940	Jonas Černius March–November 1939
	Jüri Uluots October 1939– 21 June 1940		Antanas Merkys November 1939– 15 June 1940
		Late June 1940 — early August 1940	
Soviet Emissary	**Andrei Zhdanov 17 June–6 August 1940	**Andrei Vyshinskii 17 June–5 August 1940	**Vladimir Dekanozov 15 June–3 August 1940
Prime Minister	Johannes Vares 21 June– 25 August 1940	Augusts Kirhenšteins 20 June– 25 August 1940	Justas Paleckis 17 June– 1 July 1940
		August 1940 — Summer 1941	
CP First Secretary	Karl Säre 12 September 1940– Fall 1941	Jānis Kalnbērziņš June 1940–1959	Antanas Sniečkus 1936–74
Chairman of the Council of People's Commissars	Johannes Lauristin 25 August 1940– 28 August 1941	Vilis Lācis 25 August 1940–1959	Mečys Gedvilas August 1940–1956
Chairman of the Presidium of the Supreme Soviet	Johannes Vares 25 August 1940– 29 November 1946	Augusts Kirhenšteins 25 August 1940–1952	Justas Paleckis 25 August 1940–1967
CP Second Secretary	Nikolai Karotamm 1940–4	Žanis Spure August–December 1940	Icikas Meskupas-Adomas 1940–2

* Persons who were not residents of the pre-war Baltic states, or who received German citizenship between 1939 and early 1941.
** Persons with no ethnic or pre-war ties to the Baltic area.

	ESTONIA	LATVIA	LITHUANIA
		Summer 1941–1944/5	
German General Commissioner	**Karl Litzmann December 1941– September 1944	**Otto Drechsler September 1941– May 1945?	**Adrian von Renteln September 1941– January 1945?
First Director/ General Counselor	*Hjalmar Mäe 15 September 1941– September 1944	*Oskars Dankers 21 August 1941– 27 September 1944	Petras Kubiliūnas 22 August 1941–1944
Head of Provisional Government	Jüri Uluots 18–22 September 1944	Roberts Osis 7–8 May 1945	Kazys Škirpa Juozas Ambrazevičius 23 June–3 August 1941
		1944–90	
Head of CPSU CC Special Bureau for the Republic	**Nikolai Shatalin 11 November 1944–1946 **Georgii Perov 1945?–7 *Konstantin Boitsov 1947–8?	**Nikolai Shatalin 1944–6 **V. F. Riazanov 1946–7	**Mikhail Suslov 11 November 1944– Spring 1946 **Vladimir Vasilevich Shcherbakov Spring 1946–1947
CP First Secretary	Nikolai Karotamm 22 September 1944– March 1950 *Johannes (Ivan) Käbin 1950–78 *Karl Vaino 1978–88 Vaino Väljas 1988–90	Jānis Kalnbērziņš 1940–November 1959 *Arvīds Pelše 1959–66 *Augusts Voss 1966–84 *Boriss Pugo 1984–8 Jānis Vagris 1988–90	Antanas Sniečkus 1936–74 Petras Griškevičius 1974–87 Ringaudas Songaila 1987–8 Algirdas Brazauskas 1988–
Chairman of the Council of Ministers	Arnold Veimer 1944–April 1951 *Aleksei Müürisepp 1951–61 *Valter Klauson 1961–84 Bruno Saul 1984–8 Indrek Toome 1988–90 Edgar Savisaar 1990–2	Vilis Lācis 1940–November 1959 *Jānis Peive 1959–62 *Vitālijs Rubenis 1962–70 *Jurijs Rubenis 1970–88 Vilnis Bresis 1988–90 Ivars Godmanis 1991–	Mečys Gedvilas 1940–56 Motiejus Šumauskas 1956–67 *Juozas Maniušis 1967–81 Ringaudas Songaila 1981– Vytautas Sakalauskas 1985–90 Kazimiera Prunskienė 1990–1 Gediminas Vagnorius 1991–

	ESTONIA	LATVIA	LITHUANIA
Chairman of the Presidium of the Supreme Soviet (i.e. ceremonial head of state)	Johannes Vares August 1940– 29 November 1946	Augusts Kirhenšteins 25 August 1940–1952	Justas Paleckis 25 August 1940–1967
	*Eduard Päll 1946–50	Kārlis Ozoliņš 1952–9	Motiejus Šumauskas 1967–75
	August Jakobson 1950–8	Jānis Kalnbērziņš 1959–70	Antanas Barkauskas 1975–85
	*Johan Eichfeld 1958–61	*Vitālijs Rubenis 1970–4	Ringaudas Songaila 1985–7
	Aleksei Müürisepp 1961–70	Pēteris Strautmanis 1974–85	Antanas Barkauskas 1988–90
	*Artur Vader 1970–8	Jānis Vagris 1985–8	Vytautas Landsbergis 1990–2
	*Johannes Käbin 1978–83	Anatolijs Gorbunovs 1988–	
	Arnold Rüütel 1983–92		
CP Second Secretary	**Sergei Sazonov November 1944–1950?	**Ivan Lebedev 1944–January 1949	Vladas Niunka May–December 1944
	**Vassilii Kossov 1950?–August 1953	**Fedor Titov January 1949–1952?	**A. N. Isachenko 1945–6
	*Leonid Lentsman August 1953–1964	**Valentin Ershov 1952?–June 1953	**Aleksandr Trofimov 1946–52
	*Artur Vader 1964–70	Vilis Krūmiņš June 1953–January 1956	**Vasili Aronov 1952–June 1953
	**Konstantin Lebedev 1971–82	**Filipp Kashnikov January 1956– January 1958?	Motiejus Šumauskas June 1953–1955
	**Aleksandr Kudriavtsev 1983–5	*Arvīds Pelše? January–April 1958?	**Boris Sharkov 1956–61
	**Georgii Aleshin 1985–9	Vilis Krūmiņš April 1958?– February 1960	**Boris Popov 1961–7
		**Mikhail Gribkov February 1960–1963	**Valerii Kharazov 1967–78
		**Nikolai Belukha 1963–78	**Nikolai Dybenko 1978–86
		**Igor Strelkov 1978–80	**Aleksei Mitkin 1986–8
		**Valentin Dmitriev 1980–6	Vladimir Berezov 1988–
		**Vitalii Sobolev 1986–90	

TABLES

1. POPULATION AND ETHNICITY OF THE BALTIC REPUBLICS, 1939–80

Year (1 January)	Total population (in Millions)			Percentage belonging to the Republic nationality		
	Estonia	Latvia	Lithuania	Estonia	Latvia	Lithuania
1939, pre-war borders	1.134[a]	2.00[b]	2.575[c]	88.2%[a]	75.5%[b]	80.6%[c]
1939, postwar borders	1.052[d]	1.93[d]	3.1[d]	92	77	76(?)
1945	0.854[e]	1.4[f]	2.4[f]	94(?)	83(?)	80(?)
1950	1.097	1.944	2.57	76(?)	63(?)	75(?)
1955	1.157	2.010	2.61	74(?)	62(?)	75(?)
1960	1.209	2.113	2.756	74.1	61.7	79.4
1965	1.285	2.254	2.954	70.9	58.8	79.8
1970	1.356	2.364	3.128	68.2	56.8	80.1
1975	1.427	2.465	3.295	65.7	54.5	79.9
1980	1.474	2.529	3.420	64.5	53.5	80.1

Source: Data from Rein Taagepera, "Baltic Population Changes, 1950–1980," *JBS*, XII/1 (Spring 1981), pp. 35–57, except as indicated below.

Notes

a. *Eesti entsüklopeedia,* supplementary volume (Tartu, 1940), pp. 232–4.

b. Jānis Rutkis (ed.), *Latvia: Country and People* (Stockholm, 1967), pp. 293 and 302.

c. V. Stanley Vardys (ed.), *Lithuania under the Soviets, 1940–1965* (New York, 1965), p. 22.

d. Rein Taagepera, "Population Crisis and the Baltics," *JBS,* XII/3 (Fall 1981), pp. 234–44.

e. Estimate in *Eesti NSV ajalugu* (Tallinn, 1971), III, p. 601.

f. Estimate based on considerations shown in Table 2.

353

2. POPULATION CHANGES, 1939–45[a]: EDUCATED GUESSES

(in thousands)

	Estonia	Latvia	Lithuania
Population in mid-October 1939	1,130	2,000	2,950[b]
Emigration and territorial changes, November 1939–May 1941[c]	−20	−70	+50
Soviet deportations and executions, 1940–1[d]	−15	−35	−35
Soviet army mobilization, 1941 and 1944–5[e]	−35	−20	−60
Evacuation to USSR, 1941[f]	−30	−40	−20
Nazi executions and deportations, 1941–5[d,g]	−10	−90	−200
German army mobilization, 1941–5[h]	−70	−150	−50
German labor mobilization, 1941–4[i]	−15	−35	−75
Evacuation and flight to the West, 1942–5[j]	−60	−100	−50
Return from Germany and German army, 1944–5	+60	+80	+50
Soviet executions and deportations, 1944–5[k]	−30	−70	−50
Return from USSR and Soviet army, 1944–5[k]	+20	+20	+50
Territorial changes, 1945[l]	−70	−50	+25
Emigration to Poland, 1945	0	0	−150
Birth deficit	−15	−30	−35
Population in late 1945 (estimate)[m]	850	1,400	2,400
Percentage of loss since 1939	25%	30%	15%

a. The figures presented are often very approximate "guesstimates," and should not be requoted without inclusion of this warning. Presenting these guesstimates in this book serves two purposes: to give the reader *some* idea of the type and order of magnitude of the changes, and to induce scholarly readers (East and West) to come up with better-documented figures.

b. After loss of Klaipėda (150,000) and gain of Vilnius (500,000).

c. Emigration mostly to Germany (October–November 1939 and January–March 1941). Additional territory near Vilnius (August 1940): about 100,000.

d. Including executions by local henchmen.

e. Including the Baltic units existing in early 1941; excluding the Destruction Battalions. Excluding those who surrendered to the Germans and were released, or returned home otherwise, by 1942.

f. Voluntary evacuees (including Jews fleeing the Nazi terror, and the "destruction battalions"), and involuntary ones not fitting the deportation or mobilization categories (e.g. railroad workers).

g. Includes about 250,000 Jews (Lithuania, 180,000; Latvia, 70,000; Estonia, 1,000).

h. Includes those stationed in their homelands, and in military labor battalions.

i. Includes only those sent to Germany (and other parts of Central Europe).

j. Voluntary and semi-voluntary. Excludes deportees and mobilized labor and military.

k. Highly speculative figures. Soviet demobilization largely came only later.

l. Klaipėda regained; about 25,000 people remaining. Abrene, Petseri, and trans-Narva areas transferred to RSFSR in January 1945.

m. Includes non-registered local population (guerrillas etc.); excludes imported forced labor and POWs.

3. WAR AND OCCUPATION DEATHS, 1940-5[a]: EDUCATED GUESSES

(in thousands)

	Estonia	*Latvia*	*Lithuania*
Soviet executions, 1940–1	2	1.5	1.1
Soviet deportee deaths, 1940–3	15	20	20
Soviet evacuee deaths, 1941–3	10	10	5
Soviet army and Labor Battalion deaths	25	5	20
Nazi executions, 1941–5	5	65	140
German deportee deaths, 1942–5	5	10	50
German and Finnish army deaths	15	40	10
Deaths among civilians moving west	5	10	5
Bombing and other war deaths	5	10	15
Soviet executions, deportee deaths and guerrilla war losses, 1944–5	5	10	15
Totals	90	180	280
Percentage of the 1939 population	8%	9%	9%

a. Very approximate "guesstimates" — not to be quoted without this qualification. See Table 2, note a.

4. LITHUANIAN GUERRILLAS, 1944–52: ARMED FORCES INVOLVED

(in thousands)

	Guerrillas	Repression Troops
Mid-1944	10[a]	50
Spring 1945	30	110
Spring 1946	30 to 40	50
January 1947		100
February 1947	25	20[c]
Mid-1947	30	20[c]
1948	5[b]	
Early 1950		
Early 1951	0.7[b]	
Early 1952		
Battle losses suffered:		
Soviet estimates	20[d]	20[e]
Guerrilla estimates	25 to 50[bf]	80
Civilians killed by	4[f] to 13[g]	24[b]
Civilians deported by	0	310

Sources: Thomas Remeikis, "The Armed Struggle against the Sovietization of Lithuania after 1944," *Lituanus*, VIII/1–2 (1962), pp. 29–40, except as indicated below:

Notes

a. Zenonas Ivinskis, "Lithuania during the War," in Vardys (ed.), *Lithuania under the Soviets*, p. 84.

b. Stasys Žymantas, "Twenty Years of Resistance," *Lithuanus*, VI/2 (September 1960), pp. 40–5.

c. Inferred from Burlitski, in *Fourth Interim Report of the Select Committee on Communist Aggression* (US Congress, 1954).

d. George Weller, *Chicago Daily News*, 17 August 1961.

e. Vardys (ed.), *Lithuania under the Soviets*, pp. 85–108.

f. K. V. Tauras, *Guerrilla Warfare on the Amber Coast* (1962), p. 52.

g. Usual Soviet estimate, according to Benedict Mačiuika, personal communication.

5. POPULATION CHANGES, 1945–55[a]

(in thousands)

	Estonia	Latvia	Lithuania
Population, end 1945: total	850	1,400	2,400
republic nationality	800	1,200	1,900
Deportations and arrests, 1946–53	−80	−100	−260
Guerrilla war deaths[b]	−15	−25	−50
Birth excess over natural deaths: republic nationality	+50	+60	+300
others	+20	+40	+50
Immigration: republic nationality	+100	+100	+40
Russians and others	+230	+535	+160
Population, early 1955: total	1,157	2,010	2,613
republic nationality	865	1,250	1,980
Losses in home-grown population:			
1945–55[c]	−90	−125	−310
1939–45[d]	−280	−600	−700[e]
Total, 1939–55	−370	−720	−1,000[e]
1939–55 change as percentage of 1939 population	−33%	−36%	−32%[c]
Immigration as percentage of 1939 population	29%	31%	6%[e]

a. Includes some very approximate "guesstimates" — not to be quoted without this qualification. See Table, 2, note a.
b. Includes guerrilla and native repression troop losses, and executions by both sides.
c. Home-grown population losses = (1955 pop.) minus (1945 pop.) minus (immigration) minus (birth excess over natural deaths).
d. From Table 2.
e. Based on 1939 population of the Republic of Lithuania and the Vilnius region.

6. COMMUNIST PARTY SIZE AND ETHNICITY, 1930–80

(size in thousands of members and candidates)

Year (1 January)	Estonian CP[a] Size	% Est.	Latvian CP[b] Size	% Latv.	Lithuanian CP[c] Size	% Lith.
1930	0.3[d]		1.0[e]		.65[f]	
1934	0.387[d]		1.15[e]		1.10[f]	
1936	—		—		1.942[f]	
1937	—		—		1.499[f]	
1938	0.11[g]		—		—	
1939			0.4[e]		—	
1 June 1940	0.133[g]	88%[g]	0.967		1.741[i]	53.3%
1941	2.036		2.798		3.138	
21 June 1941	3.75[j]	65[k]	3.13		4.62	31.8
1945	2.41[l]		5.0		3.54[l]	
1946	7.14	48.1[m]	10.99		8.06	
1947	12.97		21.04		16.2	
1948	16.4		28.7		22.2	
1949	16.9		31.2	53%[h]	24.5	
1950	17.6		34.2		27.8	
1951	18.9		37.3		29.9	
1952	21.2	41.5[m]	40.3		34.7	
September 1952	—		42.0[c]		37.1	
1953	22.3		42.2		36.2	38.0
1954	21.2		42.7		34.5	
1955	21.5	43.6	45.1		35.5	
1956	22.5	44.6	48.5		38.1	
1957	25.7	44.8	53.9		42.2	
1958	27.7	45.6	57.3		44.8	

TABLE 6 – *continued*

Year (1 January)	Estonian CP[a] Size	% Est.	Latvian CP[b] Size	% Latv.	Lithuanian CP[c] Size	% Lith.
1959	30.5	47.5	61.4	35[h]	49.1	55.7
1960	33.4	48.6	65.9	32[h]	54.3	
1961	37.8	49.1	72.5		60.6	
1962	42.5	49.4	78.2		66.2	
1963	45.7	50.5	82.0		71.1	
1964	49.8	51.1	88.2		77.5	
1965	54.8	51.9	95.7	39(?)[p]	86.4	61.5
1970	70.2[m]	52.3[m]	122.4		116.6	67.1[n]
1975	81.5[d]		140.0[o]		140.2[q]	68.5[q]
1980	95.4[o]		158.0[o]		165.8[o]	

a. *Source*, unless otherwise indicated: Aleksander Panksejev, "EKP tegevusest partei ridade kasvu reguleerimisel, aastad 1944-1965," *Töid EKP ajaloo alalt*, vol. II (1966), pp. 149-204.

b. *Source*, unless otherwise indicated: I. M. Muzykantik (ed.), *Kommunisticheskaia partiia Latvii v tsifrakh, 1904-1971* (Riga, 1972), pp. 6-174.

c. *Source*, unless otherwise indicated: Thomas Remeikis, "Berücksichtigung . . . ," AB, X (1970), pp. 132-8.

d. G. Naan (ed.), *Npukogude Eesti: entsüklopeediline teatmeteos* (Tallinn, 1975), pp. 85, 86, 92; the 1934 figure is for August.

e. Seppo Myllyniemi, *Die baltische Krise, 1938-1941* (Stuttgart, 1979), p. 84.

f. Leonas Sabaliūnas, *Lithuania in Crisis* (1972), p. 54.

g. "On 21 June 1940, there were in Estonia 133 ECP members, 3 of them in prison." About 22 had joined since the spring of 1938. Olaf Kuuli, *Revolutsioon Eestis, 1940* (Tallinn, 1980), pp. 47-50.

h. Gundar King, *Economic Policies in Occupied Latvia* (1965), pp. 180-3.

i. Thomas Remeikis, "The Administration of Power," in Vardys (ed.), *Lithuania under the Soviets*, p. 118.

j. Johannes Jakobson et al., *Ülevaade EKP ajaloost* (1972), III, p. 94.

k. Rein Taagepera, unpublished calculations.

l. Without Red Army units.

m. Jaan Pennar, "Soviet Nationality Policy and the Estonian Communist Elite," in T. Parming and E. Järvesoo (eds), *A Case Study of a Soviet Republic* (1978), p. 118.

n. Thomas Remeikis, "Modernization and National Identity in the Baltic Republics," in Ihor Kamenetsky (ed.), *Nationalism and Human Rights* (1977), p. 128.

o. *Ezhegodnik Bolshoi Sovetskoi Entsiklopedii* (1976 and 1980).

p. The Latvian share of the LaCP would be 46.3%; if all ethnically Latvian CPSU members resided in the LaSSR (Remeikis 1970, p. 137). However, 16% of Estonian and 14% of Lithuanian CP members resided outside their own republic. Applying a 15% correction to the LaCP figure yields an estimate of 39%.

q. *Lietuvos Komunistų Partija skaičiais, 1918-1975: statistikos duomenų rinkinys* (Vilnius, 1976), p. 123.

7. INDUSTRIAL EMPLOYMENT AND INDEX OF PRODUCTION, 1940–80

Year	Employment (in thousands of workers)			Production (last 5 mos. of 1940 = 1.00)			Production (full year 1940 = 1.00)[e]		
	Est.[a]	Lat.[b]	Lith.[c]	Est.[b]	Lat.[b]	Lith.[c]	Est.	Lat.	Lith.
1940	73	114[f]	57	(2.4)	(2.4)	(2.4)	1.00	1.00	1.00
1945	52	71[h]	42[g]	0.73	0.47[j]	0.40[g]	0.30	0.20	0.17
1950	99	171[f]	97	3.42	3.03	1.91	1.42	1.26	0.79
1955	127	218[d]	153	6.7	5.85[d]	4.9[g]	2.8	2.4	2.1
1960	161	280	212	11.5	11.0	10.3	4.8	4.6	4.3
1965	207[b]	350	313	18.4	17.4	17.9	7.7	7.2	7.5
1970	226[b]	400	414	27.8	27.3	31.2	11.6	11.4	13.0
1975	234[b]	410	458	39.1	37.1	46.4	16.3	15.5	19.3
1980	240[i]	—	—	48.3[i]	45[i]	58[i]	20.1[i]	19[i]	24[i]

a. *25 aastat Nõukogude Eestit* (1965), pp. 23, 28.
b. *Narodnoe khoziaistvo LaSSR,* 1977, pp. 65 and 76; *Nar. khoz. ESSR,* 1975, p. 224; and calculations based on *ibid.,* 1978, pp. 66 and 72.
c. *Ekonomika ir kultūra* [LiSSR], 1975, pp. 56 and 78.
d. King 1965, pp. 69, 107, 124.
e. 5/12 of the five-month values. Soviet data in the previous column seem to take as baseline the 1940 production of *Soviet* Baltic republics, which only existed for five months of 1940. The proper 12-month comparison base is restored in the last column of the table.
f. *Padomju Latvijas tautas saimniecība* (Riga, 1968), p. 72.
g. Pranas Zunde, in Vardys (ed.), *Lithuania under the Soviets,* pp. 158, 164.
h. Based on the 1950 figure and the 1950/1945 ratio of 2.48, as given in A. Šumiņš, *Apcerījums par Padomju Latvijas ekonomisko attīstību, 1940-1958* (Riga, 1960), p. 46.
i. Calculations based on *Nar. khoz. ESSR,* 1980, pp. 79, 80, 86.
j. Šumiņš, p. 45.

8. AGRICULTURAL PRODUCTION AND EFFICIENCY, 1940–78

Year	Production index (1940 = 1.00)			Cereal yield (in tonnes per hectare)		
	Estonia	*Latvia*	*Lithuania*	*Estonia*	*Latvia*	*Lithuania*
1940	1.00	1.00	1.00	1.15	1.21	0.94[g]
1945	0.6	0.5[i]	—	0.89[a]	0.87[i]	0.88[g]
1950	0.88[a]	0.77	0.85	1.15[a]	0.91[d]	0.79
1955	0.8[b]	0.62[h]	0.70	0.65[a]	0.75[c]	0.5[f]
1960	1.20	1.06	1.30	1.33	1.01[d]	0.93
1965	1.32	1.15	1.51	2.20	1.52	1.62
1970	1.49	1.35	1.89	2.13	2.31	2.45
1975	1.69	1.35	2.08	2.67	1.93	2.00
1978	1.69[c]	1.38[c]	2.21[c]	2.00[c]	1.51[c]	2.50[c]

Sources: Unless otherwise indicated, obtained or calculated from *Nar. khoz. ESSR*, 1977, pp. 20, 95 and 105, and 1978, pp. 105 and 116; *Nar. khoz. LaSSR*, 1977, pp. 115 and 126; and *Ekonomika ir kultūra* [LiSSR] 1975, pp. 100 and 121, and 1977, p. 98.

Notes

a. *25 aastat* pp. 23 and 51.
b. Estimate based on *Nar. khoz. ESSR*, 1977, p. 95.
c. Based on *Nar. khoz. SSSR*, 1978, pp. 197 and 221.
d. *Bolshaia Sovetskaia entsiklopediia* (1975), vol. 19, articles on LaSSR and LiSSR.

e. Andrivs Namsons, "Die Sowjetisierung . . ." (1962), p. 75.
f. Pranas Zundė, "Die Kollektivierung . . ." (1962), p. 105.
g. Benedict Mačiuika, private communication.
h. *Padomju Latvijas tautas saimnieciba*, p. 175.
i. Calculations and estimates based on Šumiņš, pp. 18 and 143.

9. RURAL ADMINISTRATIVE UNITS, 1939–80

	Estonia	*Latvia*	*Lithuania*
1939–41[a] districts	11 *maakond*	19 *apriņķi*	23 *apskritys*
townships	233 *vald*	516 *pagasti*	261 *valsčius*
1942–4 Kreisgebiete[b]	6	5	4
1945–9[c]	11–13 *maakond*	19–25 *apriņķi*	26–37 *apskritys*
	233 *vald*	510 *pagasti*	320 *valsčius*
	637 *külanõukogu*	1,306–1,362 *ciemu padomes*	3,032–2,774 *apylinkes*
Date of introduction of Soviet units[c]	26 September 1950	1 January 1950[d]	20 June 1950
1950 *raions*/village councils	39/626	58/1,229–1,358	87/2,772
Spring 1952–April 1953, *oblasts*	3	3	4[e]
Raions/village councils			
1960	24/319	32/643	44/1,160
1965	15/239	21/564	44/623[f]
1970	15/235	26/539	44/650
Late 1970s	15/194	26/481	44/600

Sources: Main source for 1939–60: Gottlieb Ney, "Administrative Gliederung . . . ," AB, II (1962), pp. 9–34. For 1960–77: *Nar. khoz. ESSR,* 1977, p. 10; *Nar. khoz. LaSSR,* 1968, p. 22, and 1977, p. 22; *Ekonomika ir kultūra* [LiSSR], 1975, p. 9; and *25 aastat,* p. 19.

Notes

a. Because of territorial changes, the numbers are approximate. Prior to the 1939 consolidation, Estonia had 365 *vald.*

b. Superimposed on previous units. Myllyniemi, *Die Neuordnung . . .* (1973), p. 88.

c. *Eesti NSV ajalugu,* III, p. 594; *Lietuvos TSR istorija,* IV, pp. 146 and 151–2; Rutkis, pp. 165–7; Ney, "Administrative Gliederung . . . ," p. 16.

d. Rutkis, p. 167; George Carson (ed.), *Latvia: An Area Study* (1956). p. 4; Ney's date of 31 December 1948 seems questionable.

e. In Lithuania, *oblasts* were introduced as early as 20 June 1950.

f. P. Adlys and A. Stanaitis, *Soviet Lithuania: Population* (Vilnius, 1979), p. 11.

10. URBANIZATION AND LIVING SPACE, 1940-80

Beginning of Year	Percentage of Population Living in Cities and Towns				Per Capita Urban Living Space (in square meters)		
	Estonia	Latvia	Lithuania	USSR	Estonia	Latvia	Lithuania
1940	33.6%	35.2%[b]	24.0%	32.5%	15.5	17.8	—
1945	31.3	—	16.0	—	12.0[d]	—	—
1950	47.1	45.3	28.3	38.9	9.3[e]	12[h]	8.6[c]
1955	54.8	52	34.6	44.4	8.8[e,c]	—	—
1960	57.1	54[a]	39.3	48.8	11.4	12.2[c]	9.4[c]
1965	62.1	59[a]	43.9	52.6	12.4[c]	12.6[c]	10.3[c]
1970	65.0	62.5	50.2	56.3	13.6[c]	13.4[c]	11.3[c]
1975	67.7	65.5	56.2	60.0	14.8[c]	14.3[c]	12.3
1980	70.1[a]	69.0[a]	62[a]	62.8	16.6[f]	15.3[g]	13.2[g]

Sources: Urbanization data from Taagepera, "Baltic Population Changes." Living space data from *Nar. khoz. ESSR*, 1977, pp. 237 and 12; *Nar. khoz. LaSSR*, 1968, p. 399, and 1977, pp. 250 and 6; *Ekonomika ir kultūra* [LiSSR], 1975, p. 247, and 1977, p. 217.

Notes

a. Interpolations or extrapolations.

b. 1939 figure.

c. Figure for end of the year.

d. Calculated, using data in *Eesti NSV ajalugu*, III, pp. 596 and 601.

e. Calculated, using data in *Nõukogude Eesti saavutusi . . .* (Tallinn, 1960), p. 85, and *25 aastat*, p. 105.

f. *Rahva Hääl*, 20 November 1980.

g. 1979 figure, based on *Nar. khoz. SSSR*, 1978, pp. 398 and 17.

h. Figure for 1952, based on 11.7 million sq. m. total urban living space.

11. SIZE, RELATIVE WEIGHT AND ETHNICITY OF CAPITAL CITIES, 1940–79

Beginning of year	Population of capital city (in thousands)[a]			Capital population as percentage of Republic population[j]			Republic nationality as percentage of capital Population[l]		
	Tallinn	Riga	Vilnius	Estonia	Latvia	Lithuania	Tallinn	Riga	Vilnius
1940	176[b]	348[e]	209[g]	16%	17%	7%	85.6%[k]	63.0%[n]	20%[o]
1945	134	–	110[g]	16	–	4	–	–	–
1950	212	497[f]	176[h]	19.3	25.6	6.9	–	–	–
1955	261	567[p]	223[b,r]	22.6	28.2	8.4	–	–	33.6[c]
1960	288	580[c]	236[c]	23.8	28.0	8.7	60.2[c]	44.7[c]	–
1965	329	678[i]	296[h]	25.6	29.7	10.0	–	–	–
1970	363	732	372	26.8	31.0	11.9	55.7	40.9	42.8
1975	399	796	433	27.9	32.1	13.2	–	–	–
1979	436	843[d]	492[d]	29.6	33.3	14.4	51.3[m]	–	47.3[q]

a. *Eesti nõukogude entsüklopeedia* [ENE], vol. VII (1975), p. 450; *Nar. khoz. LaSSR*, 1977, p. 8; *Ekonomika ir kultūra* [LiSSR], 1975, p. 12, unless otherwise shown.

b. 1941 figure from *Nar. khoz. ESSR*, 1977, p. 13. The value of 136,000 for 1940 given in ENE applies to restricted city territory, and reflects the recent departure of the Germans.

c. 1959 figure.

d. *USSR in Figures, 1979*, pp. 13–14.

e. 1939 figure, possibly after departure of the Germans. Rutkis, p. 182, gives 385,000 for 1935, of whom 38,500 were Germans.

f. 1951 figure.

g. *Socialistinės visuomenės susiformavimas ir raida Tarybų Lietuvoje, 1940–1980* (Vilnius, 1980), p. 56.

h. Adlys and Stanaitis, p. 25.

i. 1966 figure.

j. From city population and the republic population in Table 1.

k. Raimo Pullat, *Linnad kodanlikus Eestis* (Tallinn, 1978), p. 137.

l. Unless otherwise indicated, *Itogi Vsesoiuznoi perepisi naseleniia 1970 goda*, vol. IV (Moscow, 1973), pp. 275, 283 and 320.

m. *Õhtuleht* (Tallinn), 27 February 1980.

n. 1935 census. Carson, p. 168; Rutkis, p. 182.

o. Educated guess, based on considerations in Sabaliūnas, pp. 277–8.

p. Rutkis, p. 182.

q. Algirdas Motulas, *Vilniaus dabartis ir rytdiena* (Vilnius, 1980), p. 32.

r. 1956 figure.

12. MARRIAGE AND DIVORCE RATES, 1940-78

(Per year and per 1,000 population)

Year	Marriages				Divorces			
	Estonia	Latvia	Lithuania	USSR	Estonia	Latvia	Lithuania	USSR
1940	9.6	10.8	9.7	6.3	1.1	1.1	0.0	1.1
1945	–	–	–	–	–	–	–	–
1950	9.5	9.9	9.1	11.6	0.6	0.8	0.2	0.4
1955	10.3	10.6	9.7	11.5	1.2	1.1	0.4	0.6
1960	10.0	11.0	10.1	12.1	2.1	2.4	0.9	1.3
1965	8.2	8.8	8.4	8.7	2.3	2.8	0.9	1.6
1970	9.1	10.1	9.5	9.7	3.2	4.6	2.2	2.6
1975	8.7	9.9	9.0	10.7	3.4	4.7	2.7	3.1
1978	8.5	10.1	9.1	10.7	3.8	5.0	3.0	3.5

Sources: *Nar. khoz. ESSR*, 1969, p. 23, 1977, p. 13, and 1978, p. 21; *Nar. khoz. LaSSR*, 1977, p. 19, and 1979, p. 9; *Nar. khoz. SSSR*, 1978, p. 28; *Ekonomika i kultūra LaSSR*, 1966, p. 20; *Ekonomika ir kultūra* [LiSSR], 1975, p. 17, and 1978, p. 17.

13. BIRTH AND DEATHRATES, 1940–80
(per year and per 1,000 population)

Year	Birthrate				Deathrate			
	Estonia	Latvia	Lithuania	USSR	Estonia	Latvia	Lithuania	USSR
1940	16.1	19.3	23.0	31.2	17.0	15.7	13.0	18.0
1945	15.9[a]	–	–	–	19.4[a]	–	–	–
1950	18.4	17.0	23.6	26.7	14.4	12.4	12.0	9.7
1955	17.9	16.4	21.1	25.7	11.7	10.6	9.2	8.2
1960	16.6	16.7	22.5	24.9	10.5	10.0	7.8	7.1
1965	14.6	13.8	18.1	18.4	10.5	10.0	7.9	7.3
1970	15.8	14.5	17.6	17.4	11.1	11.2	8.9	8.2
1975	14.9	14.1	15.7	18.1	11.6	12.1	9.5	9.3
1980[b]	15.0	14.0	15.1	18.3	12.3	12.7	10.5	10.3

Source: Condensed from year-to-year data in Taagepera, "Baltic Population Changes."

Notes
[a] For 1943.
[b] *Nar. khoz. ESSR*, 1980, p. 28.

14. POPULATION INCREASE, 1950–79
(in thousands)

Average for	Estonia		Latvia		Lithuania	
	Natural	Immigration	Natural	Immigration	Natural	Immigration
1950–4	5.6	6.6	9.3	3.9	28.3	−20.6
1955–9	6.8	3.6	12.7	7.9	34.5	−6.0
1960–4	6.8	8.3	12.5	15.6	36.8	2.8
1965–9	5.3	9.0	7.8	14.2	29.1	5.8
1970–4	6.3	8.0	7.4	12.8	25.4	7.9
1975–9	4.4	4.9	3.7	9.1	18.8	6.2

Source: Calculated from year-to-year tabulation in Taagepera, "Baltic Population Changes." The 1975–9 figures involve estimates for 1979.

15. THE SHARE OF PRIVATE PLOTS IN LATVIA'S AGRICULTURAL PRODUCTION, 1950–77

	1950	1960	1965	1970	1975	1977
Total cultivated land	—	5%[a]	—	4.6%[b]	—	5.0%
Total agricultural production	—	—	—	32.5[c]	—	29[d]
Grain	—	—	2%	1	2%	2
Potatoes	64%	63	60	60	61	54
Vegetables	84	66	64	58	48	32
Meat	73	49	47	35	28	24
Milk	60	49	43	39	34	31
Eggs	93	71	51	34	28	23

Sources: Main source for 1950–60: Andres Küng, *Vad händer i Baltikum?* (Stockholm, 1973), p. 125, based on *Nar. khoz. LaSSR*, 1971. For 1965–77: *Nar. khoz. LaSSR*, 1977, pp. 117 and 119.

Notes
a. Rutkis, p. 357.
b. Küng 1973, p. 125.
c. For 1972, from A Cīce, in *Padomju Latvijas komunists*, November 1975, p. 69.
d. For 1978, *Cīņa*, 23 November 1979.

Analogous data available on Estonia and Lithuania are limited, but the general pattern seems to be the same. See Elmar Järvesoo, "Private Enterprise in Soviet Estonian Agriculture," *JBS*, V/3 (Fall 1974), pp. 169–187.

16. AVERAGE YEARLY GROWTH RATES OF PRODUCED INCOME AND INDUSTRIAL PRODUCTION, 1950–80

	Produced national income				Industrial production			
	Est.	Lat.	Lith.	USSR	Est.	Lat.	Lith.	USSR
1950–55	—	10.0%	—	11.2%	14.4%	14.1%[e]	20.9%	13.1%
1955–60	—	—	—	9.1	11.4	13.5[e]	15.9	10.4
1960–65	7.4%	7.2	8.7%	6.5	9.9	9.6	11.7	8.6
1965–70	7.6	7.7	9.4	7.7	8.6	9.4	11.7	8.4
1970–75	5.5	5.8	5.7	5.7	7.1	6.4	8.3	7.4
1975–80	4.2[a]	3.8[d]	—	4.4[b]	4.4[a]	3.6[b]	5.1[b]	4.7[b]
1980–85[c]	2.8[a]	—	—	—	2.9	3.1	4.1	4.9

Sources: Produced national income (*proizvedennyi natsionalnyi dokhod*) and total industrial production calculated from *Nar. khoz. ESSR, 1977,* pp. 24–28 and 55; *Nar. khoz. LaSSR, 1977,* p. 26, *Ekonomika ir kultūra* [LiSSR], 1975, pp. 23–27; *Mažoji lietuviškoji tarybinė enciklopedija,* II, p. 899; *USSR in Figures, 1979,* pp. 28–37 and 106; Harry G. Shaffer, "Soviet Economic Performance in Historical Perspective," in Samuel Hendel (ed.), *The Soviet Crucible* (North Scituate, Mass., 1980), pp. 293–304.

Notes
[a] *Rahva Hääl,* 20 November 1980 and 26 February 1982.
[b] For 1975–79.
[c] Average goals of the 1981–85 five-year plan, *Rahva Hääl,* 2 December 1980.
[d] For 1975–78.
[e] Calculated from Table 7.

BIBLIOGRAPHY

This is not intended to be a comprehensive listing of all relevant work. Rather, it includes those sources which we have found particularly useful in our work, and a fairly extensive sampling of what is available in English and German.

Abbreviations:

AB   *Acta Baltica*
BA   *Books Abroad*
JBS   *Journal of Baltic Studies*

Documents and Statistical Collections

The Chronicle of the Catholic Church in Lithuania: Underground Journal of Human Rights Violations. Vol. I, nos 1–9 (1972–4). Chicago, 1981. Subsequent issues not yet published in book form are available in English translation through the Lithuanian Roman Catholic Priests' League of America, Brooklyn, NY. The original title is better rendered as "The Chronicle of the Lithuanian Catholic Church."
Documents from Estonia on the Violations of Human Rights. Stockholm, 1977.
Ekonomika i kultura Litovskoi SSR. Vilnius, annual since 1957 (Russian edn of *Lietuvos TSR ekonomika ir kultūra*).
Estonskaia Kommunisticheskaia Partiia v tsifrakh. Tallinn, 1983.
Fourth Interim Report of the Select Committee on Communist Aggression. 83rd Congress, 2nd Session. Washington, 1954.
Itogi Vsesoiuznoi perepisi naseleniia 1970 goda, vol. IV. Moscow, 1973.
Kancevičius, Vytautas (ed.). *Lithuania in 1939–1940: The Historic Turn to Socialism*. Vilnius, 1976.
Kollektivizatsiia krestianskikh khoziaistv Litovskoi SSR: sbornik dokumentov i materialov. Vilnius, 1977.
Latviia za gody sovetskoi vlasti: statisticheskii sbornik. Riga, 1967.
Lietuvos Katalikų Bažnyčios kronika. 5 vols, containing issues 1–39. Chicago, 1974–9 (see *The Chronicle of the Catholic Church in Lithuania*).
Lietuvos Komunistų Partija skaičiais, 1918–1975: statistikos duomenų rinkinys. Vilnius, 1976.
Lietuvos TSR ekonomika ir kultūra. Vilnius, annual since 1957 (Lithuanian edn of *Ekonomika i kultura Litovskoi SSR*).
Lithuania in Figures. Vilnius, 1966.
Narodnoe khoziaistvo Estonskoi SSR. Tallinn, annual since 1957 (bilingual, Estonian and Russian; separate issues for some years).
Narodnoe khoziaistvo Latviiskoi SSR. Riga, annual since 1957 (bilingual, Latvian and Russian; separate issues for some years).

Naselenie SSSR po dannym vsesoiuznoi perepiski naseleniia 1979 goda. Moscow, 1980.

Nõukogude Eesti saavutusi 20 aasta jooksul: statistiline kogumik. Tallinn, 1960.

Paul, I. (ed.). *Eesti rahvas Nõukogude Liidu Suures Isamaasõjas, 1941–1945: Dokumente ja materjale.* Tallinn, 1975.

Present-day Lithuania in Figures. Vilnius, 1971.

Sontag, Raymond James, and James Stuart Beddie (eds). *Nazi-Soviet Relations, 1939–1941.* Washington, 1948.

Tarybų Lietuvos dvidešimtmetis: statistinių duomenų rinkinys. Vilnius, 1960.

Tarybų valdžios atkūrimas Lietuvoje, 1940–41 metais: dokumentų rinkinys. Vilnius, 1965.

Third Interim Report of the Select Committee on Communist Aggression. 83rd Congress, 2nd Session. Washington, 1954. Reprinted as *The Baltic States: A Study of Their Origin and National Development; Their Seizure and Incorporation into the USSR.* International Military Law and History Reprint Series, vol. IV. Buffalo, NY, 1972.

Tõnurist, Edgar (ed.). *Eesti NSV põllumajanduse kollektiviseerimine: Dokumentide ja materjalide kogumik.* Tallinn, 1978.

25 aastat Nõukogude Eestit: statistiline kogumik. Tallinn, 1965.

25 let sovetskoi Litvy: statisticheskii sbornik. Vilnius, 1965.

1940. aasta sotsialistlik revolutsioon Eestis: Dokumente ja materjale. Tallinn, 1960.

Journals and Newspapers

Cīņa	Organ of the Latvian CP (daily)
Eesti Kommunist/Kommunist Estonii	Journal of the Estonian CP (monthly)
Karogs	Latvian cultural journal (monthly)
Komjaunimo tiesa	Organ of the Lithuanian Komsomol (daily)
Komunistas/Kommunist (Litvy)	Journal of the Lithuanian CP (monthly)
Literatūra ir menas	Lithuanian cultural paper (weekly)
Literatūra un māksla	Latvian cultural paper (weekly)
Looming	Estonian cultural journal (monthly)
Padomju jaunatne	Organ of the Latvian Komsomol (daily)
Padomju Latvijas komunists/ Kommunist sovetskoi Latvii	Journal of the Latvian CP (monthly)
Pergalė	Lithuanian cultural journal (monthly)
Rahva Hääl	Organ of the Estonian CP (daily)
Sirp ja Vasar	Estonian cultural paper (weekly)
Sovetskaia Estoniia	Estonian Russian-language paper (daily)
Sovetskaia Latviia	Latvian Russian-language paper (daily)
Sovetskaia Litva	Lithuanian Russian-language paper (daily)
Tiesa	Organ of the Lithuanian CP (daily)

The press of the Baltic republics was surveyed in Assembly of Captive European Nations, *A Survey of Developments in Nine Captive Countries.* 17 vols. New York, 1956–65. Three separate volumes of the survey on Lithuania are also available: Vytautas Vaitiekūnas, *A Survey of Development in Captive Lithuania.* 3 vols. New York, 1962–6.

Estonian Events (1967–72) and *Baltic Events* (1973–5), published by Rein Taagepera (University of California, Irvine) and Juris Dreifelds (Brock University, St Catherines, Ontario, Canada).

Books and Scholarly Articles

Aiszilnieks, Arnolds P. "Sovietization of Consumers' Cooperation in the Baltic States," *JBS*, V/1 (Spring 1974), pp. 40–50.

Allworth, Edward (ed.). *Nationality Group Survival in Multi-Ethnic States: Shifting Support Patterns in the Soviet Baltic Region.* New York, 1977.

Angelus, Oskar. "Die Russifizierung Estlands," *AB*, VII (1967), pp. 85–130.

——. "Die Jugend in Sowjetestland," *AB*, XVIII (1978), pp. 156–93.

Arad, Yitzhak. "The 'Final Solution' in Lithuania in the Light of German Documentation," *Yad Vashem Studies*, XI (Jerusalem, 1976), pp. 234–72.

Balodis, Agnis. *Sovjets och Nazitysklands uppgörelse om de Baltiska staterna.* Stockholm, 1978.

Bilinsky, Yaroslav. "The Soviet Education Laws of 1958–1959 and Soviet Nationality Policy," *Soviet Studies*, XIV (1962), pp. 138–57.

—— and Tõnu Parming. "Helsinki Watch Committees in the Soviet Republics: Implications for Soviet Nationality Policy," *Nationality Papers*, IX/1 (Spring 1981), pp. 1–26.

Bilmanis, Alfred. *Latvia under German Occupation.* Washington, 1943.

——. *Baltic Essays.* Washington, 1945.

——. *A History of Latvia.* Princeton, NJ, 1951.

Bokalders, Jānis. "Urbanisation und Rückgang des Lebensstandards der Landbevölkerung Sowjetlettlands," *AB*, IV (1964), pp. 92–127.

Borba za sovetskuiu Pribaltiku v Velikoi Otechestvennoi Voine, 1941–1945. 3 vols. Riga, 1966.

Bourdeaux, Michael. *Land of Crosses.* Chulmleigh, Devon, UK, 1979.

Brazaitis, Juozas. "Pirmoji sovietinė okupacija (1940–1941)," *Lietuvių enciklopedija*, XV, pp. 356–70. Boston, MA, 1968.

——. "Vokiečių okupacija (1940–1944)," *Lietuvių enciklopedija*, XV, pp. 371–80. Boston, MA. 1968.

Buchis (Bučys), Algimantas. *Roman i sovremennost: stanovlenie i razvitie litovskogo sovetskogo romana.* Moscow, 1977.

Bulavas, Juozas. *Vokiškujų fašistų okupacinis Lietuvos valdymas.* Vilnius, 1969.

Carson, George B. (ed.). *Latvia: An Area Study.* Human Relations Area Files, no. 41. New Haven, CT, 1956.

Chambon, Henry de. *La tragédie des nations baltiques.* Paris, 1946.

Clemens, Walter C. Jr. *Baltic Independence and Russian Empire.* New York, 1991.

Czollek, R. *Faschismus und okkupation.* Berlin, 1974.

Dallin, Alexander. *German Rule in Russia, 1941–1945: A Study in Occupation Policies*, esp. chapter 10, "Ostland: Lohse and the Baltic States," p. 182–7. London, 1957.

Daumantas, J. (Juozas Lukša) *Partizanai už geležinės uždangos.* Chicago, 1950.

Dovydėnas, Liudas. *Mes valdysim pasaulį.* 2 vols. Woodhaven, NY, 1970. English edn: *We Will Conquer the World.* New York, 1971.

Dreifelds, Juris. "Characteristics and Trends of Two Demographic Variables in the Latvian SSR," *Bulletin of Baltic Studies*, VIII (1971), pp. 10–17.

——. "Latvian National Demands and Group Consciousness since 1959," in George W. Simmonds (ed.), *Nationalism in the USSR and Eastern Europe in the Era of Brezhnev and Kosygin*, pp. 136–56. Detroit, MI, 1976.

——. "Belorussia and the Baltics," in I. S. Koropeckyj and Gertrude Schroeder (eds), *Economics of Soviet Regions*, p. 323–85. New York, 1981.

———. "Latvian National Rebirth," *Problems of Communism*, XXXVIII/3 (July–Aug. 1989), pp. 77–94.

Drizul [Drīzulis], A.A. *Borba latyshkogo naroda v gody velikoi otechestvennoi voiny, 1941–1945 gg.* Riga, 1970.

Eesti nõukogude entsüklopeedia. 8 vols. Tallinn, 1968–76.

Eesti NSV ajalugu, vol. III. Tallinn, 1971 (Estonian edn of *Istoriia Estonskoi SSR*).

Eesti riik ja rahvas teises maailmasõjas, vols I–X. Stockholm, 1954–62. A polemical continuation under the same title, not authorized by the publishers of the original, was published in the same format in Soviet Estonia: vols XI–XV. Tallinn, 1964–72.

Efremenko, A.P. *Agrarnye preobrazovaniia i nachalo sotsialisticheskogo stroitelstva v litovskoi derevne v 1940–1941 godakh.* Vilnius, 1972.

Ekmanis, Rolfs. "Sowjetlettische Schriftsteller in der Sowjetunion und ihre literarische Tätigkeit seit 1940," *AB*, VII (1976), pp. 171–262.

———. "Die kulturellen Probleme in Lettland Ende der sechziger Jahre," *AB*, IX (1969), pp. 229–314.

———. "Soviet Attitudes toward Pre-Soviet Latvian Writers," *JBS*, III/1 (Spring 1972), pp. 44–70.

———. *Latvian Literature under the Soviets, 1940–1975.* Belmont, MA, 1978.

Forgus, Silvia P. "Manifestations of Nationalism in the Baltic Republics," *Nationalities Papers*, VII/2 (Fall 1979), pp. 197–211.

Ginsburgs, George. "Nationality and State Succession in Soviet Theory and Practice — The Experience of the Baltic Republics," in A. Sprudzs and A. Rusis (eds), *Res Baltica*, pp. 160–90. Leiden, 1968.

———. "Soviet Views on the Law of State Succession with Regard to Treaties and Acquired Rights — The Case of the Baltic Republics," in A. Sprudzs and A. Rusis (eds), *Res Baltica*, pp. 191–229. Leiden, 1968.

Gitlerovskaia okkupatsiia v Litve: sbornik statei. Vilnius, 1966.

Glemža, Jonas. "Die Landwirtschaft Sowjetlitauens, 1960–1973," *AB*, XV (1975), pp. 211–79.

Gregorauskas, M. *Tarybų Lietuvos žemės ūkis, 1940–1960.* Vilnius, 1960.

Grinius, Jonas. "Literature and the Arts in Captive Lithuania," in V.S. Vardys (ed.), *Lithuania under the Soviets, 1940–1965*, pp. 197–213. New York, 1965.

Gureckas, Algimantas P. "The National Resistance during the German Occupation of Lithuania," *Lituanus*, VIII/1–2, (1962), pp. 23–8.

Hanchett, Walter S. "The Communists and the Latvian Countryside, 1919–1949," in A. Sprudzs and A. Rusis (eds), *Res Baltica*, pp. 88–116. Leiden, 1968.

Harrison, Ernest J. *Lithuania's Fight for Freedom.* New York, 1952.

Heine, Eerik. "Metsavennad," in R. Maasing *et al.* (eds), *Eesti saatusaastad, 1945–1960*, vol. II, pp. 66–75. Stockholm, 1963–72.

Hoover, Karl K. "The Baltic Resettlement of 1939 and Nationalist Socialist Racial Policy," *JBS*, VIII/1 (Spring 1977), pp. 79–89.

Horm, Arvo. "Balternas flykt till Sverige," *Symposium om Balterna i Sverige.* Stockholm, 1971.

Idzelis, Augustinas. "Locational Aspects of the Chemical Industry in Lithuania," *Lituanus*, XIX/4 (1973), pp. 51–61.

———. "Response of Soviet Lithuania to Environmental Problems in the Coastal Zone," *JBS*, X/4 (Winter 1979), pp. 299–308.

Istoriia Estonskoi SSR, vol. III. Tallinn, 1974 (Russian edn of *Eesti NSV ajalugu*).

Istoriia Latviiskoi SSR, vol. III. Riga, 1957.

Istoriia Latviiskoi SSR, sokrashchennyi kurs. Riga. 1971.

Istoriia litovskoi literatury. Vilnius, 1977.

Istoriia Litovskoi SSR. Vilnius, 1978.

Ivask, Ivar. "Recent Trends in Estonian Poetry," *BA*, XLII/3 (Autumn 1968), pp. 517–20.

—— (ed.). *A Look at Baltic Letters Today,* a special topical issue of BA, XLVII/3 (Autumn 1973).

Ivinskis, Zenonas. "Lithuania during the War: Resistance against the Soviet and Nazi Occupants," in V.S. Vardys (ed.), *Lithuania under the Soviets, 1940–1965,* pp. 61–84. New York, 1965.

Jakobson, Johannes, Johannes Kalits and Aleksander Panksejev. *Ülevaade Eestimaa Kommunistliku Partei ajaloost,* vol. III. Tallinn, 1972. (Estonian version of *Ocherki istorii Kommunicheskoi Partii Estonii.*)

Järvesoo, Elmar. "Die Wirtschaft Estlands und deren strukturelle Veränderungen," *AB*, IX (1969), pp. 9–45.

——. "Private Enterprise in Soviet Estonian Agriculture," *JBS*, V/3 (Fall 1974), pp. 169–87.

——. "The Postwar Economic Transformations," in T. Parming and E. Järvesoo (eds), *A Case Study of a Soviet Republic: The Estonian SSR*, pp. 131–90. Boulder, CO, 1978.

Jensen, Erik Vagn. *Ukendte naboer — Sovjetrepublikkerne Estland/Letland/Litauen.* Copenhagen, 1977.

Juda, Lawrence. "United States' Nonrecognition of the Soviet Union's Annexation of the Baltic States: Politics and Law," *JBS*, VI/4 (Winter 1975), pp. 272–90.

Jurašiene, Aušra-Marija. "The Problem of Creative Artistic Expression in Contemporary Lithuania," *Lituanus*, XXII/3 (1976), pp. 28–48.

Jüriado, Andres. "Nationalism and Socialism in Soviet Estonian Drama," *Lituanus*, XIX/2 (1973), pp. 28–42.

Kaelas, Aleksander. *Das Sowjetisch besetzte Estland.* Stockholm, 1958.

Kalniņš, Bruno. *De Baltiska staternas frihetskamp.* Stockholm, 1950.

——. "How Latvia is Ruled: The Structure of the Political Apparatus," *JBS*, VIII/1 (Spring 1977), pp. 70–8.

Kaslas, Bronis J. *The USSR-German Aggression against Lithuania.* New York, 1973.

——. *The Baltic Nations: The Quest for Regional Integration and Political Liberty.* Pittston, PA, 1976.

Kaufmann, Max. "The War Years in Latvia Revisited," in Mendel Bobe *et al.* (eds), *Jews in Latvia*, pp. 351–68. Tel Aviv, 1971.

Kazlas, Juozas. "Social Distance among Ethnic Groups," in Edward Allworth (ed.), *Nationality Group Survival in Mutli-Ethnic States: Shifting Support Patterns in the Soviet Baltic Region*, pp. 228–77. New York, 1977.

Kiik, Heino. *Tondiöömaja* (Spook Hostel). Tallinn, 1970.

King, Gundar J. *Economic Policies in Occupied Latvia.* Tacoma, WA, 1965.

Kivimaa, Ervin. "Eesti NSV põllumajanduse kollektiviseerimine aastail 1947–1950," in Edgar Tõnurist (ed.), *Sotsialistliku põllumajanduse areng Nõukogude Eestis*, pp. 69–93. Tallinn, 1976.

Klesment, Johannes. "Die Rechtsordnung in Sowjetestland," *AB*, II (1962), pp. 9–34.

Kolde, Endel Jakob. "Estonian External Trade under the Soviet Regime," *JBS*, VI/4 (Winter 1975), pp. 291–9.

———. "Structural Integration of the Baltic Economies into the Soviet System," *JBS*, IX/2 (Summer 1978), pp. 164–76.

Koropeckyj, I. S. "National Income of the Baltic Republics in 1970" *JBS*, VII/4 (Spring 1976), pp. 61–73.

Krakhmalinikova, Z. A. *Romany i romanisty*. Tallinn, 1977.

Küng, Andres. *Vad händer i Baltikum?* Stockholm, 1973.

———. *A Dream of Freedom: Four Decades of National Survival Versus Russian Imperialism in Estonia, Latvia and Lithuania, 1940–1980*. Cardiff, 1980.

Kurman, George. "Literary Censorship in General and in Soviet Estonia,' JBS, VIII/1 (Spring 1977), pp. 3–15.

———. "Estonian Literature," in T. Parming and E. Järvesoo (eds), *A Case Study of a Soviet Republic: The Estonian SSR*, pp. 247–80. Boulder, CO, 1978.

Kütt, Aleksander. "Die Wirtschaft Sowjetestlands," AB, II (1962), pp. 107–28.

Kuusik, Mall. "Die sowjetestnische Literatur heute," AB, XIV (1974), pp. 184–96.

Labsvīrs, Jānis. "A Case Study in the Sovietization of the Baltic States: Collectivization of Latvian Agriculture, 1944–1956." Unpubl. Ph.D. diss., University of Indiana, Bloomington, 1959.

Landsbergis, Algirdas. "The Organic and the Synthetic: A Dialectical Dance," in George W. Simmonds (ed.), *Nationalism in the USSR and Eastern Europe in the Era of Brezhnev and Kosygin*, pp. 181–7. Detroit, MI, 1975.

———. "Orvell i Kafka eshche zhivy v Litve," *Kontinent*, V (1975), pp. 207–19.

Latvijas PSR maza enciklopēdija. 4 vols. Riga. 1967–72.

Latvju enciklopēdija. 3 vols. Stockholm, 1950–5.

Lehiste, Ilse. "Where Hobgoblins Spend the Night," *JBS*, IV/4 (Winter 1973), pp. 321–6.

Lemberg, Adelaida. "Estonskie dissidenty — za nezavisimost," *Kontinent*, IX (1976), pp. 157–64.

Lentsman, Leonid (chief ed.). *Eesti rahvas Suures Isamaasõjas*, vol. II. Tallinn, 1977.

Levin, Dov. "Participation of the Lithuanian Jews in the Second World War," *JBS*, VI/4 (Winter 1975), pp. 300–10.

———. "Der bewaffnete Widerstand baltischen Juden gegen den Nazi-Regime, 1941–1945," *AB*, XV (1975), pp. 166–74.

———. "The Jews and the Elections Campaigns in Lithuania, 1940–1941," *Soviet Jewish Affairs*, XII (February 1980), 39–51.

Lietuviškoji tarybinė enciklopedija. Vols I–VIII published to date. Vilnius, 1972–82.

Lietuvių archyvas: Bolševizmo metai. 4 vols. Kaunas, 1942–3. An abridged one-volume edn: J. Prunskis (ed.). Brooklyn, NY, 1952.

Lietuvių enciklopedija. 36 vols. Boston, MA, 1953–69. An abridged English-language edn: *Encyclopedia Lituanica*. 5 vols. Boston, MA, 1970–1975.

Lietuvos Komunistų Partijos istorijos apybraiža, vol. II. Vilnius, 1978.

Lietuvos TSR istorija, vol. IV. Vilnius, 1975.

Loeber, Dietrich. "The Administration of Culture in Soviet Latvia: Direction of Literature and the Arts in the Mirror of Written Law," in A. Sprudzs and A. Rusis (eds), *Res Baltica*, pp. 133–45. Leiden, 1968.

Maasing, Richard, Hans Kauri, Arnold Purre *et al.* (eds). *Eesti saatusaastad, 1945–1960*. 6 vols. Stockholm, 1963–72.

Mačiuika, Benedict V. *Lithuania in the Last Thirty Years*. Human Relations Area Files, no. 18. New Haven, CT, 1955.

——. "The Baltic States under Soviet Russia: A Case Study in Sovietization." Unpubl. Ph.D. diss., University of Chicago, 1963.

——. "Die Russifizierung Litauens seit 1959: Versuch einer quantitativen Analyse," *AB*, VII (1967), pp. 289–302.

——. "Auswertung der Volkszählungsergenisse von 1970 in Sowjetlitauen," *AB*, XI (1971), pp. 87–116.

——. "The Role of the Baltic Republics in the Economy of the USSR," *JBS*, III/1 (Spring 1972), pp. 18–25.

——. "Acculturation and Socialization in the Soviet Baltic Republics," *Lituanus*, XVIII/4 (1972), pp. 26–43.

——. "Contemporary Social Problems in the Collectivized Lithuanian Countryside," *Lituanus*, XXII/3 (1976), pp. 5–27.

Mägi, Arvo. *Estonian Literature*. Stockholm, 1968.

Maltsene (Malcienė), M. *Kino sovetskoi Litvy*. Leningrad, 1980.

Mažeika, Povilas. "Die neuere Entwicklung der Industrie Litauens," AB, IX (1969), pp. 177–225.

Mažoji lietuviškoji tarybinė enciklopedija. 4 vols. Vilnius, 1966–75.

Meissner, Boris. *Die Sowjetunion, die Baltischen Staaten und das Völkerrecht*. Cologne, 1956.

Mereste, Uno, and Maimu Saarepera. *Rahvastiku enesetunnetus*. Tallinn, 1978.

Meškauskas, K. *Tarybų Lietuvos industrializavimas*. Vilnius, 1960.

—— et al. *Lietuvos dabartis ir ateitis*. Vilnius, 1973.

Misiunas, Romuald J. "Baltic Nationalism and Soviet Language Policy: From Russification to Constitutional Amendment," in Henry L. Huttenbach (ed.), *Soviet Nationality Policies: Ruling Ethnic Groups in the USSR*, London, 1990. pp. 206–20.

—— "Sovereignty without Government: Baltic Diplomatic and Consular Representation, 1940–1990," in Yossi Shain (ed.), *Governments-in-Exile in Contemporary World Politics* (New York, 1991), pp. 134–44.

Myllyniemi, Seppo. *Die Neuordnung der baltischen Länder, 1941–1944*. Helsinki, 1973.

——. *Die baltische Krise, 1938–1941*. Stuttgart, 1979.

Namsons, Andrivs, "Die Sowjetisierung des Schul-und Bildungswesens in Lettland von 1940 bis 1960," *AB*, I (1960–1), pp. 148–67.

——. "Die Umgestaltung der Landwirtschaft in Sowjetlettland," *AB*, II (1962), pp. 57–92.

——. "Stadtentwicklung und Siedlungsformen in Lettland," *AB*, VII (1967), pp. 131–69.

——. "Neue Errungenschaften in der Industrie Lettlands," *AB*, IX (1969), pp. 81–134.

——. "Die Entwicklung der Landwirtschaft in Sowjetlettland, *AB*, IX (1969), pp. 135–76.

——. "Nationale Zusammensetzung und Struktur der Bevölkerung Lettlands nach den Volkszählungen von 1935, 1959 und 1970," *AB*, XI (1971), pp. 61–8.

——. "Die bürgerliche Bewegung in Sowjetrussland und in den baltischen Ländern," *AB*, XIV (1974), pp. 138–83.

Ney, Gottlieb. "Administrative Gliederung und Verwaltungsorgane der sowjetisierten baltischen Staaten," *AB*, II (1962), pp. 9–34.

——. "Sozialistische Industrialisierung und ihre Auswirkungen im sowjetisierten Baltikum," *AB*, II (1962) pp. 129–45.

Nirk, Endel. *Estonian Literature*. Tallinn, 1970.

Ocherki istorii estonskoi sovetskoi literatury. Moscow, 1971.

Ocherki istorii Kommunisticheskoi Partii Estonii, vols II–III. Tallinn, 1963–1970 (Estonian version: see J. Jakobson *et al.*).

Ocherki istorii Kommunisticheskoi Partii Latvii, vol. II. Riga, 1966.

Ocherki razvitiia gosudarstvennosti sovetskikh pribaltiiskikh respublik (1940–1965 gg.). Tallinn, 1965.

Olt, Harry. *Modern Estonian Composers.* Tallinn, 1972.

Oras, Ants. *Baltic Eclipse.* London, 1948.

Paletskis, Iustas (Paleckis, J.). *V dvukh mirakh.* Moscow, 1974.

Panksejev, Aleksander. "EKP tegevusest partei ridade kasvu reguleerimisel (aastad 1944–1965)," in *Töid EKP ajaloo alalt,* vol. II, pp. 149–204. Tallinn, 1966.

Parming, Tönu. "Negotiating in the Kremlin: The Estonian Experience of 1939," *Lituanus,* XIV/2 (1968), pp. 45–96.

——. "Population Changes in Estonia, 1935–1970," *Population Studies,* XXVI/1 (March 1972), pp. 53–78.

——. "Nationalism in Soviet Estonia since 1964," in George W. Simmonds (eds), *Nationalism in the USSR and Eastern Europe in the Era of Brezhnev and Kosygin,* pp. 116–35. Detroit, MI, 1975.

——. "The Jewish Community and Inter-Ethnic Relations in Estonia, 1918–1940," *JBS,* X/3 (Fall 1979), pp. 257–9.

——. "Population Processes and the Nationality Issue in the Soviet Baltic," *Soviet Studies,* XXXII/2 (July 1980), pp. 398–414.

—— and Elmar Järvesoo (eds). *A Case Study of a Soviet Republic: The Estonian SSR.* Boulder, Colo., 1978.

Penikis, Janis J. "Latvian Nationalism: Preface to a Dissenting View," in George W. Simmonds (ed.), *Nationalism in the USSR and Eastern Europe in the Era of Brezhnev and Kosygin,* pp. 157–61. Detroit, MI, 1975.

Pennar, Jaan. "Nationalism in the Soviet Baltics," in Erich Goldhagen (ed.), *Ethnic Minorities in the Soviet Union.* New York, 1968.

——. "Soviet Nationality Policy and the Estonian Communist Elite," in T. Parming and E. Järvesoo (eds), *A Case Study of a Soviet Republic: The Estonian SSR,* pp. 105–27. Boulder, Colo., 1978.

——. "Reflections on Union Republics in the New Soviet Constitution," *Lituanus,* XXV/1 (1979), pp. 5–16.

Procuta, Ginutis. "The Transformation of Higher Education in Lithuania during the First Decade of Soviet Rule," *Lituanus,* XIII/1 (1967), pp. 71–92.

Pullat, Raimo (ed.). *Problemy sotsialnoi struktury respublik sovetskoi pribaltiki.* Tallinn, 1978.

Purre, Arnold. *Soviet Farming Failure Hits Estonia.* Stockholm, 1964.

——. "Teine punane okupatsioon Eestis: Aastad 1944–1950," in R. Maasing *et al.* (eds). *Eesti saatusaastad, 1945–1960,* pp. 7–65. Stockholm, 1964.

——. "A New Deal in Soviet Industrial Administration," *Lituanus,* XI/4 (1965), pp. 67–70.

——. "Territoriale Einteilung und Verwaltung der Estnischen SSR im Rahmen der allgemeinen Staatsordnung der UdSSR," *AB,* VII (1967), pp. 9–37.

——. "Estlands Industrie unter sowjetischer Herrschaft," *AB,* IX (1969), pp. 47–69.

——. "Ethnischer Bestand und Struktur der Bevölkerung Sowjetestlands im Jahr 1970," *AB,* XI (1971), pp. 41–60.

Rakūnas, A. *Klasių kova Lietuvoje, 1940–1951 m.* Vilnius, 1976.

Raštikis, Stasys. "The Relations of the Provisional Government of Lithuania with the German Authorities," *Lituanus*, VIII/1–2 (1962), pp. 16–22.

Ratnieks, Henry. "Baltic Oil Prospects and Problems," *JBS*, VII/4 (Winter 1976), pp. 312–19.

——. "Baltic Oil Shale," *JBS*, IX/2 (Summer 1978), pp. 155–63.

——. "Energy Crisis and the Baltics," *JBS*, XII/3 (Fall 1981), pp. 245–59.

Rauch, Georg von. *The Baltic States: The Years of Independence, 1917–1940*. London, Berkeley and Los Angeles, 1974.

Raun, Linda. *The Estonians*. Human Relations Area Files, no. 4. New Haven, CT, 1955.

Rei, August. *The Drama of the Baltic Peoples*. Stockholm, 1961. (The 2nd edn [1970] has an appendix by Evald Uustalu, "Events after 1940.")

Remeikis, Thomas. "The Armed Struggle against the Sovietization of Lithuania after 1944," *Lituanus*, VIII/1–2 (1962), pp. 29–40.

——. "The Communist Party of Lithuania." Unpubl. Ph.D. diss., University of Illinois, Urbana, 1963.

——. "The Administration of Power: The Communist Party and the Soviet Government," in V. S. Vardys (ed.), *Lithuania under the Soviets, 1940–1965*, pp. 111–40. New York, 1965.

——. "A Latvian in the Politbureau: A Political Portrait of Arvīds Pelše," *Lituanus*, XII/1 (1966), pp. 81–4.

——. "The Impact of Industrialization on the Ethnic Demography of the Baltic Countries," *Lituanus*, XIII/1 (1967), pp. 29–41.

——. "Natur und Prozess der Verstädterung in Litauen," *AB*, VII (1967), pp. 263–88.

——. "Berücksichtigung der nationalen und verwaltungsmässigen Interessen der Unionsrepublik im Rahmen des zentralistischen Sowjetsystems, dargestellt am Beispiel Litauens," *AB*, X (1970), pp. 121–56.

——. "The Decision of the Lithuanian Government to Accept the Soviet Ultimatum of June 14, 1940," *Lituanus*, XXI/4 (1975), pp. 19–44.

——. "Political Developments during the Brezhnev Era," in George W. Simmonds (ed.), *Nationalism in the USSR and Eastern Europe in the Era of Brezhnev and Kosygin*, pp. 164–80. Detroit, MI, 1975.

——. "Modernization and National Identity in the Baltic Republics: Uneven and Multi-Directional Change in the Components of Modernization," in Ihor Kamenetsky (ed.), *Nationalism and Human Rights: Processes of Modernization in the USSR*, pp. 115–38. Littleton, CO, 1977.

——. *"Oppostion to Soviet Rule in Lithuania, 1945–1980*. Chicago, 1980.

Rianzhin, V. A. *Krizis burzhuaznoi konstitutsionnoi zakonnosti i vosstanovlenie sovetskoi gosudarstvennosti v Estonii*. Leningrad, 1971.

Rozītis, Elmārs. "Die evangelisch-lutherische Kirche in Sowjetlettland," *AB*, I (1960–1), pp. 93–109.

Royal Institute of International Affairs. *The Baltic States*. London, 1938.

Rutkis, Jānis (ed.). *Latvia: Country and People*. Stockholm, 1967.

Sabaliūnas, Leonas. *Lithuania in Crisis, 1939–1940*. Bloomington, IN, 1972.

Salo, Vello. "The Struggle between the State and the Churches," in T. Parming and E. Järvesoo (eds), *A Case Study of a Soviet Republic: The Estonian SSR*, pp. 198–204. Boulder, CO, 1978.

Sapiets, Jānis. "The Baltic Republics," in George Schöpflin (ed.), *The Soviet Union and Eastern Europe*, pp. 217–24. New York, 1970.

Sapiets, Marite. "Religion and Nationalism in Lithuania," *Religion in Communist Lands*, VII/2 (1979), pp. 76–96.

——. "Lithuania's Unofficial Press," *Index on Censorship*, IX/4 (1980), pp. 35–8.

Savasis, J. *The War against Gold in Lithuania*. New York, 1966.

Senn, Alfred Erich. "The Sovietization of the Baltic States," *Annals of the American Academy of Political Sciences*, CCCXVII (1958), pp. 123–9.

——. *The Emergence of Modern Lithuania*. New York, 1959.

——. *Lithuania Awakening*, Berkeley, 1990.

Sharmaitis [Šarmaitis], R. "Kommunisticheskoi Partii Litvy – 50 let," *Kommunist* (Litvy), 1968, no. 9, pp. 57–73.

Sharp, Tony. "The Russian Annexation of the Koenigsberg Area, 1941–1945," *Survey*, (Autumn 1977–8), pp. 156–62.

Shtromas, Aleksandras. "The Official Soviet Ideology and the Lithuanian People," in Rimvydas Šilbajoris (ed.), *Mind against the Wall*, Chicago, 1983, pp. 57–73.

Šilbajoris, Rimvydas P. "Socialist Realism and the Politics of Literature in Occupied Lithuania," in *Mind against the Wall* (see prev. entry), pp. 74–106.

Šilde, Ādolfs. *Resistance Movement in Latvia*. Stockholm, 1972.

Simmonds, George W. (ed.). *Nationalism in the USSR and Eastern Europe in the Era of Brezhnev and Kosygin*. Detroit, MI, 1975.

Slavenas, Julius P. "Nazi Ideology and Policy in the Baltic States." *Lituanus*, VI/2 (1960), pp. 47–52.

Smith, Graham E. "The Impact of Modernization on the Latvian Soviet Republic," *Co-Existence*, XVI/1 (April 1979), pp. 45–64.

Sotsialisticheskie revoliutsii 1940 g. v Litve, Latvii, i Estonii. Moscow, 1978.

Spekke, Arnolds. *History of Latvia*. Stockholm, 1957.

Sprudzs, Adolf, and Armins Rusis (eds). *Res Baltica*. Leiden, 1968.

Stakle, Jānis. "Die Eisenbahnen und das Transportwesen Lettlands in der Zeit von 1940–1970," *AB*, XV (1975), pp. 175–210.

Šumiņš, A. *Apcerējums par Padomju Latvijas ekonomisko attīstību (1940–1958)*. Riga, 1960.

Survel, Jaak (Evald Uustalu). *Estonia Today*. London, 1947.

Swettenham, John A. *The Tragedy of the Baltic States*. London, 1952.

Taagepera, Mare. "Pollution of the Environment and the Baltics," *JBS*, XII/3 (Fall 1981), pp. 260–74.

Taagepera, Rein. "Nationalism in the Estonian Communist Party," *Bulletin* (Institute for the Study of the USSR), XVII/1 (1970), pp. 3–15.

——. "Inequality Indices for Baltic Farm Size Distribution, 1929–1940," *JBS*, III/1 (Spring 1972), pp. 26–34.

——. "The Problem of Political Collaboration in Soviet Estonian Literature," *JBS*, VI/1 (Spring 1975), pp. 30–40.

——. "Estonia and the Estonians," in Z. Katz (ed.), *Handbook of Major Soviet Nationalities*, pp. 75–95. New York, 1975.

——. "La demanda de libertad de las naciones bálticas," *Revista de Occidente*, no. 146 (May 1975), pp. 160–74.

——. "The Impact of the New Left on Estonia," *East European Quarterly*, X (1976), pp. 43–51.

——. "Nationalism, Collaborationism, and New-Leftism," in T. Parming and E. Järvesoo (eds), *A Case Study of a Soviet Republic: The Estonian SSR*, pp. 75–103. Boulder, CO, 1978.

——. "Soviet Documentation on the Estonian Pro-Independence Guerrilla Movement, 1945–1952," *JBS*, X/2 (Summer 1979), pp. 91–106.

——. "Soviet Collectivization of Estonian Agriculture: The Taxation Phase," *JBS*, X/3 (Fall 1979), pp. 263–82.

——. "Soviet Collectivization of Estonian Agriculture: The Deportation Phase," *Soviet Studies*, XXXII/3 (July 1980), pp. 379–97.

——. "A Portrait of the 'Historical Gap' in Estonian Literature," *Lituanus*, XXVI/3 (Fall 1980), pp. 73–86.

——. "Baltic Population Changes, 1950–1980," *JBS*, XII/1 (Spring 1981), pp. 35–57.

——. "The Population Crisis and the Baltics," *JBS*, XII/3 (Fall 1981), pp. 234–44.

—— "Estonia's Road to Independence," *Problems of Communism*, XXXVIII/6 (Nov.–Dec. 1989), pp. 11–26.

—— *Softening Without Liberalization in the Soviet Union: The Case of Jüri Kukk*. Lanham, MD., 1984.

Tarulis, Albert. *Soviet Policy toward the Baltic States, 1918–1940*. South Bend, IN, 1959.

Tarybų Lietuva didžiajame tėvynės kare. Vilnius, 1975.

Tarybų Lietuvos valstietija: istorijos apybraiža. Vilnius, 1979.

Tauras, K. V. *Guerrilla Warfare on the Amber Coast*. New York, 1962.

Trapans, Andris. "The Role of the Latvian Communist Party in 1940," in *Materials of the Second Conference on Baltic Studies in Scandinavia*. Stockholm, 1971.

Uustalu, Evald. *The History of the Estonian People*. London, 1952.

—— (ed.). *Aspects of Estonian Culture*. London, 1961.

——. "Events after 1940," appendix to August Rei, *The Drama of the Baltic Peoples*, 2nd edn. Stockholm, 1970.

——. "The National Committee of the Estonian Republic," *JBS*, VII/3 (Fall 1976), pp. 209–19.

Valgemäe, Mardi. "Drama and the Theater Arts," in T. Parming and E. Järvesoo (eds), *A Case Study of a Soviet Republic: The Estonian SSR*, pp. 281–317. Boulder, CO, 1978.

Valters, Nikolaus. "Soziale Veränderungen in den baltischen Sowjetrepubliken," *AB*, IV (1964), pp. 9–35.

Vardys, V. Stanley. "Recent Soviet Policy toward Lithuanian Nationalism," *Journal of Central European Affairs*, XXIII (1963), pp. 313–32.

——. "The Partisan Movement in Postwar Lithuania," *Slavic Review*, XXII (1963), pp. 499–522.

——. "Soviet Colonialism in the Baltic States: A Note on the Nature of Modern Colonialism," *Lituanus*, X/2 (1964), pp. 5–23.

——. "Soviet Colonialism in the Baltic States, 1940–1965," *Baltic Review*, no. 29 (1965), pp. 11–26.

——(ed.) *Lithuania under the Soviets: Portrait of a Nation, 1940–1965*. New York, 1965.

——. "How the Baltic Republics Fare in the Soviet Union," *Foreign Affairs*, XLIV/3 (April 1966), pp. 512–17.

——. "The Baltic Peoples," *Problems of Communism*, XVI/5 (September–October 1967), pp. 55–64.

——. "Soviet Nationality Policy as an Instrument of Political Socialization: the Baltic Case," in A. Sprudzs and A. Rusis (eds), *Res Baltica*, pp. 117–32. Leiden, 1968.

——. "Modernization and Baltic Nationalism," *Problems of Communism*, XXIV/5 (September–October 1975), pp. 32–48.

———. "The Role of the Baltic Republics in Soviet Society," in Roman Szporluk (ed.), *The Influence of East Europe and the Soviet West on the USSR*, pp. 147–9. New York, 1977.

———. *The Catholic Church, Dissent, and Nationality in Lithuania*. Boulder, CO, 1978.

——— and Romuald J. Misiunas (eds). *The Baltic States in Peace and War, 1917–1945*. London, 1978.

———. "Lithuanian National Politics," *Problems of Communism*, XXXVIII/3 (July–Aug. 1989), pp. 53–76.

Vaškelis, Bronius B. "The Assertion of Ethnic Identity in Myth and Folklore in Soviet Lithuanian Literature," *Lituanus*, XIX/2 (1973), pp. 16–27.

Vėlaikis, Jonas. "Lithuanian Literature under the Soviets," *Lituanus*, XII/3 (Fall 1966), pp. 25–43.

Venclova, Tomas. "Translations of World Literature and Political Censorship in Contemporary Lithuania," *Lituanus*, XXV/2 (Summer 1979), pp. 5–26.

Vīķis-Freibergs, Vaira. "Echoes of the Dainas and the Search for Identity in Contemporary Latvian Poetry," *JBS*, VI (Spring 1975), pp. 17–29.

Viksnins, George J. "Current Issues of Soviet Latvia's Economic Growth," *JBS*, VII/4 (Winter 1976), pp. 343–51.

———. "Evaluating Economic Growth in Latvia," *JBS*, XII/2 (Summer 1981), pp. 173–88.

Widmer, Michael J. "Nationalism and Communism in Latvia: The Latvian Communist Party under Soviet Rule." Unpublished Ph.D. diss., Harvard University, 1969.

Žagars, Ē. *Socialist Transformation in Latvia, 1940–1941*. Riga, 1978.

Zhenklis (Ženklys), T. "Proshchaias s Antanasom Snechkusom; chego my zhdem ot emigratsii, vstupitel'naia zametka A. Shtromasa," *Kontinent*, XIV (1977), pp. 229–50.

Ziedonis, Arvids, Rein Taagepera, Mardi Valgemäe (eds). *Problems of Mininations: Baltic Perspectives*. San Jose, CA, 1973.

Zīle, Zigurds. "Soviet Federalism in Criminal Law: A Case Study," in A. Sprudzs and A. Rusis (eds). *Res Baltica*, pp. 152–9. Leiden, 1968.

Zundė, Pranas. "Die Kollektivierung der Landwirtschaft Sowjetlitauens," *AB*, II (1962), pp. 93–106.

———. *Die Landwirtschaft Sowjetlitauens*. Marburg/Lahn, 1962.

———. "Lithuania's Economy: Introduction of the Soviet Pattern," in V.S. Vardys (ed.), *Lithuania under the Soviets, 1940–1965*, pp. 141–69. New York, 1965.

Žymantas, Stasys. "Twenty Years of Resistance," *Lituanus*, VI/2 (September 1960), pp. 40–5.

INDEX

Āboliņš, Elerts (b. 1928), 236
abortions, 224
Abrene district, Latvia, 74
administration:
  changes effected during Thaw, 122–3
  immobilisme in, 204–8, 274
  postwar, 72, 76–83
  rural units of, 366
  sovietization of, 25
  See also Economy, administration of
Adomas-Meskupas, Icikas. *See* Meskupas
agriculture:
  changes in during Thaw, 138–9, 147, 189–92
  contractual arrangements, 1980s, 291
  efficiency of, 189, 230–3,
  postwar, 94–107
  pre-war, 10
  production, 106–7, 190–1, 234–5, 365
  sovietization of, 34–6
  See also collective farms; MKPP; MTS; private plots; state farms
Agrogorod proposal, 139
agroindustrial committees (1985), 274
Ahonen, Heikki (b. 1956), 301–2
Akmenė district, Lithuania, 36
alcohol consumption and abuse, 106, 224–5, 237, 263, 287
Aleshin, Georgii, 280, 352
Allik, Hendrik (1901–89), 82, 148
Alliksaar, Artur (1923–66), 157, 159
Alma mater, 260
Alver, Betti (1906–89), 157
Ambrazevičius, Juozas (1903–74), 47
American-Latvian Association, 299
Amnesty International, 257
Andersons, Imants (b. 1923), 276
Andresen, Nigol (1899–1985), 123

Andropov, Iurii Vladimirovich (1914–84), 280, 286, 300
Angarietis, Zigmas (1882–1940), 173
Angelus, Oskar (1892–1979), 68
Anilionis, Petras, 300
anniversaries. *See* history, significance of
Anti-Party Group, 140, 147
Anti-semitism, 62. *See also* Jewish population
Anvelt, Jaan (1884–1937), 173
Aputis, Juozas (b. 1936), 168
Arakas, Imre (b. 1945), 208
Arbatov, Georgii Arkadevich (b. 1923), 329
Aronov, Vasilii, 353
art. *See* cultural life
Aspāzija [Elza Rozenberga-Pliekšāne] (1868–1943), 153, 163, 298
Association of Concerned Estonians, 267
Astra, Gunārs (1931–1988), 301
Atlantic Charter, 66
Audrini village, Latvia, 70
Auškāps, Jānis (b. 1894), 145
Augspils, Latvia, 36
Aukštieji Panēriai, Lithuania, 62
Aušra, 259, 270, 300
Auster, Lydia (b. 1912), 123
automobile ownership, 219
Auziņš, Imants (b. 1937), 163, 245, 250
Avdjukevičs, Longins (b. 1916), 275
Avyžius, Jonas (b. 1922), 168, 295

Bagrationovsk [Preussisch-Eylau], Kaliningrad *Oblast*, 339
Balabaev, Aleksandr, 341
Baltakis, Algimantas (b. 1930), 166
Baltic Assembly (1989), 328, 346
Baltic political cooperation (1990), 328
Baltic Entente, 14, 18